P9-CAN-499

THE

GUIDE

TO

LONG-PLAYING

RECORDS

Chamber and Solo Instrument Music

THE GUIDE TO LONG-PLAYING RECORDS

Orchestral Music

BY

Irving Kolodin

Vocal Music

BY

Philip L. Miller

Chamber and Solo Instrument Music

BY

Harold C. Schonberg

THE GUIDE TO LONG-PLAYING RECORDS

Chamber and Solo Instrument Music

BY

Harold C. Schonberg

1955

ALFRED A KNOPF

NEW YORK

TO *Rosalyn*

"If ever any beauty I did see,

Which I desired, and got, 'twas but a dream of thee."

L. C. catalog card number: 55-5608

THIS IS A BORZOI BOOK,
PUBLISHED BY ALFRED A. KNOPF, INC.

 Published simultaneously in Canada by McClelland & Stewart Limited. Manufactured in the United States of America.

FIRST EDITION

INTRODUCTION

A spot check and some hasty calculations reveal that over a recent twelve-month period more records came out than there were hours in the year to listen to them. A marvelous tribute to free enterprise, this, and a record-buyer's paradise; but, like all the great developments of mankind, such as the atom bomb, television, and the advertising industry, it carries attendant problems. Too much can be as exasperating as too little. The record-buyer, peering in dismay at the five, ten, fifteen, or perhaps even more individual recordings of a specific work, may end up flipping a coin. Which is one way to arrive at a choice, although the method would work as well for the fifth race at Santa Anita.

To incipient coin-flippers is this book directed. It is one of a series of three, by as many authors. No one man today, whatever his confidence, aptitude, or genius, can critically assess the whole field. Life is too short; eardrums are too delicate.

The book is devoted to a survey of chamber and instrumental music on LP discs. By "chamber" is meant that kind of concerted music, for two or more instruments, in which a part is written for each player (not as in an orchestral work, where the entire violin section, say, may be playing the same part).

The listings contained in the following pages are not one-hundred-per-cent complete. I can honestly say that I have listened to every domestic record that comes within the scope of the book, but I have not hesitated to ignore submarginal recordings or interpretations. When there are ten or more discs of a given piece of music, it would be a waste of paper to include the manifestly inferior offerings; and some of them are inferior indeed. "Pray, Sir," asked Dr. Morgann, "whether do you reckon Derrick or Smart the best poet?" Dr. Johnson (reports his Boswell) at once felt himself roused, and answered: "Sir, there is no settling the point of precedency between a louse and a flea."

I have been especially harsh with ten-inch discs. As matters stand at the point of writing, most ten-inch discs are not economical. Of course, if a specific ten-inch disc is a unique interpretation, or if it is priced low enough to compete with twelve-inch discs, it will by all means be discussed. At that, I venture to say that an overwhelming majority of the instrumental and chamber works available in American pressings are somewhere mentioned within. I have aimed at presenting a concise summary of many records rather than an exegetic analysis of a few.

Naturally there will be further omissions as records pile up after publication. But much time will elapse before the book is obsolete. Nor is this merely the statement of a scared author whistling in the dark. Most of the standard repertoire has been recorded by the supreme artists of our day. The Budapest Quartet on Mozart and Beethoven; Rubinstein on Chopin; Casals on Bach; Barere or Horowitz on Liszt—these are not going to date rapidly. Not unless some extraordinary new species of musician is in the offing: and there is no sign of a new birth. On the contrary. The great figures of the old generation are passing, and not many newcomers seem able to fill their shoes.

It has been found most convenient for all concerned to have the entries listed alphabetically under composer. In those cases in which a disc contains a miscellany, or even a large group of short works by one composer, it is listed in the section toward the end of the book entitled Collections, where each disc may be found under the artist's or organization's name (*e.g.*, Horowitz or New Music String Quartet). All major works, and most minor ones, have been cross-indexed, though a loose Chopin prelude or Bach fantasia has been allowed to fall by the wayside. These odds and ends have not been omitted; they are mentioned somewhere in the text, generally in the Collections section.

All discs are twelve-inch unless otherwise stated. The heading for each disc contains all pertinent information. Parenthetical items in the headings, preceded by an asterisk, refer to the contents of the reverse side of the disc. Manufacturers' names are encoded: V for Victor, C for Columbia, and so on. The code can be found facing the first page of text. A numeral enclosed in brackets specifies the number of discs in an album set.

Tonal considerations naturally play a large part in the final evaluations of the discs under consideration. I am, however, far from being one of those 15-cycle-low, 20,000-cycle-high high-fidelity men. On the whole I am more interested in the music than in the faithfulness of the sound, granted a reasonable auditory minimum on any disc. If a choice resolves down to that between a good performance on a brilliant recording or a brilliant performance on a merely good recording, the latter unhesitatingly will be selected. As a matter of fact, most chamber works these days sound fine on records, and a disc with inferior tonal characteristics is a rarity from the reputable companies (though a bad surface or a bad pressing most decidedly is not). The piano is more difficult to record than the string instruments, and many pre-1952 piano recordings are inadequate in sound; but modern engineering has solved even that problem.

I have full confidence in my record-playing mechanism. But I can vouch for the statements about record quality in the following pages *only on the basis of the individual discs I have played.* Pressings vary. A record may be perfect, as the product of an early stamping. After a thousand or so pressings from the same stamper, a batch of records may well emerge with prominent surfaces and clogged or jumped grooves. Or you may purchase a disc, on the basis of my recommendation, from a record store without knowing that it may have been handled by a hundred customers and played by that most murderous of instruments, a demonstration machine with a worn-down stylus. Naturally such a disc will be far from the factory-fresh copy that I played. Small wonder that many record buffs browse through record shops with a jeweler's loupe constantly in play.

The deciding factor in record-reproduction is of course the equipment on which the records are played. There is little that has been so misrepresented as "hi-fi." Every manufacturer of a $50 portable strenuously advertises his product as the last word in tonal splendor. It isn't; it can't be, by all the laws of physics; and high fidelity is not a conspicuous feature in the average American home. High fidelity—this may come as a surprise to some—is not cheap. I have never heard a set that cost less than $350 to assemble that could be called hi-fi. And this $350 is devoted to playback equipment alone. No radio, no television. Most engineers would agree that the minimum requirements for a high-fidelity reproducer involve a frequency range flat from 50 to 10,000 cycles per second. The average commercial console will not give that kind of performance. All cats are alike in the dark, and all records sound alike on cheap machines.

On the other hand, let me make it clear that high fidelity does not mean exaggerated emphasis of the high and low ends of the tonal spectrum. It means good balance and as close an approximation to concert-hall sound as can be achieved. Surprisingly few owners of high-fidelity equipment know how to use it. They will insist, for instance, on keeping the treble control in the "flat" position; what comes out is a shrill sound that would make a walrus quiver. The "flat" position is a myth. It may work for some records, but it is useless for most. Controls are made to be used. Use them, and do not hesitate to tinker with the bass and treble in order to achieve an honest sound. Many new records are cut too high, and the only way to control them is to take them down. Then they can be managed, frequently with sensational results.

Records, for the most part, are ahead of equipment. There is more in the grooves than most record-reproducers can bring out. This statement does not apply only to the records of the big companies like Victor, Columbia, and London, but to almost all contemporary manufacturers. Capitol, Vox, Westminster—they all make high-fidelity discs. But, lest the owners of non-laboratory equipment despair, good records will sound good on any machine that meets the minimum requirements of high fidelity. The better the equipment, the better the results. And one thing about expensive components: you can take an inferior record and make it sound, something you cannot otherwise do.

Record criticism has its own jargon. An electronic terminology enters, wrapping itself lovingly around musical terminology. Both will here be kept to a minimum. Certain possibly ungrammatical constructions are convenient to use, such as the term "LP" in a sentence like "the only LP in the catalogue"—a solecism that already has sounded the editorial call to battle among our British brethren, but which by now is commonly accepted even in the stately pages of *The Gramophone* in London.

As pertains to the names of compositions, to capitalizations, to spellings, I cheerfully admit to certain inconsistencies. For the most part I have followed common American usage: *Art of the Fugue*, not *Kunst der Fuge;* but, at the same time, the captious reader may note that I have listed the *Little Organ Book* under *Orgelbüchlein.* To inconsistencies like these I plead guilty in advance. Sometimes my spellings and capitalizations will be found to differ from record-label or liner-note copy. Those differences are deliberate. Record labels are not always accurate. In my listings I have followed the title pages of the actual music, to a large extent. Thus: *En habit de cheval*, not *En Habit de Cheval.* In the textual discussions I have made an effort to discuss records not listed in the headings. Sometimes I name the music on the reverse of the record, sometimes not. The general rule is that if a disc is not recommended, there is no point pursuing the matter further. If the disc does have points of interest, the additional information is supplied. In the headings, of course, all record listings include the contents of the reverse side; and, in nearly all cases, recordings are listed in order of preference.

Any book like this is going to be a record of the critic's prejudices. These the reader must discover for himself, discounting that which he feels to be arbitrary. Criticism is not the objective art that some practitioners make it out to be. There *are* certain objective factors, however, and quality of performance is to some degree mensurable. A performer has an identification with his instrument or he has not. Wrong notes can be ticked off; the score tells us whether the tempo and dynamic indications are observed; an experienced listener knows when the instrumentalist is uneasy technically, when he is covering up, when he is operating with complete freedom.

At a concert performance one is inclined to overlook blemishes. Not on a record, though. A record is something for the ages, and from it the listener is entitled to the very best, as established by the great artists of our time. We don't expect a scared debutante to walk onto the stage of Town Hall and reincarnate the glories of Rachmaninoff's performance of the *Carnaval*, but on a record the Rachmaninoff standards definitely do apply. Any why not? After all, he recorded the work too; and any pianist who attempts it on discs is thus putting himself into direct competition with the Russian giant. And so we again come back to Dr. Johnson's "point of precedency." The record-buyer wants the best for his money. This book attempts to recommend the best.

Harold C. Schonberg

ACKNOWLEDGMENTS

Without the co-operation of many people in the record industry, this book would have been something less than a labor of love. I wish to express grateful thanks to the following officials of record companies for making available discs I had not previously heard: Peter Bartók of Bartók Records; John Coveney of Capitol; I. Kratka of Classic Editions; Debbie Ishlon and David Oppenheim of Columbia; Saul Taishoff of Concert Hall; Morton Cahn of Decca; Jerry Newman of Esoteric; George Riemer and William Lerner of Haydn Society; Remy Van Wyck Farkas of London; Peter Fritsch of Lyrichord; Wilma Cozart of Mercury; Edward Cole of MGM; William Avar of Period; Maynard Solomon of Vanguard; Ben Kemper of Victor; George Mendelssohn, Larry Green, Eric Schuller, and Ward Botsford of Vox; and Henry Gage, Michael Naida, Kurt List, and James Lyons of Westminster. Gladys Chamberlain, Catherine Miller, and the staff of the 58th Street Music Library fed scores to me in a constant stream. To Philip Miller and Robert Darrell I am in debt for many ideas that have been developed in the following pages; and the editorial suggestions of Herbert Weinstock have been more helpful than words can express. I especially want to thank Abner Levin of the Sam Goody Record Store, who gave me carte blanche to borrow records and watched tolerantly while I went through his stock like a hungry boll weevil in a ripe cotton patch.

THE

GUIDE

TO

LONG-PLAYING

RECORDS

Chamber and Solo Instrument Music

CODE OF RECORD LABELS

Ac	*Academy*
All	*Allegro*
AM	*Audio Masterworks*
An	*Angel*
Bar	*Bartók*
BG	*Bach Guild*
Bos	*Boston*
C	*Columbia*
Cap	*Capitol*
CE	*Classic Editions*
CH	*Concert Hall*
Col	*Colosseum*
Con	*Contemporary*
CP	*Command Performance*
D	*Decca*
Dia	*Dial*
Edu	*Educo*
EMS	*EMS*
Ent	*Entré*
Ep	*Epic*
Es	*Esoteric*
HdS	*Handel Society*
HS	*Haydn Society*
L	*London*
Ly	*Lyrichord*
Mer	*Mercury*
MGM	*MGM*
ML	*Music Library*
NR	*New Records*
Oc	*Oceanic*
OL	*Oiseau-Lyre*
Op	*Opus*
Ov	*Overtone*
Ox	*Oxford*
Per	*Period*
Ph	*Philharmonia*
Pol	*Polymusic*
REB	*REB*
Rem	*Remington*
Ren	*Renaissance*
RS	*Rachmaninoff Society*
SPA	*SPA*
Str	*Stradivari*
Tel	*Telefunken*
U	*Urania*
V	*Victor*
Van	*Vanguard*
Vox	*Vox*
W	*Westminster*
Wal	*Walden*
WCFM	*WCFM*

ALBÉNIZ, ISAAC (1860-1909)

Iberia (Books I and II). Arrau, C 4194.
No better Spanish piano music has been written, even though the work does not often turn up. The writing is excessively difficult and very few pianists care to take it on. "*Triana*" is the only piece in the set which gets much play in the concert hall. Arrau, who has immense technical command at his disposal, easily handles the difficulties. He plays with authority and musicianship, strength and clarity. The only missing ingredient is an occasional touch of color: everything sounds bleak. Nevertheless, this is one of Arrau's best discs, and it is a shame that he never got around to completing the set. The recording, originally released on shellac discs in 1948, has a good quality of sound.

ANTHEIL, GEORGE (1900-)

*Valentine Waltzes. Antheil, SPA 36 (*Eight Fragments from Shelley).*
Trivial, derivative music, divided between Poulenc and Prokofiev. Antheil himself is the pianist, a fact that disposes of all questions of style, feeling, and authenticity. Not much resonance is behind the recorded sound, but it is satisfactory enough.

ARRIAGA, JUAN (1806-1826)

Quartets for Strings Nos. 1 in D minor and 2 in A. Guilet, CH 1068.
Arriaga was a Spanish composer who studied in Paris and died at the age of twenty. He was remarkably talented. These quartets may be patterned after Haydn—Arriaga was fifteen or so when he composed them—but they are fluent and assured. The Guilet Quartet presents alert, graceful performances, and the recorded sound is clear, though the *A major Quartet* suffers from a gradual pitch rise that ends the work almost in B flat.

BACH, CARL PHILIPP EMANUEL (1714-1788)

Flute Sonata in D; Flute Trio in B minor; Duo in E minor for Flute and Violin; Solfeggietto for Harpsichord; Flute Quartet in G. Collegium Pro Arte, OL 50017.

Contained here are drab, methodical performances of little-played music. None of this material has been recorded before, nor has the world suffered an overwhelming loss from its neglect. Bright, well-balanced recorded sound.

BACH, JOHANN CHRISTIAN (1735-1782)

Sonatas for Piano in E, B flat, and C minor. Tolson, WCFM 7.

This is the "London Bach" who had so great an influence on Mozart, and these sonatas are fluent examples of his style. A certain amount of charm is present, though none but a blind admirer of the period would call the music very exciting, or even very original. Tolson plays competently, generally tinkling along the top of the keys in an approved "classical" style.

*Sonata for Two Pianos in G. Badura-Skoda, Demus, W 5069 (*Mozart: Andante and Variations in G; Sonata for Two Pianos in D).*

Used as a filler for a disc devoted mainly to Mozart, this slight work is played with the unpretentious flow it deserves. The two young Austrian artists are not in a hurry to get any place, and they make a pleasurable experience of the music. Excellent recorded sound.

BACH, JOHANN CHRISTOPH (1642-1703)

Sarabande with Variations; Aria Eberliniana. See Buxtehude: *La Capricciosa* (HS 3069).

BACH, JOHANN SEBASTIAN (1685-1750)

NOTE: for LP discs containing a miscellany of Bach's organ music, see Collections: Alain (HS 104); Biggs (C 4284, 4285, 4500, 4097); Heitmann (Tel 66009); Schweitzer (C SL 175); Viderø (HS 94). For an LP album containing a miscellany of Bach's piano music, see Collections: Friskin (BG 543/4/5).

Air with Ten Variations in the Italian Style. Tureck (piano), All 117

*(*Italian concerto; 4 Duets). Wollman (piano), W 5298 (*Italian Concerto; Overture in the French Manner).*

A magnificent work not often encountered in the concert hall. Tureck plays with her usual combination of stylistic authority, free technique, and fine manual independence. Her left hand is always a joy to hear; it is completely responsive and has an amazing variety of touch. She takes the "Duets" somewhat slower than is customary, but is able to hold them together in a dignified manner. The recording is thin in sound, and the surfaces are too prominent for comfort. Wollman enjoys much the better recorded sound. Her playing of the *Air with Ten Variations* is neat and small-scaled—a long distance from Tureck's tension, flow, and organization. Despite the disparity in recording, the Tureck is unhesitatingly selected.

Anna Magdalena Notebook. Rapf, Weis-Osborn, BG 510.

Anna Magdalena was Bach's second wife. She copied a large group of short vocal and instrumental pieces into a book, hence the name of the collection. Some of these pieces are not by her husband, but they are all flowing, simple, and attractive. Rapf, the harpsichordist, does not try to make too much out of the music, contenting himself with an appropriately simple statement (and Weis-Osborn handles the vocal sections with equal simplicity). An attractive disc, with an intimate quality of recorded sound.

Art of Fugue. Heitmann (organ), 10" Cap 8121/2 [2]. *J. and G. Dichler (duo-pianists), W WAL 215* [2]. *Leonhardt (harpsichord), BG 532/3* [2].

Bach died while composing this work. It was left incomplete at the point where he was composing a fugue on the letters of his own name (BACH in German notation is B flat, A, C, B natural). He never indicated the instrumentation. Heitmann's version for organ is out of the catalogue, but worth buying if you run across it. Only twelve of the nineteen sections are played, however. Heitmann concludes, as customary, with the chorale-prelude *Von deinem Thron ich hiermit.* The Dichlers play an arrangement by Bruno Seidlhofer, a romantic arrangement full of octave doublings and pianistic reinforcements. At times the music sounds like Brahms's *Haydn Variations.* The edition omits Contrapunctus 17 of the Graeser edition, but carries the final fugue to the point where Bach left off, and ends with *Von deinem Thron.* This interpretation by the Dichlers is robust, not very imaginative, full of good intention. The best thing about it is the clarity of the part-writing. One can get a good idea of the music, even though it is not as thick or as romantic as it sounds here. Leonhardt is a Dutch harpsichordist who gives a performance of a type known as "scholarly"—only too often a euphemism for sterile. He is accurate, pedestrian, and metronomic, grimly plowing through the music with scarcely a variation of tempo or color. He also drops the Graeser Contrapunctus 17; and he does not end with the chorale-prelude, but tacks on a short chordal ending seven measures before Bach's conclusion. The recording is one of those super hi-fi affairs in which you can hear the thump of the keys in their sockets. Landowska herself could not make the *Art of Fugue* convincing on a harpsichord.

Canonic Variations on "Vom Himmel hoch." See *Variations on "Sei gegrüsset"* (D 9615). See also Collections: Viderø (HS 94); Heitmann (Tel 66009).

*Chaconne (arr. Busoni). Petri, 10" C 2049 (*Beethoven: Sonata No. 6). Brailowsky, 10" V LRM 7050 (*Vivaldi-Bach: Concerto in D Minor).*

The most famous of all Busoni transcriptions finds Brailowsky the better recorded, Petri the better played. Brailowsky's disc is low-priced, and also contains a massively played version of the Vivaldi-Bach *Concerto in D.* No arranger's name is given; it is doubtless Stradal. Despite the advantage of superior sound, the Brailowsky performance of the *Chaconne* yields to Petri's greater suppleness and authority (though one must confess that Petri is scarcely in top form). Avoid a version by Gianoli on W 5101; it is neither especially good Bach-Busoni nor especially good piano-playing. The Bertolini on Col 1024 is also rather bad.

*Chorale-Preludes (5). Viderø, HS 3063 (*Variations on "Sei gegrüsset, Jesu gütig").*

Viderø plays an organ in Sorø, Denmark. It has an intimate, reedy quality, and it is beautifully reproduced. Viderø has never been responsible for a bad disc. Here he phrases artistically, his registrations are always in the best of taste, and his tempos invariably sound natural. A splendid disc.

*Chorale-Preludes ("Schübler"). Walcha, D 9569 (*5 Chorale-Preludes). Biggs, C 4284 (*Toccata, Adagio, and Fugue in C).*

These six "Schübler" chorale-preludes, named after the publisher who solicited them, were among the few Bach works published during the composer's lifetime. Walcha makes more of a spiritual experience of the music than does Biggs, and he plays an organ with a more delicate quality of tone. One good feature about the Biggs disc is his idea of prefacing each of the chorale-preludes with the original chorale. Weinrich also has recorded the "Schübler" works on MGM 3021 (**Passacaglia; Organ Concerto in A minor*). His playing is conscientious, as always, but he scarcely conveys the drama and tenderness of the music.

Chorale-Preludes. See *Orgelbüchlein* (HS HSL D). See also Collections: Alain (HS 104); Heitmann (Tel 66009); Schweitzer (C SL 175); Viderø (HS 104).

*Chromatic Fantasy and Fugue. Landowska (harpsichord), V LCT 1137 (*Italian Concerto; Partita in B flat; Toccata in D). Valenti (harpsichord), Ly 47 (*Toccatas in D and C minor). Chasins (piano), Mer 10062 (*Brahms: 3 Rhapsodies; Mozart: Fantasy in C minor, K. 475). Serkin (piano), C 4350 (*Italian Concerto; Sonata for Cello No. 3).*

As always, the harpsichord versions sound more natural than the piano. Landowska treats the music very freely, taking the "fantasy" indication literally. She has the most drama of any of the four players, and builds the music to an unbearable pitch of excitement. This is one of her greatest achievements, and next to it all other versions pale. Valenti's driving, energetic performance lacks a comparable degree of integration, and I do not like the boomy sound of the recording. Of the piano versions I like the Chasins the best. It is beautifully articulated, the treatment of the ornamentation is interesting, and he maintains a sustained intensity. Good recorded sound, noisy surfaces. Serkin's ideas about the music are less refined than Chasins's, and his playing somehow sounds thick by comparison, though of course he plays with his expected strength and musicianship. His recording sounds twangy. Conditions at Prades in 1950 did not favor the recording engineers.

Clavierübung (complete). Kirkpatrick (harpsichord), Callaway (organ), HS HSL A [7].

The title of this work may be translated as "keyboard practice." The seven discs are divided as follows: partitas in B flat and G (HS 3056); C minor and D (3057); A minor and E minor (3058); *Overture in the French Manner,* the four "Duets," *Italian Concerto* (3059); "*Goldberg*" *Variations* (3062), all played by Kirkpatrick; and the *Organ Mass,* a collection of chorale-preludes played by Callaway (3060/1). These discs being available separately, they are discussed elsewhere, with other versions of the same works.

The set as a whole is the work of two capable and scholarly artists. All of the playing is clear and intelligent. Sometimes it sounds pedantic. Kirkpatrick, in his notes, mentions the undesirability of too many changes in registration. To that most will agree; but in his effort to avoid sensationalism or anything that might be construed as unstylistic romanticism, Kirkpatrick often allows himself to fall into an unrelieved metronomic pattern. On the other hand there are, ever present, Kirkpatrick's textual fidelity, his masculine drive and rhythmic strength, and his embracing knowledge of baroque ornamentation. The seven discs add up to a major contribution to the Bach discography.

Concerto in A minor (after Vivaldi). See Collections: Alain (HS 104).

Concerto in D (after Vivaldi). See Collections: Landowska (V LM 1217).

Concerto in D minor (after Vivaldi). See *Chaconne* (V LRM 7050). See also Collections: Biggs (C 4500).

Duets (4). See *Overture in the French Manner* (HS 3059); *Organ Mass* (D DX 115); *Air with Ten Variations* (All 117).

Eight Little Preludes and Fugues. White, 10" Mer 15027.

The recording dates back some years and shows its age. Low-level sound predominates, and there is a lack of definition. White's easy, well-paced performances have a springy quality as unusual as it is welcome in music of this sort.

English Suites (6, complete). Valenti (harpsichord), W WAL 305 [3]. *Gianoli (piano), W WAL 306* [3]. *Borovsky (piano), Vox 7852* [2].

The harpsichord version tops the two competitors on piano. Valenti goes about his work with vigor, but also with a regrettable tendency toward monochromaticism. He tends to push too hard, as in the opening of the *G minor Suite,* and he misses the warmth of many of the lyric sections. In short, a straightforward, textually accurate performance, neither particularly poetic nor imaginative, but very well recorded (keep the volume down!). Neither of the piano versions has much to offer, but if you must have one of them, the Vox is one disc cheaper. Gianoli's greater sparkle does not make up the difference, and her scholarship is open to question. Not that Borovsky is a superior stylist.

*English Suite No. 3 in G minor. Gulda, L 756 (*Prelude and Fugue in E flat minor from Book II of Well-Tempered Clavier; Mozart: Sonata in A minor: Rondo in D, K. 485).*

Gulda has an easygoing, lyric way of playing Bach. He keeps the lines in motion, has perfect finger independence and a wide variety of touch. This is fine Bach on the piano, neither cursed with pedantry nor distorted by romanticism. The crisp quality of the recorded sound is typical of London's best.

*English Suite No. 5 in E minor. Horszowski, C 4354 (*Sonata for Flute and Piano in B minor; Prelude and Fugue in E flat minor from Book I of Well-Tempered Clavier).*

Columbia recorded this disc at the 1950 Prades Festival. The sound has dull, muddy characteristics that are no help to Horszowski's turgid playing and uneven articulation. Yvonne Lefebure is the pianist in the *E flat minor Prelude and Fugue.* She enjoys a better quality of recorded sound and gives a musicianly account of the piece.

*English Suite No. 6 in D minor. Gieseking, U 7107 (*Schumann: Kreisleriana).*

Deft, flowing piano-playing highlights this performance. The pianist sounds like the real Gieseking, not the sloppy-fingered musician who plays the *Kreisleriana* on the reverse. Whether or not this is "authorized" Gieseking—and he obviously does not think so, as he instituted a suit against Urania—it is first-class work except for a few flurried, hectic moments in the gigue.

*Fantasy and Fugue in G minor ("The Great"). Biggs, C 4097 (*Prelude and Fugue in E flat; Fugue in D minor; Toccata in F).*

The Biggs is the best of several versions of the popular organ work. His conception is orthodox. He keeps the rhythm steady and achieves a powerful climax. Avoid the Dupré interpretation on L 317, which is meandering, heavy, and has a bad tape splice in the middle of the fugue. Schweitzer on C 4600 is disappointing, and his playing is too unsteady to challenge Biggs's.

French Suites (6, complete). Valenti (harpsichord), W WAL 310 [3]. *Gianoli (piano), W WAL 307* [3]. *Borovsky (piano), Vox 8192* [2].

See the general remarks about these three instrumentalists in the *English Suites* entry above. Valenti again tries for a complete linear quality, but ends up with little variation of texture. Voices that should be set off and contrasted against each other emerge with complete uniformity. But, as in the *English Suites*, there is strength, and the harpsichord version is preferable on all counts to the two piano versions. Gianoli has more spirit and dash than Borovsky. If you must have a piano set, however, the Vox will do, as Gianoli's slight advantage in performance is not worth the price of an extra disc. Avoid the Ahlgrimm disc (C 4746), a harpsichord version that gets the six suites on two sides by avoiding all repeats. The playing sounds helter-skelter, and it has been recorded half a tone flat.

"Goldberg" Variations (Part IV of Clavierübung). Landowska (harpsichord), V LM 1080. Kirkpatrick (harpsichord), HS 3062. Tureck (piano), All 3033. Demus (piano), W 5241.

Landowska's first, pre-war, "Goldberg" is considered by some connoisseurs to be superior to this 1945 version. Landowska would disagree. So do I. Her playing in the more recent set might be accused of showmanship, of over-registration—but there are more music, subtlety, and passion in her ideas than anywhere else on records. In the twenty-fifth variation she tears your heart out. Kirkpatrick is direct, to the point, and technically perfect. His is a fine performance, truer in sound than Landowska's. But it somehow appears angular beside hers. Of the piano versions, the Tureck is inferior in tonal value, and there is little color or resonance to the sound of her piano, but she displays a maturity of conception that Demus does not approach. Demus lacks tension. Some of the intense harmonies in variations like the eleventh, fifteenth, and twenty-fifth sound matter-of-fact. With all of its vague sound, the Tureck disc is preferable. A harpsichord version by Leonhardt on BG 536 is technically accurate but limited in emotional resource.

*Inventions, Two-Part. Kirkpatrick (clavichord), 10" CH 1088. Balogh (piano), Ly 1 (*Eighteen Little Preludes).*

Concert Hall here provides one of the few clavichord recordings. In the flesh the instrument has a much wispier tone than the more brilliant-voiced harpsichord. On this record it has a dull harpsichordish quality. The record must be played with the volume near minimum, at which point it will begin to sound like the actual instrument. Kirkpatrick's delicate playing displays a type of ornamentation and scholarship which young pianists and their teachers would do well to study carefully. Balogh's piano version is smoothly played and intelligently organized, but the quality of recording leaves much to be desired. The charming little *Preludes* on the reverse also are well played, but again the recorded sound is sub-par.

Inventions, Three-Part. Foss (piano), D 9634.

The talented Lukas Foss should be making more Bach records. His work here is pellucid, presented with skill and taste, with a singing line and complete finger independence. The recorded sound is quiet and intimate. Some heavy clicks mar the results.

*Italian Concerto (Part II of Clavierübung). Landowska (harpsichord), V LCT 1137 (*Chromatic Fantasy; Partita in B flat; Toccata in D). Kirkpatrick (harpsichord), HS 3059 (*Overture in the French Manner; 4 Duets). Serkin (piano), C 4350 (*Chromatic Fantasy; Sonata for Cello No. 3).*

Between Landowska and Kirkpatrick is a chasm. Landowska sings the songs the sirens sang; Kirkpatrick marches straight ahead, looking neither to the left nor to the right. She is personal, romantic, takes long ritards; he exemplifies the modern school of classic playing—objective, rhythmic, direct. He also has far superior recorded sound; the Victor is a transfer from shellac. But I'll take it, inferior recording and all, over Kirkpatrick's more angular, brittle playing. Serkin's is the best piano version. It was recorded at the 1950 Prades Festival, and has a typically soggy sound. His performance is large-scaled, exuberant, and powerful, and the slow movement has a fine flow. A gracious version by Tureck on All 117 is handicapped by highly inferior tonal characteristics. Wollman's performance on W 5298 (*miscellaneous Bach piano music) can best be described as ladylike.

Organ Mass (Part III of Clavierübung). Walcha, D DX 115 [3]. *Callaway, HS 3060/1* [2].

This long work consists of settings of the *Kyrie* and *Gloria,* and various hymns, nearly all based on chorale melodies. It opens with a prelude and ends with a fugue—the great "*St. Anne*" *Prelude and Fugue in E flat.* Callaway uses a Skinner organ in Washington Cathedral; Walcha plays a German baroque organ. The American recording sounds heavy. Walcha defines his lines with greater clarity, and his registrations are more interesting. For some reason, he does not follow the sequence in the score, and he also takes five sides to Callaway's four. The sixth side is devoted to the "*St. Anne*" *Fugue* and the four "Duets." The latter Walcha plays on a harpsichord. These "Duets" belong to the *Organ Mass*—at least, they are found in Part III of the *Clavierübung,* just preceding the closing organ fugue. With no disrespect to the fine Callaway performance, and with the realization that the Decca set is somewhat more expensive, I prefer the Walcha. I find more character in the playing and a greater feeling of tension and release to the musical line; and the recording is brighter.

Orgelbüchlein (complete). Viderø, HS HSL D [2].

Forty-five chorale-preludes make up the *Orgelbüchlein ("Little Organ Book")*. Viderø plays an old reedy, wheezy baroque organ in Sorø which was rebuilt in 1942 but managed to retain a curiously appealing tone. As always, the Danish organist plays with style and imagination. There is culture behind his conceptions, and he knows how to unfold a long melodic line (and some of these melodic lines are long indeed) so that it rises and falls. Endless variety is present in this artistic playing. The recording is very realistic, even unto the clank and clatter of the mechanism. This is a fine Bach set to have in your collection.

*Overture in the French Manner (Part II of Clavierübung). Kirkpatrick (harpsichord), HS 3059 (*4 Duets; Italian Concerto). Tureck (piano), All 114. Wollman (piano), W 5298 (*Italian Concerto; Air with Ten Variations).*

The *"French" Overture,* also known as the *B minor Partita,* is a long, massive work that may require a few hearings to assimilate. Then will come the sudden realization that this is one of Bach's keyboard masterpieces. The four "Duets," too, are magnificent music. Kirkpatrick calls them probably the most concentrated two-voice music that Bach ever wrote. Kirkpatrick presents his invariably steady playing. As the Germans say, his work is *punkt* (loosely translated as "right on the button"). Everything is strong and musical, and the recording is right on top of the player. Tureck's piano version is splendidly played, but the inadequacy of sound makes the disc hard to recommend. Wollman has very lifelike piano sound. Her playing is clear, and her intentions are pure. Yet she comes nowhere near the intensity of Tureck or Kirkpatrick. Stick to the latter.

Partitas (6) for Harpsichord (Part I of Clavierübung). Kirkpatrick (harpsichord), HS 3056/7/8 [3]. *Badura-Skoda (piano), W WAL 303* [3].

The harpsichord version is preferred. One must respect Kirkpatrick even if at times he sounds unnecessarily austere. There is a degree of organization and musical integrity which puts his discs on a high musical level. The recording is too close up; even the pedal shifts are heard. Play these records at low volume. Badura-Skoda's piano album reveals an artist still in an immature stage. Often he does little more than hit the notes, and his semi-detached style of fingering (which some pianists wrongly believe apposite to Bach) becomes tiresome. The recording has a decided ping to the upper treble; otherwise it is satisfactory.

*Partita for Harpsichord No. 1 in B flat. Landowska (harpsichord), V LCT 1137 (*Chromatic Fantasy and Fugue; Italian Concerto; Toccata in D). Lipatti (piano), C 4633 (*"Jesu, Joy of Man's Desiring"; Siciliana; 2 Chorale-Preludes; Mozart: Sonata No. 8 in A minor).*

Landowska's is a low-level re-recording, thick in sound. Her performance makes up for the tonal deficiencies; it is sprightly, imaginative, authoritative. Lipatti's performance also can have a string of nice adjectives, such as spacious, flowing, even-fingered. The comparison here is between pearls and rubies. Naturally the harpsichord is closer to Bach, and it is the version I would choose. As between Landowska and Kirkpatrick on HS 3056, the latter is a much more realistic tonal product, and musically it would grace anybody's collection. But through the inferior sound of the Landowska disc comes a quality of grace and poetry which Kirkpatrick only suggests—even if Landowska does use a couple of ritards that would have uncurled Bach's wig. Landowska is, and always has been, a romantic.

Partita for Harpsichord No. 4 in D. See Collections: Kapell (V LM 1791).

*Partita for Harpsichord No. 6 in E minor. Gieseking, C 4646 (*Handel: Suite in E; Scarlatti: 5 Sonatas). Tureck, All 67.*

Both of these are piano versions. Gieseking's is incredibly fluent, delicate, subtly adjusted, much of it presented with a feathery touch and scaled-down dynamics. Supreme artistry is contained on this disc. The recording is quiet, undistorted, and a little dull. The Tureck is a fine performance that suffers from below-par recording. She is more of a scholar than Gieseking, and her ideas are always interesting. The only harpsichord version, and a mighty fine one it is, is Kirkpatrick's, discussed above, on HS 3058.

Partitas and Sonatas for Unaccompanied Violin (6, complete). Heifetz, V LM 6105 [*3*]. *Schneider, Mer MGL 1* [*4*]. *Schröder, C SL 189* [*3*]. *Telmanyi, L LLA 20* [*3*].

The six partitas and sonatas (there are three of each) are the fiddler's lexicon. *Partita No. 4 in D minor* contains the famous *Chaconne.* Heifetz accomplishes some impossible technical feats. He makes everything sound, if not altogether easy, at least playable. That said, question can legitimately be raised about his affinity for this type of music. He is the romantic violinist *par excellence:* but this is not romantic music. The tricks that

Heifetz employs—constant variation of bowing during a given line, constant holds (even to changing the note values), an over-vibrato—are more suited to Bruch than to Bach. As can be guessed, I am not enraptured by his approach. But he has no real competition. Schneider has a harsh quality of sound, works too hard over some sections, lacks Heifetz's technical and tonal wizardry, and takes an extra disc. Schröder uses a Bach bow, which enables him to do all kinds of multiple stopping. But Schröder, a fine musician, does not measure up to Heifetz's pinkie as a violinist. What good being able to quadruple-stop if you don't do it in tune? The same general remarks apply to the Telmanyi discs. Telmanyi, who also uses a "Bach bow," is more secure than Schröder, but his playing is equally heavy, and he makes the *Chaconne* sound infinitely more difficult than, say, Heifetz does with his Bach-less bow. In any event, "it is a misconception (though popularized by so good an authority as Schweitzer) that the bow of Bach's period permitted a slackening of tension by relaxing the pressure of the thumb against the hair in the actual course of playing, thus supposedly allowing the hair to curve over the strings for three- and four-part chords.... The chief secret of four-part harmony on the violin is a bridge less steeply arched than our present average." Thus Robert Donington, in the 1955 edition of *Grove*.

Several recordings of individual partitas and sonatas might here be mentioned. Renardy plays Nos. 1 in G minor and 3 in C on 10" L 423 and 259. He sweats over the bowing and fingering, and is generally unconvincing. Campoli, in No. 4 in D minor (L 395), is over-sweet and small-scaled, presenting the music without enough rhythmic or dynamic contrast. Szigeti is heard in No. 5 in C on C 4286, playing with his customary musicianship, but without much tone or technique. Olevsky, on W 5306, plays Nos. 1 in G minor and 4 in D minor competently, but with muscle rather than grace or imagination. Brilliant, close-up recording. Segovia has a guitar version of the *Chaconne* from the *Partita No. 4* on MGM 3015 and also on D 9751. He claims that the original fits the lute, but nobody pays much attention to him. His performance is a *tour de force* that will interest guitarists, if few else. On C 4935, Francescatti plays the *D minor* and *E major Partitas*. Francescatti does not refrain from some fiddlers' tricks, *à la* Heifetz, and some may react violently to them; but at least Francescatti has tone, control, and technique. The best one-disc example of unaccompanied Bach for violin is played by Milstein on Cap 8298, where he is heard in the *Sonata No. 1 in G minor* and the *Partita No. 4 in D minor*. Milstein engages in no super-vibrato or neo-Auerisms. His performance is one of tremendous solidity, musical probity, and artistry. It is difficult to think of another living violinist who could duplicate this feat.

*Passacaglia and Fugue in C minor. Walcha, D 9560 (*Pastorale in F). Biggs, C 4500 (*Toccata and Fugue in D minor; Fugues in C and G minor). Weinrich, MGM 3021 ("Schübler" Chorale-Preludes; Concerto in A minor).*

Walcha, playing an organ at Lübeck, shows a nobility of conception and a variety of tone color not present in the other versions. Good sound, though Biggs boasts the brightest recording, and his work is forthright and entirely competent. Weinrich's playing is well defined, small-scaled, and beautifully recorded. Avoid the muddy, theater-organ performance of Asma on Ep 3025.

*Pastorale in F. Walcha, D 9560 (*Passacaglia and Fugue).*

Seldom heard, the *Pastorale* is a fairly long four-movement work somewhat resembling a suite. It is melodious and relatively simple. Walcha brings out the melody and simplicity in a penetrating performance marked by extreme clarity of registers. For another fine performance see Collections: Heitmann (Tel 66009).

Preludes and Fugues for Organ. Walcha, D DX 117 [3].

Eleven preludes and fugues are contained in this set—the ones in D (often heard in Eugen d'Albert's piano transcription), G minor, F minor, C, A, C minor, G, A minor (best known in Liszt's transcription), C, B minor, and E flat. For those interested, the Bach-Gesellschaft numbers are 2, 5, 4, 17, 6, 16, 11, 13, 15, and 14. The concluding E flat can be located in Vol. III of the *Klavierwerke*. As in the other albums of his Bach series, Walcha splits the work between baroque organs at Lübeck and Capell. The pitch of these is considerably above our 440-A. Walcha's playing features a superb clarification of the polyphony, sensitive registrations, an avoidance of great drama, and constant nobility of conception. A magnificent, well-recorded set. On 10" MGM 527, Weinrich plays three preludes and fugues—A (No. 6), C (No. 1), and A minor (No. 13). Walcha's set includes two of these. Those who want to investigate the Gothic world of Bach's organ music, but do not wish to pay the price of a three-disc introduction, might well turn to the little Weinrich disc. But get the Decca album if you can afford it.

Preludes and Fugues for Organ (individual). See Collections: Biggs (C 4097, 4285); Alain (HS 104); Demessieux (L 319).

Prelude, Fugue, and Allegro in E flat. See *Toccatas in E minor and D minor* (Ly 48). See also Collections: Landowska (V LM 1217).

Sonatas for Cello and Piano Nos. 1 in G and 2 in D. Casals, Baumgartner, C 4349.

*Sonata for Cello and Piano No. 3 in G minor. Casals, Baumgartner, C 4350 (*Chromatic Fantasy and Fugue; Italian Concerto).*

Fruits of the 1950 Prades Festival. The recorded sound is not bad, but Casals is up front to the detriment of the cello. Considering the grandeur of the Casals tone and musicianship, one ought not quibble; but the piano has an important part too. Extraneous sounds come from Casals in these recordings: from his vocal cords in addition to his bow (especially in the slow movement of the *D major Sonata*). Piatigorsky and Berkowitz also offer a good performance of the *D major Sonata* on V LM 1792 (*Prokofiev: *Cello Sonata*).

Sonatas for Flute and Harpsichord (complete). Wummer, Valenti, W WAL 216 [2]. *Baker, Marlowe, D DX 113* [2].

Two excellent flutists. Baker plays six sonatas, Wummer eight. Most standard editions contain only the six that are in the Decca set; the seventh is a disputed work. The eighth is a *Sonata for Unaccompanied Flute in A minor.* Wummer has a little more character to his playing. Baker has a stronger lip and a fuller tone. The latter here has accomplished some of the most virtuosic flute work on records, but the constant emphasis on tone and technique results in an over-brilliant approach where one is as cognizant of the soloist as of the music; and not all of Baker's control, assurance, and tonal purity keeps the music from becoming something of a bore. Both recordings are exceptionally lifelike, though the Decca is a little fuller. Both harpsichordists, too, are proficient. My choice is the Westminster set, as it offers two more works than the Decca presents, and as Wummer's musical approach is more subtle than Baker's. Some individual discs of these sonatas are worth mention here. Birkelund and Viderø, on HS 3067, play Nos. 1, 2, and 7, collaborating in performances that have relaxation and an air of competent music-making. For a one-disc introduction to Bach's flute sonatas, this is ideal. See *Trio*

Sonata in G (OL 50015) for a performance of No. 5. On C 4354 is a version of No. 1 from the 1950 Prades Festival, played by Wummer and Mannes (piano) on a catch-all disc that also contains the fifth *English Suite* and a prelude and fugue. Not much challenge to the Haydn Society disc, though Wummer plays quite beautifully. A good buy is two Allegro discs—4003/4—of the *Flute Sonata in E flat*, the *Sonata in G for Two Flutes* (4003), the *Sonata in G for Flute, Violin, and Continuo*, and the *Sonata for Unaccompanied Flute in A minor* (4004). Phillip Kaplan, Lois Schaeffer, and a continuo of harpsichord and cello participate. The performances are musical, and the recorded sound is good.

Sonatas for Violin and Clavier (6, complete). Schneider, Kirkpatrick (harpsichord), 10" C 2109/10/11 [3]. *Menuhin, Kentner (piano), V HMV 1016/17* [2].

The Columbia performance is without the velvet sheen of Menuhin-Kentner, but it has something much better: an insight into Bach's world. The harpsichord is a much better partner than the piano, and the Columbia instrumentalists go to work with plenty of solidity, strong rhythmic outline, and, in general, a decisive quality sorely lacking in the over-refined work of the Victor artists. Menuhin seems to place his emphasis on tone, on an unfailing sweetness and placidity that soon become absolutely cloying. Kentner's work at the piano is also much too smoothed-out. The result is like a pretty girl without a skeleton.

Sonata for Violin and Harpsichord in G. See *Trio Sonata in G for Flute, Violin, and Harpsichord* (OL 50015).

Sonatas for Violin and Piano in E and G minor; Partita in E minor. Stern, Zakin, C 4862.

Fine recorded sound, though the balance features the violin. Zakin is here an accompanist rather than a partner. The *E major Sonata* is well known; the other works are curiosities. Stern is a strong and brilliant fiddler with some romantic mannerisms that do not go with this music.

Suites for Unaccompanied Cello (individual):

Nos. 1 in G and 4 in E flat. Starker, Per 582.

Nos. 2 in D minor and 3 in C. Casals, V LCT 1104.

Nos. 3 in C and 6 in D. Starker, Per 543.

Uniformly fine cello-playing on these three discs. Starker whips his bulky instrument around with perfect control and a perpetually singing tone. Casals has the field to himself with No. 2. A comparison of his No. 3 with Starker's is very flattering to the younger cellist. Discounting the advantage Starker has in richer, fuller recording, his ideas are just as assertive and his mechanism is just as responsive. There are shadings in Casals's bow that Starker cannot match, and Casals gives more of a feeling of musical repose. Casals remains the king; but Starker is, at the very least, a prince of the blood. Several other recordings of the cello suites are available. Janigro is easily outclassed in his discs of Nos. 1 and 3 (W 5217) and Nos. 2 and 6 (W 5348), though he would make a good showing against any but such strong playing as Casals and Starker offer. Mainardi, in Nos. 3 and 4 (10" L 403/4 [2]), is not a good economic proposition.

*Suite for Flute and Figured Bass in C minor. Rampal, Veyron-Lacroix, HS 80 (*Vivaldi: Concerto for Flute and Oboe; Sonata for Flute and Figured Bass).*

This is a large-scale work that may or may not have been intended for flute, but the part sounds natural enough. The performances are conscientious. Rampal's tone is not always a thing of joy, and Veyron-Lacroix pounds his harpsichord relentlessly. First-class recorded sound.

*Toccata in D. Landowska, V LCT 1137 (*Italian Concerto; Chromatic Fantasy and Fugue; Partita in B flat). Valenti, Ly 47 (*Toccata in C minor; Chromatic Fantasy and Fugue).*

Landowska plays this grand work with a springy rhythm, and her unerring pace provides a forceful statement of the music. The recording shows its age, but its musical virtues are such that it automatically supersedes the choppy, spasmodic Valenti disc. Nor does the thick sound in the bass make the latter a particularly good reproduction of harpsichord tone.

Toccatas in E minor and D minor; Prelude, Fugue, and Allegro in E flat. Valenti, Ly 48.

Valenti brings to the music a rugged approach that commands respect, but sometimes one gets the feeling that it is more muscle than instinct on the harpsichordist's part. Fortunately, the approach is less spasmodic than in the *D major Toccata* on Ly 47. Thus the result is tremendous music honestly presented. The recording is good, though again one is disturbed by a few soggy basses. For a superior recording of the *Prelude, Fugue, and Allegro*, see Collections: Landowska (V LM 1217).

Toccata, Adagio, and Fugue in C. Biggs, C 4284 ("Schübler" Chorale-*

*Preludes). Eggington, OL 50012 (*Preludes and Fugues in G, C, and E minor; Fugue in D). Schweitzer, C SL 175 (*Chorale-Preludes, etc. See Collections: Schweitzer).*

Although I think that the Biggs performance is the best of the three under consideration, I am not happy with his unimaginative treatment of the music. In any case, however, it must be preferred to the small-scale Eggington version; and Eggington plays the other music on his disc much the same way. Schweitzer has the grandeur of conception that Biggs lacks, but he no longer has the manual ability to articulate the music clearly, and he is forced to take inordinately slow tempos. I'd avoid the noisy, over-reverberant version by Asma on Ep 3025; and the Demessieux on L 946 is too mannered for my taste.

Toccata and Fugue in D minor. See Collections: Biggs (C 4500); Demessieux (L 319).

Trio Sonata No. 1 in C. See Collections: Harpsichord Quartet (ES 528).

Trio Sonata in G for Flute, Violin, and Harpsichord; Sonata in E minor for Flute and Harpsichord; Sonata in G for Violin and Harpsichord; Trio in D minor for Flute, Oboe, and Harpsichord. Collegium Pro Arte, OL 50015.

Several things combine to make this disc less than exhilarating. The music is altogether routine Bach—if it *is* Bach. The musicians obviously mean well, but their unyielding, metronomic, four-square approach will make more enemies than friends for the composer. Performances like these put the curse on music as a living force.

Trio Sonatas for Organ (6, complete). Walcha, D DX 114 [2].

Some of Bach's finest organ music is present here. It is varied in mood and content; and if there is a more moving melody anywhere in Bach than the andante from the *Fourth Sonata* I don't know where it is. Walcha plays thoughtfully, and the recorded sound has beautiful color and quality. My only complaint about the performance is a tendency toward over-deliberate tempos which sometimes robs the music of the contrast it should have. The relation, for instance, between the two sections of the first movement of the *Fourth Sonata* is hardly the adagio-vivace indicated in the Bach-Gesellschaft; and even granting that Bach's own indications have not come down to us, the nature of the music calls for greater variety than Walcha offers. Withal, a sensitive job, and a required album for Bach-collectors.

*Variations on "Sei gegrüsset, Jesu gütig." Viderø, HS 3063 (*5 Chorale-Preludes). Walcha, D 9615 (*Canonic Variations on "Vom Himmel hoch, da komm' ich her").*

"Sei gegrüsset" is a magnificent set of chorale-variations for organ. Viderø plays a Danish instrument with bright, reedy characteristics. Walcha's interpretation is softer, and his registrations are more conventional. Viderø's ideas are more rhythmically decisive than Walcha's; the latter's whole approach is quieter and more restrained. As played by the two organists, some sections sound almost like two different pieces of music. Both are imaginative musicians; I prefer Viderø because of the slightly clearer recording and his more decided ideas about the music. In the *Canonic Variations*, Walcha uses an organ pitched about a half-tone high. It is music of amazing ingenuity, and Walcha handles it with complete linear independence. For another version of these *Canonic Variations*, see Collections: Viderø (HS 94).

Well-Tempered Clavier (complete). Landowska (harpsichord), V LM 1017 (Nos. 1-8); V LM 1107 (9-16); V LM 1136 (17-24); V LM 1152 (25-32); V LM 1708 (33-40); V LM 1820 (41-48). Tureck (piano), D DX 127 [3] *(Book I); D DX 128* [3] *(Book II).*

The Landowska series started coming out in 1950 and spread out, disc by disc, until 1954. It is no discredit to Tureck's remarkable artistry to place the Landowska discs on top. If nothing else, the harpsichord serves the music better than the piano. And Landowska remains unique. However debatable her ideas may be, she invariably supports them with a musical *raison d'être.* As an executive artist she is flawless: independent left hand, articulation as efficient as a Geiger counter, linear freedom. These are as close as interpretations can come to being definitive. For those who want a piano version, the Tureck will more than fill all needs. The recording is clear, and the playing contains style, scholarship, and technique—a fairly unbeatable combination. Tureck is among the smoothest of Bach-players, with a legato like oil and an entire battery of finger weights at her command. Another harpsichord version of Book I, in addition to Landowska's, is in the catalogues, played by Isolde Ahlgrimm on C SL 191 [3]. She plays a pedal harpsichord for no particular reason; and either the recording is slow or the harpsichord is a half-tone down. The envelope notes are silent on the point. In any case, her interpretation is considerably below the Landowska level.

I have listened to the test pressings of the Demus piano recording of *The Well-Tempered Clavier* (Westminster). Those I heard—and it is not fair to Westminster to make any final judgment on the basis of test pressings—were very clear piano recordings with a bad ping in some fortissimo treble sections. Some of Demus's best playing is on these discs. At the same time, I do not find anything approaching the ease and stylistic authority of Tureck. Nor do I find much except a well-drilled, methodical approach. Demus does not maintain much tension in the melodic line, and he has some inexcusable mannerisms; one is the sudden speed-up toward the end of the *C minor Prelude* of Book I. Obviously Demus considers it in the nature of a stretto, but the end effect is merely eccentric.

BALAKIREV, MILY (1837-1910)

Islamey. See Collections: Barere (Rem 199-141).

BARBER, SAMUEL (1910-)

*Four Excursions. Firkusny, 10" C 2174 (*Knoxville, 1915).*

Pleasant, idiomatic piano pieces that achieved a short vogue several years ago. Firkusny plays them elegantly. The reverse of the disc contains a work for soprano and orchestra. Firkusny receives acceptable recording, though the sound is a far cry from what Columbia can accomplish today.

*Quartet for Strings (Op. 11). Stradivari, Str 602 (*Cello Sonata; Wolf: Italian Serenade).*

Barber composed the quartet in 1936. The slow movement, later arranged for string orchestra, is best known in that form as the *Adagio for Strings.* The quartet is a conservative work in two movements, full of promise, and is well played by the Stradivari group. Tonally the recording will serve, but is lacking in color and definition. The earlier (1932) *Cello Sonata* is a student work after the best romantic models. George Ricci, an unusually fine cellist, is the artist here. Dated-sounding recording, with the piano in bad relation to the stringed instrument. This sonata also has been recorded by Garbousova on CH 1092 (*Thompson: *Quartet* *in D minor)*, a warmer example of recorded sound, and a thoroughly acceptable performance.

Sonata for Cello. See *Quartet for Strings* (Str 602).

*Sonata for Piano in E flat minor. Horowitz, V LM 1113 (*Chopin: Sonata in B flat minor).*

Barber, in this work, obviously set out to compose a big, splashy, neo-romantic display piece. What resulted, however, is a synthetic that goes through all the motions but has no inner life. In Horowitz the composer has an interpreter who can do as much as anybody alive for the music. (The pianist was once asked if the sonata is as difficult as it sounds. He shrugged his shoulders. "Not too hard—like the Chopin *B minor Sonata.*") It's an electrifying performance, well recorded, but what one carries away is the piano-playing rather than the music.

*Souvenirs (1952). Gold and Fizdale, C 4855 (*Haieff: Sonata for Two Pianos).*

Although this disc is available separately, it belongs in the 3-disc "Music for Two Pianos—1900-1952" album. For complete contents see under Collections: Gold and Fizdale (C SL 198). Barber's work consists of six fairly short pieces, all in dance form—waltz, tango, two-step, etc. I find them tiresome. After several playings, the slick, superficial elegance wears off and the poverty of invention is laid bare. The Haieff work is an expected synthesis of Stravinsky, complete with the neo-classic patterns and abrupt rhythmic shifts of the old master. Gold and Fizdale treat this pair of works efficiently. Their playing is brisk, their ensemble perfect, their outlook attuned to the idiom.

BARTÓK, BÉLA (1881-1945)

*Bagatelles (Op. 6). Kozma, Bar 918 (*6 Romanian Folk Dances; 20 Romanian Christmas Carols).*

The fourteen *Bagatelles* date from 1909. Though most of them use original themes, they are saturated with the Hungarian melos. Both Romanian sets are frankly folkloristic. The *Folk Dances,* close translations of Romanian fiddle tunes, are often heard in concert. Kozma treats this material with a fairly percussive touch, a minimum of pedal, and a strong rhythm—exactly the way the music should be treated. The recorded sound is bright and colorful. Lili Kraus has recorded the *Six Dances* on D 4011, together with the *Three Rondos on Folk Tunes*. This 10" disk is nowhere nearly as vital in sound as the Kozma, and it has prominent surfaces, but if you are interested in the *Dances* alone it is a good buy.

"Bartók Plays Bartók." Bartók, 10" Bar 003.

The contents are: *Romanian Dance* (Op. 8a, No. 1); *Burlesque No. 2* ("A Bit Drunk"); *Allegro Barbaro; Bagatelle* (Op. 6, No. 2); *Suite* (Op. 14). Bad recorded sound here, but the disc has great interest. Bartók was a fine pianist, and he plays his music in the romantic tradition of the nineteenth century, with plenty of sweep and bravura. (It is interesting to note that he came in second to none less than Wilhelm Backhaus in the International Rubinstein Competition for Pianists in 1905.) A more up-to-date version of the *Suite* and the *Allegro Barbaro* is played by Sandor; see Piano Music (C 4868). See also the listings under *Mikrokosmos* (C 4419), "*Contrasts*" (C 2213), and *Sonata for Two Pianos and Percussion* (Vox 6010), in all of which Bartók himself is soloist.

*Contrasts for Violin, Clarinet, and Piano. Mann, Drucker, Hambro, Bar 916 (*Sonata for Unaccompanied Violin). Szigeti, Goodman, Bartók, 10" C 2213 (*Rhapsody No. 1; Portrait). Ritter, Kell, J. Rosen, D 9740 (*Milhaud: Suite for Violin, Clarinet, and Piano).*

The Columbia is the famous pre-war set with the composer at the piano. It was, and is, a notable performance. But as an example of recorded sound it is nowhere near the Bartók disc, one of the most lifelike recordings in the catalogues. The Bartók is also an equally brilliant performance. A choice is hard to make. Myself, with all due respect to the musical and nostalgic values of the Columbia, I'll take the newer version; and one determining reason is Mann's magnificent performance of the *Sonata for Unaccompanied Violin* on the reverse. Kell and his colleagues, on the Decca disc, have been well recorded and present a smooth performance, but their playing lacks the bite heard in the other versions.

Duos (44) for Two Violins. Aitay, Kuttner, Bar 907.

Originally these pieces were released on two Period discs, but Bartók took them over and re-recorded them on one. The work is a series of miniatures, as well they would have to be to get forty-four on one disc. All are based on Hungarian folk patterns and can best be described as a sort of *Mikrokosmos* for two fiddles.

Only a devoted Bartókian would want to hear them all through at one sitting. Taken in small doses, the music is piquant, exotic, and appealing. Aitay and Kuttner, both Hungarians, are excellent violinists. One of the most pleasant features of their performance is the pure intonation they employ.

For Children (79 Pieces for Piano). Kozma, Bar 919/20 [2]. *Pressler, MGM 3009, 3047* [2].

Bartók composed two books. Vol. I contains forty short pieces based on Hungarian folk tunes; Vol. II has thirty-nine based on Slovakian tunes. He originally composed eighty-five, but in a revised edition cut them down to the seventy-nine played by Kozma and Pressler. Like the *Mikrokosmos,* the *For Children* sketches were intended as teaching material; they are simple and tuneful, but contain a high degree of harmonic and rhythmic sophistication. Both pianists have received clear recordings, but the edge goes to the Bartók disc, which is fuller and brighter, and which has clearer surfaces. Pressler on the whole is softer and more delicate, Kozma more rhythmic, stronger, more percussive. The Kozma version is more to my taste, though anybody who ends up with Pressler will not regret the choice. Béla Bartók has recorded ten of the pieces on Vox 6010; these were taken from an air check in 1945 (see *Sonata for Two Pianos and Percussion*). And on C 4868, Sandor has recorded twenty (see Piano Music).

Hungarian Peasant Songs. See *Sonatina for Piano* (Vox 6410); *Piano Music* (C 4868).

*Mikrokosmos (excerpts). Bartók, C 4419. Katchen, L 759 (*Rorem: Sonata).*

Altogether, Bartók composed six volumes (153) of these pieces, which were intended as teaching material for children. The Columbia disc, with the composer at the piano, offers thirty-five. It was recorded around 1940, and the LP transfer has a good deal of surface noise, though the piano sound itself is quite listenable. Katchen plays but eight of the sketches, and so if it's the *Mikrokosmos* in which you are interested, the Columbia is by far the better choice. Tibor Serly's arrangement of five of the *Mikrokosmos* for string quartet is on Bar 901. The transcription appears unnecessary, well played as it is by the New Music String Quartet.

Out of Doors Suite; Improvisations (Op. 20). Hambro, Bar 902.

Aside from excess surface noise, this is an admirably defined piano recording. *Out of Doors,* composed in 1926, is not pictorial program music, but an evocation of the countryside in general. Section IV, "Night Music," is one of the composer's remarkable studies of night noises. The *Improvisations* are based on Hungarian folk melodies. Hambro presents a vigorous, mettlesome performance that does honor to his musical instincts. There is a constant propulsive quality to his work, and he never lets either the notes or the musical plan get out of hand.

Piano Music (miscellaneous). Sandor, C 4868.

The contents: *Allegro Barbaro;* six *Romanian Folk Dances;* twenty excerpts from *For Children;* fifteen *Hungarian Peasant Songs.* Sandor has a flair for this music. He plays with force, directness, and a technique that is more than merely able. Excellent recorded sound here; and if one is too conscious of a percussive quality, it is less a characteristic of the disc than of Sandor's style of attack. For another disc of miscellaneous pieces, see "Bartók Plays Bartók" (10" Bar 003).

Quartets for Strings (6, complete). Juilliard, C 4278/9/80 [3].

The much-discussed, much-written-about quartets by Bartók are a cross-section of his career from 1907 to 1939, during which period the composer went his own uncompromising way. These are not easy listening. The writing is savage, dissonant, full of strange effects. But they are tremendous conceptions and authentic masterpieces, and every intelligent music-lover should at least give them a chance. Such robust, red-blooded music cannot fail to make its impact after a few hearings. There is little to complain about in the performances by the talented young members of the Juilliard Quartet. Like many of the eager younger generation, they revel in the complexities and difficulties of modern music. Perhaps they lack color, and they certainly are inclined to rush headlong into the music. Yet they have a bracing, sure-handed, and confident way with music like this. I like the cocky way they dispose of the formidable writing and the intelligence with which they organize their material. Columbia has given them sparkling, well-balanced sound. The New Music String Quartet has recorded the *Third Quartet* on Bar 901. Theirs is a warmer, less objective approach, but the coupling (Serly's arrangement for string quartet of several *Mikrokosmos* pieces) favors the Juilliard.

*Rhapsody No. 1 for Violin and Piano. Szigeti, Bartók, 10" C 2213 (*Contrasts; Portrait for Orchestra).*

This transfer of a pre-war recording to LP shows its age. Considerations of recording, however, are unimportant in view of the beautiful performance by the two Hungarian musicians. Szigeti's gypsy blood comes to a boil; he uses a pronounced portamento and a vibrato that must have come close to melting the varnish from his fiddle. Quite a memento of Szigeti and the composer, this disc. Bartók also transcribed this *Rhapsody* for cello and piano, and it is so played by Starker and Herz on Per 715 (*Hindemith: *Cello Sonata;* Weiner: *Lakodalmas*). Starker's performance is lively, but the work does not sound lively as a cello solo; it needs the more effervescent fiddle. The Weiner filler on Starker's disc is gypsy-ish and pleasant.

Romanian Folk Dances; Romanian Christmas Carols. See *Bagatelles* (Bar 918); *Piano Music* (C 4868).

Sonata for Piano (1926). See Collections: Skolovsky (C 4871).

*Sonata for Two Pianos and Percussion. Yessin, etc., V LM 1727 (*Goeb: Symphony No. 3). Bartók, etc., Vox 6010 (*10 Pieces from For Children; Evening in Transylvania; Bear Dance).*

In the Vox disc, Bartók and his wife, Ditta Pasztory, are the pianists. The recording, made from an air check in 1941, is muffled and characterless in sound. As an indication of tempos, musical approach, and details of performance, the version is of course invaluable. The reverse of this disc contains some solo pieces played by the composer on a Hungarian radio hour in 1945. He announces his own selections. Victor's disc is a much clearer recording, and sections of the scoring that are obscured in the Vox emerge with brilliance in it. The Victor, then, is preferable, unless you have a sentimental interest in hearing the composer himself. A word of warning: the music, composed in 1937, is barbaric, complex, extremely dissonant, and is definitely not for the listener who thinks the *Liebestraum* the last word in musical daring.

*Sonata for Unaccompanied Violin. Mann, Bar 916 (*Contrasts). Menuhin, V LM 1087 (*Prokofiev: Sonata in F minor). Gertler, An 35091 (*Berg: Violin Concerto).*

The Mann version is the choice here, without ifs, ands, or buts. The young leader of the Juilliard Quartet plays this knotty work with sweep, color, amazingly perfect intonation and control. This disc displays a type of lifelike recording which puts the player right in your living-room. Neither Menuhin nor Gertler displays the incisive command of Mann; compare the opening of the fugue, where Mann is completely assured and not afraid of a fast tempo. Both of the other violinists hold back, and their performance sounds tentative by contrast.

Sonata for Violin and Piano No. 1. Stern, Zakin, C 4376. Menuhin, Baller, V LM 1009.

Completed in 1923, this is an experimental work, a study in rhythm, sonority, and dissonance. It has tremendous power, little melodic attraction. Stern gives a sinewy performance that shows an impressive grasp of the musical and technical fundamentals. He is inclined to be steely; certainly he could have achieved more nuance and variety in the opening solo of the second movement. The recorded sound leaves much to be desired. Surfaces are poor; a heavy background noise intrudes during the slow movement, and there are details in the complicated writing that simply do not come through. The Victor disc has better balance and a more realistic sound to both instruments. Menuhin, though, lacks the strength and slashing rhythm of Stern, who makes a much more exciting experience of the sonata. Despite its inferior recording, the Stern performance is recommended.

*Sonata for Violin and Piano No. 2. Druian, Simms, Mer 70000 (*Ravel: Violin Sonata). Spivakovsky, Balsam, CH 39 (*4 Romanian Dances).*

Another advanced, barbaric-sounding work, full of glides, swoops, strange effects, bitter harmonies: a typical middle-period Bartók conception. Spivakovsky's performance is brilliant, but the defects of the recording nullify his efforts. The sound is thin, the piano is tinny, and there is a good deal of distortion and surface noise. Druian, not as strong or exciting a protagonist as Spivakovsky, nevertheless plays with a good deal of conviction, and he has the benefit of up-to-date recording. His version therefore takes priority. To fill out the last side, Spivakovsky plays four *Romanian Dances*. The complete set of six has been recorded in its original form by Kozma. See *Bagatelles* (Bar 918).

*Sonatina for Piano; 15 Hungarian Peasant Songs. Foldes, Vox 6410 (*Rhapsody for Piano and Orchestra).*

Both works date from around 1915, Bartók's second period (it has been labeled "Of Authentic Folklore and Of Imaginative Folklore"). They are nationalistic, sounding like lots of music Bartók composed before and after; and sometimes one wonders if his ethnologic interests did not get the better of him. Foldes is a most persuasive exponent of this music. He plays with remarkable surety and clarity, and with more tonal virtue than he elsewhere shows. Ilona Kabos, on Bar 917, also is heard in the *Sonatina* (in addition to the *Three Rondos* and eight of the *For Children* sketches). But the reverse of her disc contains the boring *Seven Pieces* by Kodály, while the *Rhapsody* that Foldes plays is a lot of fun. And although the Vox sound is not as bright as the Bartók, it is perfectly satisfactory.

BARTOŠ, FRANTIŠEK (1905-)

Incidental Music to Le Bourgeois Gentilhomme. See Janáček: *Youth Sextet* (Mer 15009).

BAX, ARNOLD (1883-1953)

*Quintet for Harp and Strings. Newell, Stuyvesant, Ph 102 (*Ibert: Harp Trio; Malipiero: Sonata a cinque).*

The Bax is an example of vague British impressionism, vintage 1919. It is in one long movement—a *very* long movement. Ibert's *Trio* is a pedestrian piece of writing, though the composer's irrepressible temperament occasionally peeps through; and the Malipiero score contains more atmospheric effects than music. Not an exhilarating group of pieces, in short. The performances sound fine, but the recording is low-level, lacking definition and instrumental color.

BEETHOVEN, LUDWIG VAN (1770-1827)

Andante Favori. See *Sonata for Piano No. 32* (C 4335).

Bagatelles (complete). Johannesen, CH 1199.

In addition to the standard *Bagatelles*—the seven of Op. 33, the eleven of Op. 119, and the six of Op. 126—Johannesen plays a pair that were discovered in the late nineteenth century and date from 1797. All of this music has been under-appreciated. It consists of imaginative, whimsical sketches that often approach a Schumannesque form of romanticism (the A major of Op. 33, or the first of Op. 119, for example). The two last sets relate to the last five piano sonatas—but the *Bagatelles* are the microcosm rather than the macrocosm. Johannesen is disappointing here. His work is skillful enough, but it lacks imagination and tends to be colorless. The suggestions—and they are frequent—of Beethoven's elephantine humor scarcely come through. At least Johannesen does not misrepresent the music, and the recording has a good quality of piano sound. Dirksen has recorded Op. 126; see *Variations for Flute and Piano* (Es 525/6).

Octet for Winds in E flat (Op. 103). See *Sextet for Winds in E flat* (W 5003).

Octet Rondo for Winds in E flat. See *Trio for Winds in E flat* (W 5262).

Quartet for Piano and Strings in E flat (Op. 16). See discussion of *Quintet for Piano and Winds in E flat (Op. 16).*

Quartets (3) for Piano and Strings (Grove 152). Balsam, Pascal, CH 1215.

Pleasant, derivative, occasionally forceful music from a boy of fifteen. There is some material here that Beethoven later used in some other works. The Pascal Quartet, sparked by Balsam's precise playing, presents the music with competence. Not many favorable things can be said about the recorded sound, which has a considerable amount of distortion.

*Quartet for Strings in C (Op. 2, No. 3). Pascal, CH 1201 (*Quartet No. 1).*

Here is Beethoven's *Piano Sonata No. 3* (Op. 2, No. 3) in a transcription by one Alexandre Brand for string quartet. It is a skillful, if altogether supererogatory, piece of work. The performance by the Pascal Quartet is excellent, and the recording has a realistic texture of string tone.

Quartet for Strings in F (Op. 14, No. 1). Another transcription, this one by Beethoven himself. See *Sextet in E flat*, Op. 81b (CH 1216).

Quartets for Strings (complete). Budapest, C SL 172 [3] *(Op. 18, Nos. 1-6); C SL 173* [4] *(Op. 59, Nos. 1-3; Op. 74, 95); C SL 174* [5] *(Op. 127, 130, 131, 132, 133, 135). Vegh, HS HSQ N* [3] *(Op. 18); HS HSQ O* [3] *(Op. 59, 74, 95); HS HSQ P* [4] *(Op. 127, 130, 131, 132, 133, 135). Pascal, CH 1201/12* [12].

Of the three sets, the Vegh enjoys the best recording; it is as fine an example of string-quartet tone as one can hear on discs, and virtually the only defect is some annoying "ghosts" throughout the *Grosse Fuge*. The Budapest has clear recording, but is a little thinner and has an occasional shrillness that cannot be equalized out. The Pascal recordings are variable; some are full and resonant, others tend toward thinness, and some of the surfaces will not bear inspection.

As an all-around proposition I would select the Budapest, an organization that has no peer in German classic and romantic music. They play with a degree of strength and aristocracy, suppleness and tensile grace which puts them above the more stolid Vegh interpretations. The Vegh ensemble is forceful enough, and plays with considerable musicianship, but does not always shape a line with the instinct of the Budapest. Compare the codas of the second movement of the *C minor Quartet:* B. is all elegance and refinement; V. is stolid and deliberate. This is admittedly an extreme example. Without attempting to detract from the fine work of V., the competitive version has just as much solidity and is at the same time consistently smoother. The Pascal Quartet plays with a rugged bite and vigor, and some of its performances are splendid. On the whole, though, its intonation and ensemble are less exact than either V. or B., and while the Concert Hall recording at its best is clear and intimate, individual discs in this series sound harsh and not a little overamplified. Two of the discs, too, have pitch trouble: Op. 127 and Op. 130 are both a half-tone high.

Quartets for Strings (individual).

The Budapest, Vegh, and Pascal series are also available on single discs. Several other groups have a number of Beethoven quartets to their credit. The Barylli Quartet has recorded Nos. 1 and 2 (W 5203), 3 and 4 (5211), 5 and 11 (5140), 6 (5212), 13 (5129), 14 (5144), 16 and the *Grosse Fuge* (5151). These are well recorded and played with considerable spirit, but the leader's tone is inclined to be scratchy and he is not at all bashful about featuring it. The Vienna Konzerthaus has recorded the other five quartets for Westminster in a stodgy, uninspired manner. On a series of Victor discs the Paganini Quartet holds forth in Beethoven, with Nos. 1 and 2 (LM 1729), 4 and 5 (LM 1052), 7 and 8 (10" LM 7000/1 [2]), 9 and 10 (LM 1722), 14 (LM 1736) and 16 (10" LM 24). One thing this quartet does have, and that is tone. Even though the group suffered some personnel changes during the series, it never lost its juicy sound. The performances always have taste, though the interpretations never match those of the Budapest or Vegh in intensity or integration. On L 673 the

Quartetto Italiano present a songful interpretation of the *Quartet No. 7* (the first "Rasoumovsky"), but the same group is distressingly sentimental and affected in a recent Op. 130 on An 35064. Mention must be made of an old recording of No. 7 by the Busch Quartet on C 4155. This is a magnificent, regal conception, and the recorded sound retains its vitality.

*Quintet for Strings in C (Op. 29). Barylli, Huebner, W 5212 (*Quartet No. 6).*

This is early Beethoven, a large-scale, spirited work with an imaginative finale. It receives a musicianly, brilliant-sounding performance. The Pascal Quartet and Gerhard present an even smoother job on CH 1214, but on the Westminster disc you can get two works for Concert Hall's one.

*Quintet for Piano and Winds in E flat (Op. 16). Serkin, Philadelphia Wind Quintet, C 4834 (*Mozart: Quintet for Piano and Winds, K. 452).*

An uncomplicated, jolly, extroverted score. Beethoven was showing his muscles. Here we have a superb performance, sparked by Serkin's exact, rhythmic playing. Few chamber-music records have approached this one in matters of tonal fidelity and balance. Frugoni and the French Woodwind Ensemble have recorded the work on Vox 9090 *(*Concerto in E flat, 1784)*, a clear performance, but without the authority of Serkin and his group. An older version on Str 616 is automatically superseded. On the reverse of the Stradivari disc, it is interesting to note, is this very work, with the same opus number, as arranged by Beethoven himself for piano and strings (and it does not sound nearly as interesting or colorful as it does in the piano-winds version). The best recording of the work as a piano quartet is played by Horszowski and the New York Quartet on C 4627 (*Mozart: *Piano Quartet in G minor*).

Rondos in C and G (Op. 51, Nos. 1, 2). Kempff, 10" D 4086.

Two chips from Beethoven's workshop. The music almost verges on the salon. Kempff's performances are magnificently regulated, and the recorded sound is clear, with smooth surfaces. Too bad that Kempff's series of Beethoven piano sonatas was not turned out with equivalent electronic success.

Septet in E flat (Op. 20). Vienna Philharmonic Wind Group, W 5377. Pro Musica, Vox 6460.

The scoring is for clarinet, bassoon, horn, and string quartet. In its day this was the most popular piece Beethoven ever wrote.

Today we recognize it as a charming but essentially derivative effort. Neither recorded performance sets the music off to best advantage. The Westminster has good recorded sound, but there is some unsteady playing, especially from the first violinist (not to mention the other strings), whose intonation is not a model of accuracy. A routine performance, on the whole. And neither as a performance nor as a recording does the Vox disc stand up. A group of French musicians dutifully goes through the notes—and that is all. The recording, which dates back some years, is unresonant. Toscanini conducts the *Septet* in a blow-up for orchestra on V LM 1745.

Serenade in D (Op. 8). See *Trio for Strings in D* (W 5219).

*Serenade for Flute and Strings in D (Op. 25). Baker, J. and L. Fuchs, D 9574 (*Trio for Strings in C minor).*

The three musicians collaborate in a pert-sounding, well-coordinated reading, though one could wish that Baker paid more attention to the dynamic indications, such as the *forte-piano* contrasts at the beginning of the minuet. Realistic recording, marred by gritty surfaces. Better recorded sound is found on 10" C 2124, where the work is played by Wummer, Schneider, and Katims. Wummer plays with more nuance than Baker, but the Columbia disc is not good enough to spot the Decca an extra work.

Sextet for Winds in E flat (Op. 71); Octet for Winds in E flat (Op. 103). Vienna Philharmonic Wind Group, W 5003.

Despite the advanced opus numbers, these are fairly uninteresting early works. They receive smooth, tonally rich performances by the Viennese wind-players, than whom there are no better. The *Sextet* on this disc sounds more faithfully reproduced than the companion work. It is mellow and well balanced, whereas there are some strained highs in the *Octet.*

*Sextet in E flat for Two Horns and Strings (Op. 81b). Speth, Rawyler, Pascal, CH 1216 (*Quartet in F, Op. 14, No. 1).*

A pair of Beethoven curiosities is on this disc. The early *Sextet* (middle 1790's), energetic and derivative, contains some bearish lumberings indicative of the giant to come. A fine performance and a smooth-sounding recording. The horn parts are not easy, and Messrs. Speth and Rawyler come through superbly. On the reverse is a transcription by Beethoven himself of his *Piano Sonata in E* (Op. 14, No. 1), taken up a half-tone for the convenience of the string-players. The music sounds quite quartet-ish, though anybody who has studied the piano version will find it uncomfortable—even if interesting—listening.

Sonatas for Cello and Piano (5, complete). Casals, Serkin, C SL 201 [3] *(*"Bei Männern" Variations; "Ein Mädchen" Variations). Starker, Bogin, Per 562* [2]. *Janigro, Zecchi, W 5170, 5173, 5180.*

The couplings in the Columbia set are: Nos. 1 in F (Op. 5, No. 1) and 5 in D (Op. 102, No. 2) on C 4876; No. 2 in G minor (Op. 5, No. 2) and the two sets of variations from Mozart's *Magic Flute* on C 4877; Nos. 3 in A (Op. 69) and 4 in C (Op. 102, No. 1) on C 4878. The first and third discs are available also as single records. No. 2 and the variations originally were released on C 4572, and can be purchased by that number. These releases, made at the 1952 and 1953 Prades festivals, are excellent both tonally and in matters of balance. Two perfectly matched musicians operate here. For every bold stroke of the Casals bow there is an equivalently authoritative gesture from Serkin. The cellist was seventy-six years old in 1952, and naturally one cannot expect perfect control from his bow arm; nor is his tone the warm and accurately produced phenomenon it once was. But the virility of his playing is amazing, and the sonatas are played with a personal quality that is altogether moving. Listen carefully, and at odd intervals you can hear the great man grunt and groan. Period, ignoring the *Magic Flute* variations, gets the five sonatas on two discs. Westminster takes three, though part of one disc is devoted to the *"Bei Männern."* I prefer the Starker-Bogin collaboration. In general, Starker is smoother than Janigro and has a more pleasant, more rich-voiced tone. The factor of economy is a strong consideration, too. As a matter of fact, if the glamour of Casals-Serkin-Prades does not mean too much to you, the cheaper-priced Period set should prove a perfectly acceptable substitute.

Sonatas for Cello and Piano (individual).

Nos. 1 and 5, 2 and 4, 3 and the *Magic Flute* variations are available as separate discs played by Serkin and Casals (see above). The Starker and Janigro sets also can be had as single discs. Several other cellists are represented in the Beethoven sonatas. On C 4678, Feuermann and Hess join forces in No. 3 in A (*"*Bei Männern" Variations;* Reger: *Suite for Unaccompanied Cello in G*). It is a transfer to LP, and is marred by heavy surfaces and background noises. Yet I think it is my favorite performance of a Beethoven cello sonata on records. Warm, spacious, lyric sounds come from Feuermann's bow, and Hess in her prime was one of the most elegant of ensemble pianists. Fournier and Schnabel also recorded the A major, together with Nos. 4 and 5, on V LCT 1124. This too is a transfer to LP, but it was recorded some years after the Feuermann-Hess, and the recording, though not brilliant in sound, is clear and well balanced. The playing carries authority, even if one has reservations about Fournier's tone, the purity of his intonation, or his emotional rapport with the pianist. Schnabel is the big brother here, and always takes the lead.

*Sonata for Flute and Piano. Wanausek, Brendel, SPA 28 (*Trio for Flute, Bassoon, and Piano).*

The *Trio* seems to be authentic Beethoven, but there is some doubt about the *Flute Sonata*. Neither has much to recommend it. The writing is pleasant but undistinguished and extremely derivative. Steady performances here, and barely passable recorded sound.

*Sonata for Piano No. 1 in F minor (Op. 2, No. 1). Solomon, V LM 1821 (*Sonata No. 3). Backhaus, L 949 (*Sonatas Nos. 26, 27). Kempff, D 9583 (*Sonata No. 3).*

Because of the inferior quality of the piano tone on the Decca disc, the choice lies between Solomon and Backhaus. Both of these are excellent. Solomon plays the sonata with exquisite finish and elegance. Backhaus probably gets a little more into the music, and his perfectly articulated passagework is a joy to hear. My preference is the Solomon, though the choice is admittedly arbitrary. Kempff takes surprisingly deliberate tempos that are surprisingly effective. His playing here, however, lacks the volatility that makes Solomon's performance so interesting. I was disappointed with Gulda's versions of Sonatas 1 and 2 on L 996. His playing is precise but superficial; he goes through all the motions, and most skillfully, managing somehow to sound small-scaled and unconvincing.

*Sonata for Piano No. 2 in A (Op. 2, No. 2). Backhaus, L 948 (*Sonata No. 11). Kempff, D 9585 (*Sonata No. 15). Casadesus, C 4622 (*Sonata No. 23). Schnabel, V LCT 1155 (*Sonatas Nos. 14, 26).*

Backhaus provides the choice version. In the slow movement he achieves a big frame that neither Kempff nor Casadesus suggests, and his skittish, mettlesome quality in the third movement is full of character. Casadesus, as always, plays fluently (though with a surprising amount of dropped notes). Kempff is closer to the musical content; his is a stronger, more purposeful type of playing. Unfortunately his recording has nowhere near the clarity and color of the competing versions. Schnabel's LP transfer has dated recording sound, and the playing lacks the precise fingerwork of the other pianists. An alarming number of textual errors is present. But shining through the performance are a powerful musical message and a complete identification with the spirit of the music.

*Sonata for Piano No. 3 in C (Op. 2, No. 3). Solomon, V LM 1821 (*Sonata No. 1). Backhaus, L 627 (*Sonata No. 17). Kempff, D 9583 (*Sonata No. 1). Gulda, L 999 (*Sonatas Nos. 19, 20).*

To my taste, the Solomon has most life. The British pianist brings to the music an air of excitement that pushes the music smartly along. His is a better-recorded version than the Backhaus or the Kempff, though there is nothing wrong with the sound that Backhaus receives. Kempff is a little heavier in his approach than Backhaus, who adopts sharper, more incisive patterns. Gulda's keyboard manipulation is excellent, but his ideas lack the focus and intensity of those of the other three pianists.

*Sonata for Piano No. 4 in E flat (Op. 7). Backhaus, L 950 (*Sonata No. 7). Kempff, D 9588 (*Sonata No. 9).*

Backhaus turns in a powerful performance that is aided by excellent piano sound. Kempff's playing is typically vigorous and healthy, but no piano-playing could survive this type of recording. The level is low, and the disc sounds as though it had been pressed on sandpaper.

*Sonata for Piano No. 5 in C minor (Op. 10, No. 1). Backhaus, L 393 (*Sonatas Nos. 6, 25). Kempff, D 9587 (*Sonata No. 32).*

Again, as between the two great German pianists, there is little to choose pianistically; but there is much to choose *re* the recorded sound. The Decca is low-level, with poor surfaces. London has a degree of color that is truer to the piano and to the pianist.

*Sonata for Piano No. 6 in F (Op. 10, No. 2). Backhaus, L 393 (*Sonatas Nos. 5, 25). Kempff, D 9591 (*Sonatas Nos. 22, 30).*

The London has the better sound despite some bass boom and background noise. Those who can put up with the thin Decca sound, however, will own an expertly played version of the sonata. Petri has also recorded the work, on 10" C 2049 (*Bach-Busoni: *Chaconne*), but this is not a fortunate venture. The sound is uncontrollably harsh, and the two versions above remain superior choices.

*Sonata for Piano No. 7 in D (Op. 10, No. 3). Backhaus, L 950 (*Sonata No. 4). Kempff, D 9584 (*Sonata No. 13).*

Backhaus exploits the sonority of the sonata, immeasurably aided by his amazing ability to "get inside" the keys. Resonant recording. Kempff's recording is one of the better in his series; the level is higher and the surfaces not so annoyingly prominent. His performance has vigor, light-fingered articulation, and breadth of conception.

*Sonata for Piano No. 8 in C minor ("Pathètique," Op. 13). Rubinstein, V LM 1072 (*Schumann: Fantasiestücke). Solomon, V LM 1222 (*Sonata No. 32). Backhaus, L 952 (*Sonatas Nos. 9, 15). Gieseking, An 35025 (*Sonata No. 14). Kempff, D 9578 (*Sonatas Nos. 24, 25).*

Several fine *"Pathètiques"* are available. One of Beethoven's most romantic sonatas, it responds beautifully to Rubinstein's romantic treatment. He plays it with tension, drama, a singing line, and variety of color. The recording, though it dates back some years, still has vitality of sound. Solomon's performance is elegantly turned, fluent, and clear. Good sound, some background noise. The Gieseking version is plastic, perfectly controlled, and Grecian in outline. It is handicapped by a thick quality of sound and a thumpy bass. Backhaus is surprisingly flip in the introduction. Elsewhere he has some very original ideas. Agree or disagree with them, they are expressed in piano-playing of immense authority. Kempff is heavy, playing as though he had lost interest in the work years ago. Several other versions should be mentioned. A good low-priced disc is played by Dorfmann on V LBC 1029 (**Sonata No. 14*). Badura-Skoda on W 5184 and Frugoni on Vox 7160 offer three sonatas on one disc—the *"Pathètique,"* "Moonlight," and *"Appassionata."* Both discs are well recorded and neatly played. Yves Nat has also recorded the three sonatas on HS 109. His *"Pathètique"* has considerable power, and despite some rather rough playing it is an interesting version, well worth owning. The recording is too close-up, but reducing the highs helps.

*Sonata for Piano No. 9 in E (Op. 14, No. 1). Backhaus, L 952 (*Sonatas Nos. 8, 15). Schnabel, V LCT 1110 (*Sonatas Nos. 13, 30). Kempff, D 9588 (*Sonata No. 4).*

Backhaus has recorded the finest modern version. The Victor is a transfer to LP from the old Beethoven Society set. Naturally the tonal results leave something to be desired, but one is happy to ignore the sound in the light of Schnabel's mastery. The notes roll off his fingers in an inevitable sequence; everything has logic, organization, and feeling. And, inferior as the recording is, it possesses a better quality of sound than is found in the Decca disc. Nothing is wrong with Kempff's playing, but the pressing is too bad to be recommended. Beethoven himself transcribed this sonata for string quartet: see *Sextet in E flat* (Op. 81b).

*Sonata for Piano No. 10 in G (Op. 14, No. 2). Backhaus, L 603 (*Sonatas Nos. 22, 24). Kempff, D 9592 (*Sonata No. 31).*

Once more there is such a disparity in recording that the result is one-sided. Both pianists play well, but the clear, bright London sound is the deciding factor. Backhaus has a few moments to fill at the end of his disc, so he plays Schumann's "*Warum.*"

*Sonata for Piano No. 11 in B flat (Op. 22). Backhaus, L 948 (*Sonata No. 2). Kempff, D 9590 (*Sonatas Nos. 19, 20).*

Two different ideas about the music are presented here. Backhaus plays with more ardor and much more color, in an interpretation that has a lively, almost frolicsome quality. Kempff offers a lean, carefully shaped performance. He is altogether more objective than Backhaus. The London recording is much the better in sound.

*Sonata for Piano No. 12 in A flat (Op. 26). Backhaus, L 265 (*Sonata No. 21). Kempff, D 9589 (*Sonata No. 16). Gieseking, C 4334 (*Grieg: Lyric Pieces).*

Backhaus has the liveliest sound of the three versions, and he plays in a hearty manner, with considerable drive and power. Kempff's expert, more restrained ideas about the music present the sonata in a different, though equally valid, light. Gieseking does not have much luck with his recording, which has a heavy sound characteristic of many British Columbias of the middle forties. His interpretation is dependable, but he plays as though he were not particularly interested, and one hears little of the rippling quality that he can supply when he wants to.

*Sonata for Piano No. 13 in E flat (Op. 27, No. 1). Backhaus, L 705 (*Sonatas Nos. 14, 19, 20). Kempff, D 9584 (*Sonata No. 7). Schnabel, V LCT 1110 (*Sonatas Nos. 9, 30).*

If the treble is sharply reduced, the Decca disc can be made to reproduce tolerably well. Kempff gives a masterly performance, one with imagination, flexibility, and strength. Backhaus does not appear to be interested in the broader aspects of the sonata. His accents are sharper, his rhythms more clipped, his tempos faster. The Schnabel, a transfer from the old Society set, is a superb performance, somewhat allied to the Backhaus in its crispness. Here we have three views of the sonata by three masters, and anybody who can say "this is the best version" has more confidence than I have. If, however, you want to make the quality of recording the determining factor, the London leads the field.

*Sonata for Piano No. 14 in C sharp minor ("Moonlight," Op. 27, No. 2). Novaes, Vox 8530 (*Piano Concerto No. 4). Gieseking, An 35025 (*Sonata No. 8). Horowitz, V LM 1027 (*Mozart: Sonata in F, K. 332). Backhaus, L 705 (*Sonatas Nos. 13, 20). Kempff, D 9582 (*Sonata No. 26). Schnabel, V LCT 1155 (*Sonatas Nos. 2, 26).*

Beethoven's most popular sonata, which he did not name the "Moonlight," has a spontaneous character under Novaes's fingers. There is nothing capricious about her playing—she keeps a steady rhythm throughout the three movements—but her delicate dynamic adjustments infuse the sonata with a degree of poetry which gives a rhapsodic effect. Gieseking's version also is worth owning. The thick-sounding quality of his recording is nothing to cheer about, but the purity of the playing makes this a most desirable item. Horowitz displays most tension, though it is tension under careful control. There is a fine, spacious feeling to his performance and, not unexpectedly, his version is the most pianistic (*i.e.*, most clearly conceived in terms of the potentialities of the pianoforte). Neither the Kempff nor the Backhaus disc offers much beyond a fairly routine run-through. Among other available "Moonlights," the Serkin on C 4432 sounds turgid. The Dorfmann performance on low-priced V LBC 1029 (*Sonata No. 8*) is an excellent buy. Both Frugoni and Badura-Skoda have recorded this work in a perfectly able manner on Vox 7160 and W 5184, along with the "*Appassionata*" and "*Pathétique*"—all on one disc. Schnabel's performance is not recommended to any but aficionados of the pianist. The low-level recording, in its LP transfer, has a heavy background and some waver in the piano tone. A grand intellectual stature marks the playing, which is a combination of heart and mind. The massive performance by Nat on HS 109 (*Sonatas Nos. 8, 23*) has points of interest despite some rough pianism. Close-up recording, of an explosive nature.

*Sonata for Piano No. 15 in D ("Pastorale," Op. 28). Backhaus, L 952 (*Sonatas Nos. 8, 9). Kempff, D 9585 (*Sonata No. 2). Frugoni, Vox 8650 (*Sonatas Nos. 21, 25, 26). Schnabel, V LCT 1154 (*Sonatas Nos. 19, 31).*

The three German pianists present poised readings that the much better-recorded Frugoni cannot match. Between Backhaus and Kempff, the recorded sound is the determining factor, and Backhaus has the edge. The Schnabel is a collector's reissue, with dated sound that starts a half-tone down (though the pitch rises by the time the sonata is ended). Schnabel is in top form here, and the notes roll out with inexorable logic and style. Despite its lack of fidelity, the disc merits strong consideration. For most people, however, the Backhaus disc will be the more logical choice.

*Sonata for Piano No. 16 in G (Op. 31, No. 1). Backhaus, L 951 (*Sonata No. 18). Kempff, D 9589 (*Sonata No. 12).*

Only the inertia of most pianists keep this joyous sonata from appearing more regularly in the concert hall. Backhaus's performance is masterly. If you want to hear piano-playing about as perfect as human fingers and mind can make it, listen to the last movement. Kempff also enters into the spirit of the music with a bouncing interpretation, replete with pianistic resource, but here he is a little below the standard set by Backhaus.

*Sonata for Piano No. 17 in D minor (Op. 31, No. 2). Novaes, Vox 6270 (*Sonata No. 26). Kempff, D 9586 (*Sonata No. 18). Backhaus, L 627 (*Sonata No. 3).*

Novaes has the most interesting ideas about this sonata. She brings to the music an improvisatory quality expressed in constantly fluid pianism. Next to this, the more orthodox readings of Kempff and Backhaus are prose against poetry. Conceivably the purist will find much to irritate him in Novaes's free approach, but most listeners will react agreeably to her spontaneity. Vox has given her eminently satisfactory recorded sound. As between Kempff and Backhaus, I prefer the former despite recording that is nowhere near the quality of that on the London disc. Kempff more closely achieves the rhapsodic character of the music. Backhaus is too reticent for my taste.

*Sonata for Piano No. 18 in E flat (Op. 31, No. 3). Backhaus, L 951 (*Sonata No. 16). Rubinstein, V LM 1071 (*Sonata No. 23). Kempff, D 9586 (*Sonata No. 17).*

The best all-around version is supplied by Backhaus, who offers his usual combination of style and pianistic security. A little cold, perhaps; but what mastery! The Kempff version is beautifully played, and as an interpretation I prefer it to the Rubinstein. But the inferior quality of the Decca pressing, as against the admirably engineered Victor, plus Rubinstein's colorful and vigorous performance, leave one little choice.

*Sonatas for Piano Nos. 19 in G minor and 20 in G (Op. 49, Nos. 1, 2). Backhaus, L 705 (*Sonatas Nos. 13, 14). Kempff, D 9590 (*Sonata No. 11). Gulda, L 999 (*Sonata No. 3).*

There is little to choose, interpretatively, between Backhaus and Kempff. Both play the short sonatas with taste, etching the lines clearly, avoiding overstatement. The London disc, however, is more truly representative of piano tone. Gulda has recorded both sonatas in a performance that sounds oversimplified and unrolls in a tensionless manner. This is one of Gulda's most characterless discs; he just doesn't seem to get into the music. Schnabel has recorded the *G minor Sonata* on V LCT 1154 (*Sonatas Nos. 15, 31*). Of all the recorded versions, this has greatest maturity of conception. Neither sonata is important Beethoven, but Schnabel invests the G minor with power and intellect that make it quite an experience. Unfortunately the recorded sound is very thin. Victor, of course, makes no claims for the transfer and we are in the company's debt for the chance to re-hear Schnabel's magnificent treatment.

*Sonata for Piano No. 21 in C ("Waldstein," Op. 53). Solomon, V LM 1716 (*Sonatas Nos. 22, 30). Serkin, C 4620 (*Sonata No. 30). Kempff, D 9581 (*Sonata No. 28). Backhaus, L 265 (*Sonata No. 12).*

If you are interested in bargains, the Solomon is the only one of the four versions under consideration that offers three sonatas. The British pianist plays the "Waldstein" with mature artistry. Everything is technically exact, logically planned, consistent in approach. The recorded sound is good, though far from outstanding. Serkin's is the most personal and dramatic of the interpretations. For one with such a reputation as a Beethoven stylist, he takes a remarkably free view of the music. Sometimes it does not work out; here it emerges in an exciting manner. Kempff goes about the music with an emphasis on its large contours. The result is a performance of magnificent breadth. Backhaus's disc, though assured and strong, somehow lacks the life of the others.

Among other performances available on LP, the Gorodnitzki on Cap 8264 (*Sonata No. 23*) offers brilliant sound and a traditional reading that may be too objective for some tastes. Gieseking is represented by two versions. C 4774 (*Sonata No. 23*) is a reissue of the 1939 set, too feeble in sound to be strongly recommended; and his newer version on An 35024 is a surprisingly dull-sounding recording.

*Sonata for Piano No. 22 in F (Op. 54). Solomon, V LM 1716 (*Sonatas Nos. 21, 30). Kempff, D 9591 (*Sonatas Nos. 6, 30). Backhaus, L 603 (*Sonatas Nos. 10, 24).*

Each of these performances has something to recommend. Solomon's playing is delicate, elegant, forceful when force is needed, and well recorded. Kempff has the most dashing notions about the music. Backhaus's interpretation is the largest-scaled of all. He puts plenty of body behind his playing, and he also has received the most natural-sounding piano tone. You can't go wrong on any of these.

*Sonata for Piano No. 23 in F minor ("Appassionata," Op. 57). Backhaus, L 597 (*Sonata No. 28). Casadesus, C 4622 (*Sonata No. 2). Kempff, D 9580 (*Sonata No. 27). Rubinstein, V LM 1071 (*Sonata No. 18).*

Immense authority and sweep are found in the Backhaus performance, and the recording is fine. There may be other "*Appassionatas*" as good, but there is none better. The Casadesus version is notable for its finish. The refinement he brings to the music makes his disc the most elegant of all; and it also enjoys resonant, firmly centered recording. Kempff moves with heavy grandeur. Rubinstein is the most pianistic. We are never allowed to forget for a moment that a high-powered virtuoso is at work, and this version has more horse-power and chromium than all the others. The catalogues list many other versions. Gieseking's pre-war set has been transferred to C 4774 (*Sonata No. 21*). This LP is muffled in sound and lacks definition, but the Gieseking suavity and finesse cannot be hidden. A more recent Gieseking version on An 35024 (*Sonata No. 21*) is well played. The recording, however, lacks the color and tonal vitality that contemporary piano discs should have. Gorodnitzki has a steady performance on Cap 8264 (*Sonata No. 21*). Both the Frugoni on Vox 7160 and Badura-Skoda on W 5184 are, more or less, economy versions, offering the "Moonlight" and "*Pathètique*" as well as the "*Appas-*

sionata." Neither of these young pianists can match the grandeur of several versions listed above, but they play tastefully and have been well recorded. Yves Nat, on HS 109, is another who is heard in a "Moonlight"-"*Pathétique*"-"*Appassionata*" coupling. His "*Appassionata*" is interesting: a little rough technically, but fiery, full of strength and drama. The close-up recording makes his playing sound more explosive than it is. Try reducing the highs.

*Sonata for Piano No. 24 in F sharp (Op. 78). Backhaus, L 603 (*Sonatas Nos. 10, 22). Kempff, D 9578 (*Sonatas Nos. 8, 25). Schnabel, V LCT 1109 (*Sonatas Nos. 27, 32).*

Backhaus has the best recording and gives a fleet performance of this strange little sonata. The Kempff recording is not at all bad, considering some of the others he has had to put up with. Kempff's work has contrast and a delicious helter-skelter quality toward the end. The sound of the pre-war Schnabel recording is amazingly good. The interpretation has a masculinity characteristic of Schnabel's Beethoven, with a logic that goes straight to the point.

*Sonata for Piano No. 25 in G (Op. 79). Kempff, D 9578 (*Sonatas Nos. 8, 24). Backhaus, L 393 (*Sonatas Nos. 5, 6).*

I prefer the more controlled Kempff playing to Backhaus's impulsive quality here. The music is not so big as the latter's strenuous efforts would suggest, and Kempff keeps it in a proper framework. The Decca recording is not bad, either. A version by Frugoni on Vox 8650 (**Sonatas Nos. 15, 21, 26*) is not in this class, though the piano tone sounds exceedingly lifelike.

*Sonata for Piano No. 26 in E flat ("Les Adieux," Op. 81a). Novaes, Vox 6270 (*Sonata No. 17). Kempff, D 9582 (*Sonata No. 14). Serkin, C 4432 (*Sonata No. 14). Backhaus, L 949 (*Sonatas Nos. 1, 27). Schnabel, V LCT 1155 (*Sonatas Nos. 2, 14).*

Novaes presents a spontaneous-sounding, extremely pianistic interpretation. Warmth and lyricism mark her work, and in the slow movement she achieves a piercing intensity. Compared with this, the Kempff sounds formal and befrocked, though certainly it is a strong enough piece of work to be accepted gladly on its own terms. The Columbia disc is well recorded, and Serkin plays with the security one invariably gets from him. Superb piano sound features the Backhaus disc, but I find the playing a little overstressed and too massive. With all of its masculinity, the performance lacks the poetry of the Novaes. The little hold-backs and expressive devices that Backhaus displays in the slow movement are not very convincing. Certainly it is magnificent pianism, and yet the message fails to come across. Mention should be made of Solomon's sensitive performance on V LM 1733. On this disc, *"Les Adieux"* is really a filler for the *Sonata No. 29.* The talented young Gulda has recorded *"Les Adieux"* on L 322 (**"Eroica" Variations and Fugue*). He neatly lays out the sonata, but at this stage of his career his playing lacked the individuality of a Novaes or the experience of a Kempff. His recording is marred by a sudden level drop in the last movement. Schnabel's recording betrays its age by lack of color and much surface noise that stems from the original shellacs. The pitch is bad, and the sonata ends in D instead of E flat. But Schnabel is magnificent here. Every note is charged with meaning, and the slow movement has a searching profundity. It was for performances like this that Schnabel achieved his reputation as a great musical thinker.

*Sonata for Piano No. 27 in E minor (Op. 90). Backhaus, L 949 (*Sonatas Nos. 1, 26). Kempff, D 9580 (*Sonata No. 23). Schnabel, V LCT 1109 (*Sonatas Nos. 24, 32).*

Backhaus handles this sonata with subdued fire. I have a feeling that this recording dates from before the other two sonatas on the disc; it is on a lower level, without comparable definition, though perfectly satisfactory in sound. By the standards of most of the discs in his Beethoven series, Kempff receives good recording here. He plays with considerable thrust and, in the last movement, grace and lyricism. The pre-war Schnabel also is a beautifully direct performance, somewhat more intellectualized than the other two, organized like a company of marines at Saturday-morning inspection.

*Sonata for Piano No. 28 in A (Op. 101). Backhaus, L 597 (*Sonata No. 23). Kempff, D 9581 (*Sonata No. 21).*

This work ushers in the last five sonatas. It is the most cryptic work in the form which Beethoven had composed up to that time. I prefer the Kempff performance to the Backhaus; it has more humanity and graciousness. But, alas, the unfortunate Kempff is handicapped by inferior sound. If you do decide on it, watch out for a defective pressing that may throw your pickup. The mishap occurs throughout sections of the first movement.

Sonata for Piano No. 29 in B flat ("Hammerklavier," Op. 106). Solo-

*mon, V LM 1733 (*Sonata No. 26). Kempff, D 9579. Gulda, L 422. Backhaus, L 602.*

The most heroic of all the *"Hammerklavier"* discs is Kempff's. This is piano-playing on a very high level. It is handcuffed by thin sound and noisy surfaces. Solomon also has noisy surfaces to contend with, though his quality of sound is much brighter. Not so powerful a pianist as Kempff, Solomon offers more in the way of nuance. His version is probably the best choice. By some miracle of compression, Victor has managed to include the *"Les Adieux" Sonata* on the disc. The Backhaus performance is disappointing: all technique, little emotion, and as dry an exposition of the fugue as you will ever hear. Gulda maintains more tension, and his performance is an amazing achievement from so young a pianist. Both of these London discs have a break in the slow movement, which is something one does not expect in these LP days. I have memories of Petri doing fabulous things with the *"Hammerklavier"* in the concert hall, but on C 4479 he sounds flurried and has to fight the notes. The same can be said of Horszowski on Vox 6750. Knowledge and style are present, but the pronounced effort that he has to put into the fugue makes for a nerve-racking experience.

*Sonata for Piano No. 30 in E (Op. 109). Kempff, D 9591 (*Sonatas Nos. 6, 22). Solomon, V LM 1716 (*Sonatas Nos. 21, 22). Hess, V HMV 1068 (*Sonata No. 31). Schnabel, V LCT 1110 (*Sonatas Nos. 9, 13).*

Several excellent performances are available. Heading the list are Kempff for a remarkably fluent version (but thin recorded sound, with the pitch about a quarter-tone up); Hess, for her unhurried, spacious, mellow, and reflective interpretation (fine recorded sound); Solomon for his combination of style, musicianship, and all-around workmanship (good sound); and Schnabel, for his careful shaping of phrases and meticulous fingerwork (we can ignore a few rough spots toward the end). Backhaus on L 266 sounds perfunctory, and an inferior performance of Chopin's *B flat minor Sonata* on the reverse of the disc disqualifies it. Serkin on C 4620 (*Sonata No. 21*) is well recorded. His playing here has breadth, and yet he dawdles over slow sections in a way that becomes an annoying mannerism after a few hearings.

*Sonata for Piano No. 31 in A flat (Op. 110). Hess, V HMV 1068 (*Sonata No. 30). Backhaus, L 953 (*Sonata No. 32). Kempff, D 9592*

*(*Sonata No. 10). Casadesus, C 4388 (Schumann: Études symphoniques). Schnabel, V LCT 1154 (*Sonatas Nos. 15, 19).*

Some lovely features are contained in the Hess performance. It is beautifully proportioned, poised, and personal; and it also has a singing line of seraphic purity. Her playing is feminine in the best sense of the word. If you want a stronger performance, the Backhaus will supply the need. He takes firm hold of the phrases in a majestic rather than poetic way (though it is hard to agree with his hasty peroration at the inversion of the fugue). Kempff has a mellow outlook on the sonata. Casadesus's smooth, facile work is well recorded, but musically it does not strike as deep as the other versions. If inferior recorded sound does not bother you, I would strongly suggest that you investigate the Schnabel performance. Victor has done a public service by transferring the old Beethoven Society sets, made by Schnabel during the thirties, to LP. Seldom did this pianist, or any other, rise to greater heights than in the slow movement, which is surcharged with emotion; and a comparable maturity pervades the entire interpretation. Forget about the struggles with technique in the fugue. This is one case where idea and intent are immeasurably more important than execution.

*Sonata for Piano No. 32 in C minor (Op. 111). Backhaus, L 953 (*Sonata No. 31). Kempff, D 9587 (*Sonata No. 5). Solomon, V LM 1222 (*Sonata No. 8). Schnabel, V LCT 1109 (*Sonatas Nos. 24, 27).*

Backhaus supplies the most massive account of this great work. He really digs in. His recording has an annoyingly prominent swish and a ghost or two, though the piano tone itself is fine. Kempff ends his series with a magnificent performance, and also with his usual bad luck as regards recorded sound. Solomon is smaller-scaled, but completely in command of the music and the notes. Schnabel's pre-war conception has nobility, but technically he never was equipped to handle the last five sonatas. Some glossed-over sections and some muddy ones may well cause raised eyebrows among those listeners who are coming to his work for the first time. Lateiner has recorded the sonata on C 4335 (**Andante Favori*). He rushes in to grapple with the music and achieves some impressive moments, but on the whole his performance is too impetuous and knotted. He plays the *Andante Favori* in a determined manner, ignoring the implicit charm of the piece.

Sonatinas for Piano in G and E flat; 6 Country Dances; 6 German Dances; 6 Minuets; 6 Variations on a Swiss Song. Zeitlin, Op 6002.

Most of these pieces date from Beethoven's youth. They are not very interesting, but this disc does fill a gap in the discography, and Zeitlin plays with competence. The recorded sound is exceptionally realistic.

Sonatas for Violin and Piano (complete). Heifetz, Bay (in all but the "Kreutzer"; Moiseiwitsch in the "Kreutzer"), V LM 6701 [5]. *Fuchs, Balsam, D DX 150* [5].

A choice between these versions will depend on what you are looking for. Heifetz is closer to the fiddle and has better recording; Fuchs is closer to the music and has inferior recording. Heifetz's incomparable technical perfection shines through all of these sonatas (not that Fuchs is a technical weakling; he is as strong as a fortress, but nobody makes playing the fiddle sound as easy as Heifetz). Heifetz is all curves, Fuchs is more angular. Undoubtedly Fuchs digs more into the music. His accents are sharper, he shapes a phrase with more strength and conviction, and in Artur Balsam he has a pianist who is a partner, not an accompanist. In the Heifetz interpretations the listener is always conscious of effects of one kind or another: tiny changes of color during a long bow, an occasional portamento, a phrase played more sweetly than the musical context suggests. Fuchs's musicianship ignores these details. He concentrates more on what the ad boys call The Big Picture. The one thing missing from his work is repose; there is an unrelieved nervous tension. Superb playing, in any case. Unfortunately the sound of his violin often emerges in a harsh, ferocious-sounding manner not typical of his work in the concert hall.

Sonatas for Violin and Piano (individual).

All of the Fuchs-Balsam discs are available separately. Many other violinists have contributed to the Beethoven violin-sonata discography. Fournier and Doyen have recorded all ten for Westminster. The couplings are 1 and 10 (W 5176), 2 and 9 (5275), 3 and 5 (5247), 4 and 6 (5164), and 7 and 8 (5292). All of these are musical performances and have been well recorded. But Fournier is not so strong a violinist as many of his competitors. His tone is likely to be thin and shrill, his intonation far from perfect. These defects show up especially in the bigger sonatas, such as the C minor and the "Kreutzer." Francescatti and Casadesus have recorded Nos. 3 and 4 (C 4478), 7 and 8 (4861), and 9 (4327). Not one but is a mettlesome, alert, brilliant performance. Their approach is non-Teutonic. No grappling with the infinite here; rather a suave collaboration in the best of taste. And what elegant instrumental playing! Szigeti and Horszowski, playing Nos. 5 and 6 (C 4870), 7 (10" 2097), and 10 (4642), lack equivalent instrumental finesse. One hesitates to recommend these interpretations. Szigeti's tone is wiry and far from pleasant, and his bow arm does not have the control it once had. Exciting performances of Nos. 5 and 9 are played by Oistrakh and Oborin on Per 573 and Van 6024 respectively. These are exceptionally brilliant recordings by Russian standards, and the discs approach most American ones in tonal fidelity. Oistrakh's powerful work in No. 9 (the "Kreutzer") makes it as good a version as any on records (unless you are violently antithetic to the neo-Auer school of violin-playing). Rostal and Osborn have a series on London which I find well played but lacking in imagination: no sweep, no rapture, little tension. Ricci and Gulda play Nos. 7 and 10 on L 1004. They work deftly together, but in No. 7 Ricci tries for a big interpretation that, I feel, is alien to his nature. He forces a bit, and his tone occasionally wavers. I would like more purity of style here and in No. 10, though it must be said the latter comes off most lyrically. Gulda makes a superb ensemble pianist.

Trio for Flute, Bassoon, and Piano. See *Sonata for Flute and Piano* (SPA 28).

Trio for Piano and Strings No. 2 in G (Op. 1, No. 2). Istomin, Schneider, Casals, C 4573.

Like many of the festival performance, this one from Perpignan in 1951 has a pleasant feeling of *Gemütlichkeit.* Istomin's romanticized concepts of the slow movement, however, may become annoying after a few hearings. First-class recorded sound.

*Trio for Piano and Strings No. 4 in B flat (Op. 11). Istomin, Schneider, Casals, C 4571 (*Trio No. 6). Kell, Miller, Horszowski, D 9543 (*Mozart: Trio for Clarinet in E flat, K. 498).*

Beethoven composed this with a clarinet alternate for the violin, and the Decca recording presents the alternate version. The two versions have the same notes, but with the clarinet it actually sounds like a different score. Not many people would want to invest in both versions. My choice would be the Columbia, both for its superior tonal quality and for the more idiomatic sound of the performance. It may be conditioning on my part, but the music seems to fit the violin better than the clarinet.

*Trio for Piano and Strings No. 5 in D ("Ghost," Op. 70, No. 1). Albeneri, Mer 10139 (*Trio No. 6). Busch, Serkin, C 4128 (*Sonata for Piano No. 24; Fantasia in G minor). Santoliquido, D 9691 (*Trio No. 6).*

The Albeneri group has the field pretty much to itself here. Busch's attack on the violin is harsh-sounding, sometimes actually brutal. The Decca disc presents an impetuous reading lacking repose or breathing-space. Excellent recorded sound marks the Mercury disc, and the Albeneri Trio play with a flexibility, tonal purity, and feeling for line not apparent in the other versions.

*Trio for Piano and Strings No. 6 in E flat (Op. 70, No. 2). Albeneri, Mer 10139 (*Trio No. 5). Istomin, Schneider, Casals, C 4571 (*Trio No. 2). Santoliquido, D 9691 (*Trio No. 5).*

Again the Albeneri is preferred. The playing of this group is more supple than that on either the Decca or the Columbia from the 1951 Perpignan Festival. I also prefer the firm sound on the Mercury disc to the more diffused Columbia.

Trio for Piano and Strings No. 7 in B flat ("Archduke," Op. 97). Heifetz, Feuermann, Rubinstein, V LCT 1020. Albeneri, Mer 10140. Fournier, Janigro, Badura-Skoda, W 5131. Schneider, Casals, Istomin, C 4574.

The Victor reissue, which dates back to the early forties, is not bad in sound, though naturally it cannot be compared to that of more recent versions. Some snide remarks have been made against this set (and its LP transfer), but I don't subscribe to the notion that because you are a great virtuoso you cannot, *ipso facto*, be a great musician. The three instrumentalists sound as though they had been playing together all their lives, and they offer a lean, brilliant performance that is more bracing than any recorded version I know. The well-recorded Albeneri disc lacks the excitement present in the Victor, but it has rock-like solidity and directness of purpose. It really doesn't matter, but as a point of interest did somebody in the room have a coughing fit in the third movement? The curious can consult measures 143 *et seq.* and hear some pianissimo coughs. (These are nothing as unto Casals's heartfelt murmurs, groans, and gulps.) Best of the four recordings in sound is the Westminster, and it is a well-paced interpretation with a genial musical outlook. The 1951 Perpignan

Festival recording on the Columbia disc sounds exactly like what it is—the work of three musicians who have never before appeared as a professional unit sitting down to make music. A relaxed quality is apparent, also at times a somewhat sluggish one. I'll stick to the old Victor. If you want a more modern-sounding version, the Mercury or Westminster should take care of your needs. A version of the "Archduke" on L 599 should be avoided.

*Trio for Piano and Strings No. 8 in B flat (Grove 154). Mannes, Gimpel, Silva, D 9555 (*Clara Schumann: Trio).*

This piece fills out the last side of the Clara Schumann *Trio.* Very little is known about it. Although the date of composition has been placed at 1812, it sounds much earlier. Not much of interest is present, and the musicians on this disc do all that is required of them.

Trio for Strings in E flat (Op. 3). Pougnet, Riddle, Pini, W 5226.

Trios for Strings in D (Op. 8) and C minor (Op. 9, No. 3). Pougnet, Riddle, Pini, W 5219.

Trios for Strings in G and D (Op. 9, Nos. 1, 2). Pougnet, Riddle, Pini, W 5198. Bel Arte Trio, D 9635.

All of the Pougnet-Riddle-Pini discs are examples of stylish playing, beautifully recorded. This British group has culture, not to mention perfect ensemble and intonation. The music is lesser Beethoven, but contains many charming things. Most popular of these five works is the *Trio in D* (Op. 8), better known as the *Serenade in D.* It also has been recorded, and most brilliantly, by J. and L. Fuchs and Rose on 10" D 7506. In W 5219, by the way, both works start on pitch, but end nearly a half-tone flat; the pitch in the Decca is perfect. Also worth consideration is a recording of the *C minor Trio* by J., L., and H. Fuchs, coupled with Beethoven's *Serenade in D* (Op. 25), on D 9574. The *Trios in G* and *D* played by the Bel Arte group are well recorded and played in a sensitive, suavely modulated manner. Nevertheless, the Westminster disc has juicier tone and a more assertive quality of performance. If you do get the Bel Arte recording, watch out: the labels may be reversed.

Trio for Winds in E flat (Op. 87); Octet Rondo in E flat; Variations on "Reich mir die Hand, mein Leben." Vienna Philharmonic Wind Group, W 5262.

In some respects an A & R (artists and repertoire) man for any record company these days must feel like a fisherman dredging an exhausted oyster bed. You don't come up with much; and often what does come up is not worth the trouble. This disc has some quaint items that should have been allowed to sleep undisturbed. "*Reich mir die Hand*" is more readily identified as "*Là ci darem la mano,*" from Mozart's *Don Giovanni*. These prentice works are well played and recorded, with a noticeable assist from the recording engineers in some pianissimo sections toward the end of the *Rondino*.

*Variations and Fugue for Piano in E flat ("Eroica," Op. 35). Arrau, 10" D 4067. Gulda, L 322 (*Sonata No. 26).*

If you are interested only in the *Variations and Fugue*, the Decca disc is the better buy. It is less expensive than the London, and Arrau's performance is clear, competent, beautifully articulated. With the Gulda version comes a Beethoven sonata that you may or may not want. Gulda was a very young man when he made this disc, and while his ideas are interesting, he lacks the steadiness of Arrau.

Variations (32) in C minor. See Collections: Keene (Mer 10138).

Variations for Flute and Piano (Op. 105, 107). Mann, Dirksen, Es 525/6 [2] *(*Bagatelles, Op. 126; 5 Piano Pieces, posth.).*

Of all the oddities! These are variations on Russian themes, yodeling themes, and on some of the tunes Beethoven wrote for the Scotch and Irish collections put out by Thomson in Edinburgh. He composed these sets around 1818–20 for flute or violin with piano accompaniment. Sometimes the results are howlingly funny, as when Beethoven takes a simple Scotch tune (such as "The Last Rose of Summer") and subjects it to a typical late-period treatment: intense harmonies, abrupt stops and starts, mysterious short trills; cryptic mottos; canonic imitations; hints of themes from the last quartets and sonatas. The fourth side of this set is devoted to the Op. 126 *Bagatelles* and some posthumous piano pieces—an allegretto (1796), two waltzes (1824 and 1825), an allemande (1800), and an undated sketch. All of this music has been excellently recorded, and the playing sounds perfectly capable.

Variations on a Theme by Diabelli (Op. 120). Katchen, L 745. Horszowski, Vox 7730. Arrau, D DX 122 [2] *(*"Eroica" Variations and Fugue).*

Katchen comes up with his best record in the "*Diabelli.*" He plays with a superb digital command and a degree of concentration one would not expect on the basis of most of his other discs.

Horszowski's performance is sluggish in comparison, and he does not have comparable technical freedom. Some of the Vox copies went out with a defect—a false start in Variation 6 which should have been snipped from the tape, but wasn't. The disqualifying point about the Arrau recording is its two discs; it is not worth twice as much as the Katchen.

*Variations for Cello and Piano on "Ein Mädchen" and "Bei Männern." Casals, Serkin, C 4572 (*Cello Sonata No. 2).*

*Variations on "Bei Männern." Feuermann, van der Pas, C 4678 (*Cello Sonata No. 3; Reger: Suite in G). Janigro, Zecchi, W 5173 (*Cello Sonata No. 3).*

On his disc, Casals plays both sets of Beethoven's variations on themes from Mozart's *Magic Flute*. His assured performance makes for the best available version. The realistic sound is marred by prominent surfaces. Feuermann and Janigro play only the "*Bei Männern.*" The Feuermann is a transfer from shellac, and not bad if you can ignore the background noise. The beauties of his playing are such that the disc, inferior sound and all, is preferable to Janigro's (which also carries the *Cello Sonata in A*). A bonus on the Feuermann is Reger's *Suite for Unaccompanied Cello in G.*

*Variations on a Theme from Handel's "Judas Maccabaeus." Casals, Serkin, C 4640 (*Bach, Mozart: Vocal Works).*

These *Variations* occupy one side of the disc, which was recorded at the 1951 Perpignan Festival; the reverse has music by Bach and Mozart sung by Jennie Tourel. Casals lends his customary diligence to this by no means interesting set of variations, and the results are more notable for the breadth of the playing than for what Beethoven had to say. Good recorded sound.

Variations on Mozart's "Reich mir die Hand." See *Trio for Winds in E flat, Op. 87* (W 5262).

BEREZOWSKY, NICOLAI (1900-1953)

Suite for Wind Quintet. See Collections: New Art Wind Quintet (CE 1003).

BERG, ALBAN (1885-1935)

Lyric Suite. Juilliard, 10" C 2148. Pro Arte, Dia 5.

In view of the strange tonal combinations here, the name of the work may strike some conservative listeners as wildly optimistic. Both recordings are good, though Columbia has the edge in tonal realism. Interpretatively I prefer the Dial. The Pro Arte group is more spacious, less hectic, whereas the faster tempos of the Juilliard Quartet carry something febrile and nervous with them. Compare the endings of the first movement. On the Columbia disc the music sounds almost hysterical, which it isn't.

*Quartet for Strings (Op. 3). Juilliard, C 4737 (*Schoenberg: Quartet No. 4; Webern: 5 Movements). New Music, Bar 906 (*Casella: 5 Pieces).*

There is little to choose from. Both performances of Berg's neo-*Tristan* piece are judiciously played and excellently recorded. The couplings are the determining factor here, and Columbia's couplings are more apposite. Casella's seldom-heard pieces for string quartet are sterile affairs. Whether or not you like the Schoenberg, it is an incomparably superior and more important work, and the tiny Webern sketches are worth investigation. The Juilliard, then; but those who end up with the New Music Quartet recording of the Berg will have a fine performance.

Sonata for Piano. See Collections: Skolovsky (C 4871).

BERGER, ARTHUR (1912-)

*Quartet for Woodwinds in C; Duo for Cello and Piano. Fairfield Ensemble, Greenhouse, Makas, C 4846 (*Hill: Piano Quintet).*

The Quartet is a peppy work that moves smartly along its stylized patterns. The Duo is a much more abstract, severe composition, as carefully assembled as a chronometer. These recordings were made under the supervision of the composer under the aegis of Columbia's "Modern American Chamber Music" series. Excellent recorded sound.

BERKELEY, LENNOX (1903-)

Trio for Strings in C. See Françaix: *Trio for Strings in C* (W 5316).

BERNERS, LORD (GERALD HUGH TYRWHITT-WILSON, 1883-1950)

*3 Little Funeral Marches; Fragments Psychologiques; Le Poisson d'Or. Pressler, MGM 3081 (*Lambert: Concerto for Piano and Nine Players).*

Berners was the English Satie. You might not hear these witty little sketches in a lifetime of concert-going, and most professionals do not even know of their existence. Pressler, who makes a specialty of out-of-the-way repertoire, plays accurately and, more important in music like this, does not overplay. The sound of the piano is a delight—clear, no shatter, exceptionally well-defined bass.

BINET, JEAN (1893-)

*Quartet for Strings. Manoliu, etc., L 498 (*Brunner: Flute Sonata; Schoeck: Toccata for Piano).*

Three contemporary Swiss works make up this disc. Longest is the Binet Quartet, composed 1929, an energetic, objective piece of writing of the modern cosmopolitan school. Brunner's flute piece is fairly whimsical, fast-moving, dry. The Schoeck is a Bachian exercise that could have been composed in the nineteenth century. Good string tone in this disc, but the piano recording is tinny.

BIZET, GEORGES (1838-1875)

Jeux d'enfants (Op. 22). Vronsky, Babin, 10" C 2107.

Bizet composed this for piano four hands, and it is played here in its original form. It is as lovely a work as there is in the repertoire. Bizet, it is not too well known, was a fine pianist and a sight-reader who once made the great Liszt himself marvel. The pieces that make up the collection are composed with a deft, light touch. They are utterly charming, and "masterpiece" is not too strong a word. Vronsky and Babin present a well-adjusted performance that conveys the sparkle of the music. This disc was issued in 1950 and shows its age. Surfaces are prominent, and there is a xylophone-like characteristic in the upper treble.

BLISS, ARTHUR (1891-)

Quartet for Strings No. 2 in F minor. Griller, 10" L 299.

A broad, romantic work. The performance of the Grillers sounds dedicated, which is as it should be, for the work was dedicated to them. Low-level, not too clear recording.

BLOCH, ERNEST (1880-)

*Baal Shem. Szigeti, Farkas, C 4679 (*Violin Concerto).*

Columbia has also placed this performance on 10" 2122, backing it with music by Stravinsky. The present coupling is more consistent, especially as it contains the only LP version of the *Violin Concerto*. *Baal Shem* is subtitled "Three Pictures of Chassidic Life." When the Szigeti-Farkas performance was issued some years ago, it immediately achieved a just fame. Szigeti never sounded more fervent, nor his tone richer. Though dated in sound, the recording nevertheless conveys that fervency. The "*Nigun*" from *Baal Shem* has been recorded by Milstein; see Collections: Milstein (Cap 8259).

Enfantines. See Collections: Pressler (MGM 3010).

Quartet for Strings No. 1. Roth, Mer 10145.

1916 was the year of composition. This, like the later quartets, is rugged and uncompromising, with strongly Hebraic traits and a sheer granitic quality. The Roth Quartet achieves a forceful performance that captures the grandeur of the music without neglecting its lyric aspects. The group is especially impressive in the slow movement, where it projects a singing line without ever becoming sentimental. It is no mean order of musicianship to carry through so extended a conception without flagging. Superb recorded sound.

Quartet for Strings No. 2. Musical Art, Van 437.

Composed in 1945, this work has had musicians and critics like Ernest Newman talking in terms of the late Beethoven quartets. It is not one of Bloch's avowedly "Hebraic" studies, though the long plaint that opens the first movement has a quality of cantillation, and its echo at the opening of the third movement is not far removed from the spirit of the synagogue. To the Musical Art Quartet, nothing but praise for a strong reading that conveys the maturity of Bloch's conception. The group engages the work with technical proficiency, steadiness of tone, and unanimity of idea. Clear recorded sound.

Quartet for Strings No. 3. Griller, 10" L 840.

Like the *Quartet No. 2*, this is not easy listening. It is a strong and uncompromising work, reflective of a powerful musical personality, sternly dissonant, melodically bleak. Yet it decidedly is worth making the effort to know. The Griller Quartet attacks the work with muscle rather than inner force. The players strain too hard; and while they do achieve a chamber-orchestra sonority, it is at the expense of smoothness. London has not given the group very good recording. String tone is shrill (though some of that is due to the playing), and the highs have a tendency to blast.

Quintet for Piano and Strings. Chigi, L 382.

This powerful and impressive work is a little too big for the Chigi Quintet, which gives a fluent performance but is unable to rise to the big moments. The pianist especially has his troubles. I have the feeling that there is a permanent gap between the musical temperament of Bloch and the musical temperament of the Chigianos. London's recording is low-level with prominent background noise. Some of the writing, such as the harmonics in the *misterioso* section of the second movement, does not come through. A new LP version of the music is indicated.

*Sonata for Piano. Cumming, ML 7015 (*Cumming: Piano Sonata).*

Bloch did not spare the difficulties, and young Cumming plays the complicated work with a sure grasp that many of his older colleagues might well envy. His own four-movement *Sonata* is a talented work, not as percussively jagged as much contemporary piano writing, and not as obviously derivative. Good recording, noisy surfaces.

*Sonata for Violin. Heifetz, Bay, V LM 1861 (*Handel: Violin Sonata No. 6 in E; Schubert: Sonatina in G minor, Op. 137, No. 3).*

As testimony of Heifetz's versatility, here is an example of complete identification with a modern piece of music. Heifetz presents a strong, rhythmic reading, one that fully encompasses the brute force that Bloch poured into his writing. And yet the performance is expressed in violinistic terms. Heifetz is always on top of the notes, never forcing, managing to maintain the purity of his tone no matter how great the obstacles. A stunning disc, exceptionally well recorded.

BOCCHERINI, LUIGI (1743-1805)

Quartet for Strings in A (Op. 33, No. 6). See Collections: New Music String Quartet (Bar 911).

Quartets for Strings in A (Op. 39, No. 3) and E flat (Op. 58, No. 3). Quartetto Italiano, An 35062.

Boccherini is a composer who does not figure on many of today's programs, but on the evidence of a handful of recordings his chamber music is inferior only to that of Haydn or Mozart in the eighteenth century. This pair of quartets, composed in 1787 and 1799, are lyric, personal, and, frequently, intense—as far above most of the hack music of the time as Shakespeare was above a broadside balladeer. The Quartetto Italiano plays music like this very well, bringing considerable elegance to the phrasing and a real "lift" to the lyric sections. Beautiful recorded sound, too.

*Quartet for Strings in D (Op. 6, No. 1). New Italian, L 320 (*Haydn: Quartet in E flat, Op. 64, No. 6).*

Again the Quartetto Italiano (which used to be known as the New Italian) plays in a stylish, spirited, and well-proportioned manner, achieving special success with the elegiac slow movement. London has furnished a fine quality of recorded string tone, but the pressing I heard was handicapped by excessive background noise.

Quartets for Strings Nos. 4 in D minor (Op. 10, No. 2) and 7 in F minor (Op. 33, No. 5). Guilet, CH 43.

A pair of works with the lissome grace normally associated with Mozart. Lyric readings from the Guilet Quartet, a musicianly ensemble that can turn a phrase with delicacy and understanding. Realistic recorded sound. There is some pitch trouble: the *D minor Quartet* starts a half-tone up (though it ends in key).

*Quintet No. 1 in D for Guitar and Strings. De la Torre, Stuyvesant, Ph 101 (*Malipiero: Rispetti e Strambotti).*

Boccherini probably composed this work for a wealthy amateur. It is strongly Spanish in feeling, and the last movement is a fandango that builds to such an exciting, irresistible climax that one is tempted to yell: "*Olé!*" An unusual novelty, well worth owning, and it is too bad that Malipiero's dull work for string quartet occupies the reverse side. Both recordings are clear but rather unresonant. De la Torre, not a flashy guitarist, is content to stay in the framework of the ensemble during the Boccherini. Ordinarily such rectitude would be most praiseworthy. Here, however, one wishes for a little more extroversion.

Quintets for Piano and Strings Nos. 1 in A and 4 in D minor. Chigi, L 749.

Of these two quintets, the A major is pleasant but routine; the D minor is elegant, appealing, and has many inventive touches. Music like this perfectly fits the characteristics of the Chigi ensemble, which offers lyric, flowing performances. A fine disc that makes a valuable addition to the slender repertoire of piano plus string quartet. The recorded sound is up to London's best, with beautiful definition and perfect balance between piano and strings.

Sextets for Strings in E flat (Op. 24, No. 1) and E flat (Op. 41); Sinfonia Concertante in G. London Baroque, W 5077.

Although these pieces are played by a small instrumental group headed by a conductor, they really are chamber music. Op. 24 is scored for strings; Op. 41 for strings and winds; the *Sinfonia Concertante* for eight wind- and string-players. Karl Haas, an experienced conductor of this kind of music, leads his men in lively performances. A most attractive disc, well recorded.

*Sonata for Cello and Piano No. 6 in A. Greenhouse, Makas, Ren 11 (*Valentini: Sonata No. 4 in E).*

This is one Boccherini work without much interest, and the Valentini piece on the reverse is a standard baroque item, without style or individuality. Greenhouse presents a concert-hall treatment—romanticized, with exaggerated accents and sentimental phrasing. But the cello-playing *per se* is first-class, and the recorded sound is smooth.

Trios for Strings (Op. 35, Nos. 1, 3, 6). Schneiderhan, Swoboda, Benesch, W 5046.

Trios for Strings (Op. 35, Nos. 2, 4, 5). Schneiderhan, Swoboda, Benesch, W 5042.

These works are scored for two violins and cello. They are, for Boccherini, surprisingly conventional, sounding as though composed by the square yard. The recording is good, and the competent players do all they can—but they can't bring out what isn't there. Op. 35, No. 3, is mislabeled on both the record and the liner, as E major: E flat should be the key.

BÖHM, GEORG (1661-1733)

*Chorale Variations. Viderø, HS 3066 (*Walther: Chorale Variations).*

Three sets of variations by Böhm, and two by Walther (who was a second cousin of Bach), are on this disc. All of the music is written with the typical easy craftsmanship of the experienced baroque composer. Viderø's performances are superb. He plays with a spacious grandeur, with constant variety of registration (which does not imply over-registration or unnecessary fussiness), and with real feeling. The beautiful quality of the recorded sound perfectly sets off the baroque organ he plays.

BORODIN, ALEXANDER (1833-1887)

Quartet for Strings No. 1 in A. Vienna Konzerthaus, W 5035.
This is a pleasant, rather long-winded work, not heard often and nowhere nearly as good as the *D major Quartet.* The disc nevertheless is worth owning. Fortunately the Vienna Konzerthaus gives a competent performance in the only LP recording. The sound is shrill at the high end, and the treble needs to be cut drastically, at which point the record does not sound bad at all.

*Quartet for Strings No. 2 in D. Hollywood, Cap 8187 (*Tchaikovsky: Quartet No. 1).*
The Hollywood Quartet offers a plangent reading that just misses sentimentality. Their work is tonally rich, colorful, strong. The recording, too, is altogether lifelike. A version by the Galimir Quartet on Per 505 is not nearly so realistic, nor is it comparable in ensemble. Those who are unfamiliar with this score are in for a treat. For pure, undiluted, happy melody the Borodin *Quartet in D* is in a class by itself.

BOWLES, PAUL (1910-)

*Music for a Farce. Glazer, etc., C 4845 (*Scènes d'Anabase; Dello Joio: Variations and Capriccio).*
Bowles composed this work in 1938 for a Mercury Theatre presentation that never was put on the boards. It is scored for clarinet, trumpet, piano, and percussion. Poulenc is the big influence here. The music is a trifle that is lively, Gallic, pert, and amusing. A little of it goes a long way—but, after all, there only *is* a little of it. An expert group of musicians collaborates in the kind of slapstick performance the score needs.

*Sonata for Two Pianos. Gold and Fizdale, 10" CH 1089 (*Stravinsky: Sonata for Two Pianos; 5 Pièces faciles).*

What comes out in this sonata is a mélange of sophistication, ragtime, blues, and French influences, very much à la mode. The savage, percussive ending is a shock, and really does not belong to the score. Gold and Fizdale provide an excellent performance. The recorded sound is colorless and harsh.

BOZZA, EUGÈNE (1905-)

*Variations on a Free Theme. Copenhagen Wind Quintet, L 734 (*Nielsen: Quintet; Ibert: 3 Pièces brèves).*

Bozza, a French composer, is a Prix de Rome winner (1934). His *Variations* are slightly modal; he employs a tasteful melodic format and writes very well for the wind combination. The performance sounds like all he could have asked for. But the recording is low-level, and hardly one of London's liveliest examples of tonal quality.

BRAHMS, JOHANNES (1833-1897)

Allegro in C minor. See Collections: Milstein (Cap 8259).

Caprices. See *Piano Music.*

Chorale Preludes (Op. 122). White, organ, Mer 10070.

White plays the complete set of eleven. It is one of the most beautiful collections in the repertoire: Brahms at his most autumnal. The organist plays a responsive instrument of Aeolian-Skinner design, and turns in a sensitive performance. This recording was released in 1950, before LP techniques became stabilized. Some shrillness is apparent, and occasionally a lack of definition. But the disc on the whole can be made to sound quite well; and the musical content is priceless.

Fantasies. See *Piano Music.*

Intermezzos. See *Piano Music.*

Piano Music: 8 Piano Pieces (Op. 76); Fantasies (Op. 116). Gieseking, An 35028.

2 Rhapsodies (Op. 79); 6 Piano Pieces (Op. 118); 4 Piano Pieces (Op. 119). Gieseking, An 35027.

*Intermezzos (Op. 117). Gieseking, C 4540 (*Schumann: Kinderscenen).*

Intermezzos in B flat minor and C sharp minor (Op. 117, Nos. 2 and 3); in A and E flat minor (Op. 118, Nos. 2 and 6); in E minor and C (Op. 119, Nos. 2 and 3); Caprice in B minor (Op. 76, No. 2); 2 Rhapsodies (Op. 79); Rhapsody in E flat (Op. 119, No. 4). Rubinstein, V LM 1787.

Nearly all of Brahms's mature piano music is on the three Gieseking discs, and the eminent German pianist is in fine form. His performances have a spacious quality. Gieseking is the most aristocratic and gracious of pianists even when he is technically careless, drops notes, and indulges in some sloppy work. Somehow he gets away with it. Thus these discs are to the LP catalogue what the mid-1930 Backhaus shellac discs were in the 78-rpm days. Unfortunately the Angel quality of sound is not too well defined, what with a heavy boom in the bass and a lack of color. The Columbia disc of *Intermezzos* sounds a little better, but it remains 1950 vintage. On the Rubinstein disc is a grouping of the more popular Brahms piano pieces. His warm, masterly playing makes this the best one-disc introduction to Brahms's piano music which you can get. Rubinstein looks on the music with more romanticism than Gieseking, and the singing line he employs is something that no other present-day pianist seems able to duplicate. Victor's recording has a brilliant sound, marred somewhat by noisy surfaces.

Kempff has recorded much of the Brahms piano music for London. I'd avoid those discs; he plows his way through in a heavy manner. For a good version of the three *Rhapsodies*, see Collections: Chasins (Mer 10062). Battista on MGM 3056 storms through Op. 118. He is talented, but has a long way to go. Nor have the Mercury discs of Brahms piano music played by Magda Rusy much to recommend.

For other Brahms piano music, see *Sonatas, Variations*, and *Waltzes*.

Quartet for Piano and Strings No. 1 in G minor (Op. 25). Horszowski, Schneider, Katims, Miller, Mer 10011. Serkin, Busch Quartet, C 4296.

Though the Mercury disc has a thin and unresonant sound, it is preferable to the muffled characteristics of the Columbia. With all due respect to Serkin's masterly playing and to the musical ideals of the members of the Busch Quartet, I'll take the competitive version, on which one can at least hear everything, and which is a thoroughly musical, technically accomplished interpretation.

Quartet for Piano and Strings No. 2 in A (Op. 26). Curzon, Budapest, C 4630. Hillyer, Albeneri, Mer 10090.

The Columbia is preferred here. It has much the better recording, with more detail and instrumental color, and also is a more exciting performance. To cite one example, the passionate B minor episode in the slow movement comes off with much more spontaneity as Curzon and the Budapest members handle it.

Quartet No. 3 for Piano and Strings in C minor (Op. 60). Szigeti, Katims, Tortelier, Hess, C 4712. Schneider, Katims, Miller, Horszowski, Mer 10010.

The Mercury disc originally came out on shellac in 1948. The transfer to LP is not bad, but the recorded sound can't begin to approach that of the more recent Columbia, which was made at the 1952 Casals Festival at Prades. Szigeti & Co. present a cultured reading with fairly leisurely tempos. More tension is present in the Mercury disc, and a greater degree of musical strength. The Columbia, however, is the better choice by virtue of superior recorded sound and an entirely reliable interpretation.

*Quartet for Strings No. 1 in C minor (Op. 51, No. 1). Budapest, C 4799 (*Dvořák: Quintet for Strings in E flat).*

Originally issued on a 10" disc, the Brahms was later transferred to this disc in company with the Dvořák. The playing has the typical Budapest polish, and there is no better version in the catalogues. On L 588 the Vegh Quartet is rougher in ensemble, and London has devoted the entire disc to the Brahms. A competent version by the Amadeus Quartet on W 5084 also contains Schubert's *Quartettsatz* as a filler. In this recording the pitch of the first movement on the disc I heard was a half-tone down. Westminster says that the pitch deficiency occurs only in early pressings.

*Quartet for Strings No. 2 in A minor (Op. 51, No. 2). Curtis, W 5152 (*Quartet No. 3). Hollywood, Cap 8163.*

The Westminster disc offers two Brahms quartets, and the more brilliantly recorded Capitol is not good enough to overcome that handicap. Though the Curtis group is never exactly exhilarating, it offers sober, dependable performances. Strength and rhythm are present, rather than any great nuance. The dependable music-making of the Curtis has been clearly recorded.

*Quartet for Strings No. 3 in B flat (Op. 67). Curtis, W 5152 (*Quartet No. 2).*

For general remarks about the Curtis's playing, see the entry above. The only recorded competition worth noting is presented by the Busch Quartet on C 4330. It is one of the Busch's best jobs, but the two-for-one Westminster is economically the more feasible. This, by the way, is the least-played of Brahms's three string quartets, but it is far from the least in worth. Certainly the composer never surpassed the melodic perfection of the themes that open the last two movements

Quintet for Clarinet and Strings (Op. 115). Wlach, Vienna Konzerthaus, W 5155. Kell, Fine Arts, D 9532. Boskovsky, Vienna Octet Members, L 858.

This has been called Brahms's greatest chamber work. It may well be. Each of these recordings has something to recommend. Wlach, I think, is the most musical and accomplished of the three clarinetists. The Vienna Konzerthaus, which backs him up, is stodgy and draws things out, though never to the point of musical distortion. Kell is the most fluent of the three instrumentalists. Some may object to his vibrato, and his playing *is* awfully tricky: one's attention is focused with fascination on the player rather than the music. Boskovsky I find too smooth; his performance lacks backbone. Little of the passion in the coloratura flourishes of the slow movement is conveyed; it's all very beautiful and mellow, but not, I think, what Brahms intended. All of these versions are well recorded. I think that the Westminster will have the most staying power, and it's the one I am retaining, with regret that a more imaginative and responsive ensemble than the Vienna Konzerthaus was not selected.

Quintet for Piano and Strings in F minor (Op. 34). Aller, Hollywood, Cap 8269. Curzon, Budapest, C 4336. Demus, Vienna Konzerthaus, W 5148.

Aller and the Hollywood Quartet offer a spacious, vigorous reading that should satisfy all tastes. Curzon and the Budapest also turn in a clear performance that nobody will ever regret owning. Between these two discs there really is very little to choose. The Westminster is very much in the Teutonic tradition, but lacks the force it should have: somehow there is a dead quality about it. Like the others, this is a high-quality example of recorded sound.

Quintet for Strings No. 1 in F (Op. 88). Stangler, Vienna Konzerthaus, W 5027.

Somehow Brahms's two string quintets, masterpieces each, have been lost in the LP shuffle. There is only one version of each at the time of writing. This one in F major is given a quite respectable treatment by the Vienna Konzerthaus. The recording has a shrill tone in the upper frequencies characteristic of so many early LP discs. A good amplifier can take care of the problem, however. The music is eminently worth owning.

*Quintet for Strings No. 2 in G (Op. 111). Stern, Schneider, Katims, Thomas, Tortelier, C 4711 (*Schumann: Piano Quintet).*

This was recorded at the 1952 Prades Festival. It is a bright-sounding performance, as well it might be with such an illustrious assemblage of chamber-music players. The recording is excellent. Brahms is at his most genial in this work, which is crowned with a slow movement as hauntingly beautiful as anything in the repertoire.

Rhapsodies. See *Piano Music.*

Sextet for Strings in B flat (Op. 18). Stern, Schneider, Katims, Thomas, Casals, Foley, C 4713. Vienna Konzerthaus, Stangler, Weiss, W 5063.

The Columbia comes from the 1952 Prades Festival, and those responsible for recording the disc must have found conditions ideal. Here the string tone has a shining quality that is more flattering to the players than the drier quality of sound offered by Westminster. Similarly, the warmth and spontaneity of the Columbia recording make the disc superior to the competent but never-off-the-ground interpretation by the Viennese group.

Sextet for Strings in G (Op. 36). Vienna Konzerthaus, Huebner, Weiss, W 5263.

A lack of volatility mars this performance. Everything sounds thick and unvaried. Even the scherzo emerges like a continuation of the first movement. As this is the only LP version of the score, there is not much choice; but keep on the watch for an alternate. The recorded sound is excellent.

Sonatas for Cello and Piano Nos. 1 in E minor (Op. 38) and 2 in F (Op. 99). Starker, Bogin, Per 593.

Those who invest in this disc need look no further. Piatigorsky has done both—the E minor for Victor, the F for Columbia—but the monetary outlay for them would be almost twice as much as the cost of the Period disc. The latter is a fine recording, with plenty of "presence" to the sound. Starker is one of the steadiest cellists in the business. His bow arm is infallible, his intonation perfect. Both sonatas emerge with breadth, style, and musicianship, and Bogin is a skillful partner. It is hard to overpraise the playing in this release.

Sonatas for Clarinet and Piano in F minor and E flat (Op. 120, Nos. 1, 2). Kell, Horszowski, Mer 10016. Wlach, Demus, W 5236.

Westminster has the better recording, Mercury the better performance. Most of the deficiencies in the Westminster come from the pianist. Demus lacks spirit and imagination. Wlach, a supple clarinetist who is closer to the Teutonic style of the music than Kell, does not seem to be able to free himself entirely. As for Kell, some critics (and clarinetists) have attacked his constant use of vibrato; and, indeed, it is sometimes kittenish in these performances. But such lovely, limpid playing! Traditionalists, however, might better stick to the Wlach version. I'd avoid the coupling on OL 50030, where Jacques Lancelot plays listlessly, with a reedy tone.

*Sonata for Piano No. 2 in F sharp minor (Op. 2). Battista, MGM 3056 (*Intermezzi, Op. 118).*

Battista rolls up his sleeves and goes to work. His playing has its frenetic moments, but on the whole it is a powerful conception often delivered in a really impressive manner. The recording is a little too close-up, and the highs have a tendency to assume xylophone characteristics. Nevertheless, a better-than-average piano recording, and the bass is exceptionally realistic.

*Sonata for Piano No. 3 in F minor (Op. 5). Rubinstein, V LM 1189. Badura-Skoda, W 5245. Katchen, L 122. Fischer, HMV 1065 (*Schumann: Fantasy in C).*

It is difficult to keep this sprawling sonata in order. I prefer the Rubinstein for its vitality and constant air of musical excitement. The Badura-Skoda is a dependable job, though the young pianist lets the ending get away from him. Katchen also has trouble with the coda of the finale; otherwise he presents a praiseworthy performance that stands up very well. Fischer has a mature conception, and his is the only version that gets the sonata on one side. But the recorded sound does not match that of the other versions. Rubinstein remains the best all-around choice.

Sonatas for Violin and Piano (3, complete). Stern, Zakin, C SL 202 [2].

In addition to the three violin sonatas (No. 1 in G, Op. 78; No. 2 in A, Op. 100; No. 3 in D minor, Op. 108), Stern and Zakin include the so-called F.A.E. *Sonata* composed by Brahms, Schumann, and Dietrich. The work was composed in honor of Joachim, whose motto was *Frei aber einsam* ("Free but lonely"). Hence the *F.A.E.* title; and the three notes play a prominent part in the music. Brahms composed the third movement, Dietrich the first (he was a pupil of Schumann's), and Schumann the second and the last. The second is an *Intermezzo,* which also has been recorded by Milstein; see Collections: Milstein (Cap 8259). Stern's performance of these four works is hard to overpraise. He has never sounded better on records. Technically he is perfect, tonally he is rich without resorting to an overdone vibrato, and musically he is muscular without becoming knotted. The music emerges with sweep and assurance in an exceptionally large framework. A major accomplishment, this. Both discs are also available individually; the couplings are Nos. 1 and 3, No. 2 and *F.A.E.* Mellow recording, good relation between violin and piano.

*Sonata for Violin and Piano No. 3 in D minor (Op. 108). Stern, Zakin, C 4912, (*Sonata No. 1). Milstein, Horowitz, 10" V LM 106. Oistrakh, Yampolsky, Col 148 (*Tartini: "Devil's Trill" Sonata).*

The Stern disc, from the two-disc set of all the sonatas, is available individually and supersedes an earlier pressing on C 4363. It is easily as good a performance as any available LP version, and it is a truer-sounding recording than any other. Stern plays in a big style, with considerable thrust and immense technical security. Oistrakh and Yampolsky do not get nearly comparable sound. The guess here is that their recording was derived from 78-rpm masters; the surfaces are poor, the sound is dull and without real clarity. A fiery performance like this deserved better from the engineers. On the Victor disc two formidable virtuosos hold themselves in restraint for a beautifully played but surprisingly untemperamental performance. A previous Victor 10" V LM 71, with Heifetz and Kapell, has been withdrawn. It was a poor recording, with the piano far in the background. Elman-Rosé on 10" V LM 30 is to be avoided, and the Ferras-Barbizet version on Tel 66014 has little to recommend.

*Trio for Clarinet, Cello, and Piano (Op. 114). Wlach, Kwarda, Holletschek, W 5146 (*Trio for Horn, Violin, and Piano). Forrest, Greenhouse, Balogh, Ly 9 (*Mozart: Trio for Clarinet). Kell, Miller, Horszowski, D 9732 (*Clarinet Concerto).*

Of these recordings, the Westminster has the best sound. The

Decca is a little thin but clear and well-balanced. The Lyrichord also is perfectly adequate. Wlach, first clarinetist of the Vienna Philharmonic, has a forthright melodic line and a strong rhythm. Kell likes to juice up the line with all kinds of subtle variations and inflections. He displays tremendous virtuosity, but Wlach is closer to Brahms. Forrest is more on the Wlach order: musical, "straight," and more directly a part of the ensemble. The Westminster version is best, and it also has the most apposite coupling.

*Trio for Horn, Violin, and Piano (Op. 40). Jones, Schneider, Horszowski, C 4892 (*Schumann: Piano Quartet in E flat). Koch, Barylli, Holletschek, W 5146 (*Trio for Clarinet).*

Both versions are satisfactory. If I prefer the Columbia, it is for the disc's slightly rounder and more pleasant quality of sound. The Westminster has the horn a little too much in the background. But this too is an authoritative performance that will not disappoint anybody who likes the music.

Trio for Piano and Strings in B (Op. 8). Fournier, Janigro, Badura-Skoda, W 5237. Stern, Casals, Hess, C 4719. Trio di Trieste, L 955.

Three fine versions of this work are available. The Westminster is the smoothest and best regulated, and the participants present a lyric reading that makes the work as palatable as I have ever heard it. Stern, Casals, and Hess recorded the work during the 1952 Prades Festival. Their performance contains some beautiful details, and the recording is fine. A few sections, however, drag. On the London disc the Trieste group emphasizes the rugged contours of the music. It is one of the ensemble's most impressive attempts. The members play with breadth, avoiding the superficial prettiness to which it sometimes surrenders.

Trio for Piano and Strings in C (Op. 87). Szigeti, Casals, Hess, C 4720.

Another Prades souvenir, one of the less successful recordings of the series. Often a sluggish feeling is present, and the intonation is not as accurate as it should be. The players make the writing sound thicker than it is, and it is very thick to begin with. A version of the work played by the Alma Trio on 10" All 4035 can't fill the gap; it is a thin-sounding performance that is pitched high (C sharp instead of C).

Trio for Piano, Cello, and Violin in A (posth.). Harand, Huebner, Holletschek, W 5058.

An untitled manuscript, the work of a copyist, turned up in Germany in 1924. Dr. Ernst Buecken, a professor at Cologne University, became interested in it and put his methodical German mind to work. After much investigation he decided that it was an early work of Brahms, composed in 1853. The results are only guesswork; but if the manuscript is not by Brahms, it's a fine imitation. All of his youthful characteristics—latent nobility, self-consciousness, turgid piano writing, deference to classical models without a knowledge of how to compress ideas, melodies that wiggle on the ground instead of flying, a general feeling of ponderous integrity—all are present. The performance sounds fine, and the recording is good.

*Variations on an Original Theme (Op. 21, No. 1). Foldes, D 9708 (*Schumann: Fantasy in C).*

One of Decca's most successful piano discs, this has clear sound and quiet surfaces. Foldes handles the rather uninteresting music with his usual skill—and his usual coolness. He doesn't do much to help the writing along, and it wilts on the vine because of the lack of personality in the performance.

*Variations on a Theme by Handel (Op. 24). Gorodnitzki, Cap 8227 (*Variations on a Theme by Paganini). Simon, Ep 3050 (*Variations on a Theme by Paganini).*

Gorodnitzki gives an experienced performance in good technical order, and he has been presented with realistic-sounding recording. The Simon disc also is a good example of piano tone, and the young American pianist handles the music with considerable finesse. In some of the variations he sounds matter-of-fact, though the basic strength of his conception (and fingers) makes his interpretation better than merely routine. Katchen and Istomin have recorded the music on, respectively, 10" L 552 and 10" C 2211; neither is a good buy. When will Victor release, as a collector's item, the brilliant performance of the *Handel Variations* that Moiseiwitsch made in the thirties?

*Variations on a Theme by Haydn (Op. 56a). Whittemore and Lowe, V LM 1048 (*Poulenc: Concerto for Two Pianos). Bartlett and Robertson, MGM 3027 (*Schumann: Andante and Variations).*

Neither of these versions is satisfactory. The Victor two-piano team plays the notes in an energetic, superficial manner. It is a better performance, however, than the small-scaled, picky work of Bartlett and Robertson.

*Variations on a Theme by Paganini (Op. 35). Anda, An 35046 (*Schumann: Études symphoniques). Simon, Ep 3050 (*Variations on a Theme* *by Handel). Gorodnitzki, Cap 8227 (*Variations on a Theme by Handel). Wuehrer, Vox 8850 (*Liszt: Étude No. 6 after Paganini; Schumann: Concert Studies on the Paganini Caprices).*

Anda's performance is the most brilliant and effective of the LP versions. The major defect is a sizable cut: the entire coda of the last variation of Book I. Of all the places! Good recorded sound. Gorodnitzki is steady and powerful, though he almost seems to approach the music as a job of work rather than as an attempt to re-create the notes. Simon is mechanically brilliant. He plays with all the dash and confidence in the world. A fine performance, despite a few pet notions that do not come off. I find Wuehrer's treatment interesting despite his chunky, massive style. Some listeners, however, may think that his playing is too overpowering; and, true, the lack of relief or subtlety of nuance may be disturbing after a while. Nevertheless there is much to admire in his powerful work. He also had the admirable idea of putting on his disc Schumann's and Liszt's treatment of Paganini music. Fair recorded sound, with a few xylophone characteristics in the upper treble. Several other versions of the Brahms are available. Keene on Mer 10138 plays with superb flair, but she omits five variations. Goldsand on CH 1147 takes surprisingly slow (and safe) tempos, and the results are stodgy. Foldes on D 7532 offers primarily mechanical playing. A low-priced version by Rosen on 10" L 9104 is neither a very good recording (glassy in sound) nor a very perceptive performance.

*Variations on a Theme by Schumann (Op. 9). Blancard, Van 416 (*Schumann: Faschingsschwank).*

As usual, Blancard does her best work in the lyric sections. She is a pianist of sensibility, but some of the more difficult sections, such as the sixth variation, are a little too much for her technique. The disc is valuable primarily for Blancard's fine performance of the Schumann on the reverse.

*Waltzes (Op. 39). Chasins, Keene, Mer 10061 (*Chasins: Period Suite; Parade). Weisz, L 798 (*Schumann: Faschingsschwank).*

Brahms originally composed these waltzes for piano duet, and they are so played by Chasins and Keene (except for Nos. 1, 2, 11, 14, and 15, which are presented in Brahms's arrangement for two pianos). Weisz, in the solo version, plods his way through. Chasins and Keene are much more relaxed, and the obvious fun they have is communicated to the listener. Their disc is well recorded, though the surfaces are high.

BRITTEN, BENJAMIN (1913-)

Quartet for Strings No. 1 in D (Op. 25); Fantasy for Oboe and Strings. Galimir, Es 504.

The Fantasy, composed in 1932, is the earlier of this pair of works. It stretches some thin material over a very wide surface. The 1941 quartet is lively and professionally assembled, but the ideas themselves are something less than pure gold. The key of the quartet is D; in this recording it comes out closer to E flat. Harold Gomberg is the admirable oboist in the *Fantasy.* In both works the performances sound conscientious and the recorded sound is clear.

BRUNNER, ADOLF (1901-)

Sonata for Flute and Piano. See Binet: *String Quartet* (L 498).

BUXTEHUDE, DIETRICH (1637-1707)

*La Capricciosa. Viderø, HS 3069 (*J.C. Bach: Sarabande with Variations; Aria Eberliniana).*

Two baroque composers share this disc of harpsichord variations. This J. C. Bach (1642-1703) is Johann Christoph, an uncle of Johann Sebastian. His *Sarabande* has nothing particularly novel or inventive about it, but the *Eberliniana,* after going along in routine manner, suddenly slides into an amazing chromatic variation that stands out in the set like a peacock among a flock of sparrows. Johann Sebastian *must* have had this in mind when he composed the great twenty-fifth variation of the "Goldberg." The Buxtehude piece is very virtuosic; for its day, absolutely Lisztian. All the music is given deft, scholarly performance by a superb instrumentalist. Viderø plays the harpsichord as well as he plays the organ, which is superior playing indeed.

CAGE, JOHN (1912-)

Quartet (1950). See Piston: *Sonatina for Violin and Harpsichord* (C 4495).

Sonatas and Interludes for Prepared Piano. Ajemian, Dia 19.

Very posh, avant-garde stuff here. As Cage deals in sounds and timbres rather than music, no criteria for evaluation exist. Perhaps it's the music of the future. This recording was done under the supervision of the composer, which should be enough guarantee of authenticity. Good recorded sound.

CARTER, ELLIOTT (1908-)

Quintet for Woodwinds. See Collections: New Art Wind Quintet (CE 2003).

CASADESUS, ROBERT (1899-)

Danses Mediterranéennes. See Chabrier: *Trois Valses Romantiques* (C 2146).

CASELLA, ALFREDO (1883-1947)

5 Pieces for String Quartet. See Berg: *Quartet* (Bar 906).

CATURLA, ALEJANDRO GARCIA (1906-1940)

Cuban Suite No. 1. See Porter: *Quartet for Strings* (An 35105).

CHABRIER, ALEXIS (1841-1894)

*Piano Music. Doyen, W 5294 (*Saint-Saëns: 5 Piano Pieces). S. Stravinsky, All 56.*

Doyen plays seven pieces: an *Impromptu*, the *Bourrée fantasque*, and the *Cinq morceaux*. Stravinsky presents nine: seven of the *Pieces pittoresques*, the *Bourrée fantasque*, and *Ballabile*. Chabrier's music deserves to be better known. It is far in advance of its time; and these piano pieces are full of anticipations of Ravel, Les Six, and Satie. Chabrier had a Puckish sort of wit which manifested itself in strange turns of phrase as well as in a deliberate adoption of music-hall techniques. Of these two discs, the

Westminster is the better choice. Doyen is a French pianist who has a feeling for the style and enough technical ability to make her points. Here is a Paris Conservatory type of technique—elegant, right on top of the keys, somewhat glassy in sound. Next to her playing, the work of Stravinsky (the composer's son) sounds stiff and unimaginative.

*Trois Valses Romantiques. R. and G. Casadesus, 10" C 2146 (*Casadesus: Danses Mediterranéennes).*

Sophisticated music here, and it is beautifully played on two pianos by Mr. and Mrs. Casadesus. The disc is an LP transfer; it was originally recorded around 1941. In its LP form it does not sound bad, though the lack of overtone reveals its age. Casadesus's own *Danses* are a skillful, intellectualized treatment of folk melodies.

CHASINS, ABRAM (1903-)

3 Chinese Pieces; 3 Preludes; Fairy Tale; Schwanda Fantasy; Melodie; Dance of the Buffoons. Chasins, Mer 10025.

Chasins's solo playing is glittering and expert, as one might expect from a Josef Hofmann protégé. *Schwanda* is a brilliant, difficult, and ingenious transcription for solo piano. The Gluck "*Melodie*" and the Rimsky-Korsakov "*Dance of the Buffoons*" are here played in a two-piano transcription, with Constance Keene at the second piano. Fair recorded sound; prominent surfaces.

*Parade; Period Suite. Chasins, Keene, Mer 10061 (*Brahms: Waltzes).*

Both pieces are idiomatic examples of two-piano writing composed in the romantic piano tradition. They receive a thoroughbred performance. Clear recording, but without the resonance and quality of the best modern examples of piano tone.

CHAUSSON, ERNEST (1855-1899)

*Concerto for Piano, Violin, and String Quartet in D (Op. 21). Heifetz, Sanromá, Musical Art, V LCT 1113 (*Sibelius: Violin Concerto). Kaufman, Balsam, Pascal, CH 1071.*

Neither recording is new. The Victor, originally recorded in the early 1940's, is a transfer to LP. I never was happy with it.

There is a surface gloss to the playing, some of the tempos seem perfunctory, and there is a sizable cut in the last movement. And yet the fact remains that beside it the uncut Concert Hall version sounds crude and coarse. The Victor also has another work on the disc—Heifetz's incomparable performance of the Sibelius *Violin Concerto.*

Trio for Piano and Strings in G minor. See Franck: *Trio in F sharp minor* (Vox 8950).

CHERUBINI, LUIGI (1760-1842)

Quartet for Strings No. 1 in E flat; Fugal Suite in D. Aeolian, Ly 24.

No other Cherubini chamber music is available (at the time of writing). Unfortunately, the present disc does scant justice to the composer. The performance is screechy, and the pitch of the entire disc is a half-tone down. One would like to hear the *Fugal Suite* under more favorable auspices; the first of the two movements has some of the jolliest contrapuntal writing on records.

CHOPIN, FRÉDÉRIC (1810-1849)

NOTE: For LP discs containing a miscellany of Chopin's music, see Collections under the following names in the back of this book: Arrau (D DX 130); Backhaus (10" L 317); Balogh (Ly 20); Barere (Rem 199-17); Cortot (V HMV 1032); "Great Pianists of the Past" (V LCT 1038); Hofmann (C 4929); Horowitz (V LM 1137, 1235, 1707, 6014); Jonas (C 4476 and 10" C 2004); Katchen (L 558); Lipatti (C 4721); Novaes (Vox 7810); Stefanska (V LBC 1031).

*Andante Spianato and Polonaise (Op. 22). Hofmann, C 4929 (*see Collections: Hofmann). Rubinstein, 10" V LM 152 (*Polonaise-Fantasy). Horowitz, V LM 1137 (*Polonaise in A flat; Waltzes in A minor and C sharp minor; Mazurka in F minor).*

Rubinstein and Horowitz present magnificent performances. Hofmann's is transcendental. Despite the fact that his recording is inferior in sound—it was made from an acetate taken during his Golden Jubilee Concert at the Metropolitan Opera on November 28, 1937—it somehow makes the other two versions appear thick. I would unhesitatingly select it as THE *Andante Spianato and Polonaise* on records. It has a quality of aristocracy that no other pianist in my memory could bring to his music-making, and it has a degree of tonal and pianistic subtlety that disappeared when Hofmann retired in 1948. For the full contents of this disc, see Collections: Hofmann (C 4929). Of the other two recommended LP versions, Rubinstein's has an exuberant, swinging quality, and Horowitz's has breadth and superlative virtuosity. Both are fine-sounding recordings. The Rubinstein disc, however, ends in D instead of E flat (though it starts on pitch). The transfer as a filler in Rubinstein's three-disc *Mazurka* set is pitched correctly. On 10" V LRM 7051, Horowitz repeats his performance of the *Andante Spianato and Polonaise* (**Nocturne in F minor; Scherzo No. 1 in B minor*). This is a disc in Victor's "Concert Cameo" series, and was an attractive buy before the price cuts of 1955 went into effect.

*Ballades (4, complete). Casadesus, C 4798 (*Sonata in B flat minor). De Groot, Ep 3037 (*Waltzes in D flat and C sharp minor; Berceuse; Nocturne in F sharp). Wild, CH 1401.*

Columbia and Epic have supplied good recorded sound, though the former is preferable (many Epics, this included, have a thudding bass). The Concert Hall is a clear example of piano tone. None of these interpretations is the last word on the music. Of the three I prefer the Casadesus, despite its frequent matter-of-factness. Casadesus plays the music straight, without any surges of passion, but with a good deal of elegance and a tremendous mastery over the technical problems. De Groot is rather similar in his approach; he is an able technician and plays in good taste, but essentially there is little imagination in the performance. The Wild disc has some moments of real excitement lacking in the others. The young pianist, however, is unable to sustain the music as do the more experienced Casadesus and De Groot. Doyen has recorded the *Ballades* on W 5169 in a queerly affected manner. Arrau also plays them in the two-disc D DX 130 (see Collections). His mannered playing has little to recommend. On 10" V LRM 7018, Horowitz plays the *Ballades Nos. 1 and 4* (**Nocturne in F sharp; Mazurka in C sharp minor, Op. 41, No. 1*). These identical performances are also found individually on V LM 1235 *(Ballade No. 1)* and V LM 1707 *(Ballade No. 4)*. Both interpretations are exciting and have been splendidly recorded. There is some musical unease, however, especially in No. 4, where the phrasing is mannered and the musical flow is constantly interrupted. Horowitz has been heard to better advantage.

Ballade No. 1 in G minor (Op. 23). See Collections: Backhaus (L 317); Barere (Rem 199-17); Hofmann (C 4929); Horowitz (V LM 1235).

Ballade No. 3 in A flat (Op. 47). See Collections: Horowitz (V LM 1707); Katchen (L 554).

Ballade No. 4 in F minor (Op. 52). See Collections: Horowitz (V LM 1707).

*Barcarolle (Op. 60). Pennario, 10" Cap 8246 (*Liszt: Mephisto Waltz). Nat, HS 97 (*Sonata in B flat minor; Fantasy in F minor).*

Pennario doesn't have the style that Nat displays, but his agile fingers easily take care of the difficult writing, whereas Nat has to work too hard. For the best version on LP of the *Barcarolle* see Collections: Lipatti (C 4721). For still other versions see Collections: Balogh (Ly 20); Cortot (V HMV 1032); Arrau (D DX 130).

Berceuse (Op. 57). See Collections: Balogh (Ly 20); Hofmann (C 4929); Jonas (C 4476); Novaes (Vox 7810); "Great Pianists of the Past" (V LCT 1038). *Études (Op. 10 and 25, complete). Goldsand, CH 1132 (*Trois Nouvelles Études) and CH 1133 (*Hérold Variations). Uninsky, Ep 3065. Novaes, Vox 7560 (*Trois Nouvelles Études) and Vox 9070 (*Scherzo No. 1 in B minor). Brailowsky, V LM 6000* [2] *(*Schumann: Études symphoniques).*

It would be impossible to recommend any of these without reservation. Brailowsky is hard, driven, and percussive; and some of his playing is far from accurate. Goldsand's two discs are well recorded, and he plays with more imagination than Brailowsky. Occasionally a peculiar notion seizes him, such as the sleepwalking pace of the *E major Étude*, and there are many times where he persists in gilding the lily. Nevertheless, his *Études* are probably the best on LP. The *Hérold Variations* on CH 1133 is an ornamental trifle of no great importance. Uninsky gets both Op. 10 and 25 on one disc. Not much color is present, and he sounds affected in the lyric études. His rubato involves actual alteration of note values. Some first-class virtuosity is wasted in this generally unconvincing attempt. The Novaes discs of Op. 10 and Op. 25 are disappointing. Often she turns a beautiful phrase, but only too much in evidence are blurred passages, jerky accents, and an atypical routine feeling. From Novaes we have learned to expect more. To fill out the last side, Novaes plays the *Scherzo No. 1 in B minor* in a delicate, light-fingered manner. A group of *Études* from both books is played by Backhaus on L 704. These stiff, rhythmically monotonous performances are everything Chopin should not be. I wish I could work up some real enthusiasm for some of the above discs, but the sad fact is that not a single one of them conveys the poetry, passion, and technical splendor that Chopin poured into his *Études.*

Études (individual). See Collections: Cortot (HMV 1032); Hofmann (C 4929); Horowitz (V LM 1707); Jonas (C 4476); Novaes (Vox 7810).

*Fantasy in F minor (Op. 49). Novaes, Vox 7810 (*Scherzo No. 3, etc.). Nat, HS 97 (*Sonata in B flat minor; Barcarolle). Katchen, L 554 (*Scherzo No. 3; Ballade No. 3). Cherkassky, V LBC 1066 (*Nocturne in E minor; Mazurka No. 23 in D; Rachmaninoff: Paganini Rhapsody).*

This is one of Chopin's three or four supreme works. The Novaes is the best of the available recordings, though the impact she makes here is far from that she makes with the work in the concert hall (whereas some pianists, like Horowitz, sometimes sound better on records). In any case, Novaes plays with her usual color and style; and one can discount a few awkward moments. She does not have much competition on LP. The clangorous Nat recording does not present the veteran French pianist very favorably, and the spasmodic Katchen performance is more a collection of fine pianistic effects than a unified conception. Malcuzynski has recorded the work as a filler on his disc of the *F minor Concerto* (An 35030); his performance is positively weird. Cherkassky brings to the music rock like pianistics and an orthodox romantic conception. One could wish for more personality; and the obvious manner in which he emphasizes the sentimentality of the B major section makes the music wilt. Nevertheless, this well-recorded version ranks only under the Novaes as the best performance of the *F minor Fantasy* on LP.

*Impromptus (3); Fantasy-Impromptu. Balogh, Ly 20 (*Barcarolle; Berceuse; Tarantelle; Bolero).*

At the point of writing, there is no satisfactory performance of these miniatures. Balogh plays methodically, frequently with a sensitive turn of phrase. His recording is dated in sound. Horszowski plays the four *Impromptus* on Vox 7870, but his version is hardly poetic and it is accompanied by an indifferent performance of the *E minor Concerto.* For performances of individual *Impromptus*, see Collections: Arrau (D DX 130), Horowitz (V LM 1707); Jonas (C 4476); Novaes (Vox 7810); Rubinstein (V LM 1153); Stefanska (V LBC 1031).

Mazurkas (complete). Rubinstein, V LM 6109 [*3*] *(*Andante Spianato and Polonaise; Polonaise-Fantasy).*

Instead of transferring Rubinstein's pre-war sets of the complete *Mazurkas* to LP, Victor had the pianist re-record them. The results turned out as fortunately as in the epochal earlier set. If another pianist can match Rubinstein's combination of virility, finesse, and style in these great miniatures (there is no better way to describe them), he is unknown to me. His rubato is tastefully employed, and there never is any exaggeration. Rather there is a logical sequence of notes in which the essential dance flavor is never lost. The recorded sound is up to Victor's best. The first twelve *Mazurkas* from Rubinstein's complete set have been placed on 10" V LRM 7001. Those who cannot invest in the integral version will find this disc a lovely introduction to the music.

*Mazurkas (selection). Horowitz, V LM 1109 (*Schumann: Kinderscenen). Kapell, V LM 1715 (*Sonata in B minor). Novaes, Vox 7920.*

Horowitz plays seven: Nos. 20, 21, 26, 32, 38, 40, and 41. Kapell plays nine: Nos. 9, 14, 24, 25, 35, 44, 45, 48, and 49. Novaes plays twelve: Nos. 13, 15, 17, 23, 24, 25, 26, 34, 36, 37, 39, and 51. There is surprisingly little duplication in these three discs, and each is worth having. Horowitz, who has been beautifully recorded, displays an elegance that will surprise those who think of him only as a virtuoso supreme. When he wants to, he can play with a delicate subtlety; and he wants to, here. Kapell's work is more direct. While his playing does not have the resource that Horowitz brings to the *Mazurkas*, it is nevertheless eminently satisfactory. Novaes enjoys clear, ringing recording, with rather high surfaces. She is the most personal of the three pianists: her type of freedom may annoy some purists. I find it wonderful. Her playing has aristocracy, and she makes the effects she employs sound inevitable. Maryla Jonas has recorded two 10" discs of *Mazurkas* for Columbia. On C 2101 she plays Nos. 9, 11, 12, 13, 14, 22, 36, 41, and 45. On C 2036 she is heard in Nos. 16, 18, 21, 27, 29, 35, 48, 50, and the posthumous G major. These originally were shellac discs. The transfer has been smoothly accomplished, though a slight "wow" occasionally makes itself felt. These are scented, leisurely performances, with a rubato far too mannered for my taste. It must be said, however, that Jonas sometimes achieves a gracious, limpid flow, especially when her technique is not strained. Some people like their Chopin sweet. This is it. For individual *Mazurkas*, see Collections: Backhaus (L 317); Jonas (10" C 2004); Lipatti (C 4721); "Great Pianists of the Past" (V LCT 1038); Stefanska (V LBC 1031).

Nocturnes (complete). Rubinstein, V LM 6005 [2].

These *Nocturnes* are easy to despoil, and it is to Rubinstein's eternal credit that he plays the music as the night pieces they are, not as decadent hothouse flowers. His ideas are spacious and singing, and never sentimental, no matter how great the temptation. This set is one of the great examples of Chopin-playing on discs. It is also one of the finest examples of recorded piano tone. On 10" C 2143, Jonas plays five *Nocturnes:* Nos. 1 in B flat minor and 2 in E flat (Op. 9, Nos. 1 and 2); No. 6 in G minor (Op. 15, No. 3); No. 9 in B major (Op. 32, No. 1), mislabeled as B minor; and No. 15 in F minor (Op. 55, No. 1). She interprets these in drawing-room style, languishing over phrases, breaking up the rhythm, swooning over the melodic content. She manages to get away with it in some of her other discs, but here the results are ghastly.

Nocturnes (individual). See Collections: Cortot (V HMV 1032); "Great Pianists of the Past Play Chopin" (V LCT 1038); Hofmann (C 4929); Horowitz (V LM 1235; 1707; 6014); Jonas (10" C 2004); Lipatti (C 4721); Novaes (Vox 7810).

Polonaises (complete). Rubinstein, V LM 1205 and 10" LM 152. Johannesen, Vox 6840 [2].

The Rubinstein is as nearly definitive a version as we are likely to get—virile playing under superb technical control. The recording, too, has a gorgeous sound. Johannesen is a talented pianist, and his playing has many nice things about it, though it cannot stand up against the kind of competition to which it is here subjected. But one virtue of his set is that it contains the seldom heard posthumous *Polonaises* (the three of Op. 71), an undated *Polonaise in G sharp minor*, and the *Adieu à Guillaume Kolberg*. Hardly ever does one hear the Op. 71 set, which is immature Chopin but not without interest. Among other recorded *Polonaises*, there is an impressive A flat played by Horowitz on V LM 1137; and Lhevinne's performance of the same work on V LCT 1038 reminds us that there once were other giants on earth.

Preludes (complete). Novaes, Vox 6170. Gulda, L 755. De Groot, Ep 3017. Rubinstein, V LM 1163.

The degree of subtlety and nuance in the Novaes disc is such that one gladly ignores a few rough spots. Even though the recording is not of particularly good quality (it goes back to 1950, when a really good piano disc was a rarity), the volatility of Novaes's pianism and the personality with which she sets forth Chopin's great ideas put her version at the very top. Gulda approaches the music from a Teutonic point of view, one quite different from Novaes's romanticism. He plays without caprice. Everything is planned, the musical metrics are altogether steady, and few rubatos are employed. Some may find the performance lacking in charm, but it is exceedingly strong playing. De Groot's version is well manicured and never exciting. Nevertheless, his is a degree of controlled playing that can't be patronized. Rubinstein turns in one of his few unconvincing Chopin performances. Some of the *Preludes* have a flurried quality not normally associated with him, and there are sections where the pianism is not what it should be. Of the several other versions available, Brailowsky's (V LM 1150) is dry, with the pianist falling into dynamic ruts and never climbing out. Arrau presents an efficient and colorless performance on C 4420. The Petri disc in Columbia's low-priced Entré series (Ent 3040) is a reissue of an old recording that did not rank high even in pre-war days.

Preludes (individual). See Collections: Keene (Mer 10113); "Great Pianists of the Past" (V LCT 1038); Moiseiwitsch (V LBC 1038).

Scherzos (complete). Rubinstein, V LM 1132. Bolet, REM 199-161.

Rubinstein has had a virtual monopoly on the *Scherzos*. In shellac days, his was the only integral recording. Since LP, only Arrau and Bolet have challenged him in these works. Rubinstein plays with his customary mastery, and he has received glittering recording. What he puts into the music in the way of power, poetry, and grandeur is illustrative of a type of Chopin-playing that is fast disappearing from the scene. There is something big, something unfettered, about his conceptions. He furthermore has the technique to put those conceptions into effect. His performances of the *Scherzos Nos. 1* and *2* have also been placed on 10" V LRM 7015, not a very good buy in view of current prices. Arrau's recording is less fortunate. See Collections: Arrau (D DX

130). Bolet gets harsh recorded sound, though it is full and clear enough. His performance is fine when he can keep his wonderful fingers moving. Bolet is an extraordinary technician. In lyric sections he tends to worry the line and bog down a bit, as in the C sharp minor section of the second *Scherzo*. Bolet achieves some imposing moments on this disc, but his over-all conception cannot challenge Rubinstein's.

Scherzo No. 1 in B minor (Op. 20). See Collections: Horowitz (V LM 1707 and 6014); Moiseiwitsch (V LBC 1038). See also *Études, Op. 10* (Vox 9070).

Scherzo No. 3 in C sharp minor (Op. 39). See Collections: Barere (Rem 199-17); "Great Pianists of the Past" (V LCT 1038); Katchen (L 554); Moiseiwitsch (V LBC 1038); Novaes (Vox 7810).

Scherzo No. 4 in E (Op. 54). See Collections: Moiseiwitsch (V LBC 1038).

*Sonata for Cello and Piano in G minor (Op. 65). Piatigorsky, Berkowitz, C 4215 (*Schubert-Piatigorsky: Introduction, Theme, and Variations; Schumann: Fantasiestücke; Fauré: Elegy).*

Chopin's *Cello Sonata* is a work of stature, undeservedly neglected. The slow movement is as songful as anything he composed, and the chromatic last movement is concentrated essence of Chopin. Piatigorsky plays with plenty of vibrato, presenting a virtuoso reading that does not lack warmth. His accompanist could have done much more with the piano part. The recording favors the cello; the piano, especially in the bass, sounds muddy and out of focus. On the reverse of this disc is a Schubert four-hand work arranged for cello by Piatigorsky, who has not neglected opportunities for display. The well-known Schumann pieces receive a warm interpretation, and Fauré's pretty *Elegy* is sweetly sung.

*Sonata for Piano No. 1 in C minor (Op. 4). Goldsand, CH 1150 (*Variations on "Là ci darem la mano"; Variations on a German Theme).*

This prentice work is never heard in concert. Some lovely things are in it, but its neglect is deserved. Which is not to say that it doesn't belong on records, and Goldsand gives the music an expert performance. The piano tone is reproduced with plenty of color, and the record surfaces are silent. Neither of the sets of variations has held its place on the concert stage. *"Là ci darem,"* Chopin's Op. 2, was the work that so excited Schumann ("Hats off, gentlemen! A genius!"). Today it can be regarded as a bravura novelty. The *Variations on a German Theme* are of a superficial elegance.

*Sonata for Piano No. 2 in B flat minor (Op. 35). Novaes, Vox 7360 (*Sonata No. 3). Rubinstein, V LM 9008 (*Debussy: Piano Music). Casadesus, C 4798 (*Ballades). Horowitz, V LM 1235 (*Liszt: Piano Music).*

It is Novaes who, in this sonata, has most temperament. She plays with fire and color, poetry and imagination. In the strange finale she brings out inner voices that bring back the days of Josef Hofmann. Excellent recorded sound, quiet surfaces. Rubinstein generates considerable excitement with his ultra-romantic, grand-manner approach, but his recording unfortunately has a thick sound with little definition in the bass. The elegant Casadesus has been better recorded. Against Novaes and Rubinstein, however, he sounds small-scaled (and this sonata is nothing if not passionate; it demands a big approach). Horowitz is unconvincing. He manages to sound hysterical and petulant rather than grand. Of the other versions in the catalogue, it would be well to avoid the erratic, mannered Malcuzynski performance on An 35032. Nor is Backhaus's on L 266 much more satisfactory in its stolid approach. Nat on HS 97 has the style, but no longer the technical command; and Uninsky on Ep 3056 is correct, but singularly unexciting.

*Sonata for Piano No. 3 in B minor (Op. 58). Novaes, Vox 7360 (*Sonata No. 2). Kapell, V LM 1715 (*Mazurkas). Lipatti, C 4721 (*Barcarolle, etc.).*

As in the *B flat minor Sonata*, Novaes offers the version with most freedom and spontaneity. I think that hers is the most idiomatic performance on LP. But many listeners do not like her arbitrary ways. If you want a performance that has more orthodoxy, try Kapell or Lipatti. Kapell made one of his best records here, and the combination of pianistic brilliance and musical understanding is an indication of what he would have developed into. He presents firm playing with a degree of poetry that he did not always show. Beautiful piano tone. The Lipatti disc is harder to handle. It is a boomy recording. I had best results with it on the Columbia 78 equalization curve. Lipatti's playing is quite beautiful but just a shade reticent emotionally. He obviously was holding himself back, and often his work sounds tight. Yet this is piano-playing of a stature that few artists of his generation could have come near approaching. Uninsky's steady performance on Ep 3056 is competent but dull.

*Trio for Piano and Strings in G minor (Op. 8). Bolzano, Vox 8480 (*Schumann: Trio No. 2 in F).*

Hardly a trio in the classic sense, this work is more a baby piano concerto, with the piano cascading over the violin and cello. It's a lot of fun, a much more attractive work than its neglect would suggest. The Trio di Bolzano is not the group to do justice to the score. It plays in a small-scaled manner and with thin tone. What is needed—and what is missing—is an extroverted quality backed by tremendous technical equipment. If a more representative version comes around, you should find the music a real treat.

Variations on "L'a ci darem la mano" (Op. 2); Variations on a German Theme. See *Sonata No. 1 for Piano* (CH 1150).

Variations on an Air by Hérold. See *Études* (CH 1133).

Waltzes (complete). Novaes, Vox 8170. Lipatti, C 4522. Dorfmann, V LBC 1050. Brailowsky, V LM 1082.

Dorfmann's is the best low-priced version. She delivers the music with clarity and sparkle, and the recording has an exceptionally clear sound. But Novaes is artistically on a superior level. Occasionally she makes her own rules, and her ideas often take a capricious turn. No matter. Lipatti is more direct, without the color of Novaes. His is beautifully regulated playing—and yet one wishes for just a bit more. After a while his interpretations here begin to sound metronomic and four-square. It is interesting to compare the Brailowsky LP with the shellac version he made in the thirties. The early set had a degree of nuance missing from the angular work displayed on the LP disc. Pennario's superficial playing on Cap 8172 is no help to the music. For individual waltzes see Collections: Backhaus (L 317); Cortot (V HMV 1032); "Great Pianists of the Past" (V LCT 1038); Hofmann (C 4929); Horowitz (V LM 1137); Jonas (10" C 2004 and C 4476); Novaes Vox 7810).

CLEMENTI, MUZIO (1752-1832)

Four Études. See Collections: Schwalb (Ac 303).

*Four Sonatinas (Op. 36, Nos. 1, 2, 4, 6). Kraus, Edu 3003 (*Kuhlau: 4 Sonatinas).*

Both the Clementi and Kuhlau pieces are agreeable morceaux over which many students have worked at one time or another. Kraus gives them clear-cut performances. The music asks no more or no less. Good recorded sound, fairly prominent surfaces.

COPLAND, AARON (1900-)

Passacaglia (1922); Variations (1930); Sonata (1941). Aitken, Wal 101.

Through the years with Copland. All of this music represents his abstract side. The dissonance quota is high, the melodic lines have typically wide skips, and often an intellectualized set of jazz rhythms is superimposed. None of this is easy to play. Aitken handles the writing with competence, and he has received excellent recording.

*Quartet for Piano and Strings (1950). New York Quartet, C 4421 (*Clarinet Concerto).*

Like it or not, this is a powerful work that leaves a strong impression. It is easily one of the major American chamber works, fluently composed, with some imaginative instrumental interplay. The New York Quartet is heard in a superb performance. The group has not only assurance, but also a degree of color generally missing from performances of music as abstract and difficult as this. The recording has admirable tonal depth.

*Sextet for Clarinet, Piano, and String Quartet. Oppenheim, Hambro, Juilliard, C 4492 (*Kohs: Chamber Concerto for Viola and String Nonet).*

The *Sextet* is a chamber version of the *Short Symphony*. Connoisseurs consider it one of Copland's best works. It is lively, with some thematic material that later was to take more popular shape in *El Salon Mexico*. This disc, in Columbia's "Modern American Music" series, was prepared under the supervision of the composer. Tonally it has exceptional fidelity. The Kohs work contains energetic, non-melodic patterns. Its performance by Molnar and a group of string-players sounds excellent.

*Sonata for Violin and Piano. Fuchs, Smit, D 8503 (*Stravinsky: Duo Concertant).*

An ideal performance. Both musicians are specialists in the idiom, are extraordinarily solid technicians, and see eye to eye interpretatively. The recording is somewhat thin in sound, but perfectly satisfactory. Avoid a performance of the *Sonata* on All 33 by Lack and Hambro: the recorded sound is sub-par.

CORELLI, ARCANGELO (1653-1713)

*La Folia. Szigeti, Farkas, C 4338 (*Schubert: Fantasy in C; Encore Pieces).*

This is the only LP of the work worth consideration, and even it leaves something to be desired. Szigeti's bow arm is not completely steady, and his playing sounds labored. The recorded sound is true to his tone.

COUPERIN, FRANÇOIS (1668-1733)

Concerts Royaux. Kaplan, Mayes, Bodky, Ly 54.

In the 1722 score no instrumentation is indicated. The present combination of flute, cello, and harpsichord seems perfectly in accord with the music. Three good musicians are at work here, and they collaborate to steady effect. The only defect in an otherwise flawless example of recorded sound is the placement of the harpsichord, which plugs away at a distance. For a version of the third "*Royal Concert*" see *Troisieme Concert Royal* (OL 50031).

Les Fastes de la grande et ancienne Ménestrandise; Le Tic-Toc-Choc. Marlowe, MGM 538 (Rameau: La Poule; Gavotte variée).*

All of the wonderful pieces on this disc are well known. Marlowe, playing what sounds like a concert-grand harpsichord, makes the music come to life with her spirited and sensitive performances. This is a lovely disc. Chiasson also has recorded the Couperin *Fastes* on Ly 12, along with other Couperin pieces. His disc is a good buy, though his playing lacks Marlowe's finesse.

*Les Folies Françaises. Marlowe, Rem 199-136 (*Scarlatti: Sonatas; Bach: Toccata in D). Chiasson, Ly 12 (*Les Fastes de la grande et ancienne Ménestrandise; Chaconne; L'Arlequine; Passacaille).*

Les Folies, though technically a series of variations on a ground bass, is an example of early program music, and a very amusing one. The titles of the pieces are almost surrealistic: "Prudery in a Rose-Colored Mask"; or "Benevolent Cuckoos in Yellow Masks." On the Marlowe disc a voice, unidentified, announces the pieces in French as they come up. Marlowe plays with her usual sensitivity, providing an excellent value in a low-priced disc. Fine recorded sound. The Chiasson disc is workmanlike, but lacks Marlowe's spontaneity. Chiasson, however, offers a greater amount of Couperin's harpsichord music, and those who are interested in building up a collection of the French master's harpsichord music would do well to consider the disc. This is a good place to mention five Couperin pieces from various *Ordres*, capably played on the piano by Marcelle Meyer on HS 98 (along with music by Rameau, Debussy, and Ravel).

Le Parnasse, ou L'Apothèose de Corelli. See Collections: Harpsichord Quartet (Es 517).

Suites for Gamba and Harpsichord Nos. 1 and 2. Soyer, Chessid, 10" CH 1066.

Soyer plays a cello rather than the original viola da gamba. Both musicians give straightforward performances of some amazingly Bachian music. The recording is clear in sound. *Suite No. 1*, which is in E minor, sounds closer to F minor in this disc. The *Second Suite*, in G, is pitched correctly.

Suite No. 14; Suite No. 24. Harich-Schneider (harpsichord), 10" U 5003 and 5001.

Like nearly all Couperin, these suites, or *"ordres,"* are lively and individual music. More can be gotten from them than the harpsichordist suggests. Harich-Schneider plays with a minimum of grace, concentrating on a literal translation of the notes. Which is all right as far as it goes, but it stops considerably short of artistic fulfillment. Excellent recorded sound.

Troisième Concert Royal; La Steinquerque. Nef, Gerlin, OL 50031.

Two harpsichords are used for the *Concert Royal* and for the amusing *Steinquerque*, a program piece commemorating the Battle of Steinkirk in 1692. Nef and Gerlin play the former work as though it were grim business indeed. Fortunately, they relax in the battle opus, achieving a good measure of its perky naïveté.

COWELL, HENRY (1897-)

*Sonata No. 1 for Violin and Piano. Szigeti, Bussotti, C 4841 (*Shapero: Sonata for Piano Four Hands).*

Composed in 1945, this work was dedicated to Szigeti. It contains elements of pre-Revolutionary America transmuted into a sort of twentieth-century Americana. Cowell, of course, has a flair for this kind of writing, and he makes it sound convincing. Szigeti plays with the simplicity demanded by the music. Admirable recorded sound.

Suite for Wind Quintet. See Collections: New Art Wind Quintet (CE 2003).

CRAMER, JEAN BAPTISTE (1771-1858)

13 Études. See Collections: Schwalb (Ac 303).

CRESTON, PAUL (1906-)

*String Quartet. Hollywood, Cap 8260 (*Turina: Oración del Torero; Wolf: Italian Serenade).*

A bland, expertly written score with strong French influences. The brilliant Hollywood Quartet plays it very well, and also does a superior job on the pleasant Turina score. In the Wolf *Italian Serenade* the quartet offers a nervous-sounding performance. I would prefer a more relaxed approach, such as that offered by the Koeckert Quartet on D 4044.

CUMMING, RICHARD (1928-)

Sonata for Piano. See Bloch: *Sonata for Piano* (ML 7015).

CZERNY, CARL (1791-1857)

6 Études. See Collections: Schwalb (Ac 303).

DAHL, INGOLF (1912-)

Allegro and Arioso for Wind Quintet. See Collections: New Art Wind Quintet (CE 2003).

*Concerto a Tre. Lurie, Gottlieb, Shapiro, C 4493 (*Schuman: Quartet No. 4).*

Another in the "Modern American Music" series. Dahl's trio is scored for clarinet, violin, and cello. It is a busy-busy work with a Stravinskian paternity; derivative, but really a bright little piece. Beautiful performance and recording. The Juilliard Quartet plays the Schuman on the reverse. Tight, dissonant, and nervous, it will be tough going for many listeners. Again first-class performance and recording.

DANZI, FRANZ (1763-1826)

Bläserquintett (Op. 67, No. 1). See Collections: New Art Wind Quintet (CE 2010).

Sonatas for French Horn and Piano in E flat (Op. 28) and E (Op. 44). Koch, Granetman, SPA 29.

Danzi, a German composer, is entirely forgotten today. These sonatas are interesting as anticipating the incipient romanticism of the early 1800's. Koch handles his unwieldy instrument with a good degree of smoothness, but he does not entirely convince the listener that it is easy to play, and his intonation is sometimes off. The recording is unresonant; it sounds as though it was made in a dead studio.

DEBUSSY, CLAUDE (1862-1918)

*En blanc et noir. Vronsky and Babin, C 4470 (*Stravinsky: Three Movements from Petrouchka).*

Typical Vronsky-Babin two-piano work is contained on this disc. The performances are glittering, exceedingly objective, rhythmic, and technically in perfect order. Such playing fits this Debussy work. A sparkling quality of recorded sound is another aid. Babin's transcription of the Stravinsky is a virtuoso affair intended to pad out the two-piano repertoire.

*La Boîte à joujoux. Pressler, MGM 3042 (*Ibert: Histoires).*

The Debussy piece was intended as a children's ballet, but the composer never got around to scoring it (André Caplet eventually did). It is reminiscent of the *Children's Corner*, even unto actual quotation. Ibert's *Histoires*, a collection of ten piano pieces, contains the popular "Little White Donkey." Otherwise it is a completely derivative (Debussy) work. Attractive piano-playing here. Pressler, in both works, handles the music simply, with taste and style. Superior recorded sound, too, with exceptionally lifelike piano tone.

*Children's Corner. Gieseking, C 4539 (*Suite bergamasque). Casadesus, C 4366 (*Schumann: Waldescenen).*

This is the work that contains the "Golliwog's Cake Walk." Two specialists in French music have recorded it. Casadesus plays with a brighter and more detached style than does Gieseking; the latter employs more color and has a greater variety of pedal effects. Although Gieseking's recording lacks the clarity of Casadesus's, the greater atmospheric quality of Gieseking's performance makes his disc preferable. I prefer Gieseking's Columbia disc to a more recent one he made for Angel. For Debussy himself playing the *Children's Corner*, see Collections: "Great Masters of the Keyboard," Vol. I (C 4291).

Danse; Rêverie; Two Arabesques; Nocturne; Valse romantique; L'Île joyeuse; Le Petit Nègre; Masques; Danse bohémienne; Ballade; Mazurka; La plus que lente; Berceuse héroïque; Hommage à Haydn. Gieseking, An 35026.

Most of these pieces date from Debussy's youth. They are immature, and only specialists would know them (or care to know them). Gieseking's stylish performances are everything that could be asked for. A miscellany of Debussy's piano music is also played by Rubinstein on V LM 9008 (*Chopin: *Sonata in B flat minor*), where six works of Debussy's maturity are delivered with considerable artistry.

*Épigraphes antiques. Gold and Fizdale, C 4854 (*Poulenc: Sonata for Piano Four Hands; Milhaud: Concertino d'automne; Satie: En habit de cheval).*

Not heard very often, the *Épigraphes* is a perfumed work with a modal feeling. It is delicate, tired-sounding, and strangely moving. This disc, also available separately, is part of the three-disc "Music for Two Pianos" set; for complete listing of contents see Collections: Gold and Fizdale (C SL 198). The two young pianists are as efficient an ensemble as one can find before the public today. Brilliant performance; recording to match.

Estampes; Pour le piano; Images (Books I and II). Gieseking, An 35065. Arrau, C 4786.

Some of Debussy's best piano music is heard on this disc.

Estampes contains *Pagodes, Soirée dans Grenade; Jardins sous la pluie*. In the first book of *Images* are *Reflets dans l'eau; Hommage à Rameau;* and *Mouvement*. Book II contains *Cloches à travers les feuilles; Et la lune descend sur le temple qui fut; Poissons d'or*. Arrau and Gieseking have entirely different ideas about the music. Pianistically, Arrau is fine, but he underlines where Gieseking suggests; he is sharp and steely where Gieseking will pedal the same passage to throw a set of harmonies into relief. This Gieseking disc supersedes the same pianist's work on C 4773, which is an LP transfer with very heavy surfaces on *Estampes* (the *Images* are much better). Arrau's recording also has some distracting surfaces in the *Soirée dans Grenade*. If you are interested only in recorded quality, try the Gianoli set (W 214), which may not be near Gieseking's level of pianism, but which is exceptionally faithful to piano tone.

Études (complete). Haas, D 9599. Rosen, REB 6.

Each pianist plays the twelve *Études* (six in each book). Haas has more experience and obviously more poise than Rosen. She also has a smoother technique, and some of her playing is really resourceful. Though the piano sound itself is first-class, the Haas disc is low-level, with considerable surface noise.

Images, Books I and II. See *Estampes* (An 35065).

*Petite Suite. Bartlett and Robertson, 10" MGM 161 (*Ravel: Ma mère l'Oye).*

Bartlett and Robertson play the work as written—for piano four hands. It is one of Debussy's salon scores, but one with plenty of grace. The duettists do not try to overstep the bounds of this simple music; they play with appropriate simplicity. A fine disc, especially considering the original version of *Mother Goose* on the reverse.

Piano Pieces (miscellaneous). See *Danse* (An 35026).

Pour le piano. See *Estampes* (An 35065).

Préludes, Book I. Gieseking, C 4537 and An 35066.

Préludes, Book II. Gieseking, C 4538. Casadesus, C 4019.

Préludes, Books I and II. Gianoli, W WAL 214 [2] *(*Estampes).*

Gieseking competes with himself in Book I. The Angel disc, though on a rather low level and lacking in presence, is much clearer than the dead-sounding Columbia. Also, on the latter disc some of the preludes were recorded slightly off pitch. But this is nothing as to what goes on in the Gieseking disc of Book II, which is a half-tone flat in its entirety. This is one reason for recommending the Casadesus version of Book II. Not that Casadesus is a slouch at this kind of music or has to win by default. His performance has color, flexibility, style, and imagination. Casadesus is one of the supreme stylists in the French piano literature. Gieseking eventually will get around to recording Book II of the *Préludes* for Angel, at which time a comparison under more favorable circumstances can be made between his disc and the Casadesus. Gianoli, who plays both books in the Westminster set, has the benefit of the best quality of recorded sound. Neither her artistry nor her technical command is on the order of a Gieseking or a Casadesus. Her playing is reliable, however, and those to whom the first order of LP is hi-fi will naturally gravitate toward her album. Cortot has recorded Book I on V HMV 1009: a dull-sounding performance. For Debussy himself playing a group of *Préludes*, see Collections: "Great Masters of the Keyboard," Vol. I (C 4291).

*Quartet for Strings. Budapest, C 4668 (*Ravel: Quartet). Stuyvesant, Ph 104 (*Ravel: Quartet).*

The Columbia is a transfer to LP of a performance issued some time ago on shellac. Though the Philharmonia disc is a more recent recording, it is not noticeably better in matters of tone. I prefer the Budapest version for its stronger rhythm and better-defined instrumental interplay. It is not a "definitive" version; the Budapest has never shown complete rapport with French music, and here the patterns are laid out a little too mathematically. Masterful playing, in any case, and the performance will do very well until a better one comes along. A performance by the Quartetto Italiano on An 35130 is beautifully colored but a little too effeminate for my taste.

*Rhapsody No. 1 for Clarinet and Piano. Kell, Rosen, D 9570 (*Hindemith: Sonata; Stravinsky: 3 Pieces).*

Reginald Kell here upholds his claim to be considered the Heifetz of the clarinet. His playing has perfect control, the most liquid of tones, and all kinds of shadings and dynamics. Kell also teases a melodic line in the Heifetz manner. This disc is a lexicon of clarinet-playing—and a beautiful performance, too. Good recorded sound, fairly prominent surfaces.

*Sonata for Cello and Piano. Janigro, Doyen, W 5207 (*Sonata for Flute, Viola, and Harp; Violin Sonata).*

It is difficult to get a work like this on discs. The music is all delicate nuance, with the most minute dynamic adjustments. Records are not geared to this kind of musical subtlety, not even the best modern LP's. Janigro and Doyen make the music as interesting as limitations of the recording medium permit (the score, in all truth, is not one of Debussy's more interesting ones).

*Sonata for Flute, Viola, and Harp. Wanausek, Weiss, Jellinek, W 5207 (*Cello Sonata; Violin Sonata).*

A heavy-sounding performance. The tone of the viola is coarse, and none of the musicians plays with much imagination. The best that can be said is that they are conscientious. Excellent-sounding recording, which brings (for better or worse) the work of the players into clear relief.

*Sonata for Violin and Piano. Francescatti, Casadesus, C 4178 (*Franck: Violin Sonata). Heifetz, Bay, V LM 1184 (*Respighi: Violin Sonata). Fournier, Doyen, W 5207 (*Cello Sonata; Sonata for Flute, Viola, and Harp).*

If it's only the Debussy *Sonata* you want, and are not interested in what is contained on the reverse, Francescatti or Heifetz is your best bet. Both discs are examples of thoroughbred fiddling. The preference here is for the Columbia, which is better recorded (the Victor has a noticeable background hum). Westminster offers good recorded sound and the most consistent coupling. If you are interested in building up a Debussy collection, this disc belongs, as it contains, with the *Violin Sonata*, versions of the *Cello* and the *Flute-Viola-Harp* sonatas. Fournier is a good musician, though as a technician he cannot come up to Messrs. Francescatti and Heifetz. An interesting performance of the Debussy *Sonata* is contained on An 35128 (*Chausson: *Poème;* Ravel: *Tzigane*). Ginette Neveu is the violinist. The quality of recording is none too good (she made it shortly before she met death in a plane crash in 1949), but the playing has the combination of strength, clarity, and spaciousness which made her the Lipatti of the violin. A version by Ferras and Barbizet on L 909 (*Fauré: *Sonata in E minor*) is coarse-sounding against the Francescatti or Heifetz interpretations, and the better recorded sound of the London disc cannot compensate for its stylistic deficiencies.

*Suite bergamasque. Gieseking, C 4539 (*Children's Corner). Gulda, L 754 (*Ravel: Gaspard de la Nuit).*

Gieseking's is an old recording, but the transfer to LP has been satisfactorily accomplished, despite a slight ping in the upper treble. A more recent Angel disc with the same coupling is disappointingly dull in sound. Gulda's recording is by far the best tonally, and it is right good playing, though it lacks the incense of Gieseking's. Gulda's *Clair de lune* shows a cold moon; Gieseking's shines through a silvery cloud.

DELLO JOIO, NORMAN (1913-)

*Variations and Capriccio. Travers, Dello Joio, C 4845 (*Bowles: Music for a Farce; Scènes d'Anabase).*

For the most part this piece is lyric and conservative. It's all pretty eclectic. Dello Joio describes this work as "intellectually unproblematical." O.K.; no argument. The talented Patricia Travers bows the work sweetly enough, the composer supports her gallantly, and the recorded sound is first-class.

DITTERSDORF, KARL DITTERS VON (1739-1799)

*Three Partitas (in F, A, and D). French Wind Quintet, OL 50014 (*Pleyel: Fifth Concertante Symphony).*

The scoring here is for flute, oboe, clarinet, horn, and bassoon. Nothing particularly novel about the music, but it does have moments of naïve good humor. In the last movement of the F major occurs a touch of Janizary music. A charming disc in many respects (the Pleyel work on the reverse also is an agreeable novelty). The performance sounds entirely competent, and the recording is fine.

DOHNANYI, ERNST VON (1877-)

*Quartet for Strings No. 2 in D flat (Op. 15). Stradivari, Str 614 (*Serenade in C). Curtis, W 5301 (*Piano Quintet in E flat minor).*

Like most Dohnányi works, this quartet has its academic side. With all of its conservatism and derivations, though, it is honestly tuneful, never cheap, and decidedly worth living with. The Stradivari Quartet supplies the preferable version. It shows a more supple ensemble than the Curtis group, and its tone is truer to pitch. The Curtis Quartet is not heard to best advantage here, nor is it entirely successful in the juicy *Piano Quintet* on the reverse, despite some spirited piano-playing by Vladimir Sokoloff.

Quintet for Piano and Strings in E flat minor (Op. 26, No. 2). See *Quartet for Strings in D flat* (W 5301).

*Four Rhapsodies (Op. 11). Schwalb, Ac 301 (*Weiner: Hungarian Peasant Songs).*

These pieces impress as the work of a Czech Rachmaninoff. Dohnányi was once a great virtuoso, and he writes idiomatically for the piano. Schwalb supplies forceful performances. The Weiner sketches are pleasant, nationalistic, and also effectively laid out for the piano. Again Schwalb bounces energetically through. Clear recording, with a slight "wow" in the piano tone.

*Ruralia Hungarica. Campoli, Malcolm, 10" L 793 (*Paganini: 3 Caprices).*

Most listeners should enjoy these very *Ungarisch* pieces. Campoli evidently does; he brings more fervor to the music than to almost anything else he has done on records. The recording is a bit shrill, but handles well if the highs are reduced.

*Serenade in C (Op. 10). Pougnet, Riddle, Pini, W 5316 (*Françaix: Trio; Berkeley: Trio). Eidus, Mankovitz, G. Ricci, Str 614 (*Quartet No. 2 in D flat).*

Perhaps Tovey was thinking of this work when he called Dohnányi's chamber music "without flaw in the purity of its style." So melodious and beautiful a work does not deserve the neglect it has received. Its tuneful aspects are stressed by the lyric performance of the group headed by Pougnet. Excellent teamwork is heard on the Westminster disc, whereas the Stradivari players are dominated by the first violinist. Westminster also has the edge in recorded sound.

*Sonata for Cello and Piano in B flat (Op. 8). Scholz, Schwalb, Ac 305 (*Bach-Kodály: 3 Chorale Preludes).*

A conservative, expertly written work, melodious and quite unoriginal. The honors of this performance go to Schwalb, who has much more decided ideas about the music than does the cellist. The latter is curiously tentative at times; nor is his tone anything to rejoice over. First-class recorded sound.

Suite en Valse; Arrangements of Delibes's "Naila" and Schubert's "Valses Nobles." Dohnányi, Kilenyi, C 4256.

This elegant, sophisticated, and superficial evocation of *alt Wien* is a lot of fun. Dohnányi and his pupil Edward Kilenyi do an expert job with the brilliant two-piano setting of the waltz suite. The *Naila* and Schubert doctorings, both for solo piano, are flashily played by Kilenyi. In the two-piano work the recording is hard, clear, and unresonant. The solo pieces have a thicker sound.

DONIZETTI, GAETANO (1797-1848)

*Quartet for Strings No. 1 in E flat. Parrenin, Str 618 (*Lalo: Quartet; Gounod: Quartet).*

Three rarities are present here. None of them is very interesting. The Donizetti (1817) is pleasant and derivative. The Gounod lacks personality, nor does the Lalo have much profile except for a sparkling last movement. I am not very impressed with the work of the Parrenin Quartet. It demonstrates little idea of molding a phrase to its greatest extent, and it falls into monotonous rhythmic and dynamic patterns. The recording has a tendency toward shrillness.

DUPRÉ, MARCEL (1886-)

Symphonic Passion (Op. 23). Watters, CE 1020.

As the title implies, this is a program work—a big, splashy, romantic program work for organ. After one hearing, the neo-Franck writing all appears rather silly. After a few hearings one develops great respect for the workmanship and melodic ideas (especially the hushed, repetitious patterns of the *Nativité*); but under no conditions could this be called a really creative work. Watters plays on a Harrison-designed classical organ. He does all that can be done to hold the music together; and his strong musicianship makes the attempt almost successful. This disc is an example of resonant organ sound that never blasts.

DVOŘÁK, ANTONIN (1841-1904)

*Four Romantic Pieces (Op. 75). Rybar, Holletschek, W 5015 (*Violin Sonata in F).*

Each of the *Romantic Pieces* is attractive nationalism, and the last movement of the sonata is an especially sunny example of the composer at his most fluent. A most agreeable disc, this; melodious music without a neurosis within miles. The disc is early Westminster, vintage 1950, rather harsh in sound and plagued with a background of what appears to be 60-cycle hum. Rybar and Holletschek can be classified as earnest rather than inspired musicians.

*Quartet for Piano and Strings in E flat (Op. 87). Jahoda, Galimir, Str 619 (*Janáček: Quartet No. 2).*

The Dvořák is a gorgeous piece when the composer forgets about "sonata" form and lets his musical instincts carry him along. Fortunately, this constantly happens, especially in the third movement, one of the most charming Bohemian waltzes ever written. Janáček's score is subtitled "Intimate Letters." He was seventy-four when he composed it. The music exhibits a type of lyricism that some record-listeners may know through Suk's *Serenade for Strings*. The recorded sound on this disc is serviceable, though the flat and unresonant quality suggests a dead studio. Suave, idiomatic performances. Jahoda is a fine ensemble pianist who seems to have a thorough insight into the healthy structure of Dvořák's writing.

Quartet for Strings No. 3 in E flat (Op. 51). Boskovsky, L 387.

One could wish for a little more spontaneity from the Boskovsky group. Its performance encompasses the notes, and the members play together without any *gaffes*. That is all. Eventually a performance with a more sensuous tonal quality and with a more aristocratic shaping of the line will come along. The score demands no less. It is one of Dvořák's finest pieces: sturdy, lyric, inventive, and richly written for strings.

Quartet for Strings No. 4 in C (Op. 61). Gordon, CH 1075.

No longer in the catalogue, this discontinued recording is worth grabbing if you come across it. It is the only LP of a fine piece of music; and the sound, while not of top quality, can be reproduced quite faithfully.

*Quartet for Strings No. 6 in F ("American," Op. 96). Hungarian, CH 1157 (*Suite in D). Stradivari, Str 613 (*Smetana: Quartet). Koeckert, D 9637 (*Smetana: Quartet). Curtis, W 5199 (*Smetana: Quartet).*

The Hungarian and Koeckert quartets take the middle ground, turning in sober performances. The Stradivari group is more alert, save at those times the first violinist takes the lead as though playing the Tchaikovsky *Concerto.* Next to these versions, the Curtis sounds jerky. It does have the most vital quality of recorded sound, however, though there is nothing wrong with the Stradivari recording. Concert Hall and Decca do not show comparable tonal realism in their "Americans."

*Quartet for Strings No. 7 in A flat (Op. 105). Barylli, W 5337 (*Quintet for Piano and Strings). Barchet, Vox 7570.*

Though this is a magnificent piece of chamber music, it seldom turns up in concert. Fortunately on LP discs we can get the chance to imbibe its bracing nationalism, plus a quality of lyricism that ranks with Dvorák's best. Westminster has furnished much the better version. The company has placed the work on one side of a disc, coupling it with another Dvořák masterpiece, while Vox spreads the score over two sides. In addition, the Barylli performance, with its rhythm and musical intelligence, is superior to that of the rough-sounding (though spirited) Barchet. The only drawback to the Barylli Quartet is a lack of color in the string tone. As in the *Quintet* on the reverse, one notices a type of playing almost devoid of silk or sensuousness. Fortunately the positive virtues of the interpretation more than compensate.

*Quintet for Piano and Strings in A (Op. 81). Farnadi, Barylli, W 5337 (*Quartet No. 7). Curzon, Budapest, C 4825. Chigi, L 202.*

Here is the sunniest of all piano quintets. Those who do not know the music are in for a treat. Even for Dvořák this example of sustained lyricism and constant inventiveness is unusual. Each of the three versions has something to recommend it; but the fact that Westminster is the only company to offer two works on the same disc is the deciding factor. Neither of the other two interpretations is so transcendent that it can overcome such a handicap. The Westminster performance is tasteful, and Farnadi turns in a fine performance of the piano part, phrasing with considerable sensitivity. The music obviously is in her blood. On the Chigi disc one hears a smooth, gentle flow. Curzon and the Budapest members are brighter, more businesslike, and sharp in detail. But the Westminster is not only the best buy; it also impresses me as the best performance.

Quintet for Strings in G (Op. 77). Vienna Konzerthaus, W 5026.

The scoring is for string quartet and double bass. A negative feeling is obtained from this interpretation. All of the notes are played, and the dynamic indications are observed; but there is no particular identification with the style, nor is there any inner life to the playing. Released in the fall of 1950, this disc has some shrillness of sound, most of which can be tuned out. A gradual pitch rise puts the recording almost in A flat instead of G.

*Quintet for Strings in E flat (Op. 97). Katims, Budapest, C 4799 (*Brahms: Quartet No. 1).*

Originally on an entire 10" disc, this work was transferred to one 12" side early in 1954. Brahms occupies the other. This might be called Dvořák's "American Quintet." Elements in the second movement are supposed to have been inspired by Indian themes. But there is even more material that comes straight from Bohemia, including the fine, swinging finale. Everything is nice about this recording: the coupling, the performance, the quality of sound.

Sextet in A (Op. 48). Jilka, Rem 199-12.

Not a very good recording, this disc is listed here because the music is so lovely. The thin sound and noisy surfaces can be partially controlled by equalizing to the NAB curve and then reducing the treble considerably. Keep your eye out for a new recording of this exceptionally graceful, melodious work.

Sonata for Violin and Piano in F (Op. 57). See *Four Romantic Pieces* (W 5015).

*Terzetto in C (Op. 74). Classic, CE 1033 (*Kodály: Serenade).*

Composed for a group of amateur players, this work is scored for two violins and viola. The amateurs must have been very skilled; this writing is not easy. On this disc the performance misses a quality of integration that would have shown the music in a better light. It is really an enchanting score, but one would never guess it from the lack of zest and the general pedestrian air of the playing.

Trio for Piano and Strings in F minor (Op. 65). Kaufman, Cervera, Balsam, CH 1117.

A new recording of this powerful work is badly needed. This version is harsh in sound, lacks detail, and suffers from excess background noise. The performance sounds competent, but the players have to operate under too great a handicap.

*Trio for Piano and Strings in E minor ("Dumky," Op. 90). Eidus, G. Ricci, Mittman, Str 620 (*Smetana: Trio in G minor).*

The "*Dumky*" is the best-known work on this disc, though Smetana's *Trio*, with its wondrously lyric slow movement, deserves to be better known. Both works receive acceptable performances that do not reveal any special identification with the bouncing nationalistic writing. Good recorded sound, though the piano has a tendency to blot out the other instruments.

ELGAR, SIR EDWARD (1858-1934)

*Sonata for Violin and Piano in E minor (Op. 92). Tryon, La Montaine, CE 1019 (*Strauss: Violin Sonata).*

Nobody could call this splashy, post-romantic sonata a very original work. At the same time, you can't turn up your nose at such sincere writing; and in the apostrophe to the last movement Elgar speaks with his most British accent. Tryon is a good violinist. His tone is strong and clear, and his intonation is excellent. He does not employ much color, and avoids a heavy vibrato. He sounds more like a musician than a virtuoso, and there is a feeling that he sometimes holds himself too much in restraint. Accomplished playing, nevertheless, and he is assisted by an expert pianist. Good recording.

ENESCO, GEORGES (1881-)

Octet for Strings. Instrumental group led by composer, Rem 199-52.

This is a conservative and melodious work, well worth knowing; and someday we may get a better recording than this harsh-sounding disc.

*Sonata for Violin and Piano No. 3 in A minor (Op. 25). Druian, Simms, Mer 70001 (*Janáček: Violin Sonata).*

Much rhapsodic writing here, exotic-sounding, full of Hungarian flourishes (some of which are not too far removed from the tea-room). Druian plays with more conviction and tonal resource than he has shown on his other discs. The throbbing vibrato he applies is perfectly apposite to the gypsy aspects of the music. So are the slides and scoops. Beautiful recorded sound.

FALLA, MANUEL DE (1876-1946)

Piano Music (complete). Echániz, W 5218.

Included on this disc are not only Falla's original piano pieces, but also his transcriptions from *El Amor Brujo* and *El Sombrero de Tres Picos*. Much gorgeous music is present, and the *Fantasia Baetica* is one of the high spots of the literature, but it is hard to get excited about Echániz's percussive performance. He seems unable to curve a melodic line with any degree of imagination. The recorded sound is only too kind to his tone. On MGM 3071 is a collection of Falla's piano music, played by Pressler. This disc does not have as much coverage as Westminster offers, nor is the recording comparable in clarity. Pressler gets painfully sentimental in some sections (such as the "*Cubana*" from the *Pièces espagnoles*), though at least his approach has more color than Echániz's. As matters now stand, the Westminster is the better buy.

*Suite populaire Espagnole. Stern, Zakin, 10" C 2050 (*Hindemith: Violin Sonata). Odnoposoff, Antonietti, CH 1175 (*Nin: Chants d'Espagne; Ysaye: Two Sonatas).*

Both violinists play Paul Kochanski's popular transcription of the *Seven Spanish Popular Songs*. There is not much to choose from. Stern plays with color and virtuosity. So does Odnoposoff. The big difference between the two is that where Stern is rhythmic and muscular, Odnoposoff is all silken assurance. Hindemith's *Sonata* is not the most apt choice for a companion work; certainly Stern could have come up with something more apposite. On his disc Odnoposoff has selected Nin's routine example of Spanish nationalism. The unaccompanied Ysaye pieces are beloved of violinists and a very few listeners. Odnoposoff, who has never achieved in this country the recognition due him, plays with marvelous control and purity of intonation.

FAURÉ, GABRIEL (1845-1924)

*Barcarolles Nos. 1-6. Boynet, Vox 6910 (*3 Romances sans paroles; Improvisation; Clair de lune).*

Boynet plays this delicate music very well, gliding along the top of the keys in an elegant French Conservatory style. Not much tonal depth is present, but the music does not need much. She plays the other short pieces in the same way. Excellent recorded sound. This disc is recommended as a "sleeper." It contains some remarkable music that many collectors might normally pass over. Several other pianists have recorded some of the *Barcarolles*. Casadesus plays No. 5 (see *Dolly Suite*); Long has recorded Nos. 1 and 2 on L 887 in an able fashion that somehow never quite gets off the ground. For Fauré himself playing the *A minor Barcarolle*, see Collections: "Great Masters of the Keyboard," Vol. I (C 4291).

*Dolly Suite. R. and G. Casadesus, 10" C 2205 (*Nocturne No. 7; Barcarolle No. 5; Impromptu No. 5).*

Mr. and Mrs. Casadesus play *Dolly* in the original four-hand version. The other music is played by Mr. Casadesus alone. *Dolly* is a work of extraordinary tenderness, and one could not ask for a more polished performance than that which it receives here. From the superb way Casadesus plays the three solo pieces, it would be a worth-while project for him to record all of Fauré's piano music. The recorded sound on this disc is not especially colorful, but does have a clear quality.

Impromptus. See *Theme and Variations* (CH 1181); *Dolly Suite,* (10" C 2205).

Nocturnes Nos. 1-4, 6, 7. Boynet, Vox 7520.

See the entry under *Barcarolles* for general remarks about Boynet's playing. She is an artist of skill and taste, and she understands this music perfectly. Excellent recorded sound, excess surface noise. If you want a fine out-of-the-way piano disc, don't overlook this. Beware of a mistake in the label copy. Side 1 should read Nos. 1, 2, and 4; on Side 2 should be Nos. 3, 6, and 7. Several other *Nocturne* recordings are available. Casadesus plays No. 7 (see *Dolly Suite*). Long has Nos. 4, 6, and 13 on L 887. No. 13 is a haunting work that seems almost to be a rumination on the *Pelléas et Mélisande* suite. Long also has Nos. 2, 5, 7, and 8 on L 1058 (**Ballade;* Françaix: *Concertino for Piano and Orchestra*). She plays these *Nocturnes* in a perfectly musical manner that lacks ultimate refinement of style. Colorful recorded sound is present on all of her discs.

*Quartet for Piano and Strings No. 1 in C minor (Op. 15). G. Casadesus, Guilet, Pol 1007 (*Cello Sonata). Rubinstein, Paganini, 10" V LM 52.*

The Victor recording has a more superficial brilliance. Stylistically, however, the Polymusic disc is more gracious, with a greater degree of suppleness and with clear, well-balanced sound. It also offers the seldom-played *Cello Sonata* (Op. 117) in a good but colorless performance by Soyer; and one could wish for a pianist with more subtlety than Mittman.

*Quartet for Strings in E minor (Op. 121). Guilet, Pol 1008 (*Violin Sonata No. 2).*

This inbred work is not everybody's meat, though to a certain type of mind the piece will be a revelation. The Guilet Quartet plays the music fluently, achieving a murmuring quality and a type of restraint entirely in keeping with the nature of the writing. Good string tone, excellent instrumental balance.

Quintet for Piano and Strings No. 2 in C minor (Op. 115). Lev, Pascal, CH 1093.

Almost never heard, this strange work at first gives a feeling of gray monotony. Then it starts to grow on one, and finally achieves a distinct profile. The performance here is fluent. Lev plays with more restraint than is her wont, working with the Pascals like the good musician she is. The recording will never win any prizes for tonal realism, but there is no distortion.

Sonata for Cello and Piano No. 2 in G minor. See *Quartet No. 1 for Piano and Strings* (Pol 1007).

Sonatas for Violin and Piano Nos. 1 in A (Op. 13) and 2 in E minor (Op. 108). Francescatti, Casadesus, [*disc number not assigned by Columbia at time of publication*]. *Fournier, Doyen, W 5156.*

No. 1, of course, is a frequent concert-hall visitor. No. 2 hardly ever shows up though, by virtue of an exquisite second movement, it should. The Francescatti-Casadesus collaboration may come as an eye-opener to many listeners. The two French musicians do not look upon these sonatas as effeminate pieces of music or as a pleasant stroll through a carefully ordered landscape. Rather they play with passion, excitement, and color: two extraordinary musicians collaborating as one. The *A major Sonata* emerges with more strength than I have ever heard it, on records or in the concert hall. Extremely live recorded sound, though the piano is overamplified in fortissimo sections. All other recorded performances take a back seat. Fournier and Doyen treat the music with understanding, but the strained sounds from Fournier's bow are not always pleasant to hear. Guilet and Gaby Casadesus have recorded the *E minor Sonata* on Pol 1008. As the only LP recording of the interesting *Quartet in E minor* is on the reverse of the Polymusic disc, the Fauré-collector might have a problem. But I would duplicate the *E minor Sonata* rather than miss owning the Columbia disc. I suggest avoiding the Ferras-Barbizet performance of the *E minor Sonata* on L 909. Not much of the music's refinement comes through, and Ferras, not the most subtle of violinists, abuses a vibrato.

*Theme and Variations in C sharp minor (Op. 73). Johannesen, CH 1181 (*Ballade for Piano and Orchestra; Impromptu No. 3; Poulenc:*

*Nocturnes Nos. 1-8; Mouvements perpetuels). Long, L 887 (*Barcarolles Nos. 1, 2; Nocturnes Nos. 4, 6, 13; Impromptu No. 2).*

I am far from enthralled with either performance of the *Theme and Variations*, Fauré's most extended work for solo piano. Johannesen gives the music an exact, powerful reading, but his imagination is not commensurate with his grasp of the notes. Piano-playing of such solidity must be respected, however, and Johannesen's clear-cut quality is, to my ears, preferable to Long's pleasant but somewhat vaporous approach. The contents of her disc previously had resided in a pair of 10" Londons—260 and 246. In the transfer to the longer long-play, London somewhat improved the quality of recording, but it still is not as clear as that which Johannesen has received from Concert Hall.

*Trio for Piano and Strings in D minor (Op. 120). Albeneri, Mer 10089 (*Ravel: Trio in A minor).*

Dating back some years, this recording is lacking in instrumental definition and lusterless in sound. Unfortunate; for this is a warm, lyric work that nobody else has taken the trouble to record. The Albeneri Trio plays it conscientiously, as it plays everything conscientiously, but French music is not its cup of tea: it (French music) demands a type of delicacy and suppleness which seems to be foreign to the massive outlook of the group.

FINE, IRVING (1914-)

Partita for Woodwind Quintet. See Collections: New Art Wind Quintet (CE 1003).

*Quartet for Strings (1952). Juilliard, C 4843 (*Kirchner: Quartet No. 1).*

Impetus and considerable motor force, rather than personal communication, characterize this work. Kirchner's quartet, on the reverse, is played by the American Art Quartet. This too is sinewy and lean. Both performances sound first-rate. The Juilliard's brittle style well suits the Fine quartet, and the American Art provides the Kirchner with a spirited interpretation.

FRANÇAIX, JEAN (1912-)

*Quintet for Winds. Wind Quintet of French National Radio, An 35133 (*Poulenc: Sextet for Piano and Winds). New Art Wind Quintet, CE 2001 (*Nielsen: Wind Quintet).*

A most talented buffoon, Françaix has a knack for turning out irreverent scores. Here, perhaps, he owes too large a debt to Poulenc, but the score is attractive and a lot of fun, if not taken too seriously. On the Angel disc is a flexible performance, mellow in sound, well balanced, stylishly phrased. The New Art Wind Quintet offers a clear-cut performance, but the recording leaves much to be desired. Often the instrumental definition is hazy, and at one point at the end of the first movement there is a heavy overload.

*Trio for Strings. Pougnet, Riddle, Pini, W 5316 (*Dohnányi: Serenade; Berkeley: Trio).*

It would appear that the members of this fine string trio are not emotionally attuned to the Gallicisms and smart-alecisms of Françaix. They play in a heavy manner that suggests Brahms, at the very least. The Berkeley work comes through more successfully, possibly because it is in a more orthodox post-romantic vein—despite some unconvincing French suggestions—that is more germane to the Pougnet-Riddle-Pini style. Lacking any other LP version of the cute Françaix work, one must stay with the Westminster disc; but if another company takes a flier, investigation decidedly will be in order.

FRANCK, CÉSAR (1822-1890)

Chorals (3). Watters, CE 1007 [2] *(*Prière). Asma, Ep 3051 (*Pièce héroïque).*

The Franck *Chorals* are far from the Bach *Chorales.* In one respect they are miniature tone poems, and not very short ones either. For some reason Asma gets on one disc what it takes Classic Editions two to record. But that is about the only favorable feature of the Epic. Asma's organ is about a half-tone sharp and makes thick, featureless sounds. Often the passagework comes out an entire jumble. Even though the Watters version is twice as expensive, it is easily the better buy. The sound is much clearer, the balance more lifelike; and Watters's sensitive playing must be favored over Asma's heavy-handed approach.

Grande Pièce symphonique. See *Six Pièces* (CE 1014).

Pièce héroïque. See *Trois Pièces* (CE 1015).

*Prelude, Chorale, and Fugue. Rubinstein, V LM 1822 (*Schumann: Carnaval). Demus, W 5163 (*Prelude, Aria, and Finale).*

Rubinstein's version is the best (and the most lifelike recording), though it does not have the resilience of his 1945 shellac version. In the latest disc his tempos are deliberate and there is just a touch of stodginess. Withal, the results are far above those the small-scaled Demus can offer. In both of the Franck works Demus is sober, exact, and singularly without tension. Katchen on L 823 (*Schumann: *Études symphoniques*) presents hard-driven, almost spasmodic performances; and the Malcuzynski version on Ent 3031 sounds merely eccentric.

Quartet for Strings in D. WQXR, Pol 1010. Pascal, CH 1182.

In every way the WQXR performance is a superior choice. It is better recorded, and is presented with better rhythm and with a type of musicianship that ignores the all too obvious opportunities for sentimentalism. The Pascal group dwells so fondly over certain passages that the music melts like an ice-cream cone in the sun. Nor is the intonation of the Pascals equal to the tuning-fork accuracy of the WQXR Quartet.

Quintet for Piano and Strings in F minor. Aller, Hollywood, Cap 8220. Sokoloff, Curtis, W 5331.

Victor Aller and the Hollywood group give the strongest and most incisive reading of the score. Next to it the Westminster disc sounds thick. Few chamber-music organizations can boast the richness of sound that the Hollywood Quartet supplies, and in addition its ensemble is extraordinarily accurate. A performance of this quintet on L 201 by the Chigi Quintet is weaker in recorded sound than the above two versions, and it cannot match the Capitol disc in musical organization.

Six Pièces pour Orgue. Watters, CE 1014 [2].

The titles of the six pieces, which are often heard individually, are: *Fantaisie; Prélude, Fugue, et Variation; Grande Pièce symphonique; Pastorale; Prière; Final.* Watters plays them in a rather tentative manner; he does not seem to carry the conviction that he did in the *Chorals.* The recording has a muffled tonal characteristic; Classic has done better. There are recordings of individual pieces. Nies-Berger plays the *Grande Pièce symphonique* on CH 1145: a spacious reading, clearly recorded. Biggs on C 4329 has a brilliant-sounding *Prélude, Fugue, et Variation,* smoothly and mechanically played. Demessieux on L 319 plays the *Pastorale* in an ultra-romantic manner (see Collections). Dupré, on L 137, devotes a side to the *Fantaisie,* giving it a noble performance.

Sonata for Piano and Violin in A. Francescatti, Casadesus, C 4178

*(*Debussy: Violin Sonata). Oistrakh, Oborin, Van 6019 (*Prokofiev: Violin Sonata in F minor). Heifetz, Rubinstein, V LCT 1122 (*Strauss: Violin Sonata).*

Of many recordings of the popular Franck *Sonata*, the Francescatti-Casadesus is outstanding for its urbanity, its impeccable workmanship, its air of aristocracy. Fortunate is the violinist who can claim Casadesus for a partner. The recorded sound is not very bright, and there are some noisy surfaces. Technically the Oistrakh version is one of the best-sounding discs to come out of Russia (though there are a few "ghosts"). This is fluent fiddling, and the musical security is typical of Oistrakh's work. Nevertheless, a measure of the style that Francescatti gets into the music is missing here. The Heifetz-Rubinstein is a collector's issue. Obsolete sound; but not obsolete enough to hide a masterful performance. In one or two places Heifetz plays a few notes not written by Franck, including a final flourish. Something that is a curiosity is the Rose-Hambro performance on C 4652 (*Grieg: *Cello Sonata*), with the violin part transposed to the cello. Rose almost makes one forget the bulky quality of the instrument he plays.

*Trio for Piano and Strings in F sharp minor. Bolzano, Vox 8950 (*Chausson: Trio for Piano and Strings in G minor).*

Whatever the attributes of the Trio di Bolzano, the group is miscast in these two works, which need a more sensuous string tone and a more aristocratic type of musical approach. This is the only LP disc of the music at the time of writing, and therefore it does fill a need. Admirers of the scores would do well to keep an eye out for a replacement, however. Clear and lifelike recorded sound.

Trois Pièces pour Orgue; Andantino. Watters, CE 1015.

The three pieces are named *Fantaisie in A*, *Cantabile*, and *Pièce heroïque*. The *Andantino* is a simple, curiously exotic piece, and very charming. If your speaker can handle them, lots of low-frequency notes are present on this disc. Excellent, rather reserved performances by Watters, who does not wear his heart on his sleeve. On L 319 Demessieux contributes a splashily played *Fantaisie* (see Collections). Biggs, on C 4329, exuberantly stomps through the *Pièce heroïque*. Asma, on Ep 3051, has a thick-sounding performance of the same work.

FRESCOBALDI, GIROLAMO (1583-1643)

5 Canzoni per Sonar. See Collections: Harpsichord Quartet (Es 517).
Messa delli Apostoli. Noehren, All 111.

The music is taken from the *Fiori Musicali.* A noble work, it is played in a direct, sensible manner by Noehren. No over-fanciful registrations or dynamics; steady rhythm; considerable feeling. The disc is one of Allegro's better recordings, with smooth surfaces and a resonant sound.

Organ Music. De Donà, Vox 8780.

Included herein are five *Toccatas;* a set of variations; a *Kyrie e Christie;* the *Toccata Cromatica per l'Elevazione;* several short pieces. De Donà plays a thick-sounding organ. He handles it tastefully, though a few theater-organ registrations are present. I have a feeling that the work is not being heard under the most favorable auspices. Fine recorded sound.

FUX, JOHANN (1660-1741)

Keyboard Compositions. Rapf (organ, piano, harpsichord), SPA 27.

Fux is known today primarily through his theoretical works (especially the *Gradus ad Parnassum*). As a composer he had little to say, if these pieces are representative of his music. Rapf has included on this disc two suites, a sonata, a chaconne, and other odds and ends. He plays these museum specimens as museum specimens: steadily, methodically, unimaginatively, and metronomically.

GABRIELI, ANDREA (c. 1510-1586) and GIOVANNI (1557-1612)

Organ Music. De Donà, Vox 8470.

Giovanni was the nephew and pupil of Andrea. Both were composers of the Venetian school. They composed in a modal idiom, and it takes just as much experience to understand this music as it does to understand any of the present-day avant-garde moderns. Toccatas, ricercares, fantasias, and fugues are contained on the disc. De Donà is moderate in his use of registration, and he plays with clarity. He does not impart much fervor to the florid melismatic passages, however, and he is not what one would call a positive or assertive musician. Excellent recorded tone.

GIBBONS, ORLANDO (1583-1625)

2 Fantasias. See Collections: New Music String Quartet (Bar 913).

GLANVILLE-HICKS, PEGGY (1912-)

*Sonata for Piano and Percussion. Bussotti, New York Percussion Group, C 4990 (*Concertino da Camera; Lopatnikoff: Theme, Variations, and Epilogue).*

A clever, piquant-sounding score, with Oriental timbres and rhythms and an investigation of unusual sonorities. Bussotti, who was known to many listeners as Szigeti's accompanist, goes about his work with the necessary rhythmic clarity, and the able members of the New York Percussion Group enter with apparent relish into the exotic world of Glanville-Hicks. Like all the others in Columbia's "Modern American Music" series, this is a bright-sounding and well-defined recording.

GLAZUNOV, ALEXANDER (1865-1936)

*Novelettes (5). Hungarian, CH 1183 (*Tchaikovsky: Quartet in D).*

Only one of these pieces for string quartet has achieved any popularity. For the most part the writing seldom rises much above a salon level. The Hungarian Quartet plays elegantly and the recording is good, though on a rather low level.

Sonata for Piano No. 2 in E minor (Op. 75). See Prokofiev: *Sonata for Piano No. 2 in D minor* (CH 1311).

GLINKA, MIKHAIL (1803-1857)

*Sextet for Piano and Strings. Oborin, Beethoven, Col 104 (*Jota Aragonesa; Variations in F).*

Composed in 1832, this is a bouncing work, strongly Italianate in nature. One would like to hear it under better auspices than this dull-sounding recording. Apparently the LP is a transfer from inferior shellac discs. Also present are the *Jota Aragonesa* for orchestra and the piano *Variations in F*, beautifully played by Oborin. The theme of the variations later became known as "The Last Rose of Summer."

*Trio Pathétique in D minor. Wlach, Oehlberger, Badura-Skoda, W 5019 (*Rimsky-Korsakov: Quintet in B flat). Oistrakh, Knushevitsky, Oborin, CH 1306 (Rimsky-Korsakov: Trio in C minor).*

Glinka scored his work for piano, clarinet, and bassoon, and it is so played on the Westminster disc. The Russian artists play an arrangement for piano, violin, and cello by one Johann Hrimaly. The music is not important, though it breathes the oncoming romanticism (it was composed in 1827). As the Westminster disc presents the music as Glinka conceived it, the choice between the two versions is not hard to make. Westminster also offers a better quality of recorded sound. The Russian performance is ardent, romantic, and technically flawless. Those who do not worry too much about matters of authenticity will have a lot of fun with the Concert Hall disc.

GODOWSKY, LEOPOLD (1870-1938)

Paraphrases on 11 Chopin Etudes. Saperton, CP 1201/2 [2].

It may be that Godowsky had the most perfect mechanism of any pianist who ever lived. Certainly in these paraphrases he composed the most difficult piano music in the repertoire. They are devilishly ingenious too. Godowsky would take a pair of études —say the "Butterfly" and the "Black Key"—and put them together. Some people cry sacrilege. I look on them as transcendental études that typify a philosophy of pianism in which the piano was not held to be a percussive instrument; where, indeed, the piano was a way of life. Godowsky could play these pieces; nobody else could. Saperton, Godowsky's son-in-law, makes a brave attempt. The fact that he gets through them at all is cause for wonder; but one can virtually see the sweat rolling off his head in great drops. He also plays, on these discs, the original Chopin *études*, which are matched to those Godowsky paraphrased, in addition to two of Godowsky's brilliant Strauss paraphrases—*Artist's Life* and *Fledermaus.* The recorded piano tone is clear and colorful.

GOEB, ROGER (1914-)

Quintet for Woodwinds. See Collections: New Art Wind Quintet (CE 2003).

GOUNOD, CHARLES (1818-1893)

Quartet for Strings in A minor. See Donizetti: *Quartet in E flat* (Str 618).

GRANADOS, ENRIQUE (1867-1916)

*Goyescas. Valenzi, Rem 199–116. Magaloff, L 954 (*El Pelele). Echániz, W 5322 (*El Pelele).*

Some remarkably fluent and lovely piano music is contained in the *Goyescas,* and some very difficult figurations too. Magaloff received the best-sounding recording, but I prefer the Valenzi interpretation. She does not fool around with unnecessary ritards, holds, and other "expressive" devices, and her rhythm is better. Unfortunately, the glassy recording is hard to control. I had best results on the NARTB curve with reduced treble. The percussive playing of Echániz lacks charm and color.

Spanish Dances (12). Echániz, W 5181.

Echániz presents percussive performances of salon pieces that have little value. The music is not within light years of the *Goyescas.* In any case, Echániz is not the man for the dances. The close-up recording emphasizes the essentially cold nature of his playing.

GRIEG, EDVARD (1843-1907)

*Ballade in G minor (Op. 24). Rubinstein, V LM 1872 (*Lyric Pieces).*

*Pressler, MGM 3057 (*Piano Sonata in E minor). Andersen, Oc 38 (*Kabalevsky, etc.: Preludes).*

By far Grieg's most extended work for solo piano, the *Ballade* is a series of variations, and the opening theme has some intense, quite unusual (for Grieg) harmonies. The music is worth knowing, especially in Rubinstein's glowing interpretation. His playing nearly always expresses more *joie de vivre* than that of any other pianist I have ever heard, and there is something very healthy, bracing, and essentially uncomplicated about his swinging performance here. Victor's recording is exceedingly faithful to the sound of the piano. So is MGM's, which is clear and has an exceptionally well-defined bass. Pressler gives, on the whole, a fine performance, but he lacks the consistency of Rubinstein. He also has a tendency to drag phrases and, by lingering over them, retard the logical movement of the music. Andersen, on the Oceanic disc, plays the music rather stiffly, missing several opportunities for pianistic subtleties. The reverse of her disc is a mélange of preludes by Kabalevsky, Chopin, Rachmaninoff (mislabeled on the envelope, though not on the label, as G minor; should be G major), and Messiaen. Columbia should reissue as a collector's item on LP the great old Godowsky performance of the *Ballade*. It was the finest thing that master ever did on records.

*Lyric Pieces (selections). Rubinstein, V LM 1872 (*Ballade). Johannesen, Vox 7380. Gieseking, C 4334 (*Beethoven: Sonata No. 12).*

Johannesen plays twenty of the *Lyric Pieces*, devoting his entire disc to them. Rubinstein plays eleven, plus an *Album Leaf*, in addition to the *Ballade in G minor*. Gieseking has only five on his disc. Some excellent music is contained here, not all of it as salonish as *Papillons* or *To Spring* would suggest. Rubinstein's disc is the best choice. The performances move with his typical vigor and singing tone. There is manner to his playing, even in these sketches, and a vaulting musical line. Johannesen has nothing to be ashamed of in his disc. The young American pianist handles himself very well, and he has made an interesting selection among the many *Lyric Pieces* that Grieg composed. In addition, Vox has given him superb recorded sound. Gieseking's playing is very lovely, but one would hesitate to recommend a disc containing only five Grieg pieces when Rubinstein's contains over twice as many and Johannesen's four times as many (especially as Gieseking's performance of Beethoven's *A flat Sonata* is nothing to get excited about).

Slatter (Norwegian Peasant Dances, Op. 72). Foldes, Mer 10136.

In Norwegian, *slat* means "peasant's dance." There are seventeen *slatter* on this disc. They are strange works. Nothing of the salon, no "Anitra's Dance" department. Grieg here almost parallels Bartók's work in Hungarian folk melodies. One notes modal melodies, rhythmic variation, and authentic-sounding nationalism. Perhaps a certain monotony would ensue if the *slatter* were played through all at once, but it is doubtful that the composer expected the set to be played that way. Foldes sounds authoritative enough, and his performance has a pleasing crispness. Fair recorded sound.

*Sonata for Cello and Piano in A minor (Op. 36). Rose, Hambro, C 4652 (*Franck: Sonata in A).*

Time was when this sonata was heard very frequently; now it hangs on the periphery of the concert repertoire. It is a nationalistic bon-bon, and a very tasty one. Old-fashioned, yes; but if we can bow our heads in respect before the turgid adolescence of Brahms's *E minor Sonata,* there is no reason why this cannot be taken into the family. Rose plays brilliantly. His is a virtuoso performance, adding a type of dash to the sonata that helps vitalize it. A cut of several pages is taken in the last movement, section M to Q of the music. No great harm is done, though one fails to see the necessity for the procedure. Admirable recorded sound that does justice to Rose's soaring tone.

*Sonata for Piano in E minor (Op. 7). Pressler, MGM 3057 (*Ballade).*

One doesn't hear this sonata in years of concert-going. A shame; it is a pleasant work, pleasantly played in this recording. The only things not in favor of Pressler's performance are a tendency toward coyness and a remarkably slow tempo for the third movement. As he plays it, the music definitely sags; a more forceful statement was needed. But at no time does Pressler actually misstate the music, and most listeners should find this disc a rather charming experience. Typically clear piano recording from MGM.

Sonatas for Violin and Piano Nos. 1 (Op. 8) and 3 (Op. 45). Fuchs, Sheridan, D 9571.

*Sonata for Violin and Piano No. 3 (Op. 45). Kreisler, Rachmaninoff, V LCT 1128 (*Schubert: Duo in A).*

Victor supplied a priceless memento when it restored the Kreisler-Rachmaninoff collaborations to the active LP catalogue. The Grieg *Sonata* was recorded in the late 1920's, and the transfer to

LP has come out very well (better, indeed, than the Schubert on the reverse). For those who want modern versions, the Fuchs-Sheridan disc is fine. They collaborate in a musical performance, though here and there Fuchs has a tendency to drive a bit too hard. Decca's recording naturally is superior in sound to the Victor reissue, though the disparity is not as wide as one might expect.

GRIFFES, CHARLES (1884-1920)

Roman Sketches; Piano Sonata. Hambro, Wal 100.

Contained in the *Roman Sketches* is Griffes's most popular piece, "The White Peacock." The sketches, strongly influenced by the French impressionists, are quite different from the bleak, dissonant, powerful sonata. Hambro, always a reliable pianist, handles the music with skill, accommodating himself easily to the curves of the *Roman Sketches* and the angles of the sonata. Good piano sound, prominent surface noise.

HAIEFF, ALEXEI (1914-)

Sonata for Two Pianos. See Barber: *Souvenirs* (C 4855).

HANDEL, GEORGE FRIDERIC (1685-1759)

Concerti a Quatre; Cello Sonata. See Collections: Harpsichord Quartet (Es 528).

Sonatas (10) for Flute and Continuo. Wummer, Valenti, Parisot, W WAL 218 [2].

Sonatas (7) for Flute and Harpsichord. Baker, Marlowe, D DX 116 [2].

In Handel's Op. 1 are seven flute sonatas (or, more accurately, three for flute, four for recorder). Both Wummer and Baker play these seven. In addition, Wummer is heard in three flute sonatas that Handel had composed while living in Halle. The Westminster set is preferred for several reasons. Wummer's performance is warmer, the recorded sound is superior to Decca's, and the presence of three extra works is an additional factor. Westminster, too, supplies the scores of the works, and has added a cello to the harpsichord continuo, thus supplying an extra musical dimension. Baker's playing is beautiful but rather empty-sounding. He seems to emphasize tone and breath over scholarship and content. His Handel is unadorned. Frequently he drops the ornamentation entirely, and the result is a skeletonized Handel. But it also must be said that the three musicians in the Westminster set have not exactly gone out of their way to investigate the possibilities of baroque ornamentation. Many musicologists would like a more adventurous approach in both ornamentation and the realization of the figured bass (not that any two musicologists would agree on what constitutes a proper realization). The undisputable point is that in baroque scores like these the figured bass and also the melodic line itself were intended to serve merely as a guide to the performers. How the performers decorated that guide depended upon their taste and musicianship. And therefore performances like those presented by Wummer, Valenti, and Parisot are not a full realization of the composer's intention. But baroque ornamentation is almost a lost art, and Wummer's leisurely playing is as good as we are going to get in this day and age.

Sonatas for Recorder and Continuo in G minor, A minor, C, and F (Op. 1). Mann, Reimann, Elsner, Vox 7910.

The title of Handel's Op. 1 (not his first work, but his first published work) is *Fifteen Solos... with a Thorough Bass.* Of the fifteen, six are for violin, four for recorder, three for flute, two for oboe. The present sonatas are Nos. 2, 4, 7, and 11 of the set. They receive expert performances on this disc. Mann, a fine musician, gets a lot out of what basically is a limited instrument. The continuo of cello and harpsichord provides smooth support, and in the jaunty byplay of the second movement of No. 4 the players achieve a performance of real distinction.

Sonatas (6) for Violin and Figured Bass. Schneider, Kirkpatrick, Miller, C 4787. Campoli, Malcolm, L 652.

These are Nos. 3, 10, 12–15 of the Gesellschaft edition. Two or three are very popular: standard recital-openers. On the Columbia disc a continuo of harpsichord and cello backs up the soloist. Malcolm, on the London, uses a harpsichord. Campoli plays the notes as the Gesellschaft presents them. So does Schneider; but in one case—the adagio of the *G minor Sonata*—he follows the baroque custom of adding his own embellishments, building an elaborate fioritura over the bare harmonic and melodic structure.

In general his version is to be preferred. His playing is strong, his intonation fine, his rhythm powerful. Campoli, much more violinistic, is suaver, and his tone has much more sweetness. In lyric sections, however, he overdoes a vibrato, and his playing does not have the positive virtues of Schneider's.

Sonatas (4) for Two Violins and Figured Bass. W. and M. Schweyda, Behr, U 7046.

Some fine music is present here, but the performances are stiff and lumbering. The violinists saw away with determination, and the heavy atmosphere is made positively humid by a piano instead of a harpsichord continuo. Excellent recorded sound.

Suites (14) for Harpsichord. Pelleg, HdS 4, 5, 6, and 7.

As the notes to these four discs are somewhat vague and, in several cases, incorrect, it might be well to point out that not all of Handel's harpsichord suites are recorded here. Handel composed several that are not printed in standard editions. Pelleg follows the Handel Gesellschaft, which differs from the Peters edition that many pianists use. The first eight *Suites* of Book I are the same in both editions. In Book II, the Gesellschaft follows the early Walsh edition, about 1733. Pelleg plays only the first six, including the *B flat Suite* from which Brahms took the theme for his *"Handel" Variations.* The *Suite No. 5 in E* is the one known as the "Harmonious Blacksmith." Pelleg's performances are highly competent, though never very imaginative. He inclines toward a pedantic approach, missing the point of such sections as the rhapsodic, improvisatory opening of the *Suite No. 2.* He takes virtually every repeat and second ending: one can't grumble about cuts or lack of completeness. His playing is always tasteful, whatever the emotional limitations, and his registrations are well chosen. On HdS 5 he also plays a pair of fugues. Excellent recorded sound, on the whole; but in fortissimo sections the harpsichord has an uncharacteristic clang, not unlike that of heavy chains clanked together in a dungeon. When will recording companies learn not to record the harpsichord (or any other instrument) with a too-close microphone placement?

*Suite No. 5 in E ("Harmonious Blacksmith"). Gieseking, C 4646 (*Bach: Partita No. 6; Scarlatti: 5 Sonatas).*

Somewhat routine playing from Gieseking. He does not seem to be as interested in the music as he used to be. The pianist being Gieseking, however, one hears a beautiful legato and the smoothest of deliveries. Quiet-sounding, mellow recorded quality.

Trio Sonatas (Op. 5, Nos. 1-4). Copenhagen Collegium Musicum, HS 85.

The music is typically Handelian: sturdy, dignified, with long melodic arches. The four competent instrumentalists (three strings and harpsichord) play together in a musicianly manner, presenting performances notable more for a logical assessment of the notes than for any great degree of imagination. As a result, there is a decided museum-piece air about the disc. Excellent recorded sound.

HARRIS, ROY (1898-)

*Sonata for Violin and Piano. Gingold, Harris, C 4842 (*Palmer: Piano Quartet).*

Rhetoric prevails here. The music is free and rhapsodic, with much more extroversion than is generally considered fashionable among American composers at the present time. It receives an admirable performance from Gingold, who is not as well known as a violinist of his attainments should be. The composer's wife is at the piano. Palmer's *Piano Quartet* on the reverse, played by John Kirkpatrick and members of the Walden String Quartet, is quiet, lyric, and logically constructed. Clear recorded sound, admirable performance. This disc is one in Columbia's "Modern American Music" series.

HARRISON, LOU (1917-)

*Suite for Cello and Harp; Suite No. 2 for String Quartet. Barab, Lawrence, New Music String Quartet, C 4491 (*Thomson: Stabat Mater).*

Super-precious music by a young American composer. The piece for string quartet is in a type of neo-classicism; the cello work carries suggestions of Hovhaness in its Near-East-sounding repeated exotic patterns. All of the participants were selected by the composer in this disc made for Columbia's "Modern American Music" series, which vouches for the authenticity of the performances. Beautiful recorded sound.

HAYDN, JOSEPH (1732-1809)

Andante and Variations in F minor. See *Trios for Piano and Strings* (D DX 104).

*Octet in F. Vienna Philharmonic Wind Group, W 5002 (*Boccherini: Symphony in A).*

The scoring here calls for two each of oboes, clarinets, bassoons, and horns. Not particularly interesting Haydn, the work does have the virtue of novelty. It receives a typically mellifluous performance by the Viennese winds. Natural-sounding recording.

Quartets for Strings. All played by the Schneider String Quartet. Op. 1, Nos. 1–6 (and Quartet No. "zero"), HS HSQ A [3]. *Op. 2, Nos, 1–6, HS HSQ B* [3] *(with W. and K. Wilber, hornists, in Nos. 3 and 5). Op. 17, Nos. 1–6, HS HSQ E* [3]. *Op. 20, Nos. 1–6, HS HSQ F* [3]. *Op. 33, Nos. 1–6, HS HSQ G* [3]. *Op. 50, Nos. 1–6, HS HSQ H* [3]. *Op. 76, Nos. 1–6, HS HSQ L* [3]. *Op. 42, 77 (Nos. 1 and 2), and 103, HS HSQ M* [2].

No more ambitious attempt has been made by any string quartet. For the record, the personnel of the Schneider Quartet is Alexander Schneider, Isidore Cohen, Karen Tuttle, and Madeline Foley. As Spenser once said, in a slightly different connection, double were their pains; double be their praise. Judging the series as a whole, it is beautifully recorded and superbly played. Looking at individual recordings, it is apparent that as the series progressed, so did the assurance and unanimity of the players. In some of the sets that were released first, such as Op. 1 and Op. 17, Schneider obviously was the leading spirit to whom the lesser mortals deferred. And Schneider occasionally would seize upon a lyric solo like a frustrated virtuoso, teasing the melodic line with slight holds, ritards, and other devices of "expression." Almost none of those traits is apparent in the later sets. There the playing has beautiful ensemble, spirit, and a most wonderful freedom from pedanticism. And the music is glorious. The only really weak music is Op. 1 and 2, where Haydn was feeling his way. Thereafter there is hardly a quartet lacking in imagination, touches of wit, melodic invention, and sheer workmanship. One cannot overpraise the series, or the enterprise of Haydn Society in sponsoring it. Perhaps not many collectors would want to invest in the entire series at once; the monetary outlay is considerable. Two good sets to begin with are Op. 76 (HSQ L) or Op. 42, 77, and 103 (HSQ M), though Op. 50 (HSQ H), the "Sun" Quartets, also merits strong consideration as an introduction to Haydn's string quartets. Acquaintance with these should lead the music-lover to all the others in the series. Haydn Society has done itself proud with the recordings, which are full in tone but never strident.

Quartets for Strings (individual).

All of the Schneider discs are available separately. They can match the offerings of any other organization in the Haydn repertoire, and have the added virtue of consistency in coupling. One really need look no further. Several supplementary versions should be mentioned, however. The Griller has the *Quartet in F* (Op. 3, No. 5) on 10" L 656: an intimate, polite, somewhat affected reading. On C 4216 the Budapest is heard in the "Lark" (Op. 64, No. 5) and "Sunrise" (Op. 76, No. 4), both in typically fluent performances. The New Italian (better known as the Quartetto Italiano) presents a lyric reading of the *Quartet in E flat* (Op. 64, No. 6) on L 320 (*Boccherini: *Quartet in D*). Good recorded sound, excessive background noise. On a series of Westminster discs the Vienna Konzerthaus presents Op. 64 and several of the Op. 76 quartets. The faithful but plodding playing here in evidence does not challenge the Schneider performances of the same works. On HMV 1039 the Amadeus does the "Emperor" (Op. 76, No. 3) (*Mozart: *Quartet in G*, K. 387). Vigor is present here, rather than any great refinement. An excellent disc is EMS 301, where the Heifetz Quartet (Benar, not Jascha) plays Haydn's last two quartets, Op. 77, Nos. 1 and 2. (Op. 103, an unfinished work, cannot be considered a complete quartet.) Avoid the dry-sounding Haydn recordings of the Barchet on Ren 33 and Per 504. The only discs that can challenge the Schneider Quartet's supremacy are played by the Budapest Quartet, which has recorded all of Op. 76 on C SL 203 (3 discs; also available separately). Direct comparison reveals no great superiority, but it must be admitted that the Budapest's playing is a little fuller in tone and stronger in concept. The Schneider, on the other hand, is frequently more gracious and intimate-sounding. Both groups offer magnificent Haydn-playing; you can live happily with either. One extra-musical point in favor of the Schneider version is the excellent annotations (far superior to Columbia's).

Seven Last Words of Christ (Op. 51). Schneider, HS 39.

In most editions of Haydn, this work is listed as *Quartets Nos. 50–56.* It consists of seven slow movements of somewhat programmatic nature, each movement prefaced by a line from the New Testament. The Schneider Quartet is the only recording organization to get the music on one disc. There are two-disc (really three-side-plus-fillers) versions by Guilet (CH 1084) and Amadeus (W 5064/5), but neither is worth, in dollars or anything else, twice as much as the Haydn Society disc.

*Sonata for Flute and Piano in G. Baker, Arnold, Ox 106 (*Mozart: Clarinet Trio).*

A curiosity, this is an arrangement by Eberhardt Mueller of the *String Quartet in G* (Op. 77, No. 1). It was published while Haydn was alive. The unprepared listener who knows the marvelous quartet will get the shock of his life. Bright recorded sound, supple performance, singing tone from the flutist.

Sonatas for Harpsichord, Nos. 1–10. Marlowe, HS 3037 [2].

The 1–10 designation will not mean much to most music-lovers. Every edition has its own numbering. Marlowe's is the Breitkopf and Härtel, with the sequence as established by Karl Pasler. (In all the following piano sonatas, Haydn Society uses the B&H numberings.) Haydn composed these ten works "*per il clavicembalo*" (harpsichord). Not much of musical interest is present, except that which normally attaches to the name of the composer. The writing is still derivative, without the richness and invention that Haydn was to bring. Marlowe plays the sonatas simply, not trying to exaggerate the slender nature of the material. Excellent recorded sound.

Sonatas for Piano Nos. 20 in C minor and 50 in C, 10" HS 3013. Nos. 44 in G minor and 45 in E flat, 10" HS 3033. Nos. 46 in A flat and 49 in E flat, HS 3034. Nos. 48 in C and 51 in D, HS 3032. All played by Virginia Pleasants.

For music that is seldom played in the concert hall, these sonatas have amazing moments of inspiration. Some amusing anticipations are also present. The opening of No. 20, for instance, matches, note for note, the opening of the Brahms song *Immer leiser wird mein Schlummer.* The more one hears Haydn, the more one admires and wonders. Pleasants, in this series, plays tastefully—and that is about all that can be said. Her dynamic palette is limited, and she does not turn a phrase with any great degree of imagination. She is at her best in the fast movements, where she tinkles away prettily. As a whole these recordings do not match the tonal clarity of the majority of Haydn Society discs. Some excess surface noise crops up (especially in the last movement of No. 49), and here and there a bit of shatter.

Sonatas for Piano Nos. 23 in F and 32 in B minor, 10" HS 3035. Nos. 24 in D and 30 in A, 10" HS 3036. All played by Robert Wallenborn.

Wallenborn plays with a more assertive quality than Pleasants does in her series. He shapes a phrase with more conscious artistry, and his work has stronger rhythm. Again one wishes for a greater variety of touch and dynamics and a more poetic view toward the music. The important thing, though, is the fact that these fine compositions are available in intelligent performances.

*Sonatas for Piano Nos. 43 in A flat and 51 in D. Rosen, EMS 3 (*Partita for Orchestra).*

These performances encompass the notes, but add little to them. Rosen has robust ideas about the music which do not fit its slender frame. Good piano tone, noisy surfaces.

Trios ("London") for Flutes and Cello. Kaplan, Schaefer, Mayes, 10" All 4044.

Engaging pieces for two flutes and cello. Four short works are contained on the disc. They flow nicely along, and the fine musicians here go smoothly through the scores. A charming, out-of-the-way item. The recording is a little lacking in luster, and there is some distortion on the upper end.

Trios for Piano and Strings Nos. 1 in G, 28 in G, and 30 in D, W 5202. Nos. 4 in E, 17 in E flat, 27 in F, and 29 in F, W 5293. All played by Fournier, Janigro, and Badura-Skoda.

Lovely music presented in a relaxed manner. The performances are lyric, with just the proper amount of give and take. No. 1 in G, by the way, ends with the famous "Gypsy Rondo." Both discs are up to Westminster's tonal best, which is very good indeed. Some crackling surfaces mar W 5293.

Trios for Piano and Strings Nos. 3 in C, 2 in F sharp minor, and 5 in E flat. Goldberg, Pini, Kraus, D DX 104 [2] *(*Andante and Variations in F minor).*

Considering that this LP reissue was recorded in shellac days, with a consequently limited tonal spectrum, it emerges surprisingly rich and well defined in sound. In their day they were famous recordings, and their day has not yet passed. The playing is sparked by the precise work of Kraus, who displays none of the eccentricities she seems to have developed recently. On the fourth side Kraus plays the solo *F minor Andante and Variations* in a sensitive manner. Her approach is decidedly romantic but not overdone; and, in any case, this is one of Haydn's more romantic pieces.

*Trios for Strings in G, B flat, and D (Op. 53, Nos. 1-3). Pougnet, Riddle, Pini, W 5296 (*Wilton: 3 Trios).*

Intelligent, perfectly integrated playing. The music is treated with the respect and understanding it deserves. Well-balanced recorded sound, faithful string tone. Chamber-music collectors should not let this disc go uninvestigated.

HILL, EDWARD BURLINGAME (1872-)

*Sextet for Wind Instruments and Piano (Op. 39). Kallir, N.Y. Woodwind Quintet, C 4846 (*Berger: Woodwind Quintet; Duo).*

Hill cuts a rather witty caper in this French-derived score. Fauré lurks in the background, arm in arm with Poulenc; and occasionally a jazzy theme blares through. It's not music to be taken seriously, but is a lot of fun. The performers enter into the spirit of the occasion and appear to have a good time with the music. As in the others of Columbia's "Modern American Music" series, this is a clear recording.

HINDEMITH, PAUL (1895-)

*Kleine Kammermusik (Op. 24, No. 2). Fine Arts, Cap 8258 (*Poulenc: Sextet).*

When Columbia brought out this work in 1939 it caused great excitement among some collectors. The acerbic little piece for wind quintet has remained a favorite ever since. It is one of Hindemith's best: wry, bitter, distorted; a real George Grosz in tone. The Fine Arts Players, a group from Hollywood, give it a performance that could not be improved upon. (The flutist, Haakon Bergh, participated in the 1939 set.) Exceptionally sonorous and faithful recorded sound help make the disc a model of its kind. It easily supersedes an earlier recording by the Fairfield Wind Ensemble on Str 606.

Quartet for Strings No. 1 (Op. 10). Stuyvesant, 10" Ph 100.

Composed in 1919, this is a very early work, with suggestions of Reger and other late romantics, a touch of avant-gardism, plenty of force and character, and something very appealing in the slow movement. The Stuyvesant gives the work a rhythmic performance full of vitality. It is worth having in any collection of contemporary chamber music, though the recording sounds rather dull and dated, without too much definition.

*Quartet for Strings No. 3 (Op. 22). Hollywood, Cap 8151 (*Prokofiev: Quartet No. 2). Fine Arts, Mer 10105 (*Ravel: Quartet).*

A positively vicious second movement is one of the startling features of this moody, dissonant score. Like it or not, it is an impressive piece of work, and the Hollywood group plays it triumphantly. Hardly any other organization before the public has a comparable insight into the modern repertoire. Not only does the Hollywood interpret the music with imagination, but it also has perfectly centered pitch, flawless ensemble, and superb tone. Capitol has supplied exceptionally realistic sound. I would call this one of the great discs of the modern repertoire. The Fine Arts Quartet does an accomplished job, but does not begin to suggest the electricity present in the competitive disc.

Quartet for Strings No. 4. Guilet, 10" CH 1086.

The academician in Hindemith comes out in this highly polyphonic quartet. As with much Hindemith, you may not like the unlovely writing, but you have to listen to it with respect. The high spot is the third movement—a tiny, wispy "*kleiner Marsch.*" There is room for a good recording of this work. The Guilet here is handicapped by shrill recording, generally harsh sound, and a bad tape-splice in the first movement.

*Sonata for Cello and Piano (Op. 11, No. 1). Starker, Pommers, Per 715 (*Bartók: Rhapsody No. 1; Weiner: Lakodalmas).*

Hindemith's typical austerity, power, and immense compositional knowledge are present in this work. Starker plays it with strength and control. His technique is always dependable, his bow always responsive, his intonation always secure. The music emerges under the best of auspices. The recorded sound is full, though the piano tone has an unpleasant edge that I could not tune out. Unfortunate, for the piano part is quite important. Starker's tone, however, comes through in all its richness.

Sonata for Cello and Piano (Op. 11, No. 3). See Strauss: *Sonata for Cello and Piano* (SPA 8).

*Sonata for Clarinet and Piano (1939). Forrest, Tupas, Ly 15 (*Piano Sonata No. 3). Kell, Rosen, D 9570 (*Debussy: Rhapsody No. 1; Stravinsky: 3 Pieces for Clarinet).*

Kell is the smoother of the two clarinetists, and his phrasing is more delicate. Yet there is much to be said for Forrest's more direct, vibrato-less treatment of angular music like this. My preference is toward Forrest. He enjoys better recording, too, especially in his piano accompaniment.

Sonata for Flute and Piano; Sonata for Two Flutes; Sonata for Bassoon and Piano. Baker, Bennett, Sharrow, Arnold, Ox 103.

It is hard to regard this music as anything but a mechanical product of Hindemith's industry. The performances, by some of America's most polished instrumentalists, are really distinguished; and the recorded sound is as lifelike as one can encounter anywhere.

Sonatas (3) for Organ. Noehren, Ly 53.

Noehren handles these sonatas with intelligence, and he receives a very smooth recording. This is not one of those organ discs in which the aim is to blast you out of the room or disrupt your internal economy with 15-cycle low notes. Rather it is placed in a modest framework; but within that framework, everything is well proportioned and listenable.

Sonata for Piano No. 2. See Collections: Skolovsky (C 4871).

*Sonata for Piano No. 3. Tupas, Ly 15 (*Clarinet Sonata).*

An able technician with an objective philosophy of piano-playing, Tupas gives Hindemith's intellectual exercise a thorough workout. Good recording, high surfaces.

*Sonata for Piano Four Hands (1938). Gold and Fizdale, C 4853 (*Rieti: Suite Champêtre; Stravinsky: Concerto for Two Solo Pianos).*

While they do not erase memories of the grand old version of this sonata which Sanromá and Hindemith himself made for Victor in the late 1930's, Gold and Fizdale provide an expert performance that has been recorded with xylophone clarity. The disc, though available separately, is in the three-disc "Music for Two Pianos —1900–1952" set. For a complete listing of contents, see under Collections: Gold and Fizdale.

Sonata for Trumpet and Piano (1939); for Bassoon and Piano (1938); for Trombone and Piano (1941). Wilson, Garfield, Smith, Lettvin, EMS 4.

Presumably trumpet-, bassoon-, and trombone-players will find this disc of great interest. Not too many others will. Excellent performances; completely undistorted recording.

*Sonata for Violin and Piano (1940). Stern, Zakin, 10" C 2050 (*Falla-Kochanski: Suite populaire espagnole).*

Stern is ideal for music like this. He is right on top of the notes, playing with muscularity. His avoidance of sentimentality, his immense technical freedom, his purely produced tone—all these make the sonata shine in its best light. A few shrill highs can be taken care of by a slight reduction in the treble setting.

*Sonata for Violin and Piano in D (Op. 11, No. 2). Kaufman, Balsam, Cap 8063 (*Poulenc: Violin Sonata).*

A more inhibited approach would have benefited this sonata. Kaufman overdoes the virtuoso elements, and his vibrato is a bit disproportionate. Strong playing, nevertheless. The disc is an early LP, with the thin, unresonant sound characteristic of many records at that time. Fortunately, there is little actual distortion. A subsequent recording by Lack and Hambro on All 33 is also thin-sounding, and Lack's approach is too small-scaled.

Trios for Strings Nos. 1 and 2. Pougnet, Riddle, Pini, W 5299.

A spread of nine years, from 1924 to 1933, separates this pair of trios. Both contain some of the busiest string-writing to be heard on records. Pougnet, Riddle, and Pini, normally associated with the classic works of the repertoire, show their versatility by providing expert performances. First-class recorded sound.

HUMMEL, JOHANN NEPOMUK (1788-1837)

Septet in D minor. Holletschek, etc., W 5018.

Here is a minor masterpiece that has dropped from the active repertoire. Hummel, one of the best pianists of his day, was a widely respected composer, and this work will help explain how he got his reputation. Scored for piano, viola, cello, bass, flute, oboe, and horn, it has many ingenious ideas and is an attractive anticipation of the romantic movement. This disc has delighted many listeners since it was issued in 1950, and it should achieve a wider circulation than has been its lot. The performance is excellent. A few harsh sections are in evidence, but the recorded sound on the whole is serviceable.

IBERT, JACQUES (1890-)

Histoires. See Debussy: *La Boîte à joujoux* (MGM 3042).

*Trois Pièces brèves. Copenhagen Wind Quintet, L 734 (*Bozza: Variations; Nielsen: Wind Quintet).*

When a French composer writes *à la mode*, the results can be charming. Ibert has here composed one of the prettiest pieces of its kind, with an especially tuneful third movement. The Copenhagen wind-players present the music gracefully. Though there is not much color in the low-level recording, it is satisfactory enough. A better-recorded version by the Fairfield Wind Ensemble, on Str 606 (*Milhaud: *Cheminée du Roi René;* Hindemith: *Kleine Kammermusik),* does not have the nuanced quality that the London disc offers.

Trio for Viola, Cello, and Harp. See Bax: *Harp Quintet* (Ph 102).

IMBRIE, ANDREW (1921-)

*Quartet for Strings in B flat. Juilliard, C 4844 (*Mennin: Quartet No. 2).*

These two works have much in common. Both strive to avoid purely abstract design, and both works possess intellectual strength, logical organization, idiomatic workmanship. Neither has any stress on melodic personality. The Juilliard String Quartet, specialists in contemporary music, clarifies some very difficult writing. Superb recorded sound.

INDY, VINCENT D' (1851-1931)

Suite in Olden Style. See Saint-Saëns: *Septet* (MGM 3096).

IVES, CHARLES (1874-1954)

Quartet for Strings No. 2. Walden, Per 501.

Now discontinued, this disc is worth keeping in mind in case you happen to run across it. Ives has described the score as a "string quartet for four men—who converse, discuss, argue (politics), fight, shake hands, shut-up, then walk up the mountain side to view the firmament." The music is not as naïve as this program would indicate. In one respect it is sophisticated; in another it is an example of musical primitivism *à la* a ferocious Grandma Moses. People may wake up to the fact that Ives was perhaps the major musical figure that America has produced, and this disc will be one of the exhibits.

Sonata for Piano No. 1. Masselos, C 4490.

1902 is the date. The sonata is the damnedest mixture of everything under the sun. Yet it is surprising how so willful a collection of dissonance and eccentricity can hold the attention—at least, my attention. Like the *"Concord" Sonata,* it is immensely difficult. Honors to Masselos for a strong, amazingly well defined performance. Good recording.

Sonata for Piano No. 2 ("Concord"). J. Kirkpatrick, C 4250.

The remarks about the previous sonata again apply, only more so. Most likely the "Concord" never will be widely heard because it is (a) too difficult for most pianists to learn and (b) too strange and uncompromising for most audiences to assimilate. This disc is an LP transfer of the 1948 shellac set. The recording not only stands up well, but is much better in its LP form. Kirkpatrick's performance has already been widely praised. Suffice it to say that it is a miracle that he gets through the music in as good shape as he does.

Sonatas for Violin Nos. 1 and 3. Field, Mittman, Ly 17.

Both sonatas are in Ives's typically nationalistic vein. The writing is full of difficulties, and it cannot be said that Field makes light of them. The struggle is always obvious. No other version of the music is available, however; and Field manages at least to get the point of the music across. Variable recorded sound. *Sonata No. 1* is thin, with some tonal shatter. No. 3 is fuller, with more detail to the piano part and more color to the violin.

*Sonata for Violin No. 2. Magaziner, Glazer, Pol 1001 (*Largo for Trio; Orchestral Pieces). Travers, Herz, 10" C 2169 (*Sessions: Duo).*

The Polymusic disc is much the better buy and is also a good introduction to Ives's music. A miscellany of pieces is present, among them two chamber works—the *Sonata* and the *Trio for Violin, Clarinet, and Piano* (in which Weber joins Magaziner and Glazer). Good performances. One has to take them on trust, for the music is not available, but there is no cause to question the energetic work of the participants. The recording features a rather clangorous piano sound, but it could be worse.

JANÁČEK, LEOŠ (1854-1928)

Concertino for 2 Violins, Clarinet, Horn, Bassoon, and Piano. See *Violin Sonata* (W 5333).

Piano Pieces. Firkusny, C 4740.

Of the three pieces played here, "In the Threshing House" and "On an Overgrown Path" resemble Czech *Woodland Sketches.*

The piece named "Oct. 1, 1905" commemorates the death of a workman in a political demonstration on that date. Firkusny, one of the more gifted of today's pianists, plays with a singing line and an appropriate simplicity in the naturalistic studies. He changes his approach for the grimmer "Oct. 1, 1905," achieving an intense, introspective quality. Faithful piano sound, some prominent surfaces.

Quartet for Strings No. 2. See Dvořák: *Quartet for Piano and Strings in E flat* (Str 619).

*Sextet for Winds ("Youth"). Prague Wind Quintet, Mer 15009 (*Bartoš: Bourgeois Gentilhomme).*

Nothing in the envelope notes explains the "Youth" part of the title. The score is nationalistic and, like most of Janáček, expertly written. Bartoš's suite occupies about one third of the disc. It is a tongue-in-cheek take-off on old dance forms—Intrada, Bourrée, etc.—composed in a purposely stilted and archaic manner. The performances of both works sound superb—flexible in ensemble, rich in tone, strongly rhythmic. Both are dated as recordings: most likely they were transferred to LP from shellac.

*Sonata for Violin and Piano. Druian, Simms, Mer 70001 (*Enesco: Violin Sonata No. 3). Barylli, Holletschek, W 5333 (*Concertino for 2 Violins, Clarinet, Horn, Bassoon, and Piano; Dumka for Violin and Piano).*

The *Violin Sonata,* and the *Concertino* on the Westminster disc, are fluent and melodious works strongly impregnated with Hungarian nationalism. Of the two versions I prefer the Mercury. Druian has better tone and a more lyric view toward the music. On direct comparison, Barylli's tone is harsh and wiry where Druian's is silken. Barylli does have more rhythmic strength and a more assertive attitude toward the music. Nevertheless, the smoother Druian should be more rewarding in the long run. The *Concertino,* headed by Barylli, is played by a group of Viennese musicians in what appears to be a thoroughly adequate performance. Also on the Westminster disc is a short *Dumka* by Janáček, for violin and piano. Both recordings are good. The Westminster, on a somewhat higher level, has a tubbier bass than the Mercury disc.

KABALEVSKY, DMITRI (1904-)

Quartet for Strings No. 2 in G minor (Op. 44). Naumann, U 7083.

Though this is a thoroughly professional piece of writing, it manages to say next to nothing. At least it is one of the few current Soviet works that do not quote Shostakovich or Prokofiev all the way through. Kabalevsky only does so part of the time. The performance sounds competent. Good string tone and ensemble, well recorded. The Naumann Quartet knows its business.

Sonata for Piano No. 2 (Op. 45); Sonatina No. 1 (Op. 13); 3 Preludes (Op. 38, Nos. 13, 8, 6). Haien, WCFM 18.

Papa Prokofiev cast his large shadow over these pieces, which are extraordinarily derivative. The performance is extremely competent. Haien obviously is a well-disciplined, musicianly pianist, missing only a steel-like quality that would make for a hair-raising climax. That apparently is not her style. What we do get is hearty, non-percussive playing of fine tonal virtue, good rhythm, and positive ideas. The recorded sound does not have much life, lacking resonance and brilliance. Rather high surfaces, too.

*Sonata for Piano No. 3 (Op. 46). Horowitz, V LM 1016 (*Prokofiev: Sonata No. 7).*

For several seasons this work was popular; now it seems to have slipped from the repertoire. Horowitz, who introduced the sonata to America, plays it with a bronze tone and orchestral sonority. The music is perhaps not very interesting, but Horowitz's performance definitely is. A transfer from shellac, the LP is not very bright, but perfectly serviceable.

KHACHATURIAN, ARAM (1903-)

*Trio for Clarinet, Violin, and Piano. Bellison, B. and V. Urban, CE 1002 (*Ravel: Violin Sonata).*

Exotic, ethnic music; busy patterns; much activity that never strikes fire. On the whole a dull work. Vigorous performance, good recording, noisy surfaces.

KIRCHNER, LEON (1919-)

Quartet for Strings No. 1. See Fine: *Quartet* (C 4843).

KODÂLY, ZOLTÂN (1882-)

*Piano Pieces (Op. 11). Kabos, Bar 917 (*Bartók: For Children; Sonatina; 3 Rondos).*

It is hard to work up much enthusiasm for this collection of watery, Debussy-like impressionism. The performances sound capable and the recorded sound is realistic.

Quartet for Strings No. 1 (Op. 2). Roth, Mer 70004.

Unlike the piano pieces above, this score represents a decided personality, and it is one of the most attractive works of the composer I have run across. The writing has considerable strength, expressed in a post-romantic melodic speech that suggests Reger, among others. It is fluent, beautifully composed, and thematically interesting. The Roth Quartet plays the music with a full tone that never becomes forced. When this organization is in good form, as it is here, it is one of the most accomplished chamber groups before the public. Excellent recorded sound.

*Quartet for Strings No. 2 (Op. 10). Walden, Ly 22 (*Szymanowski: Quartet). Vegh, L 865 (*Smetana: Quartet in E minor).*

On the whole a cosmpolitan work, though the last sections suddenly betray the composer's Hungarian nationality. The Walden, a superior ensemble, presents the music with the rhythmic impulse it needs. This is really alert playing, well recorded. The Vegh Quartet has a little more body and rather less brilliance than the Walden group. Here the couplings play a strong part in determining a choice. There are about six versions of the Smetana quartet (some of them in preferable interpretations), but there is only one of the interesting Szymanowski.

*Serenade in F (Op. 12). Classic Trio, CE 1033 (*Dvořák: Terzetto).*

As with the Dvořák on the reverse, this work is scored for the unusual combination of two violins and cello. The slow movement is allied to the type of "night music" that Bartók excelled in—full of tremolos, crepuscular flutterings in the strings, mottoes instead of melodies, broken-up rhythms. On the whole a well-written little work, definitely worth owning (and the Dvořák on the reverse is a little gem). Performance and recording are satisfactory.

*Sonata for Unaccompanied Cello (Op. 8). Kurtz, C 4867 (*Prokofiev: Cello Sonata). Starker, Per 510.*

This long work demands as much stamina from the listener as from the cellist. Starker's is the better performance. His bow arm never tires, his intonation remains a model of purity, his tone always soars. But Kurtz is not exactly an amateur. He too plays well. He has a superior quality of recorded sound to back him up, and in addition can offer an extra work. If it's cello-playing alone in which you are interested, get the Period disc. For most people, however, the Columbia will be the better buy.

KOHS, ELLIS (1916-)

Chamber Concerto for Viola and String Nonet. See Copland: *Sextet* (C 4492).

KREISLER, FRITZ (1875-)

Quartet for Strings in A minor. See Paganini: *Quartet in E* (Ph 107).

KŘENEK, ERNST (1900-)

Sonata for Piano No. 3; Piano Pieces. Křenek, SPA 4.

The composer himself is soloist in the sonata and the two sets of piano works (1925 and 1946). Good quality of recording; the interpretations presumably are definitive.

KREUTZER, CONRADIN (1780-1849)

Septet in E flat (Op. 62). Vienna Octet Members, L 420.

The scoring is for strings, horn, and bassoon. Kreutzer was a popular opera-composer of the early nineteenth century. This six-movement work, a hangover from the divertimento days, has some Weber in it, but largely is dependent on the Mozart-Haydn school. No surprises are present. The performance is the kind you can expect when you throw a group of Vienna Philharmonic men together—thorough, serious, excellent in tone and ensemble.

KUHLAU, FRIEDRICH (1786-1832)

4 Sonatinas for Piano (Op. 20, No. 3; Op. 55, Nos. 1-3). See Clementi: *4 Sonatinas* (Edu 3003).

LALO, ÉDOUARD (1823-1892)

Quartet for Strings in E flat (Op. 45). See Donizetti: *Quartet in E flat* (Str 618).

LECLAIR, JEAN MARIE (1697-1764)

*Sonata for Violin and Piano in D (Op. 9, No. 3). Oistrakh, Yampolsky, Van 6024. (*Beethoven: "Kreutzer" Sonata; Ysaye: Sonata for Unaccompanied Violin in E).*

The Leclair and Ysaye works are fillers in the "Kreutzer" disc. Oistrakh handles the Leclair with a big, romantic style. It's all very impressive, but the results *are* a little outsized. Ysaye was responsible for some of the most successful unaccompanied violin-writing in the literature. This fine work is worth knowing, and it is brilliantly played by the Russian violinist. Good recorded sound.

LECUONA, ERNESTO (1896-)

Andalucia; Danzas Afro-Cubanas; Danzas Cubanas. Echaniz, W 5343.

The suite of six pieces named *Andalucia* contains the notorious "*Malagueña.*" No. 2 of this set also is very popular. All of these pieces are pleasant works in the Albéniz-Granados salon tradition. The two sets of *Danzas* are slick and commercial. Expert performances by Echaniz, and topnotch recorded sound from Westminster.

LISZT, FRANZ (1811-1886)

Années de pèlerinage:
Italie (complete). Balogh, Ly 14.
*Excerpts from Italie and Suisse. Kempff, L 315 (*2 Legends).*
*3 Sonetti del Petrarca, from Italie. Kempff, L 515 (*Schumann: Papillons; Arabesque).*
*Dante Sonata, from Italie. Katin, L 934 (*Polonaise in E; 6 Consolations).*

Liszt composed three books of *Années*. Book I is *Suisse*, consisting of nine pieces. Book II, *Italie*, has seven pieces, including the three *Sonetti del Petrarca* and the *Dante Sonata*. Book III, a supplement to *Italie*, contains the *Venezia e Napoli* (there is no LP recording of Book III). Balogh's is the only complete version of Book I. He plays with neatness, but is scarcely the pianist for this kind of extroverted material. Kempff has much more breadth. Sometimes he is careless about details (as in *Au bord d'une source*, some of which is sloppy), but he rises magnificently to the big moments. The *Legends* on L 315 (also available separately on 10" L 9087) are two such moments. For a pianist who has made his reputation in the German classical school, Kempff has an amazing affinity with the grand manner of Liszt-playing. These two London discs sound somewhat dated. I had best results with them on the AES curve. Katin's recording has excellent sound. He plays capably and without much imagination or dash. A careful pianist, Katin never is willing to take a chance; and a careful pianist will never make a Liszt-player. In, the *Polonaise in E* he misses the sweep entirely. The six *Consolations* are more in his style: quiet, non-virtuosic. Frugoni, on Vox 8800, has recorded the *Dante*. His flurried playing has little to recommend. Katin's will remain the best *Dante* until a more colorful pianist attempts it.

*Ballades. Farnadi, W 5321 (*2 Legends; 3 Liebestraume).*

Once very popular among the heaven-storming virtuosos, these two *Ballades* are now slipping from the repertoire. Given a pianist in the heroic tradition, they are very exciting pieces. Farnadi is not that pianist. She plays them heavily, and I find her phrasing of the Allegretto sections of the *B minor Ballade* (No. 2) far too coy for my taste. She actually changes the note values. Wild's performance of the B minor, on Str 607 (see next entry), is more authoritative. Farnadi is more comfortable in the three *Liebesträume*, though I cannot say that her ideas about the popular No. 3 in A flat are very subtle. Nor do I think that she has the technique necessary to make a convincing attempt at the two *Legends*. Even though she stomps up and down the keyboard most imposingly, her fingerwork in many places is rough. The *Legends* have been done better by Kempff; see *Années de pèlerinage* (L 315). Westminster's recording is brilliant and somewhat too close-up. The labels are confusing. On side 1 of the Farnadi disc, the *Legends* occupy the first two bands, the *Liebesträume* the other three.

Ballade in B minor; Gnomenreigen; Hungarian Rhapsody No. 2; Polonaise in E; Berceuse; Étude in D flat. Wild, Str 607.

At its best, this disc is an example of brilliant piano-playing. Unfortunately, Wild does not sustain the brilliance throughout. Sections of extraordinary fluency alternate with mere note-making. Perhaps Wild's biggest handicap is his inability to build a convincing climax. Either he starts too soon, leaving nothing in reserve, or he overstresses the whole way. But for the moments of dazzling playing the disc is worth having; and certainly Wild's performance of the *Polonaise in E* carries more exuberance and technical authority than Katin's on L 934. Good recording, just a shade thick in the bass, but perfectly satisfactory. Undue surface noise.

La Campanella. See under *Don Juan Fantasy* (Rem 199-35); *Études after Paganini* (CH 1149); also under Collections: "Great Masters of the Keyboard," Vol. I (C 4292). See also Paganini: *La Streghe* (L 1005).

*Christmas Tree. Brendel, SPA 26. Kabos, Bar 910 (*Variations on "Weinen, Klagen").*

Toward the end of his life Liszt composed a set of simple (relatively) non-virtuosic pieces which carried the seeds of Debussy's impressionism. This is a side of Liszt which not many people know. Brendel plays the entire set of twelve, but neither his performance nor the recording does justice to the music. More imagination was needed on the one hand, more resonance on the other. Kabos plays only seven. She has the benefit of immeasurably superior recorded sound, and her performance has a more idiomatic quality. Despite the omission of five pieces, her disc is the better choice.

*Consolations (6). Katin, L 934 (*Dante Sonata; Polonaise in E). Farnadi, W 5339 (*Rhapsodie Espagnole; Rhapsodies 16-19).*

As between Katin and Farnadi, there is little to choose. Both offer lyric performances, both are fairly objective in their approach, and both manage to indicate a singing line. Farnadi's recording is more close-up; Katin's is more mellow. My preference would be the Katin. A recording by Manley on NR 501 is not recommended. Cherkassky plays the third, and most popular, *Consolation* as a filler in V LBC 1041 *(*E flat Concerto; Don Juan Variations).*

Dante Sonata (Fantasia quasi sonata après un lecture de Dante). See *Années de pèlerinage* (Ly 14; L 934).

*Don Juan Fantasy. Barere, Rem 199-35 (*La Leggierezza; Valse oubliée; Sonetto 104 del Petrarca; La Campanella). Cherkassky, V LBC 1041 (*Consolation No. 3; Concerto in E flat).*

One of the fabulous piano pieces in the repertoire, the *Don Juan Fantasy* is an obstacle course hedged with booby traps and secret weapons. In a way it is a stunt, though when a great pianist plays the work, one gets up on a chair and yells. Barere is such a pianist. Against the daring and *diablerie* of his conception, Cherkassky is as a bright-cheeked boy bringing an apple to teacher. What matter if Barere, toward the end, lets things get out of hand? His is a thrilling conception, coupled with staggering pianistics. The shorter pieces on the disc also exhibit Barere's unique authority in Liszt. No more exciting *Sonetto 104* has been recorded; and even when Barere runs away with himself in *La Campanella* the results pack power. Barere was one of the great technicians of all time, and, when he wanted to be, a considerable artist. To all of which this disc will attest. Remington's recording is barely adequate, not nearly a match for the Victor in depth and color.

*Études (6) after Paganini. Goldsand, CH 1149 (*Rachmaninoff: Variations on a Theme by Chopin).*

Liszt composed these colossal studies to *épater le bourgeois* (and his fellow pianists, especially one Sigismond Thalberg). He prepared several versions of most of the studies, as the originals were so difficult that nobody could play them. Even the alternate versions are among the splashiest virtuoso pieces in the repertoire. Goldsand plays the entire set, avoiding the super-difficult first drafts. Some of the variations in the *Étude No. 6* (which uses the famous twenty-fourth *Caprice* of Paganini) are transposed from their proper order, but all are present. Goldsand has never been heard to better advantage on records. His performances have glitter and technical solidity. If, here and there, he refuses to look the notes square in the eye, who can blame him? His recording is clangorous in sound, but no shatter is present, and basically the disc is faithful to piano tone. Uninsky plays three of the Paganini studies on Ep 3066 (**Rhapsodie Espagnole;* Mussorgsky: *Pictures at an Exhibition*). His choices are the E major (*La Chasse*), the B major (*La Campanella*), and the E flat. I am not happy with the tinny quality of the recorded sound, though it does have the virtue of clarity. Uninsky plays the music with control and a great degree of virtuosity.

*Fantasia and Fugue on "Ad Nos ad Salutarem Undam." Demessieux, L 697 (*Widor: Variations from Symphonie Gothique).*

Seldom heard, this is a long organ work based on a chorale from the first act of Meyerbeer's *Le Prophète.* The theme is Meyerbeer's own. Liszt's treatment is tricky to the extreme; imagine one of the operatic paraphrases transplanted to the organ. Demessieux gives a vigorous performance. She is a technician of considerable ability, though sometimes one has doubts about her musical sensitivity. She plays a heavy-sounding romantic organ, which is as it should be (in music like this). The recording, rather blurred and thunderous in the climaxes, has on the whole a good deal of definition in some very complicated passagework. Widor's *Variations* fills out the last side. Like the Liszt, it is a large-scale romantic work; unlike the Liszt, it is routine music-making.

*Fantasy and Fugue on "BACH"; Gloria and Credo from Organ Mass. Biggs, C 4820 (*Reubke: Sonata in C minor).*

The *Fantasy and Fugue* is rated very high by some Liszt scholars. It is hard to see why—on the basis of this recording, at any rate. Liszt's *Organ Mass* is a bit theatrical and self-consciously noble. Biggs seems mismatched to this music. He is anything but a Byronic type. I have come to the conclusion that to play Liszt well you have to have in your breast a good-sized dollop of original sin. Very imposing recorded sound.

Faust Waltz. See Collections: Barere (Rem 199-17).

*Funérailles. Barere, Rem 199-85 (*Sonata in B minor). Horowitz, V LM 9021 (*Sonetto del Petrarca 104; Valse oubliée; Rákoczy March; Mendelssohn: Variations sérieuses).*

Two notable technicians and exponents of the grand manner are heard in the *Funérailles.* Barere's version, recorded on the stage of Carnegie Hall during an actual concert, is a boomy recording with heavy surface noise. Horowitz has much more realistic recording. His playing is better controlled than Barere's; it is steadier, more relentless, rhythmically stronger. And the climax he achieves is something that the weaker Barere recording cannot match. Also on the Victor disc is Horowitz's brilliant arrangement of the *Rákoczy March* (the *Fifteenth Hungarian Rhapsody*), one of the great *tours de force* of contemporary pianism. A clear-etched *Valse oubliée* and an electrifying *Sonetto 104* round out the Liszt side of the disc.

Gnomenreigen. See Collections: Barere (Rem 199-17); Keene (Mer 10113); see also *Ballade in B minor* (Str 607).

Hungarian Rhapsodies (Nos. 1-15). Farnadi, W WAL 213 [2]; also available separately on W 5230/1.

*Hungarian Rhapsodies (Nos. 16-19). Farnadi, W 5339 (*6 Consolations; Rhapsodie Espagnole).*

As Liszt-playing, these performances leave much to be desired. Farnadi has fluency but not much strength, and she misses the big, splashy, extroverted moments. I don't find much personality in her playing, and I don't like the constant semi-detached fingering she uses, or her reluctance to make use of pedal effects. Nor has she the necessary technique to handle the music, and in *Rhapsody No. 10* she plays the easier alternate rather than the difficult glissandi. These *Rhapsodies* sound remarkably thin unless the pianist can storm through the virtuosity with ease, and shape the lyric sections with absolute elegance. (For an idea about how a great virtuoso goes about playing Liszt, listen to Horowitz's recording of the *Rhapsody No. 6* on V LM 1235). Borovsky has recorded the nineteen *Rhapsodies* on Vox 8900, 8910, and 8920. These performances are unexciting and technically weak. Borovsky is singularly miscast in the flamboyant role of Liszt pianist; the Farnadi, with all of its defects, is preferable. Westminster has given her brilliant, close-up recording, often too brilliant for comfort. There also is a tremendous "ghost" just before the presto finale of the *Rhapsody No. 9.*

Hungarian Rhapsodies (individual).

Several of the *Rhapsodies* appear individually on discs containing a miscellany of other music. The most exciting, not unexpectedly, come from Horowitz, whose arrangements of Nos. 2 and 15 can be found, respectively on V LM 6014 and LM 9021. Horowitz's tremendous performance of No. 6, which sounds as though at least two pianists are at work, is contained in V LM 1235. A brilliantly played No. 11 by Kapell is found on V LM 1791. Brailowsky energetically plays Nos. 6 and 12 in a hard, dynamically monotonous manner on V LM 1772. Much interest attaches to Busoni's performance of No. 13 (see Collections: "Musicians of the Past," Vol. I). The best version of No. 2 in its original form (the Horowitz is a souped-up arrangement) is played by Wild on Str 607.

On L 1087, Katin plays Nos. 2, 6, and 15 in an able manner that could do with more flair and intensity.

Jeux d'eaux à la Villa d'Este. See *Mephisto Waltz* (V LM 1772).

Legends: St. Francis Preaching to the Birds; St. Francis Walking on the Waters. See *Années de pèlerinage* (L 315); *Mephisto Waltz* (V LM 1772). See also under *Ballades* (W 5321).

Liebesträume (3). See *Ballades* (W 5321); *Rigoletto Paraphrase* (L 1087). For the popular *Liebestraum No. 3,* see also *Mephisto Waltz* (V LM 1772) and Collections: Rubinstein (V LM 1153).

*Mephisto Waltz. Kapell, V LM 1791 (*for contents of disc see Collections: Kapell). Brailowsky, V LM 1772 (*Liebestraum No. 3; Gnomenreigen; Hungarian Rhapsodies Nos. 6 and 12; Jeux d'eaux à la Villa d'Este; Valse oubliée; St. Francis Preaching to the Birds).*

In Kapell's "Memorial Album," issued shortly after his death, the only previously issued work was the *Mephisto,* which had come out in 1946. Kapell was still in an immature stage at that time. Nevertheless, this *Mephisto* is note-perfect, with a lot of snap; and the recording has good piano sound. I prefer it to the more recent Brailowsky. The latter, an old *routinier,* expertly sweeps through the music, but omits the excitement of the writing. Brailowsky also does his usual methodical, percussive work on the other pieces in his Liszt disc. His playing certainly is not bad enough to ignore; but it is not imaginative enough to make it an indispensable item, either. The Pennario version of the *Mephisto* on Cap 8246 is all on the surface; and Farnadi on W 5266 does not have the depth of tone necessary to do justice to the piece.

Polonaise No. 2 in E. See *Années de pèlerinage* (L 934) and *Ballade in B minor* (Str 607).

*Rhapsodie Espagnole. Barere, Rem 199-41 (*see Collections: Barere). Uninsky, Ep 3066 (*3 Paganini Études; Mussorgsky: Pictures at an Exhibition). Farnadi, W 5339 (*6 Consolations; Hungarian Rhapsodies Nos. 16-19).*

Barere, with all of his extroverted bravura and technique for the sake of technique, is more convincing than Farnadi or even the better-controlled Uninsky. He had a tremendous flair for music of this sort, and was able to maintain excitement throughout, even if one sometimes questioned his taste. Not very good recorded sound is present here. While the Uninsky disc is superior in that respect, it also is not characteristic of what modern recording can do for the piano. A prevailing tinniness and lack of resonance give Uninsky's tone an edge quite different from what one hears from him in the concert hall. Uninsky plays the *Rhapsodie Espagnole* with considerable virtuosity and strength. Farnadi, who has the benefit of the best recorded sound, does not give the music what it needs. Hers is a sort of segmented pianism I do not like; it is a collection of details rather than a unified conception; and she does not really have the unlimited technique necessary for this kind of music.

*Rigoletto Paraphrase de Concert. Katin, L 1087 (*3 Liebesträume; Hungarian Rhapsodies Nos. 2, 6, 15).*

Katin apparently is an able technician with a fine tone. But where are the sweep, the fire, the extroverted elements of the music? The way Katin plays the *Rigoletto* paraphrase, all of its musical weaknesses are apparent. Whereas, when played by an exponent of the grand manner, the music sounds vital and exciting. For music like this was intended by Liszt primarily as a pianistic "vehicle," and so it should be approached. In the *Liebesträume* Katin is a little too inhibited; he seems reluctant to exploit the Lisztian line with a swagger. Nevertheless, this clear, tasteful performance remains the best version of the complete set on LP. London's recorded sound is bell-like.

*Sonata for Piano in B minor. Barere, Rem 199-85 (*Funérailles). Uninsky, Ep 3027 (*Sonetto 104 del Petrarca).*

Of the many versions of the *B minor Sonata*, only the above two are worth much consideration. Uninsky is steadier than Barere. A fine technician, he is closer to a literal translation of the notes. Nevertheless the more exciting Barere is preferable. His approach is flashier; it is pianism of a more personal and transcendental sort. Occasionally he makes a slip, but there never are any plodding moments, as there are in the Uninsky. Uninsky is much more careful. Barere was inclined to take chances, and when they came off, the results were sensational. When they didn't, the result was sloppy piano-playing. Most of Barere's chances come off in this account of the sonata. The Remington recording was made from acetates taken during an actual Carnegie Hall recital. Not too good tonally, but it serves. Of the other versions, the most lifelike reproduction of the piano is the recording by Frugoni on Vox 8800, but the small-scaled playing does not measure up to Liszt's heroics. Both Farnadi on W 5266 and Pennario on Cap 8136 are brittle. Malcuzynski on An 35031 is excessively mannered. Foldes on 10" D 7528 is no more than routine, and Magaloff on 10" L 392 is too undisciplined for comfort.

Sonetto del Petrarca No. 104.

This piece is available on several discs devoted to a miscellany of music, Liszt and otherwise. It has fared exceptionally well on LP. My favorites are the Barere, for its control and velocity, on Rem 199-35, and the Horowitz, for its tremendous breadth and virility, on V LM 9021. Kempff gives an idiomatic performance on L 515 (where he plays all three *Sonetti*), and there can be nothing but praise for Uninsky's sober, sure-fingered performance on Ep 3027. Also decidedly worth mention is Lipatti on 10" C 2216. All these are examples of extremely fine Liszt-playing. Several other versions, not mentioned here, fall considerably below the above.

Valse oubliée. See *Don Juan Fantasy* (Rem 199-35); *Funérailles* (V LM 9021); *Mephisto Waltz* (V LM 1772); see also Collections: Rubinstein (V LM 1153).

*Variations on "Weinen, Klagen, Sorgen, Zagen." Kabos (piano), Bar 910 (*Christmas Tree). Nies-Berger (organ), CH 1145 (*Franck: Grande Pièce symphonique).*

Liszt composed the organ piece first, in 1863; he transcribed it for piano in 1875. The variations are based on the basso continuo of a Bach cantata. It is a moody work with some strange harmonies. Nies-Berger emphasizes the big contours of the music. His performance is massive, a little muddy in the fortissimo stretches, but consistently alive. Excellent recorded sound. Kabos is all right in the moving sections. She doesn't seem sure of what to do in simple ones like the *lento recitativo;* and her refusal to maintain strict tempo in the chorale weakens the music. This is a far from ideal interpretation, though it will serve to make one acquainted with an important, seldom-played Liszt work.

LOCKE, MATTHEW (1632-1677)

Consort No. 6 for Viols. See Collections: New Music String Quartet (Bar 913).

LOEILLET, JEAN-BAPTISTE (1653-1728)

Sonata No. 12 for Cello and Harpsichord; Trio Sonatas Nos. 2 and 13 for Violin, Cello, and Harpsichord; Sonata No. 10 for Violin and Harpsichord. Alès, Coddée, Gerlin. OL 50018.

All of this music is standard baroque writing almost devoid of personality. The performers go about it in a rather dead fashion, making the proper sounds but never communicating much joy in doing so. The stolid interpretations are not helped by thick-sounding recording in which the harpsichord is placed too far back.

Trio Sonata in B minor. See Telemann: *Quartet in D minor* (W 5076).

LOPATNIKOFF, NICOLAS (1903-)

*Sonata for Violin and Piano No. 2 (Op. 32). Fuchs, Balsam, D 9541 (*Piston: Violin Sonata).*

The Lopatnikoff work is energetic, "busy," beautifully written, and contains everything save an original melodic impulse. Piston's sonata contains a more personal feeling, a slow movement of real lyricism, and a complete lack of musical or emotional verbiage. Admirable performances by the flawless Fuchs, and clear, well-balanced recording (some scratchy surfaces in the Piston).

*Theme, Variations, and Epilogue. N. and J. Graudan, C 4990 (*Glanville-Hicks: Sonata for Piano and Percussion; Concertino da Camera).*

This work for cello and piano has been recorded by Columbia for its "Modern American Music" series. It is a conservative, rhapsodic score, somewhat too long for the slight nature of its musical substance. The Graudans present a brilliant performance in which teamwork, impetus, and technical strength are justly mingled. Virtually the only defect is the cellist's rather stringy, dry tone. Realistic recorded sound.

MACDOWELL, EDWARD (1861-1908)

Piano Music. J. Kirkpatrick, C 4372.

Included herein are the three *Fireside Tales*, three of the *Sea Pieces*, four of the *New England Idylls*, and all of the *Woodland Sketches*. MacDowell's piano music has gone out of fashion. Perhaps the time has come for revival; there is some honest invention tucked away among some of the salon pieces. Kirkpatrick's performance is good, though he is startlingly flip and offhand in *To a Wild Rose*. Did he have his tongue in his cheek? On CH 1137 Balsam plays seven of the *Woodland Sketches* with more color and flexibility than Kirkpatrick demonstrates. Balsam's disc is otherwise devoted to the *D minor Piano Concerto.*

MALIPIERO, G. FRANCESCO (1882-)

Poemo Asolami. See Weber: *Piano Sonata No. 4* (SPA 15).
Rispetti e Strambotti. See Boccherini: *Quartet for Guitar* (Ph 101).
Sonata a Cinque. See Bax: *Harp Quintet* (Ph 102).

MARAIS, MARIN (1656-1728)

Suites for Viola da Gamba and Harpsichord Nos. 4 and 5. Heinitz, Wolff, EMS 8.

Marais was a pupil of Lully. The music played here was taken from five books published between 1686 and 1717. But two of the ten movements from *Suite No. 4* and three of the twelve from *Suite No. 5* have been omitted. An additional piece is present—a prelude taken from a suite published in 1701. The viola da gamba—at least, as heard on this disc—is not the most flexible of instruments. Even more than a cello it sounds, in the words of George Bernard Shaw, like a bee buzzing in a stone jug. We should be kind to our ancestors, but this is really very dull stuff. Here again, however, "historical interest" covers the disc, and as so few examples of viola da gamba music are available, this disc should be pointed out. Adequate recorded sound.

MARTINŮ, BOHUSLAV (1890-)

Quartet for Strings No. 6. See Piston: *Quintet for Piano and Strings* (WCFM 14).
Sonata for Flute and Piano; Six Piano Pieces. Le Roy, Reeves; Rosen (EMS 2).

The flute sonata is an eclectic, impersonal work. Rosen, the pianist in the solo pieces, has selected three études, two polkas and *Les Ritournelles* (the last-named a collection of six short pieces). Fine performances prevail. Le Roy and Reeves are as polished an ensemble as one could desire, and Rosen plays the piano works with evident enjoyment. Excellent recorded tone.

*Three Madrigals. J. and L. Fuchs, D 8510 (*Mozart: Duo No. 2).*

Not very many works for violin and viola have been written. These madrigals, for the combination, are among Martinů's most ingenious efforts. Two of America's best instrumentalists bring out the color and variety of the writing in a way that should satisfy the most captious. (They have a certain proprietary interest in the music; it was dedicated to them.) Decca's recording does justice to the string tone.

MENDELSSOHN, FELIX (1809-1847)

*Concert Pieces (2) for Bassett Horn, Clarinet, and Piano (Op. 113, 114). Bartosek, Wlach, Demus, W 5024 (*Schumann: Märchenerzählungen).*

Extremely melodious pieces for an unusual combination. The bassett horn belongs to the clarinet family; today the instrument is obsolete. This little-known disc is a connoisseur's item, and you may find it a delight. Though the recording dates from early LP days, it has superb quality. And the performances are sweet, singing, and beautifully integrated.

Octet for Strings in E flat (Op. 20). Vienna Octet, L 859.

Mendelssohn was not yet seventeen when he composed this score. He never wrote a better one. The third movement, often heard in a blown-up version for symphony strings, has been described as "elfin" by commentators since 1850; and who are we to disagree? Has anybody ever made mention of the crib from Handel's *Messiah* in the last movement? Mendelssohn picks up the "And he shall live for ever and ever" theme. The performance by the Vienna Octet, full-bodied and colorful, supersedes earlier recordings by Vox and Stradivari. It should remain the standard for some time to come.

Piano Music. Gianoli, W 5329.

The contents: *Prelude and Fugue in E minor; Rondo Capriccioso; Variations sérieuses; Perpetuum Mobile;* three *Études* (Op. 104); two *Clavierstücke; Scherzo a Capriccio.* Gianoli plays agreeably and superficially. She seldom gets inside the music, contenting herself with surface elegance and polish of execution. Sometimes these methods give good results, as in the *Rondo Capriccioso,* but they do not become the fine *Prelude and Fugue* or the great *Variations sérieuses;* and, in the latter, the indications *sf* or *p* seem to mean little to the pianist. Thus the eighth variation loses its point. Mention should be made of the adorable *Études*, which come to LP for the first time. For other Mendelssohn piano music, see *Songs without Words* and *Variations sérieuses*.

*Quartet for Piano and Strings in F minor (Op. 2). Balsam, Guilet, Brieff, Laporte, CH 1095 (*Violin Sonata in F minor).*

Another product of Mendelssohn's youth: he was fourteen at the time. His style is not yet as mature as it was three years later, when the marvelous *Octet in E flat* came around, but nevertheless the *Piano Quartet in F minor* remains a substantial achievement. Balsam provides a fine commentary, and the strings back him up strongly. This is a well-paced, thoroughly musical performance. The piano sound comes through clearly enough; the strings sound hard and shrill. All the defects of "flat" studio recording are here. Guilet and Balsam are efficient partners in the unimportant *Violin Sonata* on the reverse.

Quartets for Strings Nos. 1 in E flat (Op. 12) and 3 in D (Op. 44, No. 1). Curtis, W 5220.

The Curtis group plays with constant application, but there could be more grace and elegance. Applied to music like this, the qualities of the Curtis Quartet are misplaced; it has strength rather than the tonal sheen and delicacy of bowing one would like to hear. This, however, is the only LP coupling of the attractive quartets, and certainly the Curtis does not misrepresent the music. Excellent recorded quality, smooth surfaces.

Quartets for Strings Nos. 2 in A minor (Op. 13) and 5 in E flat (Op. 44, No. 3). New Music, C 4921.

Quartets for Strings Nos. 4 in E minor and 5 in E flat (Op. 44, Nos. 2, 3). Endres, Str 615.

These three works do not turn up very often. More's the pity. They are gracious, well-bred pieces with many ingenious touches and constant lyricism. No. 5 is present in recordings by the New Music and the Endres quartets. Both performances are good. I incline toward the New Music, which presents the music with a little more smoothness and more assured rhythm. The Endres, a little politer, offers stylistically assured performances, however. The same general remarks can be extended toward the interpretations of the other two works. No. 2 is nicely handled by the New Music, and there is no cause for complaint in the Endres treatment of No. 4. Both discs have been well recorded, with the honors to Columbia for a fuller and more realistic tone.

Quintets for Strings in A (Op. 18) and B flat (Op. 87). Pascal, Gerhard, CH 1172.

Neither of these pieces is heard much these days. The A major is a sweet, flowing work with an amazing elfin-like fugue for the third movement. The later *B flat Quintet* opens with a theme suggestive of the *Octet.* It is a work of breadth; and the slow movement is, for Mendelssohn, actually passionate. The Pascal Quartet, with Gerhard as the added violist, provides steady performances a bit on the routine side. One gets the idea, rightly or wrongly, that the musicians are almost reading the scores. Not much body is behind the recorded sound. No actual distortion is present, but by present-day standards the sound is flat.

Sextet for Piano and Strings in F (Op. 110). Pressler, Gordon, Sklar, Guilet members, MGM 3107.

Despite the high opus number, this is an early work, composed at the age of fifteen. The scoring calls for piano, violin, two violas, cello, and double bass. Like many of Mendelssohn's pre-*Octet* works this one has perfect form, lots of bustle, and nothing much in the way of original ideas. At that, the assurance and workmanship are amazing. This is an admirably adjusted performance. It has spirit and sparkle, precise phrasing, perfectly chosen tempos. The detail and clarity of the recording are perfectly in line with the performance.

Sonatas for Cello and Piano Nos. 1 in B flat (Op. 45) and 2 in D (Op. 58). N. and J. Graudan, Vox 8500.

Musicianly rather than colorful or spontaneous performances dominate this disc. Graudan's tone lacks a sensuous quality; it is rather coarse and wiry. His wife plays the piano with good rhythm and a percussive attack. The way she handles the arpeggiated opening of the slow movement of the D major is scarcely an example of musical sensitivity. On the whole these interpretations can be classified as competent and straightforward. One would like to have a little more. A recording by Albin on Tel 66015 is no better, and it contains an indifferently played version of Schubert's "Arpeggione" on the reverse.

Sonatas for Organ in F minor, A, and D minor (Op. 65, Nos. 1, 3, 6); Prelude and Fugue in C minor. Eggington, OL 50013.

Bach is the influence in these organ sonatas, which represent a less popular (and frequently sterile) side of the composer. Eggington plays an organ in a church in Paris. It is not a baroque instrument, but Mendelssohn did not write for a baroque organ. More linear independence could have been achieved by Eggington, who appears to be a sound organist and a remarkably unimaginative one. Mendelssohn's writing is not as stuffy, in these sonatas, as Eggington suggests. For another version of the *Sixth Sonata*, see Collections: Schweitzer (C SL 175).

*Sonata for Organ in C minor (Op. 65, No. 2). Elsasser, MGM 3007 (*Schumann: Four Sketches; Canon in B minor).*

Elsasser drags the music a little too much. A more controlled force was needed. He is at his best where his agile fingers can move around. This disc is valuable primarily because of the Schumann pieces on the reverse. Fine recorded sound.

Sonata for Violin and Piano in F minor (Op. 4). See *Quartet for Piano and Strings* (CH 1095).

*Sonata for Violin and Piano in F. Menuhin, Moore, V HMV 1071 (*Saint-Saëns: Violin Concerto No. 3).*

Composed in 1838, this sonata has never been published. Menuhin worked from a photostat of the original manuscript. The music does not have much of interest, though a lively third movement partly redeems the prevailing stuffiness. Menuhin's recording is excellent: vibrant tone, careful molding of phrases, sensitive support from Moore.

Songs without Words. Doyen, W 5192, 5246, and 5279.

The forty-eight *Songs without Words*, plus a forty-ninth that was discovered after the original publication of the series, can be heard in their entirety on these three discs. Much pretty music is present—we don't look down on the *Songs without Words* as much as the last generation did—and it is good to have all three discs for sentimental or browsing purposes. Doyen's performances are neatly arranged. She avoids the over-interpretation that has sometimes marred her playing. But one could wish for more elegance, more aristocracy, rather than the relentlessly accurate, unvaried, and somewhat percussive attack. Doyen convinces the listener of her skill but not of her complete identification with the music. Fine recording, save for several prominent "ghosts." On Vox 6570 (**Piano Concerto in D minor*) Pizzuto has recorded eight of the *Songs without Words* with considerable grace and fluency. As the *D minor Concerto* receives its only LP recording (by Wuehrer) on the reverse of her record, this disc is well worth owning. Clear, somewhat unresonant but faithful-sounding recorded sound.

*Trio for Piano and Strings No. 1 in D minor (Op. 49). Heifetz, Piatigorsky, Rubinstein, V LM 1119 (*Ravel: Trio).*

This is a really exciting performance. Color and taste are allied to instrumental virtuosity. The recording throws the cello a little too much into the background; otherwise the sound is sparkling. As the Ravel work on the reverse is a masterpiece of ensemble, this disc belongs in every collection of chamber music.

*Variations sérieuses; Wedding March (after Liszt). Horowitz, V LM 9021 (*Liszt: Funérailles; Sonetto 104; Valse oubliée).*

Horowitz's brilliant, brittle performance of the Mendelssohn masterpiece leaves all recorded competition far behind. The playing is nervous, unrelaxed, but intelligently planned and amazingly articulated. Absolutely formidable. The pianist's tinkering with Liszt's tinkering of the "Wedding March" is a typical keyboard cartwheel that nobody carries off as well. Pressler has recorded the *Variations* on MGM 3029 (*Schumann: *Romances*). Some good playing here, and superior recorded sound, but he falters in several sections and does not hold the music together as well as Horowitz does. Pressler's conception, incidentally, is close enough to Horowitz's to suggest that if he has not carefully studied the Horowitz recording he is at least aware of it. The MGM disc includes a deftly played performance of the *Rondo Capriccioso.* Both of these performances of the *Variations* are preferable to Gianoli's ladylike superficiality on W 5329. Pelleg, on CH 1127, and Winand-Mendelssohn, on 10" D 4080, bring up the rear.

MENNIN, PETER (1923-)

Quartet for Strings No. 2. See Imbrie: *Quartet in B flat* (C 4844).

MESSIAEN, OLIVIER (1908-)

Le Banquet céleste; Prière du Christ; Transport de joie. See Schoenberg: *Variations on a Recitative* (CE 1004).

La Nativité du Seigneur. White, Mer 10069.

Nine meditations for organ on Biblical texts make up this composition, which is a mystic mélange of Franck, Debussy, and others. I find it pretentious and tiresome. Others unhesitatingly call Messiaen one of the great composers of the day. White, one of the most accomplished organists around, plays expertly, and the organ has been reproduced with a smooth sound.

MILHAUD, DARIUS (1892-)

*Carnaval à la Nouvelle-Orléans; Les Songes. Gold and Fizdale, 10" C 2128 (*Bowles: Concerto for Two Pianos).*

The *Carnaval* is a peppy work, in line with the composer's popular *Scaramouche.* A ballet score before its transfer to the two-piano medium, *Les Songes* also is a frothy, very Gallic piece of writing. Everything about this disc is pleasant: the music, the performance, the quality of recorded sound.

La Cheminée du Roi René. See *Sonata for Flute, Oboe, Clarinet, and Piano* (EMS 6).

*Concertino d'automne (1951). Gold and Fizdale, C 4854 (*Debussy: Épigraphes antiques; Poulenc: Sonata for Piano Four Hands; Satie: En habit de cheval).*

Available separately, this disc is also part of the three-disc "Music for Two Pianos" (for contents, see Collections: Gold and Fizdale, C SL 198). The Milhaud *Concertino* is scored for two pianos and eight instruments: flute, oboe, three horns, two violas, cello. It is a typically fluent work, in which the notes progress in a logical and sophisticated manner, spiked with chic discords and polytonal patterns. Gold and Fizdale rattle easily through the score, playing in the alert, confident way one always expects from them. First-class recorded sound.

*La Muse ménagère. Milhaud, C 4305 (*Cantate de L'Enfant et de la Mère).*

Translation: "The Household Muse." It is a set of simple pieces written for amateurs. The titles include things like "Cooking," "Reading at Night," "Laundry," "Household Cares." With the composer at the piano, one can ask no more in the way of musical authority. The piano tone comes through with fine clarity, but the record surfaces are anything but praiseworthy.

*Quartet for Strings No. 1 (1912). WQXR, Pol 1004 (*Turina: Oración del Torero).*

This early Milhaud score is tincture of Ravel. It is cocksure, glib, and written with tremendous security. The French-derived Turina score on the reverse is salon-ish, with a very lovely opening theme. Both works receive excellent performances. Not many ensembles surpass the WQXR group in quality of tone and ensemble. Excellent recorded sound.

*Quartet for Strings No. 12. Quartetto Italiano, An 35130 (*Debussy: Quartet).*

Notable in this work is the slow movement, with its sliding chromatics. The Quartetto Italiano gives a warm-sounding performance (though beware of an affected, strangely played Debussy on the reverse).

Quartets for Strings Nos. 14 and 15; Octet. Budapest, C 4332.

The mathematics are simple. Write a quartet, write another quartet, put them together, and you have an octet. One would feel much more impressed if the octet sounded like anything instead of an ugly collection of dissonances. The disc is also a curiosity in that the four members of the Budapest Quartet play the two quartets and then combine for the octet, thanks (as the program notes say, awed) "to the miracle of recording."

Quintet No. 1 for Piano and Strings; Quintet No. 2 for Double Bass and Strings. Smith (piano), Thompson (bass), Stanley Quartet, 10" Con 103.

The recording company that made this disc is dedicated to the proposition of modern music recorded under the supervision of the composer. Milhaud himself approved this recording. Both performances are fluent, as the music demands, and the recordings are a model of tonal clarity.

*Saudades do Brazil. Skolovsky, C 4523 (*Concerto No. 4).*

As the title implies, these twelve piano pieces use Brazilian themes and rhythms. Skolovsky whizzes through them in grand style. He has a lot of fun playing them, and they make for enjoyable listening. Top-notch recorded sound.

Sketches (2) for Wind Quintet. See Collections: New Art Wind Quintet (CE 1003).

Sonata for Flute, Oboe, Clarinet, and Piano; La Cheminée du Roi René; Pastorale for Oboe, Clarinet, and Piano. N.Y. Woodwind Quintet, EMS 6.

Several phases of Milhaud's career are represented here, from the early (1918) *Sonata* through the later *Pastorale* and *Cheminée.* All of the works receive capable, spontaneous-sounding performances. They also receive close-up recording of such closeness that you can easily hear the players take breath. The Fairfield Wind Ensemble has recorded the *Cheminée* on Str 606, a disc that is duller in sound and not so strongly molded in performance.

Suite for Violin, Clarinet, and Piano. *Ritter, Kell, J. Rosen, D 9740 (*Bartók: Contrasts). Parrenin, Delecluse, Haas-Hamburger, Per 563 (*Poulenc: Piano Concerto; 3 Piano Pieces).*

Very much in *Les Six* idiom, this suite is one of the most charming Milhaud works on LP. Both performances are good. For slightly fuller recorded sound, you can turn to the Decca disc. The Period disc, however, is also a clear recording, and the performers, all French, play with a supple attack and plenty of instrumental color. Worth consideration is a look at the couplings. There are better versions of the Bartók *Contrasts*, which backs up the Decca disc, whereas the Period disc presents the only LP of Poulenc's *Piano Concerto.*

Touches blanches; Touches noires. See Collections: Pressler (MGM 3010).

MOMPOU, FEDERICO (1893-)

Piano Pieces. Mompou, An 35147.

The contents are: *Canción y Danza Nos. 1, 4, 5, 7, 8;* an excerpt from *Suburbis No. 1; Jeunes Filles au jardin* (from *Scènes d'Enfants No. 5); Preludes 9 and 10; Pájaro triste; Gitano; Secreto; La fuente y la campana; El lago.* In all, there are fourteen short pieces, all salon-like, composed in a French impressionist style with a Spanish flavor. Mompou is almost unknown in this country, though one or two of his pieces occasionally turn up as encores at piano recitals. The composer is heard as pianist in this recording. He is considered an extraordinary artist by those who have heard him play, but even he cannot make interesting a long succession of music composed in much the same style. Mompou has his little compositional and pianistic tricks that he repeats again and again. After a few numbers the listener is likely to be inflicted with a severe attack of boredom. The recorded sound is adequate, though some listeners may be disturbed by a boominess and reverberation in the bass.

MOORE, DOUGLAS (1893-)

*Quintet for Clarinet and Strings. Oppenheim, New Music, C 4494 (*Riegger: Quartet for Strings No. 2).*

A pair of entirely dissimilar American works are coupled here. Moore's quintet is conservative, with emphasis on an orthodox melodic contour. Riegger's quartet is nervous, muscular, and dissonant, with a low melodic impulse and a high intellectual content. Oppenheim does well by Moore's work, and the New Music equally well by both. Tops in recorded sound.

MOZART, WOLFGANG AMADEUS (1756-1791)

Adagio in B minor (K. 540). See *Sonata for Piano in F,* K. 533 (W 5153/4).

Adagios and Fugues (K. 404a). Pasquier, HS 108.

These four adagios and fugues are half original. Mozart transcribed for string trio three fugues by Bach (No. 8, Book I of *The Well-Tempered Clavier,* and Nos. 13 and 14 from Book II) and a fugue by W. F. Bach, adding a prelude, in adagio tempo, of his own composition in each instance. The preludes are brooding works, seldom heard, as sorrowful and intense as anything Mozart composed. I am not too happy about the performances. The intonation of the Pasquiers leaves something to be desired, and there is not much "lift" to the playing. But the notes are there, the music is worth knowing, and the recording is excellent.

*Andante and Variations in G (K. 501). Badura-Skoda, Demus, W 5069 (*Sonata for Two Pianos in D, K. 448; Bach, J. C.: Sonata in G).*

Only a small part of the Bach-Mozart disc is occupied by these four-hand variations, but they are worth singling out as one of Mozart's most delicious keyboard works. A simple lyric inspiration, like a Herrick poem, the music catches an emotion on the fly; and one of the variations, in G minor, is what some writers refer to when they describe Mozart's work as "demonic." Badura-Skoda and Demus combine in a sharply etched performance that avoids over-interpretation. The young pianists have the taste to keep things simple. Fine piano sound, with a prominent surface that should not disturb anybody but the listener who thinks that sound is more important than content.

*Cassazione-Quartet in E flat for Oboe, Clarinet, Horn, and Bassoon. Members of French Woodwind Quintet, OL 50016 (*Quintet for Piano and Winds, K. 452).*

The cassation was an instrumental form designed for outdoor performances. This so-called "cassation-quartet" was discovered in manuscript and played in Berlin before the First World War. It is not listed in the Köchel catalogue. Mozart or no (there seems to be some doubt about the authorship), it is a charming work, with lighthearted melodic content. Here it receives a fine performance, aided considerably by excellent balance and recorded sound. For another recording of the work see Collections: New Art Wind Quintet (CE 2010).

*Divertimento (Trio) for Strings in E flat (K. 563). Heifetz, Primrose, Feuermann, V LCT 1150 (*Duo No. 2 in B flat; Handel-Halvorsen: Passacaglia). Pougnet, Riddle, Pini, W 5191.*

Universally hailed as the greatest of all string trios, this work belongs in every record collection. Westminster's is the best modern version; Victor's is the best. The latter, which was released early in 1944, does not compare in tonal realism with recent examples of string-playing on discs. But no group that has attempted the work has shown comparable finish. The quality of workmanship that the musicians present is its own reward; and anybody who sneers at the set as a vehicle for three virtuosos is merely parroting the smart-alecisms of people who never have really analyzed the set. It is a brilliant achievement. The artists on the Westminster disc offer completely assured playing, buttressed by first-class musicianship, and their superior recorded sound will attract a wide audience. You can't go wrong with it. I have retained both discs for my permanent collection. A version by the Bel Arte Trio on D 9659 has harsh sound; nor does the actual performance offer much competition to the discs discussed above. And the Pasquier Trio on HS 114 is not only rough in ensemble but imprecise in intonation.

Divertimento for Strings No. 10 in F (K. 247). Members of Vienna Octet, 10" L 682.

Mozart scored this attractive work for string quartet, bass, and two horns. The Viennese players are entirely at home in its polished measures. Their performance is as smooth as cream and exactly in the style of the music. No fuss, no artificial dynamics, just music-making. The recording has depth and color.

Divertimento for Strings No. 17 in D (K. 334). Vienna Konzerthaus, W 5276. Members of Vienna Octet, L 235.

The dividing line between chamber and orchestral music is drawn thin here. Mozart calls for two violins, two violas, bass, and two horns. Like most of the divertimentos, this six-movement score is a relaxed work with many beautiful sections. Both groups present the music with a good deal of charm. Curiously, the Vienna Octet members, who played the *Divertimento No. 10* without any eccentricity, here feel impelled to add some unnecessary (and unmarked, in the score) retards. The results are rather sentimental. Furthermore, this recording has a cut of about eighty measures (including a lovely transition) in the last movement. No cuts are made in the Westminster disc. That, plus a more even quality of playing, gives the honors to the Vienna Konzerthaus and its supporting instrumentalists.

Divertimentos for Winds in E flat (K. 196e) and B flat (K. 196f). Vienna Philharmonic Wind Group, W 5349.

Einstein has renumbered these as K. anh. 226 and 227. The score calls for oboes, clarinets, horns, and bassoons. For the most part these divertimentos are naïve garden music, composed with a wonderful feeling for the sounds and balances of wind instruments. An excellent performance is presented by the Viennese specialists, who lag not, keep a steady pulse, and make the richest of sounds. Extremely lifelike recorded timbre.

Divertimentos for Winds Nos. 1, 4, and 5 (K. anh. 229). Wlach, Bartosek, Oehlberger, W 5213.

*Divertimento for Winds No. 2 (K. anh. 229). Wlach, Bartosek, Oehlberger, W 5022 (*Oboe Quartet; Flute Quartet in D).*

*Divertimento for Winds No. 3 (K. anh. 229). Wlach, Bartosek, Oehlberger, W 5020 (*Sinfonia Concertante in E flat, K. anh. 9).*

On these three discs are the five wind divertimentos of K. anh. 229. Each is in the key of B flat, and each is scored for two clarinets and bassoon. Innocuous music, for the most part, though No. 4 has some imaginative moments. The accomplished wind trio does all that can be done with the music, and the recorded sound is sonorous.

Divertimentos for Winds Nos. 8 in F (K. 213), 12 in E flat (K. 252), 13 in F (K. 253), and 14 in B flat (K. 270). Mayerhofer, etc., W 5103.

Here the combination is two each of oboes, horns, and bassoons. Not much of interest is present in the music, but the admirable Viennese wind-players contribute a degree of artistry which makes the playing, at least, hard to resist. A noticeable pre-echo can be observed at the opening of most of the movements. Otherwise the recording is exceptionally colorful.

*Duo for Violin and Viola No. 1 in G (K. 423). Goldberg, Riddle, D 8523 (*Sonata for Piano No. 13).*

This pre-LP recording shows its age in the transfer. Thin sound, low level, prominent surfaces. The performance is admirable. Both players go about their work in a lusty manner. There is nothing at all anemic about their conception. One might think that this instrumental combination of violin and viola would be lacking in contrast, but Mozart saw to it that interest is constantly maintained. Despite the period quality of the recording, it is decidedly worth having, preferable to the more recent Str 1001 played by Louis and Rolf Persinger. The recording is harsh and unresonant on the Stradivari disc, and the performance is not stylistically as suave.

*Duo for Violin and Viola No. 2 in B flat (K. 424). J. and L. Fuchs, D 8510 (*Martinů: Three Madrigals). Heifetz, Primrose, V LCT 1150 (*Divertimento in E flat, K. 563; Handel-Halvorsen: Passacaglia).*

Flawless string-playing is contributed here by the Fuchs combination. Intonation dead center; instinctive teamwork; strong rhythm; scrupulous musicianship. To add to this lexicon of violinistic goodness is the clear Decca recording, devoid of surface noise and rich in tone. The Heifetz-Primrose disc is an LP transfer, and the sound is nowhere near so vital. Nor do these two eminent instrumentalists convey the gusto and rhythmic vigor of the music as do the Decca musicians. What makes the Victor disc valuable is the brilliant performance of the *E flat Divertimento*, which occupies the greater portion. But if it's the *Duo* in which you are interested, the Decca disc is the better choice.

Early Mozart Keyboard Music. Zeitlin, Op 6003.

Thirty miniatures are presented. These are K. 1–5, 24, 25, and quite a few from the Köchel appendix. One can't expect much musical character from a baby, even from a baby christened Joannes Chrysostomus Wolfgangus Theophilus Mozart. (He was five when he composed the minuet known as K. 1.) The disc, of course, is absorbing from a point of view that is part sentimental, part historical, part scholarly. Zeitlin makes no more of the music than it requires, and the recording has fine piano sound.

Eight Year Old Mozart. Epstein, SPA 35.

One of the features of this disc is that Epstein uses a reconstruction of Mozart's own piano. Very nice, even if the music was composed for the clavichord. Epstein has made a selection of twenty-three of the forty-three pieces that Mozart composed in London, under the influence of J. C. Bach, at the age of eight. She plays the music tastefully, without any tricks. Clear recording.

Fantasy in C minor (K. 475). See *Sonata for Piano No. 14* (C 4356 and W 5317); see also Collections: Chasins (Mer 10062).

Fantasy and Fugue in C (K. 494). See *Sonata for Piano in F*, K. 533 (W 5153/4); see *Sonata for Piano No.16* (Bar 912 and SPA 6).

*Eine Kleine Nachtmusik. Herrmann, Vienna Konzerthaus, W 5315 (*Ein Musikalischer Spass).*

Both works are played in their original form: the *Nachtmusik* as a string quintet, the *Musikalischer Spass* ("Musical Joke") as a sextet (quartet plus two horns). The former, of course, is one of Mozart's most frequently played works, heard usually for string orchestra. Performances of the amusing *Spass* do not come up very often. These are the only LP versions of the chamber-music originals. Unfortunately the lightness of one and the humor of the other do not emerge in these stiff, unsmiling performances. Typically clear, close-up Westminster sound.

Ein Musikalischer Spass. See *Eine Kleine Nachtmusik* (W 5315).

Organ Music. Elsasser, MGM 3075.

Elsasser plays the *Andante in F* (K. 616), the *Fantasy and Fugue in F minor* (K. 608), the *Adagio and Allegro in F minor* (K. 594) —all for mechanical organ—and the *Adagio for Glass Harmonica* (K. 356). All of it is tremendous music. The mechanical organ was a pipe organ that worked on a clock mechanism. Today the instrument is obsolete, but the pieces Mozart composed for it have been arranged by non-clockwork organists into workable forms. The glass harmonica was Benjamin Franklin's contribution to the gaiety of nations. Again this is an arranged piece. It has to be. The musicians' local lists not one player of the glass harmonica. Elsasser plays with considerable ability. The recording is one of those in which, if you turn the pianissimo to a listening level, the fortissimos will blow you into the next county. Too bad, for the organ of the Hammond Museum in Gloucester comes through with fine quality. An unusual and interesting disc.

Piano Music (complete). Gieseking, An 3511K [*11*].

You take them all or you don't take any. None of these discs will be available individually until the bicentennial festivities in 1956. Sixty-three works are included on these eleven discs, and they add up to the most impressive array of solo Mozart piano-playing in the catalogues. The recordings themselves are exceptionally quiet, for the most part (two or three sides have noisy surfaces, but not inordinately so), and Gieseking's tone is captured in all its subtlety. Some of the playing is of extreme beauty. The eleventh variation of the *Sonata No. 6 in D* (K. 284) is typical. Gieseking's work is so liquid and deft that it makes one wriggle with pleasure. His articulation is a joy to hear, and the only out-of-control playing I noticed was a few muddled measures in the first movement of the *Sonata No. 17 in D* (K. 576) and quite a few dropped notes in the finale of No. 5 in G (K. 283). Otherwise a master is at work. And yet I must confess to much disappointment. I feel that Gieseking does not rise to the big sonatas and solo pieces—the *C minor Fantasy* (K. 475), the *Allegro in C minor* (K. 312), the last movement of No. 16 in B flat (K. 570), and several others. A lack of spontaneity and the absence of a really creative mind are noticeable. Often, in these particular works, what comes out is merely sequences of notes—very beautifully played, to be sure, but scarcely conveying the passion of the ideas. In the light of the general authority and keyboard finesse displayed in most of the music, my objection admittedly may be picayune. It also may be that Gieseking, who after all is one of the great pianists of our time, deliberately is trying to avoid any suggestion of passion or drama in Mozart's keyboard music. If that be the case, I think he is dead wrong. The composer himself left plenty of indications about how his piano music should be played, and his letters are full of admonitions about the necessity for strict rhythm, the employment of rubato (yes, rubato; it is not exclusively a romantic phenomenon), the need for sparkle, spirit, and a large framework. Gieseking's over-politeness suggests little of these, and one can but regret that so much finesse is coupled with so little musical conviction.

Quartets for Flute and Strings in D (K. 285), C (K. 285b), and A (K. 298). Baker, Zarief, Mankovitz, Oxman, Ox 101.

It is pleasant to have all three of the flute quartets on one disc. Though Mozart's dislike for the flute is a matter of record, he wrote some remarkably pretty music for it, and the Gluck-like adagio of the D major is Mozart at his most serene. Fine performances here. Baker has a rocklike solidity. The playing is never particularly warm or tender, but it certainly is accurate, and there never is a time when the music is misrepresented. If the highs are reduced a bit, this is a very realistic recording. On W 5022 is a recording of the D major by Reznicek and others (**Oboe Quartet; Divertimento for Winds,* K. anh. 229). They distort the slow movement by too fast a tempo. While the playing itself is good, the competitive version on Oxford remains a better interpretation and a better buy.

*Quartet in F for Oboe and Strings (K. 370). Tabuteau, etc., C 4566 (*Divertimento for Orchestra No. 11). Gomberg, etc., D 9618 (*Telemann: Oboe Partita; Oboe Sonata).*

The Columbia disc was recorded at the 1951 Perpignan Festival. Tabuteau plays with such notables as Stern, Primrose, and Tortelier. What results is a degree of instrumental security not available elsewhere. As the Decca version is quite spirited, one of the determining factors in making a choice is the couplings; and the fine Mozart *Divertimento* backing the Columbia disc is much more pleasant to own than the dullish Telemann pieces that Gomberg plays. On W 5022 Hans Kamesch and three Viennese players are heard in the *Oboe Quartet* (**Flute Quartet in D; Divertimento No. 2,* K anh. 229). Compared with the versions on Columbia and Decca, the Westminster is stiff, lacking color and resilience. Larry Adler has made a recording for harmonica and strings on CH 1161. Silly.

Quartets for Piano and Strings Nos. 1 in G minor (K. 478) and 2 in E flat (K. 493). Szell, Budapest, C 4080. Curzon, Amadeus, L 679.

Mozart composed only two works in this form. Both are masterpieces, and while the G minor is the more popular, the slender E flat is no whit inferior. The Columbia disc is an LP transfer; the original shellacs were released in 1947 and 1948. Thus the recording is a little dry, in no way comparable to the rich sounds that come from the London disc. Yet the combination of Szell's clearly articulated playing and strong sense of musical design with the Budapest's knowledgeable partnership more than holds its own. Curzon and the Amadeus offer perfectly able performances that also are well worth owning. The London disc automatically will be the choice of those who insist on the latest in tonal realism. I'll stick with the Columbia for its greater musical bite. A good performance of the G minor alone is played by Horszowski and the New York Quartet on C 4627 (*Beethoven: *Quartet for Piano and Strings in E flat,* Op. 16). The copy I heard had some skipping grooves in the last few measures of the finale.

Quartets for Strings ("Milanese"). Barchet, Vox 7480.

These "Milanese" *Quartets,* four in number are listed in Einstein's revision of Köchel as "doubtful" because no score in Mozart's hand has come down and there is no contemporary reference to them. But Einstein "unhesitatingly" accepts them and puts the date of composition at 1773. The *anhang* numbers are as follows: No. 1 in A (K. anh. 212); 2 in B flat (210); 3 in C (211); 4 in E flat (213). From the Barchet group come efficient, hard-driving performances. Rhythm rather than softness is stressed, and after a few hearings one is likely to grow restless. Nevertheless, the disc is worth owning, if only for the opportunity of having access to some rarely heard Mozart music.

Quartets for Strings Nos. 1 in G (K. 80), 2 in D (K. 155), 3 in G (K. 156), and 4 in C (K. 157). Barchet, Vox 8510.

Some charming ideas are present in these early quartets, which are more convincing pieces of music than the "Milanese" series. Also, the Barchet is heard to better advantage here. Not only do they enjoy a superior type of recorded sound, but they also seem to enter with greater relish into the style of the music (though this is hardly a spectacular example of nuanced playing). Again the disc is valuable for its material. One would hardly hear the music in years of concert-going. The Quartetto Italiano has recorded K. 155 as part of the last side of the *F major Quartet* (K. 590) on L 665. The performance is smoother than that of the Barchet; but the latter disc, with its grouping of four early and related quartets, is the better buy.

*Quartet for Strings No. 5 in F (K. 158). Barchet, Vox 8690 (*Quartets Nos. 6, 7).*

Dependable but essentially routine playing. One would like to hear a greater degree of grace and volatility. There is something stolid about the way the Barchet Quartet shapes a phrase. The music, however, is never misrepresented, the notes are all there, and so seldom does one have the opportunity to hear this fine early quartet that quibbling may be a little beside the point. Clear, well-defined recorded sound.

*Quartet for Strings No. 6 in B flat (K. 159). Barchet, Vox 8690 (*Quartets Nos. 5, 7). Griller, 10" L 656 (*Haydn: Quartet in F, Op. 3, No. 6).*

Best choice here is the Vox disc, which has a decided edge in recorded sound and the advantage of a more consistent choice of couplings. The Barchet Quartet will never thrill you with these performances, but it plays in a dependable manner. A heavy attack features the Griller performance, and in general its work here is unexciting.

*Quartet for Strings No. 7 in E flat (K. 160). Barchet, Vox 8690 (*Quartets Nos. 5, 6).*

The music goes along in typical Barchet Quartet style—competent, musicianly, rather earthbound. Much value attaches to the seldom-heard music, which should be a new experience to all but Mozart specialists. Excellent recorded sound.

*Quartet for Strings No. 8 in F (K. 168). Griller, L 658 (*Quartet No. 17).*

The Griller approaches the work dutifully, and there is a lack of volatility, especially in the spread-out slow movement. The recorded sound is excellent.

*Quartet for Strings No. 11 in E flat (K. 171). Loewenguth, Vox 6420 (*Violin Concerto No. 3).*

This disc is mentioned here because it is the only recording of an interesting early work. The recording goes back some years, and sounds it: thin sound, background noise, prominent surfaces. It fills a gap in the Mozart discography, but an up-to-date version is long overdue.

Quartets for Strings Nos. 14 in G (K. 387), 15 in D minor (K. 421), 16 in E flat (K. 428), 17 in B flat ("Hunt," K. 458), 18 in A (K. 464), and 19 in C ("Dissonant, K. 465). Budapest, C SL 187 [3]. *Roth, Mer MGL 8* [3].

Mozart dedicated these six quartets to Haydn, and posterity knows them as the "*Haydn*" *Quartets.* Each is a masterpiece, and any collector casting around for ideas about starting a chamber-music collection would be well advised to investigate the series. As between the Budapest and Roth versions of all six, the Budapest has a decided edge. The Columbia recording has a smoother sound, the Budapest Quartet a smoother ensemble. Where the Roth group is sometimes a little off in its intonation, the Budapest invariably is perfect; and where the Roth sometimes sounds a little rough, the Budapest always is aristocratic and refined in its musical approach. The Budapest recordings, like the Roth, are available in individual couplings (14 and 15; 16 and 17; 18 and 19). One need look no further than the Columbia discs. Other individual recordings of the "*Haydn*" *Quartets* are available, but none is on a comparable level of achievement. The Quartetto Italiano has Nos. 14 and 15 on An 35063, presented with considerable polish and weak rhythm (as witness the flabby phrasing of the third movement of No. 14). No. 14 is also played by the Barylli on W 5265 (**Quartet No. 22*): a strong, musical performance not as tonally agreeable as the Budapest. Still another No. 14 is delivered by the Amadeus on V HMV 1039 (Haydn: "*Emperor*" *Quartet*). It is a good routine reading, with the exception of a minuet phrased as though it had hiccups. The Griller in No. 17, L 658, is dependable and unexciting. Nos. 16 and 17 are played by the Amadeus on W 5099; and the same group is heard in No. 18 on W 5092 (**Quartet No. 23*). All of these are strong and assertive readings. In No. 16 the pitch of the first two movements is a little flat; the rest of the disc is exactly in tune. No. 17 also is pitched about a quarter-tone flat. I mention this because many string-players like to play along. Westminster completes its series of "*Haydn*" *Quartets* with a performance by the Vienna Konzerthaus of Nos. 15 and 19 (W 5175). No threat to the Budapest version is contained in these stodgy readings.

*Quartet for Strings No. 20 in D (K. 499). Barylli, W 5356 (*Quintet in D. K. 593). Stuyvesant, Ph 105 (*Quartet No. 21). Roth, Mer 10133 (*Quartet No. 21).*

Both the Stuyvesant and Roth groups present more "natural" couplings (especially as the *D major Quintet* is available in a preferred version by the Budapest), but it cannot be denied that the Barylli is the best modern version. In matters of tonal realism none of the competing discs can match it. Musically it is a dependable performance, with a fine choice of tempos, complete respect for the music, and steady rhythm throughout. Those who would prefer having the *Quartet No. 21* on the reverse will be satisfied with the Stuyvesant interpretation, which also has a mellow recording characteristic. The Roth is harsher in sound. On C 4863 is a coupling of Nos. 20 and 21 played by the Juilliard Quartet; it should be avoided. Mozart is not the Juilliard's cup of tea. The phrasing is stiff, and there are some strange tempos, such as a prestissimo ending to the allegro finale of No. 20.

*Quartet for Strings No. 21 in D (K. 575). Stuyvesant, Ph 105 (*Quartet No. 20). Roth, Mer 10133 (*Quartet No. 20).*

There is little to choose interpretatively between these two versions. Both are well played, mature in approach, carefully articulated. The Philharmonia disc has the edge in recorded sound. It is less wiry than the Mercury, and its better instrumental definition makes it the preferred version. The Juilliard Quartet, on C 4863, has the most faithful sound of all, but as Mozart-playing it is out of the running.

*Quartet for Strings No. 22 in B flat (K. 589). Barylli, W 5265 (*Quartet No. 14). Barchet, Vox 8260 (*Quartet No. 23). Roth, Mer 10134 (*Quartet No. 23).*

The Barylli Quartet has the most success in letting the music flow. Despite a tendency for the hard tone of the leader to take undue prominence, it overcomes serious criticism by virtue of natural tempos, spirit, and excellent ensemble. Next to it the Roth sounds stolid. The Barchet brings considerable elegance to the performance, but the Barylli is in general the most musical and convincing version and easily the most faithful example of recorded string tone.

*Quartet for Strings No. 23 in F (K. 590). Amadeus, W 5092 (*Quartet No. 18). Italiano, L 665 (*Quartet No. 2). Barchet, Vox 8260 (*Quartet No. 22). Roth, Mer 10134 (*Quartet No. 22).*

There is a spacious quality to the Amadeus performance which I prefer to the more subdued, almost effeminate, ideas of the Quartetto Italiano. Both versions are excellent in sound, though the Westminster disc has one blemish: a slight pitch drop. It starts right on key and ends almost a half-tone flat. The Vox disc is to be approached with caution. "A few" copies, according to the company, were released with the first six measures of the first movement missing: make certain that the disc you buy is complete. The performance is well conceived and firm in outline. Some nice things can be said about details of the Roth performance, but on the whole it is tonally rough and not absolutely secure in intonation.

Quintets for Strings (complete):

*B flat (K. 46). Pascal, CH 1188 (*Horn Quintet, K. 407).*

*B flat (K. 174). Pascal, CH 1185 (*Quintet in C).*

*C minor (K. 406). Budapest, C 4143 (*Quintet in D). Pascal, CH 1186 (*Quintet in G minor).*

*C (K. 515). Budapest, C 4034. Pascal, CH 1185 (*Quintet in B flat).*

*G minor (K. 516). Budapest, C 4469 (*Quintet in E flat). Pascal, CH 1186 (*Quintet in C minor).*

*D (K. 593). Budapest, C 4143 (*Quintet in C minor). Pascal, CH 1187 (*Quintet in E flat).*

*E flat (K. 614). Budapest, C 4469 (*Quintet in G minor). Pascal, CH 1187 (*Quintet in D).*

Milton Katims is the added violist in the Columbia discs. Walter Gerhard joins the Pascal Quartet, which throws in a couple of early quintets and the *Horn Quintet in E flat.* Some of Mozart's very greatest music is contained in the group beginning with the *Quintet in C minor* (K. 406). Into that work, and the four which followed it, Mozart poured everything he knew about music and life. An exaggerated statement? Wait till you become familiar with the music! The Budapest discs, transfers to LP, are quite successful. Some bad surfaces are present (as in the minuet of the *C major Quintet*), but on the whole the sound retains a lively quality. Nevertheless the Pascal Quartet series, which came along later, has a more colorful and realistic type of reproduction. Both versions do honor to the composer. As always, the Budapest Quartet plays with elegance. A stronger quality is offered by the Pascal. Tempos usually are a little slower, the phrasing is more positive and is inflected with less subtlety, and the general feeling is more powerful. Depends upon what you're looking for. I prefer the greater polish of the Budapest. The Pascal, however, has something to say and says it quite well; and its recorded sound certainly has a more realistic quality.

Of other recordings of the Mozart quintets, the Barylli Quartet has recorded the C major on W 5271 and the D major on W 5356 *(*Quartet No. 21).* Spirited performances, rather dry in tone, beautifully recorded. But what happened in the great slow movement of K. 593, where the musicians play as though they were walking in molasses? I see no point in getting the *G minor Quintet* on either W 5086 (Amadeus) or L 132 (Griller), when Columbia and Concert Hall offer it backed by another quintet. Nor can the Vienna Konzerthaus performance of K. 614 on W 5007 (**Quintet for Piano and Winds)* be endorsed; it is dated in sound and there is a general lack of musical spontaneity.

Quintet for Clarinet and Strings in A (K. 581). De Bavier, New Italian, L 573. Goodman, American Art, C 4483. Kell, Fine Arts, D 9600. Wlach, Vienna Konzerthaus, W 5112.

Each version has its points, but I prefer the luminous-sounding London disc. De Bavier and the New Italian (known these days as the Quartetto Italiano) are the most elegant in approach. They do not favor the extreme dynamics heard elsewhere, and yet their performance has as much tensile strength as any Mozart on discs.

The Benny Goodman-American Art interpretation is good, though alongside the London one it sounds foursquare. This recording dates back some years. You'd never guess it. Goodman plays the music "straight"; he is solid, dependable, and a bit characterless. I prefer it to the Kell-Fine Arts version. Kell is a magnificent clarinetist with a sensuous tone: but is his cute and tricky playing really what Mozart intended? On the Westminster disc, Wlach is a graceful clarinetist with style and tradition. So far so good; and the recording has first-rate sound. But one wishes that the Vienna Konzerthaus had Wlach's kind of nuance. They are sincere enough musicians, but not very imaginative ones, nor are they blessed with subtlety. Their idea of "expression" is to slow down, as they do in the famous third variation, in A minor, of the finale. There is absolutely nothing in the score to indicate a change of tempo. Mention might be made of the Forrest-Galimir version on Ly 10. Some fine clarinet-playing is encountered here, but the quartet accompaniment is little more than routine. The Duques performance on Str 601 does not belong in this company; and the Etienne-Vegh performance on HS 96 *(*Clarinet Concerto)*, the only version to get the *Clarinet Quintet* on one side, moves in a ponderous manner.

*Quintet for Piano and Winds in E flat (K. 452). Serkin, members of Philadelphia Wind Quintet, C 4834 (*Beethoven: Quintet for Piano and Winds). Raupenstrauch, Vienna Philharmonic Wind Group, W 5007 (*Quintet for Strings in E flat). Veyron-Lacroix, members of French Wind Quintet, OL 50016 (*Cassazione-Quartet).*

What with Serkin's masterful playing, the Philadelphia players' resonant support, and the beautifully balanced recorded sound, the Columbia disc is in a class by itself. The musicians present a spacious reading that is classic in contour, romantic in conception—which is as it should be, for this is one of Mozart's most intense works. In one breathtaking moment in the *larghetto*, directly after the first repeat, Mozart just about skates off the edge of a black precipice. The Westminster disc, one of the earliest in that company's catalogue, has harsh sound; and the piano (played very well by an artist with the Graustarkian name of Roland Raupenstrauch) has a tendency to "wow." The performance comes through with understanding, however. A thick quality of sound is found in the Oiseau-Lyre disc; and while Veyron-Lacroix knows his business, he is no Serkin. Nor do the other instrumentalists show the unanimity of purpose exhibited by the first-desk men of the Philadelphia Orchestra (especially the horn-player, not in the same league with Mason Jones).

Rondo for Piano in A minor (K. 511). See *Sonata in F*, K. 533 (REB 5).

Rondo for Piano in D (K. 485). See *Sonata in F*, K. 533 (W 5153/4); *Sonata No. 16* (SPA 6); *Sonata No. 8* (L 756). See also Collections: Landowska (V LM 1217).

*Sonata for Piano No. 1 in C (K. 279). Kraus, HS 127 (*Sonatas Nos. 2, 16; Rondo in A minor, K. 511).*

What is most bothersome about this performance is Kraus's rhythmic unsteadiness. She does not seem to be able, or to want, to hold a basic rhythm, and she overloads the melodic line with unnecessary contrivances. I would not call this a successful performance, nor is the recorded sound nearly as good as others in the Mozart series that Kraus has made for Haydn Society. The bass is too boomy, for one thing.

Sonatas for Piano Nos. 2 in F (K. 280), 4 in E flat (K. 282), and 6 in D (K. 284). Hambro, All 54.

Hambro, a fine pianist, does not seem to have too much affinity for these sonatas. His performance is accurate and businesslike, but he could just as well be reading them off. The recording is not of the best quality, and the copy I played had some strange scraping noises. Nevertheless, I prefer Hambro's approach to the gilded-lily presentation of Kraus, who has recorded No. 2 on HS 127, No. 4 on HS 121, and No. 6 on HS 124. Kraus drags the music, imposing her own personality on it, and her fingerwork is not invariably of the crispest. Nos. 4 and 6 are good recordings, tonally; No. 2 has a boomy bass that cannot be equalized out.

*Sonatas for Piano Nos. 3 in B flat (K. 281) and 5 in G (K. 283). Blancard, L 529 (*Sonatas Nos. 15, 16).*

For the most part, this is unaffected, flowing playing. Blancard has a light touch and a sensitive musical outlook. Once in a while she uses a romantic rubato that is a bit unstylistic, though applied with the best of taste. Her treatment of the appoggiaturas is unconventional and not very scholarly. London has supplied a singing piano sound. Kraus has recorded No. 3 on HS 126 and No. 5 on HS 121. Neither of these performances has the gracious quality that Blancard brings, and in the slow movement of K. 283 Kraus is inexcusably affected.

*Sonata for Piano No. 8 in A minor (K. 310). Lipatti, C 4633 (*Bach: Partita No. 1; Chorale Preludes). Gulda, L 756 (*Rondo in D; Bach: English Suite in G minor; Prelude and Fugue in E flat minor).*

Lipatti displays poise, serenity, and more inner strength than Gulda, who tinkles prettily through this intense sonata without once ruffling the surface. Gulda's liquid performance of the *Rondo in D* is more in keeping with the nature of the music. Lipatti's performance of the sonata is much the better, and the recorded sound is colorful. People who heard him in Europe tell me that this disc gives a good idea of his tone. Kraus, who has recorded the sonata on Vox 6310, is a little too mannered for my taste (she does better in the complete version for Haydn Society); and the noisy surface of the Vox disc is an added deterrent.

*Sonata for Piano No. 9 in D (K. 311). Kraus, HS 126 (*Sonatas Nos. 3, 11; Fantasy in D minor, K. 397).*

A typical Kraus performance: broad layout, occasional sparkle, many mannerisms superimposed on the music. The hold-backs and hesitancies in the slow movement would be unstylistic in any music. I am afraid that Kraus is not a very subtle pianist these days. Fairly clear recording, though the bass is not as firm as it should be.

*Sonata for Piano No. 10 in C (K. 330). Dumont, CH 1115 (*Sonata No. 17; Fantasy in D minor). Balsam, CH 1116 (*Piano Concerto No. 13).*

Concert Hall is in competition with itself here. The Dumont disc will fill most needs. It is a clear recording and a lively performance. Dumont has sharp execution and keeps the patterns clear. Fine piano-playing as well as fine Mozart-playing. Balsam also enjoys good recorded sound. His accurate performance is slightly marred by some idiosyncrasies in the slow movement. I would keep away from a superficial version by Boynet on 10" Vox 6400. Kraus has a good performance on HS 121, but it is accompanied by questionable versions of *Sonatas Nos. 4* and *5*.

*Sonata for Piano No. 11 in A (K. 331). Badura-Skoda, W 5317 (*Fantasy in C minor, K. 475; Sonata No. 14). Hambro, Rem 199–135 (*Haydn: Sonatas in D and E flat). Kraus, Vox 6310 (*Sonata No. 8).*

This is the popular "Turkish March" Sonata, so named because of the *Rondo alla Turca* finale. Badura-Skoda gets the most singing quality. His performance is slightly affected, but not annoyingly so; and in the "Turkish March" he really achieves an unhurried, marchlike quality. Hambro is musical, direct, and not very imaginative. His steadiness and clear articulation, however, make the playing enjoyable. Remington's recording here is lifelike, but the surfaces are high. Kraus romanticizes the music.

Some listeners like her approach. I find that after a while it becomes more mannerism than manner. In any case, one objective mark against the Vox is a thick-sounding piano tone coupled to much surface noise. The Kraus performance on HS 126 *(*Sonatas 3, 9)* is impossible to recommend.

*Sonata for Piano No. 12 in F (K. 332). Horowitz, V LM 1027 (*Beethoven: Sonata No. 14). Kraus, Vox 7040 (*Sonata No. 17).*

It's Kraus who is the romanticist here. Horowitz is determined to be a good boy and avoid excess of any kind. He succeeds, even if some of the dynamics are a bit outsized. I prefer Horowitz's performance to that of the less disciplined Kraus. The Victor disc has a better piano sound, too: clear and ringing. This, by the way, is one of the more popular sonatas, frequently encountered in the concert hall. A more recent version by Kraus, on HS 123 *(*Sonata No. 17)*, enjoys fine recorded sound, but is essentially the same type of performance as that found on the Vox disc.

*Sonata for Piano No. 13 in B flat (K. 333). Kraus, HS 122 (*Sonata No. 15; Allegro in G minor, K. 312; Variations in E flat, K. 353).*

This disc supersedes Kraus's performance on D 8523. The latter is an LP transfer with prominent surfaces, nowhere comparable to the modern Haydn Society recording, with its bright tone and feeling of presence. Kraus presents a broad performance that has warmth without eccentricity; and the singing line she displays in the slow movement is something that has not been common in her post-war discs. A version by Dumont on CH 25 is pitched almost a semitone flat in the first movement, and only this sonata is present on the disc. Kraus is by far the preferable buy.

*Sonata for Piano No. 14 in C minor (K. 457). Badura-Skoda, W 5317 (*Fantasy in C minor, K. 475; Sonata No. 11). Gieseking, C 4772 (*Sonata No. 15; Schumann: Carnaval). Firkusny, C 4356 (*Fantasy in C minor, K. 475; Fantasy in C minor, K. 396).*

In both the Badura-Skoda and Firkusny versions, the sonata is preceded by the *C minor Fantasy* (K. 475). We don't know if Mozart intended them to go together, but emotionally the two pieces fit, and there is evidence to show that Mozart himself coupled the works in performance. Gieseking is undoubtedly the most mature of the three pianists, but his version has several drawbacks. One is the omission of the *Fantasy;* another is a dated quality of sound; a third involves some strange goings-on in the slow movement (specifically, measure 12, if anybody is interested). Gieseking's latest recording of the sonata, in the eleven-disc album (see *Piano Music*, An 3511 K), is much better in every aspect. Badura-Skoda's recording is the most lifelike, and he gets a good element of drama into his playing. I find his ideas very interesting. Firkusny's approach is considerably more polished (though not necessarily better). His limpid performance is certainly worth having; and he includes the seldom-played, utterly magnificent *C minor Fantasy* (K. 396). Kraus's performance on HS 124 *(*Sonata No. 6)* lacks the evenness of the other versions.

*Sonata for Piano No. 15 in C (K. 545). Blancard, L 529 (*Sonatas Nos. 3, 5, 16). Kraus, HS 122 (*Sonata No. 13; Allegro in G minor, K. 312; Variations in E flat, K. 353). Gieseking, C 4772 (*Schumann: Carnaval).*

To my way of thinking, this is one of the Gieseking Mozart recordings which is almost entirely devoid of charm. He made it in France shortly after the war, and it may be that he had other things on his mind. Naturally the playing is accomplished, but Gieseking's particular style and magic are missing. The recorded sound is thick and noisy, with a heavy bass. Blancard's performance is tasteful, simple, and clear. It is a much better example of piano sound and, all things considered, the best choice for this sonata. The Kraus disc has a few romantic mannerisms in the way of retards and expressive devices, especially in the G minor section of the slow movement. Nor am I enamored of her heavy approach to the *E flat Variations*. She has the most lifelike quality of recorded sound. The London disc is a mellow recording, however.

*Sonata for Piano No. 16 in B flat (K. 570). Kirkpatrick, Bar 912 (*Suite in C, K. 399; Fantasy and Fugue in C, K. 394). Blancard, L 529 (*Sonatas Nos. 3, 5, 15). Epstein, SPA 6 (*Fantasy and Fugue in C, K. 394; Minuet in D, K. 355; Rondo in D, K. 485; Variations: "Salve Tu Domine," K. 398).*

Blancard plays a modern grand. Kirkpatrick and Epstein play a reconstruction of an eighteenth-century piano, with scaled-down, looser action. Kirkpatrick has more strength (inner strength; it does not involve brawn or dynamics) than the two ladies. His exact, rhythmic interpretation keeps the music constantly interesting. Epstein is less assertive, but quite musical and technically competent. Blancard, as always, is sensitive and artistic.

Both Kirkpatrick and Epstein have some uncommonly interesting short Mozart works on their discs. Kirkpatrick plays the *Suite in C,* a work composed in the manner of Handel, but with intense, almost passionate, harmonies that belong to Mozart alone. Listen carefully, and you will hear some whispering just before Kirkpatrick starts the *Fantasy and Fugue.* This is an explosive work with some clashing harmonies. It would be interesting to learn whether or not Mozart was acquainted with Bach's "*Chromatic Fantasy*"; the *Fantasy and Fugue* has much in common with the earlier work. Epstein also plays the *Fantasy and Fugue,* though without the concentration that Kirkpatrick applies to it. The elaborate "*Salve Tu*" *Variations* are of interest; and the wistful *Minuet in D* is a tiny masterpiece. The popular *Rondo in D* is expertly played. Some extraneous noises are present; and, unless my ears deceive me, Epstein—or someone else—faintly hums parts of the minuet.

*Sonata for Piano No. 17 in D (K. 576). Dumont, CH 1115 (*Sonata No. 10; Fantasy in D minor, K. 397). Kraus, HS 123 (*Sonata No. 12; Ten Variations, K. 460; Adagio in C minor, K. 396).*

Dumont's is a good recording and a better performance. Her pianism is direct and simply stated, backed by admirable articulation. Kraus's Haydn Society recording supersedes an earlier one on Vox 7040. The new one has a clearer sound, but the two are alike in lack of volatility and an alarmingly sentimental approach toward the F sharp minor section of the slow movement. This sonata is nothing if not volatile. Its scampering measures (first and last movements, anyway; the slow movement is touched with tragedy) are popular in the concert hall. Only four or five Mozart sonatas get much play from the professionals these days. On her disc Dumont is also heard in the *D minor Fantasy,* one of the Mozart pieces every young piano student gets. She handles the assignment with quality and assurance.

*Sonata for Piano in F (K. 533). Badura-Skoda, W 5153 (on Mozart piano) and 5154 (on modern piano) (*Adagio in B minor, K. 540; Rondo in D, K. 485; Fantasy and Fugue in C, K. 394). Rosen, REB 5 (*Gigue in G, K. 574; Rondo in A minor, K. 511; Suite in the Style of Handel, K. 399).*

Strictly speaking, this sonata should be listed as K. 494-K. 533. The Rondo (K. 494) came first; later Mozart tacked on an Allegro and Andante (K. 533) to precede the Rondo. The work, however, is generally recognized as K. 533. It is not numbered in the sequence of sonatas, though, to be logical, it should be called No. 18. On W 5153, Badura-Skoda plays the sonata (and the other works) on a reconstruction of a 1785 instrument, complete with lowered pitch. On W 5154 the same pieces are played on a modern concert grand. This is an interesting idea, and those who can afford it should get both discs. Those who are willing to be content with one should get the modern version, which has extraordinary clarity of sound. The performance is tasteful and intimate. K. 533 is a remarkable sonata, with more polyphony than any in the series. The *Fantasy and Fugue,* which Kirkpatrick and Epstein also play (see *Sonata No. 16*), is a moody, explosive masterpiece that Badura-Skoda does not carry off well. Both the *Adagio in B minor* and the *Rondo in D* are among Mozart's better-known piano pieces, and are nicely played here. Badura-Skoda plays the sonata more smoothly than Rosen, and the Westminster disc has superior sound. Rosen has some interesting pieces for his second side; but the *Suite in the Style of Handel* is available in a better performance by Kirkpatrick (see *Sonata No. 16*). The strange *Gigue in G* almost carries the day for Rosen's disc. It is the only LP version at the time of writing (if we except the one in Gieseking's eleven-disc Angel set), and is decidedly worth owning.

Sonatas for Piano Four Hands Nos. 1 in G (K. 357), 2 in B flat (K. 358), and 3 in D (K. 381). Badura-Skoda, Demus, W 5060.

Unlike the fourth and fifth of the four-hand sonatas, these three are light, charming in content, and easy to play. The one in G (K. 357) is a rarity, not included in the standard Peters edition of Mozart's four-hand music. It is a two-movement fragment, the second movement of which contains a glorious romantic theme. Also present is some amusing byplay: Mozart stops and starts abruptly, purposely trying to throw the players off balance. These are nice, easygoing performances from Badura-Skoda and Demus, who think alike on the important particulars. Good recording, a little over-reverberant on the bass end. Vronsky and Babin have recorded Nos. 2 and 3 on C 4667. They benefit from a better quality of sound, but their interpretation does not have much sparkle, and some of their tempos are much over-deliberate.

Sonatas for Piano Four Hands Nos. 4 in F (K. 497) and 5 in C (K. 521). Badura-Skoda, Demus, W 5082.

Duettists know these; not many others do. The F major is a masterpiece, from the brooding introduction to the last chord.

None of the solo piano sonatas, not even the C minor, can approach it. The C major is also a brilliant, large-scale work for four hands. Badura-Skoda and Demus offer a well-bred performance. They do not penetrate deeply into the F major, which has more than they bring out. But their pleasant, lyric approach and their smooth pianism are always enjoyable. This is a more than merely adequate introduction to a pair of superb works. Fair recording that lacks the "presence" it might have.

*Sonata for Two Pianos in D (K. 448). Badura-Skoda and Demus, W 5069 (*Andante and Variations in G; Bach, J. C.: Sonata in G). Luboshutz and Nemenoff, Rem 199-147 (*Saint-Saëns: Variations on a Theme by Beethoven; Debussy: Lindaraja; Falla: Ritual Fire Dance).*

The two young Viennese pianists play with nicely co-ordinated ensemble. They don't try to impress; they go about the music as though they are having a good time. The result is a relaxed performance, with leisurely tempos, and plenty of tradition behind it. Very fine. Luboshutz and Nemenoff play expertly, but their recording has harsher sound, and the other pieces on the disc do not have as much interest as the works Badura-Skoda and Demus have included. (The Westminster is worth owning for the adorable *G major Variations* alone.) José and Amparo Iturbi have recorded the sonata on V LM 1135. Touches of Iturbi's old magic occasionally come up, but on the whole this brittle performance has little to recommend.

Sonatas for Violin and Piano Nos. 18 in G (K. 301), 21 in E minor (K. 304), 26 in B flat (K. 378), and 27 in G (K. 379). De Klijn, Heksch, Ep 3034.

Heksch uses a reconstruction of the Stein piano on which Mozart played. These four sonatas are among the most popular, and best, of Mozart's works in this form, and the disc is as good an introduction to the sonatas as you could desire. De Klijn is a most accurate violinist. His tone does not have much color—it is, indeed, rather steely—but his intonation and musicianship are impeccable. Both artists keep good rhythm, play with spirit, and know how to shape a phrase. Excellent recorded sound. The Mozart piano, incidentally, is considerably closer to Mozart's intentions than the harpsichord Kirkpatrick uses on his discs.

Sonatas for Violin and Piano Nos. 17 in C (K. 296), 25 in F (K. 377), 26 in B flat (K. 378), 27 in G (K. 379), 28 in E flat (K. 380), and 33 in E flat (K. 481). Goldberg, Kraus, D DX 103 [3].

These discs, originally shellacs, go back years, but the sound is not bad at all (except for No. 27, which is inferior all the way around). Naturally one cannot expect the realism encountered in a modern violin-piano recording. Famous interpretations in their day, these discs hold their vitality. Both artists express considerable character in their playing. The sonatas emerge with warmth, instrumental finesse, and expert planning. Goldberg and Kraus keep things moving; no pauses for "expression" here. The set is decidedly worth owning.

Sonatas for Violin and Piano Nos. 17 in C (K. 296), 21 in E minor (K. 304), and 18 in G (K. 301), W 5130. Nos. 25 in F (K. 377), 22 in A (K. 305), Sonata in E flat (K. 58), W 5145. Nos. 27 in G (K. 379) and 32 in B flat (K. 454), W 5109. All played by Barylli and Badura-Skoda.

On these three discs the performances are invariably cultured. Barylli and Badura-Skoda have an element of graciousness missing from many of the other discs of Mozart violin sonatas. They never rush, and they lovingly curve a melodic line. One could easily imagine a better tone and a smoother technique than Barylli shows; but he makes music so agreeably that one gladly overlooks his deficiencies as a solo instrumentalist. Splendid recorded sound. The *E.flat Sonata* on W 5145 is a spurious work now listed as K. anh. 209 f in Einstein's revision of the Köchel catalogue.

Sonatas for Violin and Piano Nos. 17 in C (K. 296), 26 in B flat (K. 378), 27 in G (K. 379), 19 in E flat (K. 302), and 23 in D (K. 306), C SL 152 [2]. *Nos. 22 in A (K. 305), 24 in F (K. 376), and No. 34 in A (K. 526), C 4617. All played by Schneider and Kirkpatrick.*

Kirkpatrick plays the harpsichord on these three discs. Mozart composed these sonatas for piano and violin, not harpsichord and violin. It can be said, in partial extenuation of Kirkpatrick, that the piano was not in universal use in the 1780's, and that the sonatas often *were* played on the harpsichord in those days. Schneider and Kirkpatrick, old partners, work very well together. They play the music with considerable propulsion, style, and knowledge. Not much grace or aristocracy is present, however. Schneider's tone often sounds harsh, and in a few double-stopped passages he sounds as though he is tearing his fiddle apart. The emphasis here is not on tone, but on rhythm and clear-cut patterns. In C 4617 the numbers of the sonatas are given on the record label as 1, 7, and 17. These numbers are incorrect; they pertain to the placement of the sonatas in the Peters edition. The correct numbers are given above.

Sonatas for Violin and Piano Nos. 21 in E minor (K. 304), 26 in B flat (K. 378), and 33 in E flat (K. 481). Langbein, Jones, L 1069.

Suave, smooth playing, and fine partnership between violinist and pianist. So far, so good; but why the textual variants that Langbein introduces? In one or two cases he plays different notes from those Mozart wrote. These points aside, the performances have considerable validity, and the disc can gratefully be admitted into the Mozart violin-sonata discography. Excellent sound save for a slight "wow" that occasionally appears in the piano tone.

Sonatas for Violin and Piano (individual).

Several recordings of individual sonatas are worth mentioning. Heifetz and Bay, on V LM 1022 (*Beethoven: *Sonata No. 5 in F*), play No. 17 in C (K. 296; mislabeled on the record as No. 8) with inevitable smoothness. Heifetz is sweet without being cloying, and his work here is irresistible. The recording has a somewhat dated sound, but it is clear enough and the balance with piano is excellent. Stern and Zakin, on C 4301 (*Haydn: *Concerto in C*), play No. 26 in B flat (K. 378) crisply. It is a beautiful performance save for a tendency to press too hard. Just a little more relaxation and breathing-space were needed. Menuhin and Kentner are heard in No. 32 in B flat (K. 454) on V HMV 1053 (*Beethoven: *Sonata No. 5 in F*). The violinist is sweet, sentimental, and rather lacking in rhythmic impetus. His record mislabels the work as No. 40. The same sonata (No. 32 in B flat) is played by Grinke and Taylor on L 739, along with the *Sonata No. 34 in A* (K. 526). Less emphasis on tone is present, and there is more spirit to the playing. The mellow-sounding recording is up to London's best.

*Trio for Clarinet, Viola, and Piano in E flat (K. 498). Kell, Fuchs, Horszowski, D 9543 (*Beethoven: Clarinet Trio). Brody, Lifshey, Arnold, Ox 106 (*Haydn: Flute Sonata). Forrest, Cooley, Balogh, Ly 9 (*Brahms: Clarinet Trio).*

The Decca musicians play this melting work with enormous nuance. Kell actually gets a viola-like timbre that winds around Fuch's tone like morning glories around a trellis. Some purists might call this performance effeminate, and they might have a point. But the beauty of the interpretation is incontestable. For no particular reason I enjoy Kell's clarinet-playing here as much as I dislike it in the *Clarinet Quintet.* Decca's recording is not easy to reproduce, what with an occasional tonal shatter and poor surfaces. The Oxford has a much finer quality of recorded sound, and the musicians do a rattling good job. Yet the Decca has something special in the way of artistry which makes it unique, bad recording and all. The Lyrichord is a steady performance, well recorded, but (like the Oxford) it does not approximate the subtlety of the interpretation that Kell & Co. offer.

Trios for Piano and Strings (6, complete). Fournier, Janigro, Badura-Skoda, W 5242, 5267, and 5284. Aitay, Starker, Jambor, Per 524 [3]. *Trio di Bolzano, Vox 8493* [3].

Work-by-work comparison between the Westminster and Period recordings gives the edge to the former. Westminster's superior recorded sound will mean a lot to people with high-fidelity equipment. The Period is lower-level, with some gritty surfaces and a lack of instrumental color. Musically, I prefer the choice of tempos in the Westminster discs. The finale of the last movement of the *Trio No. 1* is a case in point. Mozart has marked it *allegretto.* It goes at a good *allegro* clip as played by the Aitay group; by adhering to Mozart's own indication, the Fournier ensemble sounds much more elegant. Generally, throughout the six trios, the Westminster tempos are slower, even very much slower. (But it must be said that in at least one instance, the opening of No. 4, the Period musicians have more life.) Most listeners will find the Westminster discs the best choice for the music. The Trio di Bolzano, which not only plays the six trios on its discs but also throws in the *Clarinet Trio* (K. 498), lacks the smooth finish of the other versions, mostly because of the limitations of the violinist. Available separately, the Westminster discs are coupled as follows: Nos. 1 in G (K. 496) and 2 in B flat (K. 502) on W 5242; Nos. 3 in E (K. 542) and 4 in C (K. 548) on W 5267; Nos. 5 in G (K. 564) and 6 in B flat (K. 254) on W 5284.

*Variations on "Unser dummer Pöbl meint" (K. 455). Seemann, D 9568 (*Concerto No. 25).*

This piece is a filler on the concerto disc. It is worth knowing. Mozart took the theme from a Gluck opera (and later Tchaikovsky used the Mozart theme for his *Mozartiana*). The melodious, ingenious music is typical of Mozart at his most *galant.* Seemann, a fine artist, gives the music a knowledgeable performance. Low-level, but perfectly satisfactory piano sound.

MUSSORGSKY, MODEST (1839-1881)

*Pictures at an Exhibition. Horowitz, V LM 1014. Uninsky, Ep 3066 (*Liszt: Rhapsodie Espagnole; 3 Paganini Études). Katchen, L 330. Pennario, 10" Cap 8266.*

All except Horowitz play the music as Mussorgsky wrote it. Horowitz, believing that the original is not very pianistic (and how right he is!), has touched it up. The results are mildly stupendous. Horowitz, who has the deepest sonority of any pianist before the public, actually gets orchestral effects from his instrument. Before his kind of authority all other versions pale. Purists who want the original can turn to Uninsky, who, despite recording that makes his tone sound tinny, plays the work with breadth and power. He has a more solid grasp of the material than either Katchen or Pennario. Of the latter two, Katchen is to be preferred. Pennario plays brightly but superficially.

NIELSEN, CARL (1865-1931)

Chaconne (Op. 32). Ellegard, 10" L 9065 (Liszt: La Campanella; Liebestraum No. 3).

Is all of Nielsen's piano music as interesting? This piece has considerable imagination and harmonic ingenuity, with a couple of faint suggestions of the Grieg *Ballade.* It was composed in 1916. Ellegard turns in an efficient performance. The Liszt pieces are also capably played, but scarcely more than routine. Surely music more pertinent to the Nielsen piece could have been found to place on the reverse.

*Commotio (Op. 58). Fjelrad, L 1030 (*Motets).*

Nielsen composed this long work for organ a few months before his death in 1931. In one movement, it has four sections, two of them fugal. The writing is very individual, with a basically romantic personality peering through the dissonances. Fjelrad's performance sounds excellent. His registrations are tasteful, he keeps a steady rhythm, and he molds a phrase with artistry. He plays a heavy-sounding organ, but the recording has managed to maintain clarity of texture without excess reverberation.

*Quintet for Winds (Op. 43). Copenhagen Wind Quintet, L 734 (*Bozza: Variations on a Free Theme; Ibert: Trois Pièces brèves). New Art Wind Quintet, CE 2001 (*Françaix: Wind Quintet).*

Seldom heard, this is a work with plenty of character and some unexpected melodic twists. Nielsen uses old forms to a certain extent (minuet, praeludium, *etc.*), but there is nothing neo-classic about the writing. The music is worth looking into; it stands up well on repeated hearings. Of the two recordings I prefer the London for its clearer instrumental definition, though you won't go wrong with the Classic disc. I also prefer the London coupling. The Françaix quintet can get pretty boring after you've heard it a couple of times.

NIN, JOAQUIN (1879-)

Chants d'Espagne. See Falla: *Suite populaire Espagnole* (CH 1175).

PAGANINI, NICOLO (1782-1840)

Caprices (Op. 1). Ricci, L 264 and 252. Rabin, 10" C 2168.

In their original form the *Caprices* were written for unaccompanied violin. Ricci and Rabin so play them. Ricci is heard in the entire set of twenty-four on his two discs; Rabin plays eleven. The former accomplishes some remarkable things in the way of multiple stopping, staccato attack, and gymnastics in general. It is real virtuoso playing. And yet Ricci's intonation is not invariably pure. One also feels the tremendous strain under which he is operating. Those who want a one-disc introduction to the *Caprices* are referred to Rabin, who is amazingly deft and assured. He was in his teens when he made the disc. On C 4219, Francescatti plays eight of the *Caprices* with piano accompaniments supplied by Mario Pilati and played by Artur Balsam. Brilliant playing here; but you might as well get the original versions for unaccompanied violin. The reverse of Francescatti's disc is devoted to Kreisler favorites: material that hardly goes with the athletics of Paganini.

*Quartet for Strings in E. Stuyvesant, Ph 107 (*Kreisler: Quartet in A minor).*

Two of the great violinists of all time are represented by chamber music on this disc. The Paganini is his only work in the form (he composed several quartets for guitar and strings). It is pretty tame. The staccato bowing in sections of the finale is strongly reminiscent of those in the *D major Concerto;* it is about the only place in the quartet where the devil shows his horns. Kreisler's quartet, composed in 1949, is salon-ish and sentimental, graceful and superficial. The Stuyvesant presents excellent performances that have been well recorded.

La Streghe; Fantasia on the G string; Moto Perpetuo; Variations on "Nel cor più mi sento"; Variations on "God Save the Queen"; La Campanella; Sonata in E minor; I Palpiti. Ricci, Persinger, L 1005.

Most of these pieces have been out of the repertoire for years. It is pretty terrible music, but, then again, it doesn't pretend to be much more than a stunt for the violin. And, given the proper violinist, the pieces can be a lot of fun. Ricci is the proper violinist. He goes up and down the scale in a grand sweep, nothing bothers him, and he turns in some hair-raising feats. The only thing that keeps him from perfection is intonation that once in a while is flawed. London's recording is exceptionally realistic.

PALMER, ROBERT (1915-)

Quartet for Piano and Strings (1947). See Harris: *Sonata for Violin* (C 4842).

PERGOLESI, GIOVANNI (1710-1736)

Violin Sonata No. 12. See Collections: Milstein (Cap 8259).

PERSICHETTI, VINCENT (1915-)

Pastorale for Winds (Op. 21). See Collections: New Art Wind Quintet (CE 2003).

PETER, JOHANN FRIEDRICH (1746-1813)

Quintets for Strings (6). Moravian Quintet, 10" NR 2013/14/15 [3].

Peters was a minister-musician who came to this country from Europe in 1770. He wrote these six quintets in Winston-Salem in

1789. They are innocent and naive and completely unimportant, though the second movement of No. 2 has its lyric moments. The Moravian Quintet has no relation to the Pennsylvania sect; they are good Local 802 members who got together under this name for the recording session. They play very well, too, and the recording is excellent.

PHILLIPS, BURRILL (1907-)

Sonata for Cello. See Swanson: *Suite for Cello and Piano* (SPA 54).

PISTON, WALTER (1894-)

*Quintet for Piano and Strings. Wild, Walden, WCFM 14 (*Martinů: Quartet No. 6).*

Few sturdier, better-written chamber-music works have been composed by an American. Piston, as usual, is a little reserved, and does not wear his heart on his sleeve, but this quintet has real quality. The Martinů quartet is eclectic, utterly professional, and without very personal characteristics. Sparked by the brilliant work of Earl Wild, the Walden Quartet gives a superb performance of the Piston work. They also do a first-class job on the Martinů. Excellent recorded sound.

Sonata for Violin and Piano. See Lopatnikoff: *Violin Sonata No. 2* (D 9541).

*Sonatina for Violin and Harpsichord. Schneider, Kirkpatrick, C 4495 (*Cage: String Quartet).*

One of the reasons why Piston is held in such high repute among his American colleagues can be seen in this attractive violin-harpsichord sonata, which is beautifully assembled, to the point, and full of interesting ideas. The performance sounds ideal. On the reverse of the disc Cage's *Quartet* is played by the New Music String Quartet. An extremely amusing thing about this enterprise is the program notes for the Cage work, which read like one of those fliers for an avant-garde art show. Cage's music is very, very advanced stuff. So far advanced is it that it may even leave music far behind.

Three Pieces for Flute, Clarinet, and Bassoon. See Collections: New Art Wind Quintet (CE 2003).

PORTER, QUINCY (1897-)

*Quartet for Strings No. 6. Pascal, An 35105 (*Roldán: Ritmica No. 1; Caturla: Cuban Suite No. 1).*

These three works were recorded during a series of concerts over the French radio. They were sponsored by the International Music Council of UNESCO. Porter's quartet is an example of smooth, sure writing that somehow lacks individuality. Caturla and Roldán were Cuban composers who died around 1940. Caturla's suite is scored for eight wind instruments and piano; the Roldán calls for wind quintet and piano. Both works are strongly nationalistic, with a dissonant cosmopolitan style (mostly Boulanger-derived) superimposed on the Cuban themes and rhythms. The Pascal Quartet plays the Porter work with vigor and finesse. Musicians of the French radio system participate in the other works. They seem to have fun with the exotic writing. Beautifully resonant recorded sound.

POULENC, FRANÇOIS (1899-)

*Mouvements perpetuels; Eight Nocturnes. Johannesen, CH 1181 (*Fauré: Theme and Variations; Impromptu No. 3; Ballade for Piano and Orchestra).*

One hears the *Mouvements* often in concert, the *Nocturnes* less often. The latter are attractive, melodious sketches in varied mood, from flippant to serious. Johannesen plays them accurately. His work is a little reserved, but always in order. A touch of humor, of effervescence, of relaxation—these were needed to make his performance really distinguished. Good recorded sound; high surfaces. Poulenc himself can be heard playing the *Mouvements* (not very well); see *Suite Française* (C 4399).

Sextet for Piano and Winds; Trio for Piano, Oboe, and Horn; Sonata for Clarinet and Bassoon. Fairfield Chamber Group, REB 7.

*Sextet for Piano and Winds. Lurie, Fine Arts Ensemble, Cap 8258 (*Hindemith: Kleine Kammermusik). Françaix, Quintet of French National Radio Orchestra, An 35133 (*Françaix: Quintet for Winds).*

Listening to the works on the REB disc may give you the feeling you get while looking at the ads in a 1925 *Vanity Fair*. So smart then, so *à la mode;* and so dated today! But also so nostalgic! I admire these Poulenc pieces no end. The *Sextet* is the most ambitious work, and it has a juicy theme in the first movement that will just about melt the vinyl from the record. This dates from 1932–9. The 1926 *Trio* has wit and charm, and the *Clarinet-Bassoon Sonata* (1922) is a sassy little piece. Of the three recordings of the *Sextet*, the Capitol has the most realistic sound and greatest all-around brightness. I also like the performance best of all. Occasionally the French players on the Angel disc are more gracious, but they lack the snap, sparkle, and precision of the Hollywood group on the Capitol disc. Nor does the Fairfield group match the excitement that the Hollywood players bring to the music. But it can be said that all of the versions are certainly acceptable, by any standards; and, to complicate matters, the Fairfield Chamber Group has on its disc the only LP versions of the *Trio* and *Clarinet-Bassoon Sonata*, while on the Angel disc is the best LP performance of the Françaix *Quintet*. The only solution might be to get the three discs, pocketbook permitting. If it's the *Sextet* alone in which you are interested, I think that you will find the Capitol the best choice.

*Sonata for Piano Four Hands (1918). Gold and Fizdale, C 4854 (*Debussy: Épigraphes antiques; Milhaud: Concertino d'automne; Satie: En habit de cheval).*

This disc, available individually, is part of the three-disc set "Music for Two Pianos—1900–1952." For complete contents see Collections: Gold and Fizdale (C SL 198). The Poulenc is an early work, but contains most of the elements that went into the later ones. Nothing but praise can be given Gold and Fizdale for their well-integrated work. They play the music with considerable elegance, and adhere strictly to the rhythm. The latter may not sound like much praise, but it is surprising how easy it is to get off the rails in Poulenc. Ringing clarity to the recorded sound.

*Sonata for Violin and Piano (In Memory of García Lorca). Kaufman, Balsam, Cap 8063 (*Hindemith: Violin Sonata in D).*

Sections of the score have a grimmer quality than one associates with Poulenc. It is given a vigorous performance. Kaufman plays everything much the same way: big tone, heavy vibrato, not much subtlety, emphasis on the technical elements of the work. The disc is an early LP, without much color or depth, though there is no distortion.

*Suite Française; Mouvements perpetuels; Nocturne in D. Poulenc, C 4399 (*Satie: Piano Pieces).*

Poulenc is curiously uneven in his performances of this music. He sounds out of practice, and in the third *Mouvement* he drops notes all over the place. The pieces are very pretty, however; and a disc of a composer playing his own music always contains more than routine interest. Johannesen has also recorded the *Mouvements perpetuels* on CH 1181. His playing is more exact than Poulenc's, and the recorded sound is a trifle clearer.

*Trio for Trumpet, Trombone, and Horn. Glantz, Pulis, Berv, Str 605 (*Saint-Saëns: Septet).*

Composed in 1922, this trio is one of those impertinent pieces *Les Six* were madly turning out. It contains elements of music hall, the circus, jazz—everything that would be a shock to those brought up in the orthodox tradition. The performance here is excellent: properly rowdy, yet with the order inherent in the music. Bright, metallic recording sets off the brass very realistically.

PROKOFIEV, SERGE (1891-1953)

Music for Children (Op. 65). See Collections: Pressler (MGM 3010).

Overture on Hebrew Themes (Op. 34). See *Quintet for Winds and Strings* (D 8511 and Per 512).

*Quartet for Strings No. 1 (Op. 50). Guilet, MGM 3113 (*Shostakovich: Quartet No. 1).*

The year of composition was 1930. This is a typically vigorous and well-written work. Those who are responsive to Prokofiev's idiom should have a very good time with the *First Quartet*. It receives an excellent performance from the Guilet group, which plays with plenty of rhythmic ardor and with a lean type of tone that is a perfect vehicle for music like this. Very smooth recorded sound.

*Quartet for Strings No. 2 in F (Op. 92). Hollywood, Cap 8151 (*Hindemith: Quartet No. 3). Fine Arts, Mer 10045 (*Shostakovich: Trio in E minor).*

If you want to impress your friends, you can tell them that this work was composed on Kabardino-Balkarian themes. Composed with Prokofiev's immense technical security, the writing contains some exotic sounds, all kinds of rhythmic devices, and a heavy underlay of Mother Russia. It receives a magnificent performance by the brilliant Hollywood Quartet, a group that plays modern music as well as or better than anybody else in the business. The recording is top-notch—clear, well balanced, exceptionally "alive." No comparable sound is present in the Mercury disc, which dates back some years and which occasionally makes the Fine Arts Quartet sound like a string orchestra. The disparity in recording alone would be enough to make the Hollywood version the recommended one.

*Quintet for Winds and Strings (Op. 39). New York Ensemble, D 8511 (*Overture on Hebrew Themes; Swanson: Night Music). Goetgluck, etc., Per 512 (*Overture on Hebrew Themes).*

Three works on the Decca disc; two on the Period. But that is not the only reason to choose the Decca. For the *Quintet,* and for the *Overture on Hebrew Themes,* the New York Ensemble, some of whom are members of the New York Philharmonic, are directed by Dimitri Mitropoulos. He leads a typically energetic performance marked by his usual sympathy for modern music. The *Quintet,* scored for oboe, clarinet, violin, viola, and bass, is a six-movement, sardonic work, basically nationalistic, with a nod toward Stravinsky's *Sacre.* Dullish recorded sound on the Decca disc, and the copy I heard had several jumping grooves. Nevertheless, it is preferable to the Period version. Those players are less secure in their intonation, and the performance as a whole lacks verve. Prokofiev's adaptation for small orchestra of the *Overture on Hebrew Themes* is heard on the Period disc. The Decca presents the chamber score, written for piano, clarinet, and string quartet.

*Sonata for Cello and Piano in C (Op. 119). Kurtz, Balsam, C 4867 (Kodály: Sonata for Unaccompanied Cello). Piatigorsky, Berkowitz, V LM 1792 (*Bach: Sonata No. 2 in D).*

Toward the end of his career Prokofiev often wrote essentially elaborate salon pieces assembled with immense skill and authority. This is one of them, and its content is really very thin. Between these two performances there is little to choose. Both are under complete technical control; both are fine examples of recorded cello tone. Piatigorsky finds a few things that Kurtz either misses or does not care to bring out. I would select the Victor disc, but the choice is purely arbitrary.

*Sonata for Piano No. 2 in D minor (Op. 14). Gilels, CH 1311 (*Glazunov: Sonata No. 2 in E minor; Tchaikovsky: Three Pieces).*

Gilels, on the evidence of a few recordings, would appear to be a major pianist. Certainly he is a supreme virtuoso. His Prokofiev has a big sweep, absolute pianistic security, and an identification with the musical elements. In the second movement his work suggests that of Horowitz, and not to Gilels's disadvantage, either. He has the iron fingers needed for music like this, and the rhythmic propulsion to keep it moving along. He also gives a grand performance of the big, empty post-romantic sonata by Glazunov, piling heartily into the massive writing with thrilling effect. The three Tchaikovsky pieces are from Op. 19; they are named *Scherzo humoristique, Nocturne,* and *Capriccio.* Stravinsky used part of the *Nocturne* for his *Baiser de la fée.* Gilels deftly handles the salon-like music. The Russian-made recording—at least, the tapes emanated from Russia—lacks definition and is a rather dull-sounding affair, but the piano-playing makes one gladly overlook tonal deficiencies.

Sonatas for Piano Nos. 2 in D minor (Op. 14) and 5 in C (Op. 38), L 553. Nos. 3 in A minor (Op. 28), 4 in C minor (Op. 29), and 8 in B flat (Op. 84), L 748. Nos. 6 in A (Op. 82) and 7 in B flat (Op. 83), L 902. All played by Robert Cornman.

Seven of the eight piano sonatas by Prokofiev are on these three discs. Nos. 2 and 5 are seldom played in concert. No particular reason why; they are just as good as the others. Cornman makes a brave attempt, but only hints at the force and electrical rhythm of the music. His small-scaled playing is too weak for the task at hand; and his technique, while accurate, does not have the steel to etch Prokofiev's patterns. A better performance of No. 3 is played by Weissenberg on 10" C 2099, along with a brilliantly played *Suggestion diabolique* and several Scriabin pieces. On CE 1032, Di Bonaventura comes closer than Cornman to the heart of *Sonata No. 8.* Di Bonaventura's is not by any means a finished conception, but his playing has so much more vitality that it is preferable, even taking into allowance the fact that Cornman has three sonatas on his disc.

Sonata for Piano No. 6 in A (Op. 82); Visions fugitives (Op. 22). Pennario, Cap 8113.

Pennario has a facile technique, but his tone is percussive and he plays with more force than poise. Not much organization is present in his breathless, impulsive attack. The recording, one of Capitol's early LP's, has a glassy sound that is hard to control. Pennario is more successful in the twenty short *Visions fugitives,* those skillful little prelude-like sketches. But the best version on LP of the *Visions* is played by Francois on An 35045 *(*Piano*

Concerto No. 3). His mechanism is more erratic than Pennario's, but he is more successful in conveying the wit and whimsy of the pieces. When will Victor bring out as a collector's reissue the recording of nine of the *Visions fugitives* which Prokofiev himself made in the 1930's?

*Sonata for Piano No. 7 in B flat (Op. 83). Horowitz, V LM 1016 (*Kabalevsky: Sonata No. 3).*

Here is *the* recording of a Prokofiev piano sonata. It is one of Horowitz's specialties. Nobody plays it quite as he does. Nobody can, because Horowitz can achieve a type of sonority unmatched today (and possibly at any time in the history of piano-playing). His ability to maintain tensile force is ideal for age-of-steel music like this, and he builds the toccata-like finale to a shattering climax. The recording was originally released in 1946. Its transfer to LP has been entirely successful. No tonal shatter is encountered, even in the biggest moments of the finale, and Horowitz's tone comes through with almost concert-hall brilliance.

*Sonata for Violin and Piano in D (Op. 94). Ricci, Bussotti, L 770 (*Strauss: Violin Sonata). Szigeti, Hambro, C 4257 (*Violin Sonata in F minor). Stern, Zakin, C 4734 (*Violin Sonata in F minor).*

Ricci has the most lyric approach to this sonata, which is one of Prokofiev's most songful pieces. Needless to say, Ricci also has the technical strength to do complete justice to the music. Some listeners may be attracted by the more logical couplings of the other versions. If so, the Szigeti is recommended. Stern is too unrelaxed in his approach. Certainly the second movement has more grace than he even begins to convey. Szigeti has made this work one of his specialties, and he plays it with complete understanding. This sonata was originally composed for flute and piano. It can so be heard on Bos 208, played by Dwyer and Sanromá. The music does not sound as convincing as a flute work: or is this opinion the result of conditioning? I can conceive of better performances. If Dwyer were a singer, I would say that her voice lacks focus. But her musical approach is spirited and competent, and the disc, with Roussel's *Flute Trio* on the reverse, is an interesting novelty.

*Sonata for Violin and Piano in F minor (Op. 80). Oistrakh, Oborin, Van 6019 (*Franck: Violin Sonata). Szigeti, Levine, C 4257 (*Violin Sonata in D). Stern, Zakin, C 4734 (*Violin Sonata in D).*

Russian-made tapes are variable. This one from which Vanguard worked has good violin sound and a somewhat tubby quality to the piano. Nothing really bad, however. Oistrakh's performance has more virility than the competing LP versions. His playing has bravura sweep, musical intensity, and complete identification with the idiom. Stern tries to overpower the music. He is all muscle, and lacks the warmth that Oistrakh brings. Szigeti has knowledge and all the musicianship in the world, but technically and tonally he is not in Oistrakh's class. A version by Menuhin and Gazelle on V LM 1087 is weak and lacks profile.

*Sonata for Two Violins (Op. 56). Persinger, Eidus, 10" Str 1001 (*Mozart: Duo No. 1).*

A noncommittal piece. It doesn't say much; and, in all truth, there does not appear to be very much behind the impeccable workmanship. Persinger and Eidus fiddle manfully, playing with plenty of rhythm and violinistic solidity. The recording is rather thin and harsh.

*Tales of the Old Grandmother (Op. 31); Four Pieces (Op. 32). Foldes, Vox 6590 (*Piano Concerto No. 1).*

The *Tales* are pleasant pieces in folk idiom. The *Four Pieces* are based on old dance forms, and the set contains a minuet strongly suggestive of sections of the *Classical Symphony.* Foldes plays this kind of music very well. He brings to it an incisive quality. Everything is sharp, well organized, impeccably fingered. The recording is an early LP, thick in sound, with a heavy bass and prominent surfaces. A good amplifier can control it, however.

Visions fugitives. See *Piano Sonata No. 6* (Cap 8113).

PURCELL, HENRY (1659-1695)

Pavane and Chacony. See Collections: New Music String Quartet (Bar 913).

Suites for Harpsichord, Nos. 1-8. Nef, OL 50011.

Each of these short suites consists of dance movements *(Allmand, Corant, Hornpipe,* etc.). Purcell composed little harpsichord music; this disc contains about half his output. Some fine things are here. Remember, Bach was ten years old at the time of Purcell's death. At that, the Prelude to the *Suite No. 8* sounds very much like a short Bach toccata. Nef plays this music without much imagination or flexibility. Her approach is rather plodding, relieved by a few (fortunately a very few) unstylistic romanticisms in the way of rubatos and retards. The music has more life than Nef suggests. What happened in the *Corant* of No. 7? As in the other suites, Nef takes all the repeats and second endings, but here she repeats each section *three* times. Should there have been a tape snip?

Trio Sonatas (1697). Ciompi, Torkanowsky, Koutzen, Chessid, Per 572.

Seven *Trio Sonatas* are presented, including the famous *"Golden" Sonata.* They are taken from a set of ten published in 1697. This music will not appeal to all tastes. It has a delicate modal flavor, and many will find the workmanship restricted or monotonous. The writing is very British in its turn of phrase, though one needs a certain acquaintance with early English music to note the parallels. Three strings and a harpsichord continuo are heard in this recording. The performance sounds excellent. A quiet, intimate, and unostentatious approach is adopted; the players exhibit fine ensemble; and they play in perfect tune. Good recorded tone and balance.

RACHMANINOFF, SERGEI (1873-1943)

Études-Tableaux (Op. 39). Thew, RS 3.

About the best that can be said for this disc is that it presents some seldom-heard music. Otherwise, the pianist is not ready for this type of virtuosity, and the recording is submarginal in sound. There are nine in this set. For the Op. 33 set of the eight *Etudes-Tableaux*, see *Sonata for Piano No. 2* (RS 1).

Piano Pieces (miscellaneous). See Collections: Keene (Mer 10113); Rachmaninoff (V LCT 1136).

Piano Pieces (Op. 3, 10); Polka de W. R. Reisenberg, W 5344.

Among the favorites in these two sets are the *Prelude in C sharp minor, Polichinelle, Sérénade,* and *Humoresque.* The *Polka de W. R.* also is a pleasant trifle. All of these performances are worth hearing. Reisenberg is a good technician and a musicianly artist. She plays the music in a manner that suggests its emotion without overdoing it. Clear recorded sound. If you collect Rachmaninoff, don't miss this disc (and especially don't overlook V LCT 1136, where Rachmaninoff himself plays a large selection of his own pieces, including several contained on the Westminster disc; see under Collections for a discussion).

Preludes for Piano (24). Lympany, L 328/9 [2].

Among others in this set is *the* Prelude in C sharp minor (for another version see above, *Piano Pieces,* Op. 3 and 10). Lympany handles the music very well. She is more than merely a fine technician; she is a real virtuoso, and some of the most difficult piano-writing in the repertoire rolls right off her fingers. The one reservation that could be mentioned about her performance is an adolescent-like quality that makes her dawdle over lyric sections, re-gilding the lily. Rachmaninoff would not have liked this. But, to compensate, Lympany shows that she can play with grace *(E flat Prelude),* abandon (G minor), and fluency (G major). These two discs are well worth having. Despite the cultivated sneers of some present-day critics, the music manages to hold up very well. London has given realistic sound to Lympany. A slight hum, noticeable when pianissimo sections are played, is not bothersome.

Sonata for Cello and Piano in G minor (Op. 19). Kurtz, Kapell, V LM 1074. Schuster, Pennario, Cap 8248.

Anybody who likes plangent scores like the *C minor Piano Concerto* should revel in this long cello work. Others may get restless at the chromatic stream and constant sentimentality. (In some respects, Rachmaninoff was almost a Russian Franck). The Victor recording is the better choice. It has a more mellow sound than the over-bright Capitol. Both cellists know their business, but Kapell brings more to the important piano part than does Pennario. He is smooth where Pennario is spasmodic, and his contribution helps make the Victor disc go with more life and sparkle.

*Sonata for Piano No. 1 in D minor (Op. 28). Thew, RS 6 (*Powder and Paint).*

Thew makes a brave try, but the music needs a bigger, more imaginative pianist, and also a more secure technician. The recording is good. Chief point of interest on this disc is the short filler, in which Rachmaninoff himself accompanies the diseuse Nadejda Plevitskaya in "Powder and Paint," an arrangement of a Russian folk song. This is a real collector's item, and many enthusiasts have gladly put down the price of the disc for the one short band.

Sonata for Piano No. 2 in B flat minor (Op. 36); Études-Tableaux (Op. 33). Weiser, RS 1.

The trouble with pieces like this, as far as most pianists are concerned, is that Rachmaninoff tailored them to his own specifications, and the specifications of a Rachmaninoff are fulfilled once every generation or so. Lesser mortals must needs fight the music. Weiser has to concentrate all of his energies on meeting the technical problems, and little is left over for interpretative subtleties. Fair recording, rather low-level, with considerable surface noise.

Suites for Two Pianos Nos. 1 in G minor (Op. 5) and 2 in C (Op. 17). Vronsky and Babin, C 4379.

No. 1 is seldom played, though the fascinating bell-like sonorities in the last movement are worth knowing. Did Rachmaninoff have Mussorgsky's "Coronation Scene" in mind? No. 2, with its popular waltz, is an old concert-hall favorite. Vronsky and Babin are at their best here. Crisp fingerwork, scintillating sound, perfect co-ordination, rhythmic propulsion—all are present. This is one of the best discs of its kind.

*Variations on a Theme by Chopin (Op. 22). Goldsand, CH 1149 (*Liszt: Paganini Études).*

For his theme Rachmaninoff selected the chordal *C minor Prelude*. It may be that there is more piano music than music in the *Variations*; the workmanship certainly is ingenious, even if the content is thin. Those who respond to fleet pianism will enjoy Goldsand's way with the music. The recorded sound is a little overamplified. No tonal shatter is present, but if your stylus is not in good condition you may get a considerable amount of distortion. Weiser has also recorded the *Variations on a Theme by Chopin* on RS 4 *(*Variations on a Theme by Corelli).* He does not approximate Goldsand's fluency.

RAMEAU, JEAN PHILIPPE (1683-1764)

*Piano Pieces. Casadesus, C 4695 (*Scarlatti: 6 Sonatas). Meyer, HS 98 (*Couperin: 5 Pieces; Ravel: Le Tombeau de Couperin; Debussy: Hommage à Rameau).*

Casadesus plays a gavotte, *Le Rappel des oiseaux*, *Les Sauvages*, and *Les Niais de Sologne*. Meyer's selection is *L'Entretien des Muses*, *Les Sauvages*, *Les Tendres Plaintes*, *Le Rappel des oiseaux*, and *Les Cyclopes*. Casadesus has no superior in this kind of music. His work has taste, polish, and the most finished execution. For bewitching piano-playing, listen to his performance of *Le Rappel des oiseaux.* (*Le Rappel* is a movement from the *E minor Suite;* for a complete version see following entry.) Meyer lacks the touch and flexibility of Casadesus, but there is nothing wrong with her competent playing or her musicianship.

Suites for Harpsichord Nos. 2 in E minor and 4 in A minor. Valenti, W 5128.

The *E minor Suite* contains some of Rameau's most popular music: *Le Rappel des oiseaux, Tambourin, Musette, Rigaudon.* The A minor is seldom heard. I find Valenti less than convincing here. His phrasing is stiff, and he chops the line. Some of these pieces are humorous, but little of the humor comes through. Westminster has provided close-up recording. Even with the volume reduced, the sound is unnatural.

RAVEL, MAURICE *(1875-1937)*

Alborado del Gracioso. See Collections: Lipatti (10" C 2216).

*Gaspard de la Nuit. Gieseking, C 4773 (*Debussy: Estampes; Images). Casadesus, C 4519 (*Ma Mère l'Oye, etc.). Gulda, L 754 (*Debussy: Suite bergamasque).*

When Gieseking made this recording of *Gaspard* in 1939 it immediately achieved fame. It is rightly considered one of the great piano recordings, and this despite the fact that "*Scarbo,*" the last of the three movements, is far from impeccable technically. Nobody else has brought to the music a comparable degree of style, color, and understanding. The transfer to LP is low-level, with prominent surfaces. Casadesus's version is part of his three-disc complete piano music of Ravel. This amazingly fluent performance runs Gieseking a close second, and the recorded sound is infinitely superior. For most listeners it should be the preferred interpretation on LP. The London disc played by Gulda is also a superior example of recorded sound. Gulda takes care of the notes easily enough, but he doesn't approach Gieseking or Casadesus in smoothness, subtlety, or identification with the music. Several other versions of *Gaspard de la Nuit* in the LP catalogues come nowhere near those listed above.

*Introduction and Allegro for Harp, Flute, and String Quartet. Stockton, Gleghorn, Lurie, Hollywood, 10" Cap 8154 (*Debussy: Danses sacrée et profane). Amsterdam Chamber Music Society, 10" L 621 (*Debussy: Danses sacrée et profane).*

Each of these will do. The London recording has a mellow quality; the Capitol is sharper, with better instrumental definition. As interpretations, the discs are the product of two different schools. The Amsterdam players have a little more nuance and are less aggressive. A more propulsive quality is found on the Capitol disc. Here the feeling is one of seven brilliant instrumentalists working together, whereas one is conscious primarily of ensemble from the Amsterdam group. Which is not to say that the American players lack good ensemble. They play together beautifully; but one is never allowed to forget that each instrumentalist is a virtuoso.

*Ma Mère l'Oye. R. and G. Casadesus, C 4519 (*Habanera, etc.). Bartlett and Robertson, 10" MGM 161 (*Debussy: Petite Suite).*

In English, this is the *Mother Goose Suite.* It is played here in its original form as a piano duet (one piano, four hands). Mr. and Mrs. Casadesus present the best LP performance of the utterly charming work. The disc is part of the three-disc complete piano music of Ravel, but is also available separately. Bartlett and Robertson play simply, and the results are attractive, but they lack the elegance that the French pianists bring to the music.

Piano Music (complete). Casadesus (with Gaby Casadesus in the four-hand works), C 4518/19/20 [3].

These three discs are available separately. The contents are Vol. I: *Pavane, Sonatine, Miroirs,* a pair of minor pieces; Vol. II: *Ma Mère l'Oye, Habanera* (both four-hand works), *Jeux d'eau, Gaspard de la Nuit, Menuet antique;* Vol. III: *Le Tombeau de Couperin, Valses nobles et sentimentales, Prélude en la mineur,* and *Menuet sur le nom d'Haydn.* If you want to begin with one of these, Vol. II is a good choice. It is hard to think of a better pianist for this project. Casadesus is a man of unlimited tone and technique. He has as much subtlety and color as any living pianist, and he knows more about the pedals than nearly any other pianist before the public. His playing sometimes has been called lacking in force, and with good reason. But nobody has ever questioned his affinity with the French school of composition. This he plays with complete authority, and the type of elegance he brings even to such an overworked piece as the *Pavane pour une infante defunte* is an example of supreme artistry. Fortunately Columbia has given him clear recording that brings out the nuance of his touch and the subtlety of his musical approach. These discs are classics. For Ravel himself playing the *Valses nobles et sentimentales,* see Collections: "Great Masters of the Keyboard," Vol. I (C 4291). For additional piano music, see *La Valse* (Cap. 8294).

*Quartet for Strings in F. Pascal, CH 1123 (*Sonata for Violin and Cello). Budapest, C 4668 (*Debussy: Quartet). Stuyvesant, Ph 104 (*Debussy: Quartet).*

Though not the best version from a sonic point of view, the Concert Hall disc presents a performance that has more elegance and refinement than any other on LP. The quality of recording is far from obsolete, however. A greater degree of tonal clarity is found on the Columbia disc, even though this is a transfer from shellac. It may be that many listeners will find the superb integration of the Budapest Quartet enough reason to prefer it over the slightly less exact ensemble of the Pascal group. French music, however, has never been one of the Budapest specialties, and here the Pascal brings a degree of rapport that the more objective Budapest Quartet lacks. At that, the Columbia performance has more of an assertive quality than one notes in the Stuyvesant Quartet version. A recording by the Fine Arts Quartet on Mer 10105 (*Hindemith: *Quartet No. 3)* is routine, and the sound tends toward overamplification.

*Sonata for Violin and Cello. Shumsky, Greenhouse, CH 1123 (*Quartet).*

Even Ravel's admirers hedge about this work. To put it bluntly, it is dull. Shumsky and Greenhouse do what they can with it, and those who are interested will find this a good performance, well recorded.

*Sonata for Violin and Piano. Druian, Simms, Mer 70000 (*Bartók: Violin Sonata No. 2). B. Urban, V. Urban, CE 1002 (*Khachaturian: Clarinet Trio). Eidus, Smith, Str 1005 (*Trio in A minor).*

Like the *Sonata for Violin and Cello,* this work has never succeeded in taking a place on the concert stage. It was experimental, in a way, and its jazz sections are pretty well dated. Druian's version is the best, though he bears down a little too hard. I would have liked to hear less emphasis on tone, more on musical shadings. The other two performances are about on a par, but neither approaches the Mercury disc in tonal realism.

*Trio for Violin, Cello, and Piano in A minor. Heifetz, Piatigorsky, Rubinstein, V LM 1119 (*Mendelssohn: Trio in D minor). Alma, All 3091 (*Stravinsky: Piano Sonata; Serenade). Albeneri, Mer 10089 (*Fauré: Trio in D minor).*

A lovely work. The first movement is of an unsurpassed lyricism, and I'm not so sure but that it's the most beautiful thing Ravel ever wrote. Victor's is the best-sounding recording (even with a weakly placed cello) and easily the most accomplished performance. Ravel's writing is difficult, and it needs brilliant instrumentalists. Of the brilliance of Messrs. Heifetz, Rubinstein, and Piatigorsky, nobody need be told. The question is: how well do they combine as chamber-music players? Fortunately the answer is a resounding affirmative. Next to this kind of virtuosity and musical nuance, all other versions pale. The Albeneri recording is on the dullish side, and its performance is stodgy. In the second movement, for example, the *assez vif* quality hardly comes through. Somewhat better is the Alma Trio's performance, but here again it does not capture the subtle, intellectually pointed quality that the Victor musicians convey. A performance by Eidus, Ricci, and Smith on Str 1005 does not have much color and is further handicapped by a muddy quality of recording.

*La Valse; Valses nobles et sentimentales. Pennario, Cap 8294 (*Delibes-Dohnányi: Naila Waltz; Strauss-Dohnányi: Sweetheart Waltzes from Fledermaus).*

After composing *La Valse,* Ravel made a transcription for two pianos and for solo piano. Neither is much heard in concert (and Casadesus does not play the solo version in his three-disc set of Ravel's "complete" piano music). Immensely complicated and difficult, the solo requires a superhuman technique and considerable musical elegance. For Pennario's performance, nothing but praise. This is by far the young American's best disc. The glittering, objective music seems to suit his temperament exactly, and he skates through it not only with enormous virtuosity but also with musical refinement. He also does well with the *Valses nobles et sentimentales,* which he plays in a neat, crisp manner that never permits the music to degenerate into a sequence of clichés. In the Dohnányi transcriptions he again is master of the situation. An extremely impressive example of piano-playing all around. Typical Capitol recording—clear, brilliant, a little glassy.

REGER, MAX (1873-1916)

*Introduction, Passacaglia, and Fugue. Luboshutz, Nemenoff, Rem 199-143 (*Encore Pieces).*

This large-scale work will delight those listeners responsive to such juicy Reger works as the *Mozart Variations.* It abounds in rich sounds, a heavy patina of chromaticism, and idiomatic writing for the two pianos. The fugue, with a subject about as long as the *Queen Mary,* is a puckish affair, brilliantly handled. Luboshutz and Nemenoff, one of the best ensembles anywhere for the romantic two-piano literature, handle the music with complete authority. Unfortunately the recording does not do justice to their smooth tone; it is clangorous and lacking in quality. On the reverse of this disc is a group of fluffy encore pieces that could not possibly interest anybody who wants to own an *Introduction, Passacaglia, and Fugue* (and vice versa). The one exception amid the fluff is Chopin's *Rondo in C.*

*Suite for Unaccompanied Cello. Feuermann, C 4678 (*Beethoven: Sonata No. 3; Variations on "Bei Männern").*

Columbia has made an LP transfer of these shellac discs. The sound is not bad. Certainly more than enough is present to show clearly why Feuermann was one of the greatest cellists of this century. Tone, style, technique, variety of bowing and attack, musical imagination—everything.

REICHA, ANTON (1770-1836)

Bläserquintett (Op. 88, No. 2). See Collections: New Art Wind Quintet (CE 2010).

RESPIGHI, OTTORINO (1879-1936)

*Sonata for Violin and Piano in B minor. Heifetz, Bay, V LM 1184 (*Debussy: Sonata).*

Heifetz seems to have a fondness for this work. He programs it often (and is about the only violinist who does so). Most people will find it a rambling sonata of more interest to the player than to the listener. Heifetz gives it the works: throbbing tone, heavy portamento in the slow movement, golden sounds in general. It can safely be said that under his auspices the sonata is being heard under the most favorable circumstances.

REUBKE, JULIUS (1834-1858)

Sonata in C minor on the 94th Psalm. Biggs, C 4820 (*Liszt: Fantasia and Fugue on BACH).

Reubke, a pupil of Liszt, conceivably could have developed into a composer of consequence (he died at the age of twenty-four). This large-scale work, however, is full of romantic ditherings and clichés. Biggs plays the sonata on the organ of the Memorial Music Hall in Methuen, Massachusetts. This recording probably has an extended frequency range, but frequently all that I heard was a massive jumble of sound. Perhaps the characteristics of the organ are too bulky, or the acoustics of the hall over-reverberant. Or are Biggs's registrations too thick?

RICHTER, FRANZ XAVER (1709-1789)

Quartet for Strings in C (Op. 5, No. 1). New Music, Bar 915 (*Stamitz: Quartet in A, Op. 14).

Honest *Kappellmeistermusik* here. Richter and Stamitz were composers of the Mannheim school. As in much of the minor music of the period, the writing is professional, and there always is musical purity. Otherwise, the scores do not have much individuality or invention. In both works there is nothing especially to like, and certainly nothing to dislike. Again the LP-collector is presented with one of those "historically important" items. The New Music String Quartet, an able and intelligent group, handles the assignment with complete musicianship, and the recording is realistic in sound.

RIEGGER, WALLINGFORD (1885-)

Quartet for Strings No. 2 (Op. 43). See Moore: *Clarinet Quintet* (C 4494).
Quintet for Woodwinds (Op. 51). See Collections: New Art Wind Quintet (CE 2003).

RIETI, VITTORIO (1898-)

Second Avenue Waltzes. See Collections: Gold and Fizdale (10" C 2147).

*Suite champêtre (1948). Gold and Fizdale, C 4853 (*Stravinsky: Concerto for Two Solo Pianos; Hindemith: Sonata for Piano Four Hands).*

Three peppy movements, French-derived plus a soupçon of Stravinsky, deceptively simple, expertly designed for two pianos: that is the *Suite champêtre*. The music has much charm despite its obvious derivations. Gold and Fizdale play it with a light hand and an aristocratic sense of line, managing to avoid the "cuteness" that many another two-piano team would bring out. Top-notch recorded sound. This disc, available separately, is part of the three-disc "Music for Two Pianos—1900-1952." For complete contents, see Collections: Gold and Fizdale (C SL 198).

RIISAGER, KNUDAGE (1897-)

Sonata for Two Violins; Sonata for Violin, Cello, and Piano. Tworek, etc., 10" L 785.

Riisager, a contemporary Danish composer, knows his Prokofiev well. Both of these pieces were composed in 1953; they sound as though they had been composed by a talented amateur. The performances by a group of Danish instrumentalists appear entirely in order, and the recording has typical London smoothness.

RIMSKY-KORSAKOV, NICOLAI (1844-1908)

*Quintet for Piano and Winds in B flat. Wlach, etc., W 5019 (*Glinka: Trio Pathétique).*

Here's a novelty for you. It is a dated example of static Russian academism, with a few Russian folk themes occasionally penetrating the Westernized Mendelssohnian treatment. The score calls for flute, clarinet, bassoon, horn, and piano. On this disc a group of Viennese musicians presents the music with sympathy, though one imagines that participants with Slavic blood in their veins would get a little more color out of the writing. It's all quite expert, however. The recording, which goes back to early LP days, could hardly be mistaken for a modern example, but holds up reasonably well.

*Trio for Piano and Strings in C minor. Oistrakh, Knushevitsky, Oborin, CH 1306 (*Glinka: Trio Pathétique).*

Not only is this work Mendelssohnian, but one of the themes directly calls to mind the opening of Mendelssohn's *Octet*. Brahms also plays a part; so does Schumann; and there is a quotation from a late Beethoven quartet. Eclectic? Oh, my! Technically this is not a good recording. Some piano shatter is present, and the sound is on the dull side. The performance appears to be magnificent. Three of the Soviet's best musicians participate, and they play with fervor, perfect co-ordination, and instrumental virtuosity.

ROLDAN, AMADEO (1900-1939)

Ritmica No. 1 for Piano and Wind Quintet. See Porter: Quartet No. 6 (An 35105).

ROREM, NED (1923-)

Sonata for Piano No. 2. Katchen, L 759 (*Bartok: *Mikrokosmos*).
A mixture of Poulenc and Prokofiev is present in this difficult virtuoso piece. It is very effective in its derivative way. Katchen has a flair for brilliant, objective playing, and his performance contains a happy mixture of technique, color, and sheer pianistic finesse. Excellent recorded sound.

ROSENMÜLLER, JOHANN (1619-1684)

Sonata No. 2 in E minor. See Collections: Harpsichord Quartet (Es 517).

ROSSINI, GIOACCHINO (1792-1868)

Quartets for Wind Instruments (6). New Art, CE 1010 [2].
The first five of these six works were not originally for winds. Rossini composed five string quartets at the age of sixteen, while he was at the conservatory in Bologna. According to Noel Straus of the *New York Times*, these five quartets were arranged for wind quartet by one Friedrich Berr and first published in that form in 1829. No. 6 appears to have been conceived for winds. Rossini used classical models, but his Italian temperament constantly was breaking through. Bubbling, melodious, utterly disarming music results. In the third movement of No. 5 (and elsewhere) there is

real buffo quality coupled with some typical operatic cadences. The quartets are not easy to play; the horn especially has a rough time, and one can sense it in this recording. But the players go about it with plenty of spirit and good ensemble, and the recorded sound is clear. This unusual, off-the-track item is highly recommended for some pleasant listening.

ROUSSEL, ALBERT (1869-1937)

Quartet for Strings in D (Op. 45). Loewenguth, 10" D 4026.

This is an entry in Decca's "4000" series. It is lean and wiry music with considerable forward momentum. Some ingenious ideas and workmanship are present, and the score is one of the best examples of the modern French school of chamber music. In striving to get the power of the music across, the Loewenguth Quartet sounds hectic; it pushes too hard. Nevertheless, the playing conveys the nature of the music, and the disc is a very good buy. The recording is rather harsh in sound, though some of that may be the tonal quality of the Loewenguths.

RUBBRA, EDMUND (1901-)

Quartet for Strings No. 2 in E flat (Op. 73). Griller, 10" L 657.

Rubbra, a composer much talked about in England, is represented in this country by very few recordings or live performances. If this quartet is typical of his work, he writes in a basically conservative, post-romantic idiom despite a heavy outlay of dissonance. The work has intensity, and one is happy to make its acquaintance. As the Griller Quartet commissioned the work and has played it throughout the world, it is fairly certain that the group (a) has familiarity with the score, and (b) likes it. Both familiarity and liking are present in this clear, accomplished reading. Mellow recorded sound, with transparent texture throughout.

RUGGIERI, GIOVANNI MARIA (fl. 1693)

Sonatas da Chiesa (Op. 3). Steinbauer, etc. SPA 18/19 [2].

Spawn of LP. Ruggieri is completely unknown to most specialists, and standard sources of reference do not list him. The notes with the discs are no help either. These notes, written in a language somewhat resembling English, state that Ruggieri composed ten church sonatas in 1693. Most of these ten are scored for two violins and viola da gamba, with continuo. On these discs the continuo is filled by various combinations of cello, bass, lute, guitar, piano, harpsichord, organ. It is all orthodox, unexciting baroque music, played here with dogged determination (one is reminded of the old phrase about certain baroque composers being poor and pious men who wrote poor and pious music).

SAINT-SAËNS, CAMILLE (1835-1921)

*Étude en forme de valse; Toccatas (Op. 72 and 111); Thème varié; Allegro Appassionata. Doyen, W 5294 (*Chabrier: 7 Piano Pieces).*

These pieces, somewhat out of fashion today, are brilliant, effective, superficial, and ever so much fun. Saint-Saëns could be the salon composer *par excellence*. Doyen turns in some exciting pianistics. Her playing, glib and accurate, is just what the music needs. She illustrates the French Conservatory style: all on the top of the keys, rather brittle tone, elegance, monochromaticism, little depth. It would be a pity if this disc were to be neglected because of the unfamiliarity of the music. It's a charming departure from the standard repertoire; and the fine Chabrier music on the reverse makes for an ideal coupling. I think you'll enjoy this record. Brilliant, close-up recording. For several piano pieces played by Saint-Saëns himself, see Collections: "Musicians of the Past," Vol. I (AM 1203) and "Great Masters of the Keyboard," Vol. II (C 4292).

*Septet for Piano, Trumpet, Bass, and String Quartet. Pressler, Glantz, Sklar, Guilet, MGM 3096 (*D'Indy: Suite in Olden Style).*

In this score Saint-Saëns anticipated the neo-classic trend. He also cribbed a theme from the first movement of Schumann's *Fantasy in C* and used it prominently throughout the work. All is urbane, well constructed, and very melodious. The players on the MGM disc present a spirited, clean-cut performance that supersedes an earlier version on Str 605. MGM also has supplied extremely realistic sound. The D'Indy work, for trumpet, two flutes, bass, and string quartet, is played by Glantz, Baker, Monteux, Sklar, and the Guilet Quartet. Less interest attaches to this well-made but sterile effort. The performance is superb.

Sonata for Violin and Piano in D minor (Op. 75). Heifetz, Bay, V LM 9007 (Bruch: Violin Concerto in G minor).

Heifetz has never sounded better, and his performance can best be described as soaring. This disc is no less than a lexicon of violin perfection. The Saint-Saëns work, out of fashion as it is, nevertheless remains considerably more than a museum piece, and the lovely third movement is as graceful and elegant as anything composed during its period. But for violin-fanciers the main interest will be Heifetz's incredible suavity. Fine recorded sound.

SARASATE, PABLO DE *(1844-1908)*

Danzas Españolas (8); Caprice basque; Introduction et Tarantelle; Ziguenerweisen. Ricci, Persinger, L 962.

A notable virtuoso violinist, Ricci has a fine time with these showy, attractive, showpieces. Nor is this said condescendingly: these Sarasate works are among the best specimens of their kind, and they contain a species of musical invention of no mean order. Needless to say, they are brilliantly conceived in terms of violin technique. It is interesting to compare Ricci's ideas about several of these pieces with Sarasate's own: see Collections: "Musicians of the Past," Vol. I (AM 1203). Without attempting to disparage Ricci's superb work, I can say that you have never heard the *Ziguenerweisen* or the *Caprice basque* until you hear Sarasate flip through them in an unearthly, facile manner.

SATIE, ERIK *(1866-1925)*

*Piano Music. Poulenc, C 4399 (*Poulenc: Suite Française; Mouvements perpetuels; Nocturne in D).*

The names of the pieces in this collection will give an idea of their tongue-in-cheek mood: *Descriptions automatiques; Gymnopédie No. 1; Sarabande No. 2; Avant-dernières pensées* ("Next-to-last thoughts"); *Croquis et agaceries d'un gros-bonhomme en bois* ("Sketches and enticements of a fat wooden man"). Some of the jokes wear pretty thin after a few hearings, but the music continues to exert its strange fascination. Satie was an original, in the truest sense of the word. Poulenc, a pianist-composer who came under the influence of Satie, is the able instrumentalist here. Plenty of musical authority is present, and while the piano-playing is a little rough, it is eminently satisfactory. Good recording; prominent surfaces.

*En habit de cheval (1911). Gold and Fizdale, C 4854 (*Debussy: Épigraphes antiques; Poulenc: Sonata for Piano Four Hands; Milhaud: Concertino d'automne).*

This disc, available separately, is in the three-disc "Music for Two Pianos—1900-1952." For complete listing see Collections: Gold and Fizdale (C SL 198). The notes to this record do the remarkable feat of presenting two full columns about Satie without mentioning the piece that is being recorded. It is one of Satie's flaunting works, deliberately stripped to bare essentials: mostly block harmonies, with a simple line above them. Satie intended the work for orchestra, but never got around to scoring it. The satiric title, according to one biographer, "without doubt evokes the liberty with which he breaks the rules of composition." Gold and Fizdale play expertly, as always. Their anti-romantic way of interpretation is admirably suited to music like this. By anti-romantic I mean strict rhythm, musical objectivity, avoidance of pedal and color effects, and under- rather than over-statement.

Piano Music. Masselos, MGM 3154.

By far the best collection of Satie's piano music ever recorded, this disc presents a large-sized dollop that includes: *3 Gymnopédies; 3 Préludes flasques* ("Flabby Preludes"); *3 Gnossiennes; Chapitres tournés en tous sens* ("Chapters Turned Every Which Way"); *Embryons desséchés* ("Dessicated Embryos"); *Sports et divertissements; Nocturne No. 5.* None of these works is heard much in the concert hall, an especially surprising fact in view of the attention paid to Satie in recent years. This disc will help the listener make up his own mind, and the informative program notes by Edward Cole should be of real assistance. Masselos presents the music sympathetically. He has a singing line, a lyrical approach, and the musical intelligence to know when not to push Satie's drollery too hard. Superb recorded sound. Also on this disc is an arrangement for piano by Hans Oudine of *La Diva de l'Empire*, a music-hall song subtitled *Intermezzo Américain.* It is an attractive piece of buffoonery.

*Trois morceaux en forme de poire. R. and G. Casadesus, C 4246 (*Saint-Saëns: Piano Concerto No. 4).*

"Three pieces in the form of a pear." Thus did Satie rebuke

those critics (specifically, Debussy) who told him that his music was formless. It is one of Satie's most successful works. Forget the tomfoolery of the title. Fresh melodic ideas are present, and the workmanship is that of a composer with true originality. The performance on two pianos by the Casadesus combination is beautifully stylish. One cannot imagine a better interpretation; and what with Casadesus's scintillating performance of the *C minor Concerto* by Saint-Saëns on the reverse, this disc is very much worth having. The Satie is a transfer from shellac to LP, and is a bit unresonant in sound, but the piano tone remains perfectly clear: it is better, indeed, than in the original version.

SCARLATTI, ALESSANDRO (1659-1725)

Sonata a Quattro in D minor. See Collections: New Music String Quartet (Bar 911).

SCARLATTI, DOMENICO (1685-1757)

Sonatas for Harpsichord. Valenti, W 5106 (Vol. I), 5116 (II), 5139 (III), 5186 (IV), 5205 (V), and 5325 (VI).

Each disc contains twelve sonatas. As in the future these works will probably be identified by the new Kirkpatrick numbering, I have collated them with the familiar Longo ones. Vol. I contains L. 429 (K. 175), L. 430 (K. 531), L. 204 (K. 105), L. 37 (K. 325), L. 395 (K. 533), L. 345 (K. 113), L. 415 (K. 119), L. 252 (K. 421), L. 279 (K. 419), L. 500 (K. 545), L. 449 (K. 27), and L 262 (K. 535), *Vol. II:* L. 422 (K. 141), L. 465 (K. 96), L. 413 (K. 9), L. 232 (K. 124), L. 8 (K. 461), L. 104 (K. 159), L. 14 (K. 492), L. 263 (K. 377), L. 23 (K. 380), L. 486 (K. 13), L. 126 (K. 347), and L. 127 (K. 348). *Vol. III:* L. 25 (K. 46), L. 33 (K. 87), L. 419 (K. 484), L. 165 (K. 214), L. 420 (K. 444), L. 58 (K. 64), L. 241 (K. 54), L. 352 (K. 11), L. 432 (K. 44), L. 433 (K. 446), L. 365 (K. 401), and L. 10 (K. 84). *Vol. IV:* L. 463 (K. 430), L. 321 (K. 263), L. 209 (K. 455), L. 386 (K. 35), L. 388 (K. 2), L. 136 (K. 61), L. 418 (K. 443), L. 103 (K. 259), L. 205 (K. 487), L. 381 (K. 438), L. 475 (K. 519), and L. 323 (K. 215). *Vol. V:* L. 407 (K. 115), L. 155 (K. 271), L. 129 (K. 201), L. 375 (K. 20), L. 376 (K. 147), L. 86 (K. 520), L. 325 (K. 98), L. 327 (K. 529), L. 218 (K. 398), L. 84 (K. 63), L. 457 (K. 132), and L. 487 (K. 125). *Vol. VI:* L. 379 (K. 7), L. 281 (K. 239), L. 324 (K. 460), L. 173

(K. 185), L. 163 (K. 176), L. 282 (K. 133), L. 135 (K. 212), L. 452 (K. 116), L. 286 (K. 427), L. 497 (K. 544), L. 274 (K. 399), L. 466 (K. 264).

It is not necessary to dwell on Scarlatti's unique genius. Of the 500-odd sonatas he composed, none is repetitive. Constant flow and invention are ever present; the man was a magician. Valenti's most satisfactory playing is to be encountered on these six discs. Unlike his work in some of the Bach he has recorded, his playing here has flexibility, color, a quality of musical excitement, and superb rhythm. This is music he feels and understands, and his ideas are supported by a technique that enables him to sport with the music. It might be mentioned that, simple as it sometimes sounds, Scarlatti's writing can be extremely difficult. He favored, at times, wide skips that call for unerring marksmanship on the part of the player; and all of the running figurations demand, in addition to agile fingers, a perfectly equalized scale. In some romantic music the player can put his foot down on the pedal and manage to get through, if he has the style. In Scarlatti, no; the slightest flaw stands out almost as Everest would in the middle of the Sahara. Which is what keyboard players mean when they refer to Scarlatti's writing as "naked." These six Westminster recordings are too close-up. Even with the volume down, the reproduction sounds overamplified.

Several other harpsichordists have made some Scarlatti recordings. Landowska has a pair in her "Treasury of Harpsichord Music": see Collections: Landowska (V LM 1217). A good low-priced disc is Marlowe's performance of seven sonatas on Rem 199-136. Of the piano versions, the best are those of Gieseking, who plays five on C 4646 (*Bach: *Partita No. 6*), and Casadesus, who plays six on C 4695 (*Rameau: *Piano Pieces*). Both know how to play the piano without pounding, both are masters of touch and legato. Haskil on W 5072 and Long on 10" L 314 and 524 present a conventional, fairly accurate Scarlatti that can just as well be avoided, all the more so since the fine harpsichord versions by Valenti are available.

SCHEIDT, SAMUEL (1587-1654)

Selections from the Tabulatura Nova. Noss, Ov 3.

Scheidt was a major pre-Bach figure. His *Tabulatura Nova* is a strongly modal collection of sacred and secular organ pieces. These works are very impressive formally. Scheidt, like nearly all the professionals of his day, was a superb craftsman and technician. On this disc the *Magnificat Noni Toni* is prefaced by a brief announcement of each chant, sung in Latin by an unnamed male group. Noss, a recognized authority on the subject, presents the music in a devotional spirit, playing with fairly subdued registrations. It sounds like a splendid performance. The recording of the organ is altogether realistic, and there are some very low frequencies on this disc, if you go in for that sort of thing.

SCHNABEL, ARTUR (1882-1951)

Piano Pieces (7); Rêverie. H. Schnabel. Piece in Seven Movements. Newlin, SPA 13.

Two pianists share the disc: Helen Schnabel (daughter-in-law of the composer) and Dika Newlin. The early *Rêverie* could have been composed by, say, Chaminade. The others are of Schoenberg's school. Schnabel in his maturity favored an extremely advanced, dissonant style of composition. The performances are in good order, but not much can be said for the dull-sounding recording.

SCHOECK, OTHMAR (1886-)

Toccata for Piano. See Binet: *String Quartet* (L 498).

SCHOENBERG, ARNOLD (1874-1951)

*Piano Pieces (Op. 11); Suite (Op. 25). Field, Per 568 (*Piano Concerto).*

Op. 11 is atonal; Op. 25 is twelve-tone. Field's affinity for this type of music is not demonstrated by this disc. It can be said that one gets a good idea of the music, but more was needed: a degree of control and lightness that Field cannot meet. The piano tone, clear and rather clanging, is not inappropriate to Schoenberg's writing. These piano pieces are not recommended to those whose ideal are the Chopin waltzes.

Piano Pieces (Op. 19 and 23); Fantasy for Violin and Piano. Steuermann; Koldofsky and Steuermann, Dia 14.

Some people find this music analogous to the New Testament; others find it neurotic, intellectual, and unlovely. Here it is on records for you to make your own decision. The performances are played by two Schoenberg specialists, and the recorded sound ranks with the best in the Dial series.

Quartets for Strings (4, complete). Juilliard, C SL 188 [3].

These discs are available separately. On the reverse of the final one are Berg's *String Quartet* (Op. 3) and Webern's *Five Pieces for String Quartet.* As Berg and Webern were Schoenberg's two most talented pupils, the coupling is entirely apposite. Schoenberg's four quartets are extremely difficult music, technically and aurally. They span the period between 1905 and 1936. No. 1 is in one long movement, strongly allied to the Wagner-Mahler nexus. No. 2 is more experimental. The last two movements are settings of poems by Stefan George, sung here by Uta Graf. No. 3 is twelve-tone, and No. 4 is concentrated twelve-tone. These Juilliard discs are not the only recordings of the quartet of quartets. Some years ago the Kolisch Quartet did all four for Alco. But those recordings are now dated in sound, and the playing does not have the technical finish that the younger ensemble brings to the fiendish writing (though some twelve-tone authorities believe that the Kolisch had more of an insight into the music). I prefer the eager, impulsive way that the Juilliard goes about its work, and the security with which it plows through the writing. The recording is a bit on the shrill side: nothing that a good amplifier cannot handle.

Quintet for Winds (Op. 26). Metropolitan, Dia 13.

A strict twelve-tone work composed in 1924, the quintet is scored for flute, clarinet, oboe, bassoon, and horn. The performers do not make the music sound any less difficult than it is, and one can sense them fighting to line up the notes in cohesive order. Nevertheless, a lucid exposition of the score comes through. Good recorded sound.

Suite (Op. 29). Schuller, etc., Per 705.

Here the score calls for clarinet, E flat clarinet, bass clarinet, violin, viola, cello, and piano. The seven instrumentalists are conducted by Gunther Schuller. In view of the complexity of the writing, one well understands the need for a conductor to hold things together. Schuller keeps the music in constant motion, and he is working with an expert group of musicians. More definition in the recording would have helped his work. The low-level sound lacks resonance, and the piano is tinny.

Trio for Strings (Op. 45). Koldofsky, Dia 3.

Not a successful performance. Schoenberg's dynamic indications in the printed score run the range from *pppp* to *fff* and *sfz*. Little of those extremes comes through. The playing is much on one dynamic level, with the performers apparently so preoccupied with meeting the textual demands that they forget all else. The recording also has a heavy background noise that sounds like a subway train in the distance.

*Variations on a Recitative (Op. 40). Watters, CE 1004 (*Messiaen: Le Banquet céleste; Prière du Christ; Transport de joie).*

This is Schoenberg's only organ work. It is atonal, not twelve-tone. Watters, a fine technician, presents the knotty score with a vigorous and understanding performance. On the copy I played the surfaces were pronouncedly gritty. The Messiaen works on the reverse are stupefying examples of triteness hidden behind a façade of mysticism.

Verklärte Nacht (Op. 4). Reher, Dinkin, Hollywood, 10" Cap 8118.

Several recordings of the score are available, but this is the only one in its original form as a string sextet. It would be difficult to imagine a better job. The performance is rich without being sloppy, songful without becoming sentimental, and supported by firm ensemble playing. It might be pertinent to point out, for the benefit of those who are not familiar with the score, that it is an early work, ultra-romantic, non-dissonant, and as sensuous as anything in the repertoire. Some listeners may recognize it as *Pillar of Fire*, the Tudor ballet that was one of the most successful productions of Ballet Theatre.

SCHMIDT, FRANZ (1874-1939)

Quintet for Piano and Strings in G. Demus, Barylli, W 5158.

What the Viennese call *Kitsch*, and what we call "cute," is represented on this disc. Schmidt was no forceful intellect, and contented himself with a lightweight score, sentimental and melodious, that has a few charming moments. It is played here by an able group of Viennese musicians. Typically bright Westminster sound.

SCHUBERT, FRANZ (1797-1828)

Divertissement à la Hongroise (Op. 54). Vronsky and Babin, 10" C 2125.

Schubert composed this for piano four hands. It is the ancestor of every Hungarian Rhapsody that Liszt ever composed. The sprightly and often amusing measures are played by Vronsky and Babin in a way that fully brings out the music's sparkle. They preserve Schubert's rhythmic bounce, and shape the melodic line with cultivated art. Exceptionally fine recorded sound, too.

Duo for Violin and Piano in A (Op. 162). See *Sonata for Violin and Piano in A.*

*Fantasy in C ("Wanderer"). Curzon, 10" L 83. K. U. Schnabel, WCFM 17 (*20 Dances).*

The London recording dates back years. The sound is thick, and its lack of color is characteristic of many early LP discs. So is the heavy background. Curzon gives a fine, thoughtful performance, but a new recording from him would be a fine idea. Schnabel has the benefit of much more up-to-date piano sound, but neither as an executant nor as a stylist can he approach Curzon. His playing is steady, however, and the clarity of the recording may attract many purchasers who ordinarily would select the London disc.

Fantasy in F minor (Op. 103); Rondo in D (Op. 138); Rondo in A (Op. 107); Marche caractèristique in C (Op. 121, No. 1). Badura-Skoda, Demus, W 5047.

Much of this music was unknown, except to piano duettists, until Westminster had the enterprise to bring it to the public. When it was issued, early in 1951, the disc immediately attracted an enthusiastic coterie. It should be in every collection of piano music. Schubert never composed a more beautiful theme than that which opens the great *F minor Fantasy*, and the other pieces on the disc are extremely enjoyable, in a lighter way. Badura-Skoda and Demus play nicely, respecting each other's wishes, working together in perfect accord. They do not take a heroic view of the *F minor Fantasy*, contenting themselves with bringing out the lyric aspects. What they miss in strength they make up in grace. Faithful piano sound, some slight surface noise.

*Fantasy for Violin and Piano in C (Op. 159). Szigeti, Levine, C 4338 (*Encores; Corelli: La Folia).*

One of the main themes of the *Fantasy in C* is the song *Sei mir gegrüsst,* one of Schubert's great lyric inspirations. The work is a masterpiece, and it is regrettable that the reverse of this disc contains fluff like *Clair de lune* and Tchaikovsky's *Valse sentimentale* and others. There may be a place for such music, but not on this disc. Szigeti plays the *Fantasy in C* with considerable vigor, but his tone is not a very pleasant experience, and his technique—here, at least—does not flow as easily as of yore.

Grand Duo (Op. 140). Badura-Skoda, Demus, W 5093.

Some scholars insist that this is a reduction for four hands of the lost "*Gastein*" *Symphony;* it probably isn't, however. The work is more interesting in its original form than in the Joachim orchestration. By no means very strong Schubert—it is similar in style and feeling to the *Sixth Symphony*—it nevertheless contains a breathtaking moment in the trio of the third movement which is excruciatingly poignant (and which Badura-Skoda and Demus could have brought out with much more conviction). Otherwise this is a well-played, completely dependable performance, recorded with clarity.

Impromptus (Op. 90 and 142). Schnabel, V HMV 1027. Firkusny, C 4527. Badura-Skoda, W WAL 205 [2] *(*Sonata in A, Op. 120).*

Schnabel brings to the music a type of authority that no competing LP pianist can match. He does not look on the music as pretty miniatures, and his playing has power (internal, not external). What matter a few awkward fingerings? One cut is present: some measures toward the end of Op. 90, No. 4. Firkusny presents the music in its entirety. His well-turned and polished playing is agreeable, even though it lacks the insight that Schnabel conveys. Some sensitive moments are encountered in the Badura-Skoda set. Not enough, however, to spot Schnabel or Firkusny an extra disc, even with Op. 120 thrown in. Goldsand has recorded the eight *Impromptus* on CH 1146. These are well played, but why all the cuts? He takes a large one in Op. 142, No. 1, and others in Op. 90, Nos. 1 and 4. Curzon plays the Op. 142 set on L 720. Fine performances and superlative sound; but here again Schnabel has both books of *Impromptus* on a single disc, and the Curzon interpretations are not *that* good.

Ländler. See Collections: Kapell (V LM 1791).

*Moments musicaux (Op. 94). Goldsand, CH 1148 (*Sonata in A, Op. 120). Fischer, V HMV 1055 (*Beethoven: Sonata No. 23).*

Fischer's performance is not up to his pre-war standard, and Goldsand's version easily is preferable. He plays with delicacy, fine-spun melodic line, and appealing simplicity. Good recorded sound. The HMV disc is a little flat (about a quarter-tone), and Fischer sometimes is inexcusably deliberate. He takes No. 4, for instance, at little more than a practice tempo.

*Nocturne in E flat for Piano, Violin, and Cello (Op. 148). Mannes, Gimpel, Silva, D 9604 (*Schumann: Trio in D minor). Wuehrer, Barchet, Vox 8970 (*Quintet for Piano and Strings).*

Schubert did not thus name this movement for trio. The languorous mood of the piece undoubtedly gave the publisher the idea for the title. The music improves on hearing. At first it doesn't seem to get anywhere; afterward, a coherent design appears. Decca offers a good performance, even if tonal virtue is not one of its main points. Harsh sound prevails. The Vox performance is a clearer recording, but, as in the Decca disc, the players do not make very ravishing sounds. In both recordings the *Nocturne* serves as a filler for the last side of the disc.

Octet in F (Op. 166). Vienna Octet, L 1049. Vienna Konzerthaus, etc., W 5094. Vienna Symphony Octet, Vox 6970. Duques, etc., Str 603.

Four reasonably good versions, none of them outstanding. The Americans on the Stradivari disc are, in general, the briskest and most objective in their approach. More culture is behind the Viennese versions, though none is the last word in subtlety. Of these three discs, one eliminating factor might be that the Vox breaks the *scherzo* movement. The London and Westminster discs also are superior in sound. But why do all of the Viennese groups lag over the slow movement, "interpreting" it with all their might? Other annoying mannerisms are present: changes in basic tempo, rubatos that do not fit, kittenish ideas. This superb *Octet,* after all, is not *Kitsch.* I have no strong preference between the London or Westminster discs; both are about on a par. The Chamber Music Ensemble of the Berlin Philharmonic plays the *Octet* on D 9669. This is a low-level recording, lacking the color and definition of the others.

Quartet for Flute, Guitar, Viola, and Cello in G. Mess, etc., Per 518.

This is Schubert only by courtesy. One Wenzel Matiegka wrote a *Nocturne* for flute, viola, and guitar which Schubert expanded into the present work in 1814. Presumably he used the transcription for the entertainment and edification of a visiting guitar virtuoso. Pretty feeble stuff, but the fourth movement in B minor has an intense feeling not characteristic of anything else in the score. The performance is competent, the recording fair, and if you want a novelty that you will probably never hear in the concert hall, here it is.

Quartets for Strings Nos. 1 in B flat, 2 in C, and 3 in B flat, W 5204. Nos. 4 in C, 5 in B flat, and 12 in C minor ("Quartettsatz"), W 5210. Nos. 6 in D and 9 in G minor, W 5224. Nos. 7 in D and 8 in B flat (Op. 168), W 5110. Nos. 10 in E flat and 11 in E (Op. 125, Nos. 1 and 2), W 5222. All played by the Vienna Konzerthaus.

Schubert's first twelve string quartets are contained on these five discs. Nos. 1-7 and No. 10 are schoolboy works, composed in 1813. Haydn is the chief influence. No. 8 dates from 1814; it is a little masterpiece. No. 9 was composed in 1815, No. 11 in 1816, and No. 12, the great *Quartettsatz,* in 1820. With the last work we hear Schubert at his most intense, in music prefiguring the last great chamber works. This is a valuable set of records, not so much for the music (some of which is, as might be expected, immature) as for the opportunity to trace the musical development of a genius. The Vienna Konzerthaus group, never exciting or imaginative, is competent all the way through. In music like this a lack of passion is not too noticeable. On L 669 the Italian Quartet takes two sides to play No. 8; that alone disqualifies it from consideration. In addition, the players miss the point of the perpetual-motion-like last movement. (The greatest recording ever made of the beautiful No. 8 was done on three shellac discs by the Busch Quartet in 1940. If you ever come across that old Victor set, grab it.)

Quartets for Strings Nos. 13 in A minor (Op. 29), 14 in D minor ("Death and the Maiden"), and 15 in G (Op. 161). Budapest, C SL 194 [*3*].

It is difficult to think of a better introduction to chamber music than this set of three magnificent quartets so well played by the Budapest, so well recorded by Columbia. In the German repertoire from Mozart through Brahms, the Budapest Quartet remains unsurpassed. One will not dogmatically say that it is the best group in that particular repertoire before the public, but certainly none is superior. In the three Schubert works, it is sane, always fluent and musical, full of subtle touches, devoid of eccentricity. Its tempos are perfectly chosen. It does not Interpret with a capital "I," but lets the music flow logically and naturally. Columbia's bright-sounding recording helps the good work.

As these three quartets are also available on separate discs as played by the Budapest, the purchaser can make his investment one disc at a time, if he so desires. Many other recordings of the last three Schubert quartets are available. *No. 13:* The Italian Quartet on L 668 has some peculiar notions about the first movement, dragging it no end. Otherwise the playing has a most elegant polish. The Vegh on L 587 is satisfactory but tonally a little rough. Neither it nor the Vienna Konzerthaus on W 5115 has the "lift" of the Budapest. *No. 14:* The Koeckert on D 9567 offers a spirited "Death and the Maiden" handicapped by recorded sound that is relatively lifeless and lacking in presence. There also is an annoying break in the second movement. The Hungarian Quartet on CH 1152 is a thick-sounding recording weighted on the bass end. The interpretation itself is excellent. Both the Barchet on Vox 8810 and the Amadeus on V HMV 1058 present lyric performances, and both have been beautifully recorded. Also well recorded is the Vienna Konzerthaus on W 5052 (though in spots a little overamplified); this is one of its best discs, played with force and assurance. "Death and the Maiden" is fortunate in its LP interpreters. *No. 15:* Budapest is supreme here, with a combination of polish, virility, and lyric tenderness which neither the Vienna Konzerthaus on W 5041 nor the Fine Arts on Mer 10104 can match.

*Quartettsatz in C minor. Koeckert, 10" D 4044 (*Wolf: Italian Serenade).*

Several organizations have recorded this great quartet movement, but this is the only version that presents it complete on one side of a disc. The Koeckert handles its assignment with accomplishment. Vitality is present in the playing, plus a fond shaping of the lyric elements. Excellent recorded sound. What with an equally fine performance of Wolf's delicious *Italian Serenade* on the reverse, this is a disc very much worth owning.

*Quintet for Piano and Strings in A ("Trout," Op. 114). Aeschbacher, Koeckert, D 9707. Pressler, Guilet, MGM 3128. Amsterdam, Ep 3046. Badura-Skoda, Vienna Konzerthaus, W 5025. Horszowski, Budapest, C 4317. Wuehrer, Barchet, Vox 8970 (*Nocturne in E flat).*

None of these can be unreservedly recommended. At the same time, each is a musicianly account of the score. The Aeschbacher-

Koeckert collaboration is a little overdeliberate, a little lacking in spontaneity, but it is a remarkably steady performance, guided by the controlling force of Aeschbacher. MGM's is the best quality of recorded sound. Pressler and the Guilet Quartet, on the MGM disc, present a bright, lightweight, lyric performance. I find the tone of the string-players somewhat thin and unresonant; otherwise there is little about which to complain. Epic's version, with the Amsterdam Quintet, is not too well recorded. Musically it is much in the Koeckert vein: reliable, sober, well co-ordinated. Badura-Skoda and the Vienna players are often bracing and effervescent. What spoils this disc is the tendency of the Vienna Konzerthaus to slow down when it wants to be "expressive." Too many changes in tempo are present, especially in the variation movement. Columbia's recording sounds dated. The piano often is in the background, the strings lack resonance, and there is excess surface noise. The performance, as can be expected of such participants as Horszowski and the Budapest, is good. The Vox disc offers fine piano-playing from Wuehrer and rather unattractive tonal support from the strings. This is a stiff performance, but an undeniably powerful one. A version with a combination of Vox's steadiness and Westminster's charm has yet to be recorded. Members of the Vienna Octet play the "Trout" on L 223: a straightforward interpretation lacking imagination; and the recorded sound is thick and undefined in the bass (though a lovely string tone is present elsewhere). When will Victor release as a collector's item the magnificent performance of Schnabel and the Pro Arte?

Quintet for Strings in C (K. 163). B. Heifetz, Budapest, C 4437. Stern, etc., C 4714.

One of the sublime works in the repertoire, this *Quintet in C* is represented on LP by a near-definitive performance by the Budapest ensemble. An aristocratic quality is present on this disc. The playing is suave but never weak, and it is distinguished by the perfect Budapest co-ordination. I find more flexibility here than in any comparable recorded version. Clear, well-balanced recording. The other Columbia disc, recorded at the 1952 Prades Festival, has the services of some redoubtable string-players: Stern, Schneider, Katims, Casals, and Tortelier. An impressive array, this, and a fine performance. Quite a difference in conception is present between the two versions. The Budapest is

Grecian in its approach; the Prades group is darker and more intense. I prefer the elegance of the Budapest, but those who end up with Stern & Co. will have no cause for regret. Other versions include one by the Vienna Konzerthaus on W 5033, in which the players are up to their old trick of slowing down and changing tempos to suit themselves. What they do to the second subject of the first movement is absurdly sentimental. The Amadeus Quartet on V HMV 1051 is never at odds with the music, but never particularly revealing or exciting. The Hollywood Quartet on Cap 8133 plays without the character and affinity it shows for the modern repertoire. Its ideas about the *Quintet in C* are much too sweet for my taste.

*Rondo Brillant in B minor (Op. 70). Szigeti, Bussotti, C 4642 (*Beethoven: Violin Sonata No. 10).*

Szigeti plays this sprightly work with his customary spirit. The technical aspects give him some trouble, however. He has to work audibly hard, and some of the results are, to say the least, rough. Clear recording.

Rondo for Violin and String Quartet in A. See *Trio for Strings in B flat* (W 5223).

*Sonata for Cello in A minor ("Arpeggione"). Feuermann, Moore, C 4677 (*Haydn: Cello Concerto). Gendron, Françaix, L 654 (*Schumann: Romances; Fantasiestücke).*

Schubert originally composed this for the arpeggione, a now obsolete instrument that had a brief vogue in the early nineteenth century. For some reason, many critics and musicologists have turned up their nose at this exceedingly lovely score. Both of these recordings are admirable. The London is the best modern version, with rich-sounding recording and accomplished playing that is songful, perfectly in tune, mellow in tone. Gendron appears to be an aristocratic player. The Columbia disc, transferred to LP from shellacs, has a heavy surface, and cannot be considered a good example of the recording art. But it contains Feuermann's magnificent playing, in a performance that is volatile, gracious, and sinuous. If the dated quality of this recording scares you away, you will find the Gendron a perfectly acceptable substitute. Several other cellists have attempted the work. Mainardi and Borciani offer a musical interpretation on 10" D 7539, but the cause is not helped by Mainardi's dry tone. Some beautiful playing by G. Ricci (the brother of Ruggiero) on Str 612 is handicapped by dullish recorded sound. Albin, in Tel 66015, goes about his work with spirit, but lacks the controlled artistry of a Feuermann or a Gendron.

NOTE: The following numbers of the piano sonatas follow the chronological order as set forth in the Clough and Cuming World's Encyclopedia of Recorded Music.

*Sonata for Piano No. 5 in B (Op. 147). Wuehrer, Vox 8420 (*Sonata No. 19).*

Hardly ever is this early sonata heard in concert. Many fine things are contained in it, and all are brought out by Wuehrer, who gives a virtual blueprint of the music. You could write down the work from his performance. Every dotted eighth note is meticulously observed, every phrase is in place, every chord is clearly balanced. Wuehrer is a superb pianist for music like this, and his projected series of all the Schubert sonatas should prove one of the most valuable contributions to the piano discography. Excellent recorded sound.

Sonata for Piano No. 6 in E flat (Op. 122). See *Sonata No. 17* (Vox 8820).

*Sonata for Piano No. 13 in A (Op. 120). Wuehrer, Vox 8590 (*Sonata No. 18). Goldsand, CH 1148 (*Moments musicaux).*

The only reservation about Wuehrer's performance involves the last movement, in which he sounds unnecessarily pedantic. Admirable artist though he is, Wuehrer has a tendency to lack sparkle, and his slow tempo in one of Schubert's more gossamer pieces of piano-writing makes the music more ponderous than it is. Nevertheless it is the best version of the sonata, though Goldsand's playing has a degree of lightness that Wuehrer lacks. Goldsand, however, does not have the German pianist's steadiness and technical solidity. Badura-Skoda has recorded the work as the last side of his two-disc *Impromptus* album (W WAL 5); it is not available from him on a single disc.

*Sonata for Piano No. 14 in A minor (Op. 143). Wuehrer, Vox 8210 (*Sonata No. 21).*

On this disc the *A minor Sonata* occupies part of the last side; the posthumous *B flat Sonata* has most of the space. Short and, for Schubert, compact, No. 14 is a superb piece of music with a lyric theme in the last movement which is close to heaven. Wuehrer's performance is powerful and manly. He has excellent recorded sound. A note on the jacket of the disc suggests NAB equalization, but I had much more success with the old Orthophonic curve. Lili Kraus has recorded this work on D 8506. She plays sensitively, but without Wuehrer's authority; and the recorded sound is nowhere near so good.

*Sonata for Piano No. 16 in A minor (Op. 42). Kempff, L 792. Kraus, D 8518 (*Valses nobles).*

From nearly every point of view the London disc is better: quality of sound, breadth of performance, and musical style. Decca's recording is low-level, without much color or resonance. The *Valses nobles*, which fills out the last side of the Decca disc, has a more realistic piano sound, and Kraus plays the lovely sketches with taste. Applebaum has recorded the sonata on W 5313 (**Sonata No. 6*). His ideas about the music (and also the accompanying *E flat Sonata*) are intense and sincere—but ever so ponderous. I don't find much imagination in his work, and would consider the Kempff version a better choice even though his disc contains one work in contrast to the other pianists' two.

*Sonata for Piano No. 17 in D (Op. 53). Wuehrer, Vox 8820 (*Sonata No. 6). Aitken, EMS 108.*

On the Vox disc you can get two sonatas as against the D major only on the EMS. In addition, Wuehrer is a more convincing Schubert-player than Aitken. The German pianist maintains more of a flow, particularly in the slow movement. His style is big but not muscle-bound. Aitken, trying to get a big style, sounds merely labored. His slow movement is flabby compared to Wuehrer's, and his insistence on taking every repeat and second ending in the third movement makes it sound intolerable. For some reason Wuehrer is less satisfying in the *E flat Sonata* (Op. 122) on the reverse of his disc. As in his recording of No. 13 in A (Op. 120) he seems to lack the volatility for the less imposing sonatas. Apparently he is a man for the long run, not the sprints. I wish that Vox had given him better recording. This is the only poor example of recorded sound in Wuehrer's Schubert series. The *D major Sonata* lacks resonance and thins out badly on top, while the E flat has some shatter. EMS has given Aitken much superior fidelity.

*Sonata for Piano No. 18 in G (Op. 78). Wuehrer, Vox 8590 (*Sonata No 13). Jolles, HS 81 (*3 Klavierstücke).*

Also known as the *Fantasy-Sonata* or *Sonata-Fantasy*, this work is one of Schubert's finest keyboard pieces. Wuehrer, as usual, offers a performance that has style, dignity, and pianistic resource. He shapes a phrase with the utmost intelligence and never lets the attention flag. Jolles has gathered many admirers for his performance of this work. I am not one of those admirers. I find the playing stolid and heavy, scarcely hinting at the poetry of the musical ideas. One attractive feature about his disc is the inclusion of the seldom-played posthumous *Klavierstücke* —magnificent compositions, almost morbid, like thunderheads with lightning playing around the edges. Aitken has recorded the *G major Sonata* on EMS 109. A reason for disqualification is economic: the other versions offer two works on one disc, whereas Aitken presents only the sonata.

*Sonata for Piano No. 19 in C minor (posthumous). Wuehrer, Vox 8420 (*Sonata No. 5). Aitken, EMS 110.*

Aitken suffers by being represented with a disc containing one work as against the two played by Wuehrer. Even at best, however, Aitken cannot match Wuehrer's bigger style and more comprehensive grasp of the notes. Wuehrer is a pianist of skill and integrity. He is never especially graceful; nor do tenderness or charm appear to play a major part in his emotional make-up. What he does have is musicianship, sweep, power, and an ability to integrate Schubert's rambling measures such as few pianists have had since Schnabel. Wuehrer gets marvelous things out of the massive slow movement, with its many enharmonic changes, and displays a steel-like tension that is almost hair-raising.

Sonata for Piano No. 20 in A (posthumous). Aitken, EMS 111. Kraus, Vox 6940.

Neither of these versions fills the bill, and prospective buyers had better wait until Wuehrer records it (Vox has announced Wuehrer in all the Schubert piano sonatas), or until Victor decides to release the great old Schnabel interpretation. Aitken's work is careful but never passionate, and the tremendous slow movement under his fingers is more related to a hill in Central Park than to the Matterhorn. Nor is Kraus able to rise to the big moments. Sensitivity there is, but music on this scope demands something monumental.

*Sonata for Piano No. 21 in B flat (posthumous). Wuehrer, Vox 8210 (*Sonata No. 14). Kempff, L 307.*

Vox gives you more for your money: two well-played sonatas, as against the single work contained on the London disc. Kempff and Wuehrer are pianists very much in the same style. Both exhibit the Teutonic school of playing; both work in broad, massive strokes; both have strength and integrity. I prefer Wuehrer in these sonatas for his more careful workmanship and closer adherence to the text. Vox also has a brighter quality of recorded sound. Haskil, on Ep 3031 (*Schumann: *Bunte Blätter*), has recorded the *B flat Sonata* quite tastefully, though without the concentration that Wuehrer brings. Aitken on EMS 12 has some interesting ideas, but not always the authority to put them across. Worth consideration is the Horowitz version. Horowitz plays the sonata as part of his Carnegie Hall concert: see Collections: Horowitz (V LM 6014).

Sonatas (Sonatinas) for Violin and Piano Nos. 1 in D, 2 in A minor, and 3 in G minor (Op. 137). Mischakoff, Balogh, Ly 7.

Of these three, only No. 1 is familiar. All are worth knowing. They were published as "sonatas" but are more commonly known as "sonatinas." Two good musicians participate in this disc, but Mischakoff's imprecise intonation and unyielding tone are scarcely the best medium for these gentle, lyric works. Or for any other. Clear-sounding recording, fine balance. Szigeti has an attractive performance of No. 1 on C 4133 (*Beethoven: *Sonata in D*, Op. 12, No. 1). Heifetz has recorded No. 3 on V LM 1861 (*Bloch: *Violin Sonata;* Handel: *Violin Sonata No. 6 in E*). Heifetz is incredibly suave and fluent.

*Sonata (Duo) for Violin and Piano in A (Op. 162). Kreisler, Rachmaninoff, V LCT 1128 (*Grieg: Violin Sonata No. 3). Oistrakh, Oborin, Per 573 (*Tartini: Violin Sonata in G minor; Beethoven: Violin Sonata in F, Op. 24). Szigeti, Hess, C 4717 (*Variations for Flute and Piano on "Trock'ne Blumen").*

Kreisler and Rachmaninoff recorded the *Sonata in A* (or, as it is better known, the *Duo*) in 1928. The transfer to LP sounds amazingly vital. The violin comes through well and the piano, while tubby, is clear. I wouldn't swap this version for any other ever made, even in consideration of the excellent disc that Szigeti and Hess recorded at the Prades Festival in 1952, or of the more positive, virile performance of Oistrakh and Oborin (which is well recorded, though far from the last sonic word). The grace and tenderness that Kreisler and Rachmaninoff display are a unique experience in this day of knock-'em-dead instrumentalism. If you feel that you will not be content with what is, after all, dated recorded sound, I suggest looking into the Oistrakh version, which has a little more control and tonal beauty than that encountered in the Columbia disc.

*Trio for Piano and Strings No. 1 in B flat (Op. 99). Heifetz, Feuermann, Rubinstein, V LCT 1017. Albeneri, Mer MG 10106. Thibaud, Cortot, Casals, V LCT 1141 (*Schumann: Trio in D minor). Fournier, Janigro, Badura-Skoda, W 5188.*

Much sentimental interest attaches to the Heifetz-Feuermann-Rubinstein disc, and even more to the Thibaud-Cortot-Casals. Many veteran collectors were weaned on the latter, which was recorded in 1926 (a really early electrical recording). Its sound is primitive. Moreover, you'd think that Victor might have checked the pitch. On the LP transfer, the work starts a whole tone down, in A flat instead of B flat, and it ends in A major, a half-tone down. (The Schumann on the reverse is right on key.) Much more successful is the transfer on V LCT 1017, which gives a good idea of the sound of the three virtuosos (though naturally one cannot expect, from a 1942 recording, anything approximating the color and balance of a late LP). Elegance and extreme polish mark this interpretation—and, of course, impeccable playing. Of the modern versions I prefer the Albeneri. It has consecutive flow, fine organization, considerable spirit. The performance on the Westminster disc does not have the homogenous quality that Badura-Skoda, Fournier, and Janigro have elsewhere achieved. Nothing really is wrong with their playing, but it lacks the split-second sense of timing, attack, and release which it should have; and tonally it is nothing to get excited about. I am not an admirer of the Schneider-Casals-Istomin performance, from the 1952 Prades Festival, on C 4715. Istomin's work at the keyboard does not match the volatile quality of the score. The performance sounds heavy, with more application than spontaneity.

Trio for Piano and Strings No. 2 in E flat (Op. 100). A. Busch, H. Busch, Serkin, C 4654. Fournier, Janigro, Badura-Skoda, W 5121. Schneider, Casals, Horszowski, C 4716. Albeneri, Mer 10107.

Each of this quartet of performances has something to recommend. I think that the Busch-Serkin collaboration is the best all-around choice, with a combination of authority and lyricism which is hard to beat. And Serkin's work is above that of any pianist who has played the *E flat Trio* on LP. Generally good recording, though some of the highs are shrill. The Westminster artists present the most relaxed reading. This is chamber music in the best sense: genial, unpretentious, and very musical. Something very gracious and *gemütlich* surrounds the slow movement as they deliver it. The Mercury disc goes along with sweep, style, and strength.

Good recording, marred by an excessive amount of pops, snaps, and crackles. Schneider, Casals, and Horszowski made their recording at the 1952 Prades Festival. It is not the last word in ensemble playing, but remains a well-planned, serious performance. The grunting noises that Casals makes during the course of the slow movement are an interesting supplement to the music.

Trio for Strings in B flat; Trio Movement in B flat; Rondo for Violin and String Quartet in A. Vienna Konzerthaus, W 5223.

Three fairly early and fairly routine pieces. The *Rondo* is sometimes heard in an arrangement for violin and string orchestra; here it is presented in its original form. Dry performances, skillful but routine, well recorded.

Variations in A flat (Op. 35); Introduction and Variations in B flat (Op. 82, No. 2); Lebensstürme (Op. 144). Badura-Skoda and Demus, W 5147.

All of these works are for piano four hands. Not well known, they are exceedingly lovely; and if you want to hear some intense harmonies, even for Schubert, listen to the seventh variation of the Op. 35 set. Excellent performances here. There is a constant flow that is devoid of artificial build-up or artificial dynamics. Not the least hint of slickness is present; just music. The recording is excellent in quality: clear, bell-like, well balanced. If you get this disc you will have a little gem. Piatigorsky has made a cello transcription of the *Introduction and Variations:* see Chopin: *Cello Sonata* (C 4215).

*Variations for Flute and Piano on "Trock'ne Blümen." Wummer, Mannes, C 4717 (*Sonata for Violin and Piano in A).*

A chip from the 1952 Prades Festival. Schubert took the theme from one of the songs in *Die schöne Müllerin.* It is an appealing work. Wummer's performance is nothing less than masterful, displaying the kind of tone and breath control which can be set up as a model. The recorded sound is clear in the high register, muddy and ill-defined in the bass.

SCHUBERT-LISZT

Die Forelle; Gretchen am Spinnrade; Barcarolle; Auf dem Wasser zu singen; Der Lindenbaum; Der Erlkönig; Soirée de Vienne No. 6; Liebesbotschaft. Petri, C 4436.

Also on this disc is Carl Tausig's transcription of an *Andante and Variations.* (Tausig was Liszt's favorite pupil; he died in 1871 at the age of thirty.) Some people think that Liszt's tinkering with the Schubert songs amounted to an act of musical vandalism. Others, myself included, put up a strong brief for them as effective, ingenious, original compositions that stand on their own as significant contributions to the piano literature of the nineteenth century. Petri is one of the great Liszt pianists of our time, and we are fortunate to have these examples of his art on records. His rather massive style, big technique, and authoritative phrasings are models of what can be done to these pieces without vulgarizing them. There are many flashy effects here, but Petri does not play them as flashy effects. Rather he conceives them as part of the musical scheme; and it is amazing, after all the insensitive pounding to which this music has been subjected by many other pianists, to see how well the music holds up when it is approached by a real artist.

SCHUBERT-PIATIGORSKY

Introduction, Theme, and Variations. See Chopin: *Cello Sonata* (C 4215).

SCHUMAN, WILLIAM (1910-)

Quartet for Strings No. 4. See Dahl: *Concerto a Tre* (C 4493).

SCHUMANN, CLARA (1819-1896)

*Trio for Piano and Strings in G minor (Op. 17). Mannes, Gimpel, Silva, D 9555 (*Beethoven: Trio in B flat).*

As being by the wife of Robert Schumann, Clara's music has been dwarfed. She wrote many pretty piano pieces, songs, a piano concerto, and other works. This *Trio in G minor* is more than an amateurish attempt, and very many composers of the century would have been glad to call it their own. The shadow of Robert lies over it. He was, of course, much the stronger musical personality of the two; and Clara absorbed his romanticism, his pet harmonies, and some of his melodic devices. Yet there are many spontaneous moments, and the second movement is something quite individual. (Five dollars will get you ten that Robert carefully edited and touched up the score.) Good recorded sound is present, and the performance sounds entirely accurate, if rather stolid.

SCHUMANN, ROBERT (1810-1856)

*Abegg Variations (Op. 1). Demus, W 5410 (*Faschingsschwank aus Wien; Arabesque; Blumenstück). Foldes, Mer 10122 (*Impromptus on a Theme by Clara Wieck; Papillons; Toccata).*

Of the two pianists, Demus is the more spontaneous, and he has more grace in his conception. Foldes plays the notes accurately but with coolness, missing the romantic ardor of the music. The *Impromptus* on Foldes's disc is a weak work, and there are better versions of the *Papillons* and *Toccata.* On the other hand, Demus's disc contains a good performance of the *Arabesque* and a very fine one of the *Faschingsschwank.* He also plays the seldom-heard *Blumenstück* ("Flower Piece"), an ultra-melodic invention which he handles quite lyrically. A ten-measure cut does not mar the *Blumenstück;* indeed, it improves the music (Harold Bauer used to advise the cut that Demus takes). Clear recording.

Album for the Young (Op. 68). Zeitlin, Op 6004.

All forty-three short pieces are contained on this disc. Zeitlin's playing is precise and not very colorful. Pedantic might be the word. Everything is much on a single dynamic plane. Take No. 3 as a typical example: she makes no attempt to build up the melodic line, avoiding any hint of crescendo-decrescendo. The recorded sound is startlingly lifelike.

*Andante and Variations for Two Pianos (Op. 46). Appleton and Field, Vox 7740 (*Konzertstück for 4 Horns and Orchestra). Bartlett and Robertson, MGM 3027 (*Brahms: Variations on a Theme by Haydn).*

The Vox version goes back some years. Appleton and Field play the original score, for two pianos plus horn (Barrows, in this recording) and two cellos (Oxman, Sarser). I am not overly fond of this performance. It is a little finicky, more than a little percussive, and does not convey the pulsating romanticism of the music. But Appleton and Field remain superior to the Bartlett-Robertson combine, which lacks flow. The field is wide open for a modern recording.

Arabesque (Op. 18). See *Abegg Variations* (W 5410); *Papillons* (L 515).

Blumenstück (Op. 19). See *Abegg Variations* (W 5410).

*Bünte Blätter (Op. 99). Haskil, Ep 3031 (*Schubert: Sonata No. 21).*

Fourteen short pieces make up this set. Haskil plays only the first eight, as a filler on the last side of the Schubert sonata disc. The *Bünte Blätter* are pretty sketches that Schumann had hanging around; he put them together under the present title. Too bad Haskil could not get the entire work on her disc. She plays the music well, and the recorded sound is good.

*Carnaval (Op. 9). Rachmaninoff, 10" V LCT 12. Novaes, Vox 7830 (*Papillons). Gieseking, C 4772 (*Mozart: Sonatas Nos. 14, 15). Rubinstein, V LM 1822 (*Franck: Prelude, Chorale, and Fugue).*

I realize that the aged Rachmaninoff recording has nowhere near the luster of sound present in the other versions, but no pianist on records has achieved comparable results with Schumann's kaleidoscopic writing. The performance is amazing. Some of the tempos are very fast—probably faster than they should be—but Rachmaninoff carries them off triumphantly. This virile, magnificent type of piano-playing is a grand testimonial to the genius of the Russian giant; and how the man could mold a phrase! Novaes's is the best modern recording. She is a stylist on quite a different plane from Rachmaninoff. She does not have his directness or his way of going straight to the heart of the musical matter. Rather she is all nuance and suggestion, seeking out inner voices, seemingly working by instinct rather than reason. Clear recording, rather noisy surfaces. Gieseking's performance is interesting. It is a bit noncommittal, and one feels that he never really warms to the task, but a vast authority is present—wrong notes and all. I find Rubinstein's version disappointing. The tempos often are on the slow side, he lacks his usual dash, and one misses the electricity and vitality that usually pervade his interpretations. Occasionally he is actually sluggish. Of several other versions in the catalogues, Badura-Skoda on W 5105 (**Sonata No. 1*) is immature and not ready for the above kind of competition. Brailowsky on V LM 9003 (**Fantasia in C*) is percussive and little more than routine. The Arrau performance on 10" D 7502 is worth mention for a formidable technical exposition of the music. Otherwise it is cold, and the recording has a highly dated sound.

*Concert Studies (6) on Caprices by Paganini (Op. 3). Wuehrer, Vox 8850 (*Brahms: Variations on a Theme by Paganini; Liszt: Étude No. 6 after Paganini).*

I had never before heard this music, and I imagine that it will be equally novel to most listeners. The Brahms and Liszt settings of the Paganini caprices are much better known. Yet Schumann's is more sensitive than Liszt's and certainly as interesting (Schumann did not, in this Op. 3, transcribe the *A minor Caprice* that Brahms used for his *Paganini Variations*). In a way the writing is equally difficult, though not as transparently flashy. Wuehrer's performance has breadth and manual security. His playing, somewhat heavy and lacking in poetry, is nevertheless exceedingly thorough. Such able pianism must be regarded with respect. Fairly good recorded sound. This is a valuable addition to the Schumann discography.

Davidsbündlertänze (Op. 6). Aeschbacher, 10" D 7531. Gieseking, U 7106.

Aeschbacher is the best buy here. His performance is really distinguished until the final dance, where he misses the point. In general the recorded sound is satisfactory, despite some bad surfaces and low-level reproduction. The Urania disc presents a most erratic Gieseking. He is careless, missing notes, blurring many passages. Withal, he has the stature of a great artist, and the way he shapes certain phrases is something that few could duplicate. (There was a big fuss when this disc was issued, followed by a lawsuit in which Gieseking charged that the recording was unauthorized.) Good recorded sound, though there is a slight "wow" in sustained tones. Neither Battista on MGM 3011 nor Demus on W 5232 displays a brand of pianism comparable to that which Aeschbacher or Gieseking is capable. I would avoid both. Demus is unimaginative, while Battista tries to overpower the writing. A curiosity is the performance by Adelaide de Lara on Apollo 1. She was a pupil of Clara Schumann and now resides in England, where the disc originally was issued. De Lara plays very slowly and sensitively, with quite a few technical slips.

*Études symphoniques (Op. 13). Anda, An 35046 (*Brahms: Paganini Variations). Lympany, V HMV 1013 (*Franck: Symphonic Variations).*

*Casadesus, C 4388 (*Beethoven: Sonata No. 31). Boukoff, Ep 3094 (*Fantasia in C).*

In general, Anda has the most romanticism. He includes several of the seldom-heard variations that Schumann composed but decided to drop from the published version. There is a short cut in the finale. A big technician with an ability to color a phrase with subtlety, Anda seems well cast as a Schumann-player. Boukoff's performance also rates high. He plays all of the five unpublished variations, and brings to his interpretation a good deal of pianistic and musical strength. I would not call his a colorful way of approaching the music, but it has taste, probity, and musicianship. This disc is worth owning. It is also a good example of piano tone. Lympany offers a well-controlled performance marred by a few kittenish ideas. She *will* become sentimental and linger over cantabile sections. Very good playing, for the most part, and excellent sound. Casadesus brings exquisite polish to the music, but he has little to say. In the third variation he skips up and down with utmost brilliance—and the emotional meaning is about nil. The other versions in the catalogue have little to recommend. Katchen on L 823 (*Franck: *Prelude, Chorale, and Fugue*) seems unable to integrate the music into a cohesive unit. The Yves Nat disc (HS 87) is technically unsteady, and anybody who gets it will have to put up with a poorly played Schumann *Fantasy* on the reverse. Brailowsky's version is available only as part of the two-disc V LM 6000, three sides of which are devoted to Chopin études.

*Fantasia in C (Op. 17). Curzon, L 1009 (*Kinderscenen). Firkusny, C 4238. Fischer, V HMV 1065 (*Brahms: Sonata No. 3). Boukoff, Ep 3094 (*Études symphoniques). Brailowsky, V LM 9003 (*Carnaval).*

Curzon is recommended here. He has the best quality of recorded sound (even with a prominent hiss in the last movement), and his music-making has more sensitivity than is found elsewhere in this work on LP. The only disappointing thing about this performance is the cautious tempo of the second movement. It may be that Curzon, like every other pianist who ever lived, is worried about the horrible skips in the coda. Nobody—well, hardly anybody—gets through that coda without slipping up somewhere along the line. Brailowsky solves the problem by slowing up noticeably. He plays it safe; the result is stodgy. On the whole, Brailowsky's performance is that of a *routinier.* Sections of the second movement also throw Fischer, whose playing elsewhere is experienced and mature, though without the color of Curzon's. The HMV recording has a thick bass and is hard to handle. Firkusny brings considerable spontaneity to the music. Unfortunately his version occupies all of a disc, which makes it less attractive economically than the Curzon. Boukoff is a little less convincing here than he was in the *Études symphoniques*. His playing is never less than competent, but there is something thick and stolid about it. A quality of musical rapture, of imagination and personality, hardly ever enters into this performance. Nevertheless, by virtue of the fine playing on the reverse, and by the fact that Boukoff makes no errors of commission, this version of the *Fantasia* will find a place in many record libraries. Yves Nat, on HS 87, has interesting ideas, but the veteran pianist is no longer up to the technical demands. Both Weisz on L 152 and Demus on W 5157 utterly lack passion in this most passionate of piano pieces, and Foldes on D 9708 also misses the poetry.

*Fantasiestücke (Op. 12). Rubinstein, V LM 1072 (*Beethoven: Sonata No. 8). Engel, Ep 3070 (*Faschingsschwank aus Wien). Blancard, 10" L 210.*

Carefully as Blancard plays, and as vigorously as Engel goes through the notes, they cannot approach Rubinstein's poise and innate romanticism; and why Blancard so rushes the first number, "*Des Abends*," is an unanswered question. Engel sounds heavy beside Rubinstein, who somehow makes most pianists sound thick. The Blancard recording has some heavy background noise, and is low-level. Rubinstein's, which dates back some years, also has excessive background noise, but is a much more lifelike reproduction of the piano. I do not care much for the heavy-sounding Epic recording. A version of the *Fantasiestücke* by Demus on W 5157 is nowhere near the romanticism and color of the music.

Fantasiestücke for Cello (Op. 73). See Chopin: *Cello Sonata* (C 4215); Schumann: *Romances* (L 654).

*Faschingsschwank aus Wien (Op. 26). Demus, W 5410 (*Abegg Variations; Arabesque; Blumenstück). Engel, Ep 3070 (*Fantasiestücke, Op. 12). Blancard, Van 416 (*Brahms: Variations on a Theme by Schumann). Weisz, L 798 (*Brahms: Waltzes).*

Meaning "Carnival Jests in Vienna." I like the Demus version best of all. He is steady, sometimes passionate, and constantly flowing. Often he pitches things a little on the loud side. Still, this is the best playing I have heard from him: a spirited, forceful interpretation, resonantly recorded. Blancard gets more of the carnival feeling than Engel or Weisz. The last plays accurately, but lacks personality. Engel is more authoritative, and technically he is stronger than Blancard, who occasionally has trouble with the notes. She seems to feel the music and identify herself with it, however, and in the Intermezzo movement she brings to the writing a multicolored touch that is a tribute to her instincts. Her disc has been well recorded save for an unpleasant ping during fortissimo attacks in the upper register. Engel's recording is rather thick-sounding, but will serve most purposes.

Forest Scenes (Op. 82). See *Waldscenen* (C 4366).

Fünf Stücke im Volkston (Op. 102). See *Trio No. 1 in D minor* (C 4718).

*Humoresque (Op. 20). Demus, W 5264 (*Sonata No. 3).*

Seldom played in concert, this is a long piece with many beautiful sections. It requires a type of sustained romanticism that Demus cannot produce. He is a good technician who offers little besides a correct outlay of note values. The Intermezzo movement sounds almost like a Czerny exercise as Demus conceives it. Beautiful recorded sound, but the field remains open for a more definitive version.

Impromptus on a Theme by Clara Wieck (Op. 5). See *Abegg Variations* (Mer 10122).

*Intermezzos (Op. 4). Johannesen, CH 1173 (*Sonata No. 3).*

Here is a really negelected piece that happens to rank with major works like the *Carnaval* and *Davidsbündlertänze.* It too is composed of short sections, and it is equally impassioned and ultra-romantic. Johannesen plays it very well. His is not a romantic temperament, but one must respect his musicianship, his technical accuracy, and his good taste. He also has a redeeming vigor that never degenerates into bombast. This well-ordered performance has clear sound. I recommend this disc very highly.

Intermezzo for Violin. See Brahms: *Sonatas for Violin* (C SL 202); see also Collections: Milstein (Cap 8259).

*Kinderscenen (Op. 15). Novaes, Vox 8540 (*Piano Concerto). Horowitz, V LM 1109 (*Chopin: 7 Mazurkas). Gieseking, C 4520 (*Brahms: Intermezzi, Op. 117). Curzon, L 1009 (*Fantasia in C).*

Each of these is an interpretation worth owning. I respond most closely to the poetry and tenderness that Novaes brings. This is playing on as high a level as anybody today is going to offer. Horowitz is on his best behavior here. He keeps everything down, and his simple, singing line is something to admire. Seldom has he displayed so sensitive and unassuming an artistry (in other discs, even where he fights to be simple, a nervous tension comes through). Only in the *"Träumerei"* does the worst in him come out; it is a performance in Technicolor seen through the wrong end of the telescope. Gieseking has charm, relaxation, and culture behind his playing. But direct comparison with Horowitz shows that the latter is no less deficient in suggesting the charm of the music (except for the above-mentioned *"Träumerei"*), and has a firmer grasp of the notes. Curzon has the best-sounding recording. He is a fine artist who is never guilty of a breach of taste, and his interpretation should attract a wide following. To my taste, however, it just misses the magic of Novaes and the magnificent pianistic discipline of Horowitz. Other recordings: Cortot on V HMV 1009 offers a slow performance, far from accurate technically, played with considerable style. It is coupled with a dull-sounding version of the Debussy *Prèludes* (Book I). Blancard, on Van 415 *(*Sonata No. 3)*, plays prettily but without stature.

*Kreisleriana (Op. 16). Demus, W 5142 (*Romance in F sharp). Gieseking, U 7107 (*Bach: English Suite No. 6).*

Strange things happen on the Urania disc. The opening is sloppy and disorganized, and some subsequent sections are not to be expected from a pianist of Gieseking's stature. In view of the technical errors that swarm through the opening measures, one can well understand Gieseking's action in seeking an injunction to prevent the sale of the disc. The prissy Demus version is at least technically exact, and he plays the *F sharp Romance* with taste. But the really romantic, fiery *Kreisleriana* is yet to be recorded.

*Märchenerzählungen (Op. 132). Demus, Wlach, Weiss, W 5024 (*Mendelssohn: 2 Concert Pieces).*

The forbidding collection of vowels and consonants that make up the title means "Fairy Tales." This is a set of four pieces scored for piano, clarinet, and viola. You won't hear them in a lifetime of concert-going; which doesn't make the music any less songful and attractive. In most cases when music has dropped from the repertoire there is a very sound reason why. But surely these Schumann pieces deserve an occasional airing. The performance here sounds properly lyrical, and the recording is excellent if you have the means to reduce the sharp highs.

*Papillons (Op. 2). Novaes, Vox 7830 (*Carnaval). Kempff, L 515 (*Arabesque; Liszt: 3 Sonetti del Petrarca from Années de pèlerinage).*

To some listeners Novaes's playing here may seem capricious. But a piece of music is more than a black-and-white series of ovals placed on ruled lines. The instinct and color with which Novaes phrases; her ability to catch a subtle, unexpected curve here, accent or inner voice there; her ravishing tonal resource—all this is a vanishing art. I would call this one of Novaes's greatest discs; perhaps her greatest. The powerful Kempff performance sounds stiff next to that of Novaes, though on all counts it is good piano-playing. He also does fine work in the *Arabesque*. Demus, on W 5232, is not remotely near these two; and Foldes, on Mer 10122, sounds methodical and colorless.

*Quartet for Piano and Strings in E flat (Op. 47). New York Quartet, C 4892 (*Brahms: Horn Trio).*

I get the impression that the group has not lived with this work very long. Four musicians as good as these (Schneider, Katims, Miller, Horszowski) cannot but give a reliable performance; and yet the extra ingredients that make an interpretation memorable are missing: an element of rapture; that last, final touch to a melodic line; an instinctive rather than technical application. Excellent recorded sound.

Quartets for Strings Nos. 1 in A minor and No. 3 in A (Op. 41, Nos. 1 and 3). Curtis, W 5166.

These are good but scarcely inspired versions. The Curtis Quartet plays with deliberate tempos, and in some places the attack is heavy. One example: the opening of the second movement of the A minor is earthbound rather than airborne. But in essence the Curtis brings out the romantic message of the music, and this pair of string quartets is music well worth knowing. As recorded sound, this disc is as faithful a reproduction of string-playing as you will find anywhere.

*Quartet for Strings No. 2 in F (Op. 41, No. 2). New Italian, L 323 (*Verdi: Quartet).*

A lyric, well-integrated reading without much contour. The playing itself is of the utmost loveliness, but one wishes that the Quartetto Italiano would dig into the music a little more. This group generally avoids passion, stressing the virtues of tone and ensemble. Good recording, though on a subdued level.

*Quintet for Piano and Strings in E flat (Op. 44). Rubinstein, Paganini, V LM 1095. Curzon, Budapest, C 4426. Hess, Stern, Schneider, Thomas, Tortelier, C 4711 (*Brahms: Quintet for Strings in G).*

The Rubinstein version goes back to 1950, but it still has resonant sound and clear piano tone, and remains a quality recording. Both Columbias are a little brighter. Nevertheless, I stubbornly cling to the Victor disc for its breadth and romanticism. Schumann's great *Piano Quintet* calls for color; and this it receives in abundance from Rubinstein and the Paganini Quartet. And, of all the pianists who have played the work, Rubinstein stands out for the finish of his style and his supreme virtuosity. Curzon, a fine artist, is heard to good advantage with the Budapest Quartet, and nobody could possibly regret owning this disc, though it lacks the *élan* of the Victor. The group headed by Hess made its recording at the 1952 Prades Festival. This is a sensitive performance, of course, but without the flow and organization present on the other discs. It does, however, offer the quintet on one side (with a superbly played Brahms on the reverse), and thus has an economy feature that the competing versions cannot boast. Still a third disc of the work comes from Columbia. On 10" C 2081 Serkin and the Busch Quartet are heard in a well-regulated but tonally rough performance.

*Romances (3) for Cello and Piano (Op. 94). Gendron, Françaix, L 654 (*3 Fantasiestücke; Schubert: "Arpeggione" Sonata for Cello).*

Old-timers will remember this work in the alternate for oboe and piano that Goossens made for Columbia in pre-war days. The three pieces are ultra-melodious, as are the *Fantasiestücke,* and they are brilliantly played by Gendron, who sounds like a cellist far above the average. He has, on records at any rate, a beautiful, rounded tone and absolutely perfect intonation. Whatever register he plays in sounds free. His musical instincts are also impeccable. This disc is superior in every way, as is the recorded sound.

*Romances (3) for Piano (Op. 28). Pressler, MGM 3029 (*Blumenstück; Mendelssohn: Variations sérieuses; Rondo Capriccioso).*

Of the three *Romances,* No. 2 in F sharp minor is the only one heard much these days, while the *Blumenstück* almost never appears on concert programs. For the most part the neglect of the latter is deserved; it is pretty repetitious. Pressler plays these works agreeably. He refrains from exaggeration and states the notes with a minimum of fuss. He also rings in some sensitive changes of color. Demus has recorded the *Romance in F sharp* (see *Kreisleriana,* W 5142). His performance sounds much more stolid than Pressler's.

*Sketches for Organ (Op. 58); Canon in B minor. Elsasser, MGM 3007 (*Mendelssohn: Organ Sonata No. 2 in D minor).*

These four *Sketches* are rarities. Schumann composed them for pedal piano. Now that the instrument is obsolete, organists have requisitioned the set. The intensely pianistic figuration does not fit the organ well, but Elsasser is an able technician, and his playing comes out with a good deal of fluency. Clearly defined recording.

*Sonata for Piano No. 1 in F sharp minor (Op. 11). Badura-Skoda, W 5105 (*Carnaval). Hoffmann-Behrendt, SPA 3.*

Not much competition here. Badura-Skoda plays better and gets the work on one side. He accomplishes this by taking a cut in the last movement (though he is not alone in this; many pianists, including no less a Schumann specialist than the late Harold Bauer, always have cut the finale). Sensitive as he is, however, Badura-Skoda is not the ideal interpreter for this kind of music—or, rather, was not when he made this disc. He has come a long way since then. His performance of the sonata is straight and lacking in color. He completely misses the point of the "*alla burla, ma pomposo*" episode of the Intermezzo, and he has trouble sustaining the finale. The recording, on a low level of sound, lacks the brightness of current piano LP's.

*Sonata for Piano No. 2 in F minor ("Concerto without Orchestra," Op. 14). Goldsand, CH 1147 (*Brahms: Paganini Variations).*

One of Schumann's less-played piano pieces, the *F minor Sonata* will not be of much interest to most listeners. It lacks the flow of the other sonatas and is extremely repetitious. Goldsand gets good piano-recording here, though the surfaces are prominent. He presents the music with a vigorous reading that is deficient in poetry. He also has to work much too hard over the technical problems of the last movement, and one feels the strain.

*Sonata for Piano No. 3 in G minor (Op. 22). Johannesen, CH 1173 (*Intermezzos, Op. 4). Blancard, Van 415 (*Kinderscenen). Demus, W 5264 (*Humoresque).*

Blancard plays the popular sonata with much force and also with some technical and tonal roughness. Johannesen is smoother technically; and while his recording is not as big in sound, it is closer to the piano than are the outsized dynamics of the Vanguard disc. On the whole, Johannesen's is the better choice. He does not have much fire, but his musicianship is incontestable and he is a technician of no mean order. The *Intermezzos* on side 2 of this disc is another factor that makes his disc the choice: no other pianist has recorded this delicious work. On the Westminster disc Demus picks at the sonata rather than plays it. Plenty of keyboard ability is present, without an equivalent musical impulse to back it up. He enjoys the best quality of recorded sound. Kathleen Long has recorded the sonata on L 188. Dated recorded quality here, and not a very perceptive performance.

*Sonata for Violin and Piano in A minor (Op. 105). Druian, Simms, Mer 70002 (*Brahms: Violin Sonata No. 2).*

For some reason this exceedingly lyric, sensitive work has never achieved much popularity. Its popularity will not be greatly furthered by this performance. Druian is not in the best of form here, and his work sounds labored. His intonation can best be described as precarious, and in some double-stopped passages he slides into the deep. The same remarks can be applied to the Brahms work on the reverse of the disc, though it must be admitted that musically Druian sounds more comfortable there. Excellent recording.

Toccata (Op. 7). See *Abegg Variations* (Mer 10122); see also Collections: Barere (Rem 199-141).

*Trio for Piano and Strings No. 1 in D minor (Op. 63). Schneider, Casals, Horszowski, C 4718 (*Fünf Stücke im Volkston). Gimpel, Silva, Mannes, D 9604 (*Schubert: Nocturne in E flat). Thibaud, Casals, Cortot, V LCT 1141 (*Schubert: Trio No. 1).*

The Victor is, of course, a reissue. It was recorded in 1928, and the sound is primitive. On the original 78's a good deal of surface noise is present. Victor has removed the noise and, in the process, has removed what little life the originals had. In this case, however, the interest is in the performance, not the recording, and a noble performance it is. The musicians play with a surging romanticism, and with a quality of tension (constant build-up and release, followed by more build-up and release) which the more modern versions do not reveal. The better of the two contemporary LP's is the Schneider-Casals-Horszowski, recorded at the 1952 Prades Festival. A better quality of sound than that encountered on the Decca disc is present; and, on the reverse of the disc,

Schumann's *Five Pieces for Cello in Folk Style* exhibit Casals's mature art. Casals plays with Leopold Mannes, the pianist on the Decca disc, who leads the Mannes-Gimpel-Silva Trio through the Schumann music with intelligence. The conception is not as robust as that which the Prades players bring, however, and the recording has a thinner sound.

*Trio for Piano and Strings No. 2 in F (Op. 80). Trio di Bolzano, Vox 8480 (*Chopin: Trio in G minor).*

About all that can be said is that the Trio di Bolzano plays the notes. Little breadth or style is encountered; certainly none of the ardent feeling that Schumann poured into the music. The stiff phrasing and unpleasant tone of the first violinist are too much of a handicap for the other members of the Trio to overcome. This is a lovely work, and should be represented more favorably on LP. Keep on the watch for another recording. One eventually will come.

*Waldscenen (Op. 82). Casadesus, C 4366 (*Debussy: Children's Corner).*

Like many of Schumann's piano works, these *Forest Scenes* are a group of short pieces bound under a generic title. Despite the competence of Casadesus's playing, I never could warm up to the interpretation. He plays with force rather than color; his attacks are inclined to be explosive; and his matter-of-factness misses the mood of such delicate sketches as *Verrufenes Stelle* or *Einsame Blumen.* To show that this is a minority opinion, Mr. Casadesus can wave a sheaf of reviews enthusiastically greeting the disc when it appeared several years ago. Clear recording, bad surfaces.

SCRIABIN, ALEXANDER (1872-1915)

Sonata for Piano No. 4. See Collections: Skolovsky (C 4871).

Sonata for Piano No. 9; Étude in B flat minor (Op. 8, No. 7); Étude in C sharp minor (Op. 42, No. 5). See Collections: Horowitz (V LM 6014).

SERLY, TIBOR (1901-)

Sonata for Violin (unaccompanied). See Stravinsky: *Suite Italienne* (Bar 908).

SESSIONS, ROGER (1896-)

Chorale No. 1; Three Chorale Preludes for Organ. See Thomson: *Variations on Sunday School Themes* (Es 522).

*Duo for Violin and Piano. Travers, Herz, 10" C 2169 (*Ives: Sonata No. 2).*

A typically intense, dissonant, close-knit work, this duo is one of those things you respect like anything but somehow never get around to re-playing. Travers goes through the music in an energetic and well-controlled manner. The recording has a dull sound. I got best results on the AES curve.

Sonata for Piano No. 2; From My Diary. Abramowitsch, ML 7003.

Both the *Sonata* and the four pieces that make up *From My Diary* are powerful, dissonant, Bartókian explosions. This recording was made under the supervision of the composer. Abramowitsch, a West Coast pianist, has the difficult writing well in hand; and if he sounds percussive, that is the nature of the writing.

SHAPERO, HAROLD (1920-)

*Sonata for Piano Four Hands. Shapero, Smit, C 4841 (*Cowell: Violin Sonata No. 1).*

To a large extent the Copland of *Our Town* is evoked here. Shapero handles his derivative material with a nice, swinging quality. He treats the piano in a percussive manner. Played unskillfully, the work could sound very hard, but Shapero and Smit, two fine pianists, never bang or overstress. Excellent recorded sound.

SHOSTAKOVICH, DMITRI (1906-)

Children's Pieces. See Collections: Pressler (MGM 3010).

Preludes (24). Pressler, MGM 3070.

The more you get to know this music, the thinner it sounds. How dated it all is! Pressler plays as though he were confident of the music's worth: plenty of musical conviction, neat layout, minimum pedal for optimum clarity. The notes are well in his fingers. Excellent recording that occasionally (as in the ending of No. 6) is too brilliant, giving the effect of a super-piano.

*Quartet for Strings No. 1. Guilet, MGM 3113 (*Prokofiev: Quartet No. 1).*

The music emerges smoothly under the capable ensemble of the

Guilet Quartet, which plays with a cool tone, fine intonation, and a good deal of rhythmic life. Excellent recorded sound. MGM makes, much more often than not, a really high-fidelity disc that can stand comparison with that of any other record company in the business.

Quartet for Strings No. 2 (Op. 69). Rudolf Schulz Quartet, U 7040.
Composed in 1944, this quartet plows the same old field. When does mannerism become cliché? The Rudolf Schulz Quartet handles the music in a thoroughly capable manner. Plenty of force is contained in its playing, together with a degree of tonal smoothness and uniformity of ensemble that are above the ordinary. Some fine quartet playing can be heard here. Resonant, well-balanced recording.

Quartet for Strings No. 3. Fine Arts, Mer 10049.
Music like this has the permanence of an ice cube in a glass of hot water. The Fine Arts Quartet handles the score with a good deal of flexibility, and if the music fails to be entirely convincing, the fault is not always that of the players. Some shrill highs in this recording can be flattened out; otherwise the sound is good.

Quintet for Piano and Strings (Op. 57). Aller, Hollywood, Cap 8171. Chigi, L 500.
Capitol has the edge here. The somewhat steely recording is appropriate to the music. Aller and the Hollywood group have a flair for the brisk, busy patterns that abound in the score. Their performance is firm, rhythmic, and sharply outlined. The Chigi performance is smaller-scaled, without the drive and intellectual force of the competitive version.

*Sonata for Cello and Piano (Op. 40). Brabec, Holletschek, 10" L 9075. Piatigorsky, Pavlovsky, Ent 3015 (*Russian Melodies).*
At its price the London is the better buy (it is in the black-label series). The recorded sound is mellow, the performance suave. The Entré also is a low-priced disc, but it was recorded by Columbia some years ago before its LP transfer. The sound is faint, and the reverse of the disc contains stuff like the *Orientale*, "Song of India," and other precious items that nobody interested in the Shostakovich could possibly want.

*Sonata for Piano No. 2 in B minor (Op. 64). Pressler, MGM 3079 (*Piano Concerto).*
A skillful performance without much depth. Pressler here is generally on the surface of the keys. More weight of tone was

needed, and more of a variation in dynamics. Excellent recorded sound, especially realistic in the bass.

*Trio in E minor (Op. 67). Shostakovich, Oistrakh, Sádlo, Mer 10045 (*Prokofiev: Quartet No. 2).*

According to the liner information, this recording was made in Prague in May 1946, during a music festival. The recorded sound is inferior: unresonant, with some tonal shatter. The major point of interest is the participation of the composer at the piano, supported by two of Eastern Europe's best instrumentalists—David Oistrakh and Miloš Sádlo. Shostakovich, by the way, is a fine pianist.

SIBELIUS, JAN (1865-)

Quartet for Strings in D minor ("Voces Intimae," Op. 56). Griller, L 304.

It is seldom that one hears the *Voces Intimae* these days. Admirers of the symphonies will find the same devices here: long ostinato sections, bleak harmonies, constant repetition. The Grillers play very well, achieving the dark mood needed by this music. Good string tone in the recording; but a pronounced hum and background noise come through strongly in pianissimo sections.

SMETANA, BEDŘICH (1824-1884)

Piano Music. Maxián, etc., Mer 10004 and 10046.

Six Czech pianists participate in these two discs. The records have been dropped from the Mercury catalogue; grab them if you happen to run across the pair. Some very interesting and very pretty piano music is offered. Imagine Liszt with a touch of Schubert and a strong strain of pure Bohemian nationalism. That, largely, is what Smetana composed. Neither of these recordings is much good technically; they were taken off 78-rpm masters; but recording considerations are not important in this case. Enough comes through, in any event, for the results to be enjoyable.

*Quartet for Strings in E minor (Aus meinem Leben). Stradivari, Str 613 (*Dvořák: Quartet No. 6). Curtis, W 5199 (*Quartet No. 6). Vegh, L 865 (*Kodály: Quartet No. 2).*

The Stradivari group presents the most supple performance of Smetana's charming work, and the recording is good, though not as realistic as the Westminster. The Curtis Quartet interpretation is more large-scale, but I do not like its heavy, stomping accents, and the ensemble is rougher than that found on the Stradivari disc. Despite some dependable playing, the Vegh version misses the close-to-the-soil quality of the music. There is something pedestrian about it, especially in the second movement, where all should be dancelike and rhythmic. A version by the Koeckert Quartet on D 9637 suffers from some questionable intonation.

Trio for Piano and Strings in G minor (Op. 15). See Dvořák: *Trio in E minor* (Str 620).

SOLER, ANTONIO (1729-1783)

Sonatas for Harpsichord (10). Valenti, W 5196.

Soler was a disciple of Scarlatti, and these sonatas are the sincerest form of flattery. They are skillfully composed, according to the precepts of the earlier master, and often contain an inventive turn of phrase that Scarlatti himself would not have disowned. Valenti plays this kind of music very well. Plenty of spirit and excellent rhythm are present, and his registrations are colorful. The recording is too close-up; keep the volume down.

SPOHR, LUDWIG (1784-1859)

*Nonet in F (Op. 31). Eidus, etc., Str 609 (*6 Songs). Vienna Octet, L 710.*

A little more daring, and Spohr would have been one of the great romantics. Some graceful and enjoyable writing is on this disc. The Viennese players adopt much slower tempos, especially in the first movement, than do the Americans. Of course, they weren't concerned with getting the work on one side. I must confess that the tempos on the Stradivari disc make more sense to me; the performance on London is over-leisurely and even dragged. Undoubtedly the Viennese show a smoother ensemble, and their recording has greater instrumental definition. The Stradivari disc, however, is not bad tonally; and the playing is lively and spirited.

For this work, then, the Stradivari version will do just fine; and there is a bonus in the form of six virtually unknown songs.

STAMITZ, KARL *(1746-1801)*

Bläserquartett (Op. 8, No. 2). See Collections: New Art Wind Quintet (CE 2010).
Quartet for Strings in A (Op. 14). See Richter: *Quartet in C* (Bar 915).

STRADELLA, ALESSANDRO *(1645-1682)*

Trio Sonatas (6). Trio di Bolzano, Vox 8380.

No other Stradella disc is available on LP at the time of writing. This music is virtually unknown, but it is safe to say that the recording does not present it in its best light. A piano instead of a harpsichord is used, and the whole approach is heavily romantic. (The music itself does not appear to be of much value; competent note-spinning, mostly.) Clear-sounding recording.

STRAUSS, RICHARD *(1864-1949)*

Quartet for Piano and Strings in C minor (Op. 13). Segáll, Figueroa, Brieff, G. Ricci, NR 201.

An early work, this is an academic product in the Brahms style. Yet a personal quality comes out in the puckish second movement, and the writing throughout is that of a master of classical form and technique. The performance on this disc is what can be expected when four good musicians get together for a session with unfamiliar music. The playing is competent and careful, lacking the freedom that only living with the music can bring. Somewhat low-level recording, of good quality and instrumental balance.

*Sonata for Cello and Piano in F (Op. 6). Stern, O'Neil, SPA 8 (*Hindemith: Cello Sonata).*

Not a successful disc. Strauss composed a luxurious, post-romantic sonata, but Stern's harsh tone and stiff attack make the music sound dry, which it decidedly isn't. Similarly, in the Hindemith work Stern grinds away; and the acid writing cannot survive this kind of treatment.

Sonata for Piano in B minor (Op. 5); Five Piano Pieces (Op. 3). Brendel, SPA 48.

Everything is present in these early works: Mendelssohn, Weber, Brahms, even a suggestion or two of Richard Strauss. Brendel does what can be done with these student pieces. The recording is fine in the treble, thick and muddy in the bass. Prominent surfaces develop toward the end of each side.

*Sonata for Violin and Piano in E flat (Op. 18). Heifetz, Sandor, V LCT 1122 (*Franck: Violin Sonata). Ricci, Bussotti, L 770 (*Prokofiev: Violin Sonata No. 2). Tryon, La Montaine, CE 1019 (*Elgar: Violin Sonata in E minor).*

If you like a big, juicy (and the word "schmalzy" could be substituted) sonata without a "problem" in it, this should entrance you. Heifetz's tremendous performance heads the list; and this despite an LP transfer that cannot hide the dated sound of the original 78-rpm version. The degree of authority with which he plays the music is unmatched by any other violinist who has attempted the work (and not only on records). Ricci plays the best modern version. He is a little more lyric than Heifetz, a little softer and rhythmically less precise. Some beautifully phrased sections make this interpretation more desirable than the tasteful but small-scaled performance on the Classic disc.

STRAVINSKY, IGOR (1882-)

Cinq Pièces faciles. See *Sonata for Two Pianos* (10" CH 1089).

*Concerto for Two Solo Pianos (1935). Gold and Fizdale, C 4853 (*Hindemith: Sonata for Piano Four Hands; Rieti: Suite champêtre).*

This disc, available separately, is part of the three-disc "Music for Two Pianos—1900–1952." For complete contents, see Collections: Gold and Fizdale (C SL 198). Several other two-piano teams have attempted the *Concerto* on LP, but this version is by far the best. The pianists play with complete rhythmic flexibility, and with a neo-classic purity that well matches the neo-classic content of the score. An unimaginative performance by Bartlett and Robertson on MGM 3038 should be avoided. Much better are Vronsky and Babin on C 4157, but the weird assortment of Stravinsky and salon encore pieces on the reverse ("Dance of the Tumblers," etc.) wipes out any attraction the disc might have.

*Duo Concertant for Violin and Piano. Fuchs, Smit, D 8503 (*Copland: Violin Sonata). Szigeti, Stravinsky, 10" C 2122 (*Pastorale; Bloch: Baal Shem).*

I prefer the Decca. It is equally strong rhythmically and more attractive tonally. It also is a neat, well-planned performance that goes with split-second integration. The Columbia disc is a 78-rpm transfer to LP, with all the attendant dated quality of sound. Szigeti and a wind quintet play Stravinsky's attractive *Pastorale* on the reverse side. It is the only LP version at the time of writing.

L'Histoire du Soldat. See *Octet* (V LM 1078).

*Octet for Wind Instruments. Members of Boston Symphony, conducted by Bernstein, V LM 1078 (*Histoire du Soldat).*

A marvelous disc. Bernstein directs a lively performance of the perky music, and the Boston musicians respond like the thoroughbreds they are. Everything is in place. The music goes with the smoothest flow imaginable; and what instrumental virtuosity! As played here, *L'Histoire du Soldat* is chamber music (seven instruments), and it comes off with equal brilliance. (Another version of *Histoire*, good but lacking Bernstein's brilliance, is conducted by Rossi on Van 452, backed by *Les Noces;* and the complete score, with narrator, is well done on Vox 7960.) Victor's recording captures the timbre of the instruments with remarkable fidelity.

Pastorale for Violin and Wind Quartet. See *Duo Concertant* (10" C 2122).

Petrouchka; Serenade; Ragtime. Meyer, HS 113.

Stravinsky made the transcription for solo piano of *Petrouchka* in 1921. It is a fantastically difficult, complicated affair, and not many pianists dare attempt it. Marcelle Meyer, long a specialist in Stravinsky's music (her discs in the 1930's attracted wide attention), handles the piece most impressively. Her technique is ample enough, and she is able to dispose of the welters of notes with confidence. Her tone is full without being percussive, and she is not afraid to infuse a bit of color with the pedal. Nor is there anything ladylike about her bold attack and surges of tone. Splendid piano-playing here, and the accompanying piano pieces on the disc have equal musical and technical authority. Brilliant recorded sound to the treble, and a rather thick bass, but not enough to spoil the generally faithful piano tone.

*Pieces (3) for Solo Clarinet. Kell, D 9570 (*Debussy: Rhapsody No. 1; Hindemith: Clarinet Sonata).*

Kell's ultra-smooth tone and technique make the music sound easy, and even tasteful. Other clarinetists within memory have worked so hard over the pieces that they sounded jagged. With Kell everything is liquid, and Stravinsky's abstract patterns in these pieces have never sounded better—on discs, at any rate.

*Pieces (3) for String Quartet. New Music, Bar 901 (*Bartók: Quartet No. 3; 5 excerpts from Mikrokosmos).*

The first of these three pieces resembles, in general style and humor, *L'Histoire du Soldat*. The others are darker and more difficult to get in focus. A fine performance is played by the New Music String Quartet, a group that obviously looks with sympathy on Stravinsky's writing and has the technique to handle it easily. Excellent recorded sound.

*Sonata for Piano (1924). S. Stravinsky, All 3091 (*Serenade in A; Ravel: Trio). Scarpini, Col 1025 (*Piano Rag Music; Bartók: Piano Sonata; 6 Bulgarian Dances).*

Neither performance can be recommended. Soulima Stravinsky's piano-playing is flaccid. While Scarpini is stronger technically and rhythmically, he too has a plodding quality, and no great understanding of the composer's aims is in evidence. Of the two, the Colosseum has the better recorded sound.

*Sonata for Two Pianos; Cinq Pièces faciles. Gold and Fizdale, 10" CH 1089 (*Bowles: Sonata for Two Pianos).*

The first movement of the sonata has one of Stravinsky's most fluent melodies (he *can* compose them when he wants to). The *Cinq Pièces* are played here in their original form for piano four hands. Despite inferior recording, Gold and Fizdale have the field to themselves. Bartlett and Robertson, who play the sonata on MGM 3038, lack assertion; and Whittemore and Lowe, on V LM 1705, do not have Gold and Fizdale's identification with the music. Both Victor and MGM offer better recorded sound, but the musical virtues of the Concert Hall set are too prominent to be ignored.

*Suite Italienne. Magnes, Garvey, Bar 908 (*Serly: Sonata for Solo Violin).*

The *Italienne*, based on the *Pulcinella* ballet, contains some of Stravinsky's most attractive melodies, thanks to Pergolesi, the composer whose music Stravinsky is here arranging. Naturally the treatment is all Stravinsky, and the suite continues to exert its wry fascination. It receives a spirited performance by the talented Magnes, who falls into a *sec* manner exactly appropriate to the neo-classic writing. Serly's unaccompanied *Sonata* is subtitled "*in Modus Lascivus.*" According to the Harvard Dictionary of

Music, Modus Lascivus is "the medieval name for the tonality of C major." Serly has composed a very difficult, complicated work, strongly rooted in the nineteenth-century idiom, which explores the resources of the violin. He may not have any striking message to convey, but at least he avoids boredom, no mean feat in a long work for solo violin. Superb recorded sound; and the performance is one that must have made the composer very happy.

SUK, JOSEF (1874-1935)

Burleska. See Collections: Milstein (Cap 8259).

*Four Pieces (Op. 17). G. Neveu, J. Neveu, An 35129 (*Sibelius: Violin Concerto).*

Most of this disc is occupied by the *Concerto;* the *Four Pieces* take up part of the last side. Neveu plays them with the masculine firmness that the brilliant young violinist brought to all of her work. The disc is a souvenir of an artist who, had she not met death in 1949 at the age of twenty-eight, would have walked with the elect.

SWANSON, HOWARD (1909-)

*Suite for Cello and Piano. Stern, Bogin, SPA 54 (*Phillips: Cello Sonata).*

Two American composers are represented here. Swanson's *Suite* is definitely romantic, with some sections verging on the salon. It is an interesting work with real quality, even if it does convey the idea that the composer's style is not fully formed. Burrill Phillips, who plays the piano part of his *Sonata,* has composed a work in the modern idiom which lacks melodic ideas. Stern plays with consistent musicianship and with a tone that brings the ear something less than pleasure. Good recorded sound.

SZYMANOWSKI, KAROL (1883-1937)

*Quartet for Strings in C (Op. 37). Walden, Ly 22 (*Kodály: Quartet No. 2).*

If you are not allergic to modernism, you should investigate this fine work. It dates from 1917, and through its high dissonance index comes a good deal of character and independence. I wish that the recording were clearer. Some of the details in the lower strings are obscured, and there is a series of thirty-second-note figurations which hardly comes through at all. The Walden, an alert and intelligent organization, presents a fine interpretation, one with plenty of technical finesse and tonal virtue.

TARTINI, GIUSEPPE (1692-1770)

Quartet for Strings in D. See Collections: New Music String Quartet (Bar 911).

Sonatas for Violin and Harpsichord in G minor, A minor, B minor, and D. Rybar, Holletschek, W 5141.

*Sonatas for Violin and Harpsichord in E and E minor. Rybar, Holletschek, W 5118 (*Concerto in D minor).*

The G minor on W 5141 is not the "Devil's Trill." All of these works are skillfully composed, but the content is a good deal less than memorable. So is the playing. Rybar is a sound but pedestrian violinist in this music. He has not the tone or musical imagination to bring it to life. First-class recorded sound.

*Sonata for Violin and Piano in G minor ("Devil's Trill"). Oistrakh, Oborin, Per 573 (*Schubert: Sonata in A; Beethoven: Sonata in F, Op. 24). Odnoposoff, Wehrle, CH 1170 (*Geminiani: Sonata in B flat; Vitali: Chaconne).*

Virtuoso fiddling of the very top rank is contained in the Period disc, and the recording is not bad. Don't confuse this disc with Colosseum 148, which also offers a "Devil's Trill," probably the very same performance, but nowhere near so clear in sound. The well-recorded Odnoposoff version is another example of secure bravura fiddling, and the violinist also is in brilliant form in the popular Vitali *Chaconne* and the less-played Geminiani piece for unaccompanied violin. In the Tartini he is accompanied by a harpsichord. Menuhin has recorded the "Devil's Trill" on V LM 1742 (*Bartók: *3 Romanian Dances;* encore pieces by Sarasate and others). The performance sounds flurried and not as pure in intonation as the Oistrakh and Odnoposoff interpretations.

TCHAIKOVSKY, PETER ILYICH (1840-1893)

Album for the Young (Op. 39). Zeitlin, Op. 6001.

This work is a collection of twenty-four short, easy pieces *à la*

Schumann. The sketches are tastefully played by Zeitlin, who leaves the music in its proper miniature framework. Fine recorded sound.

*Quartet for Strings No. 1 in D (Op. 11). Hollywood, Cap 8187 (*Borodin: Quartet No. 2). Hungarian, CH 1183 (*Glazunov: Novelettes).*

One movement in this work—the *Andante Cantabile*—developed into one of the most popular pieces Tchaikovsky ever composed. Both recordings are good. The Hollywood Quartet has more force and rhythmic propulsion; the Hungarian is softer and suaver. My preference is the Capitol, for its clearer sound and more decided musical character. The coupling also plays a strong part in the decision. On the reverse of Capitol's Tchaikovsky is the best LP version of Borodin's melodious *Quartet in D*, whereas the Glazunov work on the Concert Hall disc is merely a pleasant collection of salon trifles. On Col 10190 is a version of the Tchaikovksy labeled "as played by the Oistrakh Quartet." This shrill-sounding, low-level recording is to be avoided.

Quartet for Strings No. 3 in E flat minor (Op. 30). Burgin, Panasevich, de Pasquale, Mayes, Bos 206.

A strange key for a string quartet. It is a very Tchaikovskian work, and a very long one, and not a very successful one. Members of the Boston Symphony play the music in a careful, respectful way, but they do not have enough vitality to give the music a little extra impetus. The recording meets minimum demands and not much more; it lacks brilliance and resonance.

The Seasons (Op. 37). Wollman, W 5290.

Twelve piano pieces, one for each month of the year. Only two of the months have ever achieved much popularity—June (*Barcarolle*) and November (*Troika en traineaux*, which Rachmaninoff liked to play). For the most part they are salon pieces, slight in substance, with a thin veneer of elegance. Wollman employs a singing tone and a clean-cut technique. She handles the music very well, with enough force when needed and a continually smooth legato approach. Excellent recorded sound. For several other piano pieces by Tchaikovsky, see *Sonata in G* (W 5330); see also Prokofiev: *Piano Sonata No. 2 in D minor* (CH 1311).

*Sonata for Piano in G (Op. 37). Reisenberg, W 5330 (*Romance in F minor, Op. 5; Nocturne, Op. 10, No. 1; Humoresque, Op. 10, No. 2; Souvenir de Haspal, Op. 2).*

Expert performance of a seldom-heard work. Reisenberg plays

with a thorough knowledge of the idiom and a command of the mechanics involved. Not many listeners will find much of absorbing interest in the musical content, however. The short pieces on the reverse also are skillfully played. The *Romance* and the *Humoresque* used to be very popular. No more, except on Muzak. Ditto for the *Chanson sans paroles* that ends the *Souvenir de Haspal,* a short suite of three pieces. Still, it is pleasant to hear these salon trifles in their original form: pleasant, and even somewhat nostalgic. Clear recording.

Trio in A minor (Op. 50). Heifetz, Piatigorsky, Rubinstein, V LM1120.
Although long and redundant, this piece has many beautiful things in it. It would be hard to imagine a better performance than that presented here by the three Slavic-born virtuosos. They bring to the score considerable elegance, and just the amount of sentiment it needs (with a complete avoidance of sentimentality). The sounds produced are warm and rich, and the individual playing is a joy to hear. It has been some years since the recording was first issued, but the sound is perfectly satisfactory.

TELEMANN, GEORGE *(1681-1767)*

Fantasias (12) for Harpsichord. Elsner, Vox 8680.
Some of Telemann's best music on discs is contained here. The *Fantasias* have character and, in one or two cases, a type of melodic treatment which actually suggests the romantic period. Elsner plays them in a scholarly way, keeping close to the text without eccentricity, holding a steady rhythm. One might have wished for a little more personality; but better this type of playing than egomania. Fine recorded sound.

*Partita No. 5 for Oboe and Harpsichord; Sonata in C minor for Oboe and Harpsichord. Gomberg, Chiasson, D 9618 (*Mozart: Oboe Quartet).*
Routine baroque works. Most of the interest here is in the performance. Gomberg plays with style, fluency, and apparently unlimited breath. He is one of the finest oboists in circulation: an instrumentalist with control, smoothness, and an unfaltering lip. Fine recorded sound.

*Quartet in D minor; Trio in E minor. Wittgenstein, etc., W 5076 (*Loeillet: Trio Sonata in B minor).*
Both pieces are *Tafelmusik,* designed as sort of an eighteenth-

century Muzak as a background to dining. The music is certainly bland enough to suit such a purpose. Telemann's scoring calls for flutes, oboe, strings, harpsichord (the accompanying Loeillet calls for flute, cello, and harpsichord; it is one of those baroque scores virtually devoid of individuality). Fine performances here, with clear, well-articulated passage work backed by lifelike recorded sound.

Trio Sonatas (4); Duet for Flute, Violin, and Continuo. Middlesex Collegium Musicum, Ren 12.

The Middlesex Collegium Musicum is a collection of players from Cambridge (Mass., not England). Here the flute-player uses a German flute, similar in tone to a recorder. The performances are well balanced, the quiet timbres are beautifully reproduced, and the disc does fill a gap in the repertoire.

THOMPSON, RANDALL (1899-)

*Quartet for Strings in D minor. Guilet, CH 1092 (*Barber: Cello Sonata).*

The quartet is a well-made academic work. Not many criteria for evaluating the performance are in existence—the work has had too few performances—but obviously the fine rhythm and ensemble of the Guilet Quartet aid the cause of the composer. Clear, rather thin recorded sound, and prominent background noise.

THOMSON, VIRGIL (1896-)

Études (10) for Piano. Schapiro, D 4083.

Facile music, well recorded, with prominent surfaces. Schapiro plays well, though at times he sounds heavy and over-serious.

Synthetic Waltzes. See Collections: Gold and Fizdale (10" C 2147).

*Variations on Sunday School Tunes. Mason, Es 522 (*Sessions: Chorale No. 1; 3 Chorale Preludes).*

Thomson composed these sets of organ variations in 1927. They are very Parisian (by way of Kansas City). The Sessions pieces, composed 1924–6, are austere, complicated works, some of which sound like a neo-Bach improvisation. On the first few hearings the dry harmonic underpinning is a little forbidding, but acquaintance reveals a logic and a reluctant sort of beauty. Marilyn Mason, a talented organist who specializes in modern music, handles both composers sympathetically, and the recording is excellent.

TURINA, JOAQUIN (1882-1949)

La Oración del Torero. See Creston: *Quartet* (Cap 8260); Milhaud: *Quartet, 1912* (Pol 1004).

Piano Pieces. De Larrocha, D 9750.

Included herein are *3 Danzas Fantasticas, Ciclo Pianístico,* and *Recuerdos de la Antigua España.* This is tuneful, extremely derivative music, part Albéniz-derived, part French impressionism. Alicia De Larrocha sounds like an able pianist. She delivers the notes neatly wrapped up in clean-cut patterns, has an obvious identification with the style, and a confident way of handling the musical problems. The recording is not very bright, being low-level and possessed of noticeable surface noise. Nevertheless the sound of the piano is faithful enough.

*Scène Andalouse. L. and R. Persinger, Str 608 (*Hindemith: Trauermusik; Handel-Halvorsen: Passacaglia; Villa-Lobos: Duo).*

The Turina is a pleasant, lightweight work for violin and piano, well played here, and recorded with color. The Handel and Villa-Lobos works are for violin and viola, the viola being played by Louis Persinger (who took the piano part in the Turina). Halvorsen's arrangement was taken from the Passacaglia of Handel's *G minor Harpsichord Suite;* the Villa-Lobos is a trifle that sounds like something the composer might have turned out between breakfast and lunch. Hindemith's score is played by solo viola and a small ensemble. All of these are musicianly, technically accomplished performances and, like the Turina, have the benefit of lifelike recorded sound.

VALENTINI, GIUSEPPE (1681- ?)

Sonata for Cello and Piano No. 4 in E. See Boccherini: *Cello Sonata No. 6* (Ren 11).

VERDI, GIUSEPPE (1813-1901)

*Quartet for Strings in E minor. Paganini, 10" V LM 37. New Italian, L 323 (*Schumann: Quartet in F).*

A strange and rather moving work, composed in 1874, full of hints of the thematic subtleties of *Otello* and *Falstaff*. The slow movement is extraordinarily sweet and poignant. I prefer the Paganini Quartet here. The group plays with more virility, and it shapes a phrase with a more decided character. It also has been recorded with greater clarity. Despite the fact that the London disc is a better buy, economically, I strongly suggest the Victor.

VILLA-LOBOS, HEITOR (1881-)

*Bachianas Brasileiras No. 4 for Solo Piano. Pressler, MGM 3105 (*Bachianas Brasileiras No. 1 for 8 Cellos).*

In the opening movement the Bachian spirit is evoked. Later on come Villa-Lobos's usual nationalistic devices, complete with strange rhythms, exotic tunes, and a carefully cultivated barbarism. Much musical personality is present. Pressler vigorously goes through the music. He does not have complete identification with the medium, and some of the dancelike measures do not come through as they should, but the essence of the music is present. The piano sounds exceptionally brilliant. MGM can make one of the best piano discs on the market.

Cirandas. Battista, MGM 3020.

This is a cycle of sixteen piano pieces based on Brazilian folk tunes. It is an ingenious set, and there is something very hearty and uninhibited about it. Battista sounds very comfortable. He does not overstress (as he elsewhere does), and his playing has a good quota not only of relaxation, but also of actual geniality. If you want a colorful novelty, try this disc. Excellent recording.

Piano Music. Ballon, 10" L 531 and L 9095.

On L 531 are seven pieces: *A lenda do Caboclo, Vamos atraz de serra calunga, N'esta rua, O Polichinelo,* and three pieces from *Ciclo Brasileiro.* The six pieces on L 9095 are: *Pobre céga, O pintor de Cannahy, Choros No. 5, Impressaões seresteiras, A maré encheu,* and *Passa, passa, gaviao.* Some very attractive music is among these, especially the *Impressaões seresteiras.* Ballon has worked on them with the composer, and her playing sounds entirely competent. The recording in L 531 is good. L 9095 has a tubbier quality.

*Quartet for Strings No. 6 in E. Hollywood, Cap 8054 (*Walton: Quartet in A minor).*

Two fine modern chamber works are on this disc. The lively Villa-Lobos work, with its haunting slow movement, stands up very well. Walton's *Quartet* is one of the best examples of the contemporary British school. It is quite romantic, with an honest lyric impulse that sounds free and uncontrived. The Hollywood Quartet is up to its usual high standard in both pieces, playing with impeccable finish. Brilliant recorded sound. An old recording of the Villa-Lobos by the Stuyvesant String Quartet is superseded by the Capitol disk.

Rudepôema; The Children's Doll Suite; The Three Maries. Abram, EMS 10.

The first of these pieces is a hard nut to crack. *Rudepôema* is long, difficult, improvisatory, and rhythmically very complex. Better known as *A Prôle do Bébé*, the *Children's Doll Suite* is simple and charming. One of them, *Polichinelle*, is very well known. Villa-Lobos wrote two series; Abram plays the eight pieces of No. 1. *The Three Maries* are tiny pieces on a Brazilian fairy tale. Amazingly lifelike piano sound is present, and it emphasizes Abram's percussive attack and lack of color. He plays efficiently and methodically, but the music simply shrieks for something more. Whoever is responsible for the liner notes should have his wrist slapped. There are more misspellings present and more omission of necessary data than seemingly could be possible in such a small compass.

*Saudades das Selvas Brasileiras; Chôros No. 5; Poema Singelo; Suite Floral. Engdahl, MGM 3158 (*Milhaud: Saudades do Brasil).*

The piano music of Villa-Lobos is invariably interesting. Among the present works, *Choros No. 5* (subtitled *Alma Brasileira*, or "Soul of Brazil") is an exceptionally lyric piece of writing, and *Saudades das Selvas Brasileiras* ("Recollections of the Brazilian Forests") sustains an elegiac mood. Not one of these pieces lacks personality and melodic appeal. Engdahl sounds like a competent pianist. She plays this assortment with spirit, color, and a good technical foundation. The recorded sound is excellent. Those in the market for an unusual disc of contemporary piano music should not miss this.

Trio for Violin, Viola, and Cello. Schneider, Katims, Miller, 10" C 2214.

Villa-Lobos's heritage of French impressionism comes through the dissonances and the wild mélange of native sounds and rhythms. This interesting work is well played by three of the best instrumentalists in the chamber-music field. Sharp recording, with an unpleasant edge in the high register.

Trio for Winds; Quartet for Winds; Quintet for Winds. New Art, W 5360.

These three works illustrate the fecundity of the composer. Sometimes a musician writes out of habit, and here, one feels, is an illustration of how to turn out glib music without being troubled by anything much in the nature of musical ideas. One thing, though: these pieces have Villa-Lobos's thumbprint on every measure. Fine performances here. The New Art Wind Quintet is a group with smooth ensemble and with a rather lean but appealing sound that avoids a juicy vibrato and excessive globs of tone. The sensitive performances it offers to Villa-Lobos set his music off to best advantage. Sharp, detailed recorded sound.

VIVALDI, ANTONIO (c. 1675-1741)

Sonatas (4) for Cello and Piano. Mayes, Litwin, All 95.

Strong works with some curiously Bachian figurations. The performances by the first cellist of the Boston Symphony are competent and rather dry in tone. The recording is excellent. Smooth surfaces, fine instrumental definition, good balance between cello and piano.

*Sonata for Flute and Figured Bass in D minor; Concerto for Flute, Oboe, Violin, Bassoon, and Figured Bass in G minor. Rampal, etc., HS 80 (*Bach: Suite for Flute and Figured Bass in C minor).*

Sonata for Flute in A minor; Concerto for 5 Instruments in D ("La Pastorella"); Concerto for Flute, Oboe, and Bassoon in G minor; Sonata for Oboe in C minor. Rampal, etc., HS 82.

Sonatas and Concertos for Five Instruments in F,C,D, E minor, and D. Rampal, etc., HS 116.

Enormously sturdy music. In many respects, Vivaldi was an Italian Handel. The performances here sound carefully prepared. None of the soloists is an outstanding workman, but they collaborate well, playing with taste and musical integrity. For the record, the players are Jean-Pierre Rampal (flute), Pierre Pierlot (oboe), Paul Hongne (bassoon), Robert Gendre (violin), and Robert Veyron-Lacroix (harpsichord). Excellent recorded sound and completely noiseless surfaces.

WAGNER RICHARD (1813-1883)

Sonata for Piano in B flat; Album Sonata in A flat; Albumblatt in E flat. Karrer, Rem 199-26.

Curiosities. Wagner composed a handful of piano works. None of them is of the least importance; they are mentioned here because of their novelty. Anybody in the 1830's could have composed the music. Karrer's performance sounds well controlled. The recording, on the other hand, varies from passable to impossible.

WALTHER, JOHANN GOTTFRIED (1684-1748)

Chorale Variations. See Böhm: *Chorale Variations* (ES 3066).

WALTON, SIR WILLIAM (1902-)

Quartet for Strings in A minor. See Villa-Lobos: *Quartet No. 6 in E* (Cap 8054).

*Sonata for Violin and Piano. Menuhin, Kentner, V HMV 1037 (*Beethoven: Violin Sonata No. 1 in D).*

Family note: the score is dedicated to the wives of the players here (Mrs. Menuhin and Mrs. Kentner are sisters). The violinist fiddles away fervently in this rich-sounding, conservative work, Kentner supports him with ardor, and the results should please all. Fine recorded sound.

WEBER, CARL MARIA VON (1786-1826)

Grand Duo Concertante (Op. 48); Variations on a Theme from Silvania (Op. 33). Forrest, Hambro, WCFM 12.

Forrest and Hambro have a lot of fun with these dated virtuoso works for clarinet and piano. Their performance is flexible and bright-sounding, full of easygoing virtuosity. Exceptionally firm piano sound is contained on this disc, and the clarinet comes through with all of its color.

Sonata for Piano No. 1 in C (Op. 24). Roloff, 10" D 7543.

More of this sparkling piece could have been revealed by Roloff, who plays the music in a heavy, pedantic manner. Little of the vigor and exhilaration of the writing comes through. The recording has satisfactory sound.

*Sonata for Piano No. 4 in E minor (Op. 70). H. Schnabel, SPA 15 (*Malipiero: Poemi Asolami).*

The coupling here is a strange affair. Weber's dated but elegant work lies uneasily next to Malipiero's dreary impressionism. Helen Schnabel, who does all she can with the latter work, lacks the flair for the brisk patterns of the Weber. The recording has some shatter in the treble and is too heavy in the bass. It is worth noting that Weber's best sonata, No. 2 in A flat, is not represented on LP. Victor should release the fine old pre-war Cortot in long-play form.

Sonatas (6) for Violin and Piano (Op. 10). Ricci, Bussotti, L 1006.

Composed in 1810, these sonatas were intended as short, easy works for amateurs. The publisher returned them to Weber. Perhaps he thought they were too hard, though his excuse was they were "far too good and must be made more commonplace for sale." Violinists have been neglecting these pretty works far too long, and those who get this disc will own a charming novelty. Ricci's performance is most graceful. He employs his beautiful tone to ravishing effect, his pitch is accurate, and his ideas about the music are fortunately not overwhelming (the music could not stand an over-serious approach). Top-notch violin-playing and equally good music-making. Recording to match.

WEBERN, ANTON VON (1883-1945)

*Concerto for Nine Instruments; Variations for Piano; Quartet for Tenor Saxophone, Violin, Clarinet, and Piano. Leibowitz, etc., Dia 17 (*4 Songs).*

Pointillistic music here, advanced when it was composed in 1934, and still advanced in 1955. Chances are it always will be advanced. This is a fine-sounding, detailed recording. Leibowitz, a twelve-tone specialist, is in charge of the ensemble. The strange *Piano Variations* are well played by Jacques Monod, who also is the pianist with the group that plays the equally strange *Quartet for Tenor Saxophone*.

Five Movements for String Quartet. See Berg: *Quartet for Strings* (C 4737).

WEINER, LEO (1885-)

Hungarian Peasant Songs (Op. 22). See Dohnányi: *4 Rhapsodies* (Ac 301).

Lakodalmas (Hungarian Wedding Dance). See Bartók: *Rhapsody No. 1 for Cello and Piano* (Per 715).

WIDOR, CHARLES (1844-1937)

Symphony for Organ No. 6 in G minor. Elsasser, MGM 3056.

Symphonies for Organ Nos. 9 ("Gothique") and 10 ("Romane"). Watters, Self, CE 1012 [2].

Watters plays No. 9; Self, No. 10. The music is pretentious, secondhand stuff. But Widor, a great organist, knew all the tricks, and the writing for the instrument is the big redeeming factor. Two expert organists turn in excellent performances. Classic Editions claims a frequency response for this record of 16-16,000 cycles. Very nice. I never have heard speakers outside of a laboratory that could go down to 16 c.p.s., but it's good to know it's on the record. The MGM disc makes no claims, but it too is a fine-sounding recording, and young Elsasser plays the music with real flair.

Variations from Symphonie Gothique. See Liszt: *Fantasy and Fugue on "Ad nos ad Salutarem Undam"* (L 697).

WIENIAWSKI, HENRI (1835-1880)

Violin Music. Eidus, Flissler, Str 1003.

The popular encore pieces that Eidus plays here are a lot of good, clean fun. Included are the *Polonaise brillante in A*, the *Scherzo-Tarantelle, Polonaise brillante in D, Souvenir de Moscou,* and *Caprices* in E flat and A minor. In this recording the violin comes through fine, but the piano has a tinny sound. Eidus is all right as far as he goes, but he does not travel to the end of the line. He supplies the athletics, ignoring the breadth and the refinement of style needed to vitalize the music. Some pitch deficiencies are present: the *Polonaises* are a half-tone high.

WILTON, CHARLES (fl. 1780)

*Trios for Strings Nos. 1, 3, and 6. Pougnet, Riddle, Pini, W 5296 (*Haydn: 3 Trios).*

All that is known about this composer is that he apparently was an Englishman who flourished around the 1780's. These scores were unearthed from a private collection about 1930. The music is entirely conventional, amateurishly put together, and if it had been left neglected it would not have made an irreparable gap in musical knowledge. Top-notch performance and recording.

WOLF, HUGO (1860-1903)

*Italian Serenade. Koeckert, 10" D 4044 (*Schubert: Quartettsatz in C minor).*

For those interested in the Wolf piece alone, the Koeckert LP is a fine buy. The disc is recorded with color, it is the only version that presents the music on one side, and the interpretation is excellent. The Schubert on the reverse, too, is a masterpiece that should be in every collection of chamber music. Several other organizations have recorded the bouncing *Italian Serenade* as fillers. On C 4821 the New Music Quartet plays the Wolf as a filler on its disc of the Wolf *String Quartet;* and the Hollywood String Quartet has a version on Cap 8260, along with music by Creston and Turina.

Quartet for Strings in D minor; Italian Serenade. New Music, C 4821.

This quartet was written in 1894 by a young composer who knew his late Beethoven. In the first movement is a good deal of anguish and breast-beating. The only place Wolf's individuality peers out is in the last movement. The *Italian Serenade,* short and to the point, is an ingenious masterpiece bubbling over with good spirits. Not many groups could have sustained the long Wolf quartet as successfully as the New Music does; and if its playing does not carry complete conviction, that is not altogether its fault. Excellent recorded sound.

WOLPE, STEFAN (1902-)

Sonata for Violin and Piano; Passacaglia for Solo Piano; Quartet for Trumpet, Tenor Saxophone, Percussion, and Piano. Magnes, Tudor, etc., Es 530.

Not many criteria exist for evaluating music as avant-garde as this. Magnes, a strong fiddler, happily presents the abstract Wolpean patterns of the *Sonata,* and Tudor supports her with considerable finesse. Tudor himself makes a convincing case for the complicated piece for solo piano, and four expert musicians, conducted by Samuel Baron, seem to have the *Quartet* well in hand. The percussion goings-on at the beginning of the quartet will give hi-fiers something to play with.

YSAYE, EUGÈNE (1858-1931)

Sonata for Unaccompanied Violin in E (Op. 27, No. 3). See Leclair: *Sonata in D* (Van 6024).
Sonatas for Unaccompanied Violin in D minor and E minor (Op. 27, Nos. 3 and 4). See Falla: *Suite populaire Espagnole* (CH 1175).

ZEISL, ERIC (1905-)

Sonata for Violin and Piano. Baker, Yalta Menuhin. Sonata for Viola and Piano. Reher, Schlatter, SPA 10.

Zeisl is a Viennese composer now living in Los Angeles. He works in the massive, unsmiling Central European tradition. Nicolas Slonimsky might describe this music as somber psychologism tempered by incipient symphonicism with a touch of constructivist emotionalism. The musicians who participate in this disc are entirely competent, and the recording is fair, though not so bright or well defined as the best modern examples.

Collections

ALAIN, MARIE-CLAIR

Bach: Organ Music. HS 104.

Mlle Alain plays the following pieces: *Concerto in A minor* (after Vivaldi), two *Chorale-Preludes,* the *D minor Canzona,* the *Aria in F,* the *Preludes and Fugues in G and D minor,* and the *Trios in C minor and D minor.* Her instrument is located in a church in Paris. This organ has a thicker sound than that heard in the Haydn Society recordings by Finn Viderø or the Deccas by Helmut Walcha. It never is heavy or vulgar, fortunately, and has a dignified sound (in complete contrast to some of the cranky noises that wheeze forth from the Danish organ). Alain's interpretation are on a high musical level—sober without being inhibited, resourceful without being flamboyant. The *C minor Trio* that she plays, as the notes are careful to point out, is not by Bach but by his pupil Johann Krebs.

ARRAU, CLAUDIO

Chopin: Complete Works, Vol. I. D DX 130 [2].

Fine project, wrong pianist. Arrau's formidable technique is applied to the four *Ballades* and *Scherzos,* the three *Impromptus* and *Fantasy-Impromptu,* and the *Barcarolle.* What comes forth is, to my taste, mannered and calculated. Arrau's ideas, his rubato and notions of tone color, are to me a complete misapprehension of what Chopin intended. The strange thing is that on D 8517 he plays the *A flat Ballade* and *C sharp minor Scherzo* in a strong, direct manner, with few of the exaggerations present in the two-disc set. But those two performances were 78-rpm discs transferred to LP. Arrau has decidedly changed since then.

BACKHAUS, WILHELM

Chopin: Ballade No. 1 in G minor (Op. 23); Étude in E (Op. 10, No. 3); Mazurkas in B flat minor (Op. 24, No. 4), E flat (Op. 30, No. 3), and C (Op. 33, No. 3); Waltz in A flat (Op. 34, No. 1). 10" L 317.

Forceful, not very idiomatic Chopin-playing. Backhaus never was a good Chopin-player, though he has recorded more of the Polish master's music than most German pianists. (Has a German pianist ever played Chopin convincingly?) Backhaus's performance on this disc commands respect for its probity and for its tremendous grasp of the notes, but qualities of lightness, flexibility, and nuance elude him. The recording has a thick sound not characteristic of the more modern London discs.

"Carnegie Hall Recital." London 1108/9 [2].

The recital that Wilhelm Backhaus gave in Carnegie Hall on March 30, 1954, marked his return to America after an absence of twenty-eight years. London engineers were on hand to take the performance down for posterity. They recorded the entire program of five Beethoven sonatas and several encore pieces: the Sonatas Nos. 8 ("*Pathètique*") in C minor, 17 in D minor, 25 in G, 26 (*Les Adieux*) in E flat, and 32 in C minor; Schubert's *Impromptu in A flat;* Schumann's *Warum*; the Schubert-Liszt *Soirée de Vienne* No. 6, and Brahms's *Intermezzo in C.* Backhaus must have been stimulated by the occasion and by the reception he received. His "*Pathètique*," for example, is livelier than the performance he recorded for London on L 952; and, in general, his playing here is informed with a sense of excitement. That it is big, muscular Beethoven-playing need not be said. Backhaus's traits do not include much warmth or color. Instead, there is a monolithic quality that is, in works like the *C minor Sonata,* simply monumental. He plays with the technique of a virtuoso, the strength of a young man, and the maturity of a veteran. In short, a complete master. Future generations will find this album (and the album that Victor recorded of an actual Horowitz recital) a priceless memento of how a great artist operated under actual recital conditions. London's recording is good, and audience noises are surprisingly few.

BALOGH, ERNO

Chopin: 3 Impromptus; Fantasy-Impromptu; Bolero; Berceuse; Barcarolle; Tarantelle. Ly 20.

Aside from two or three pieces, the contents of this disc represent the less-played Chopin. Balogh's readings are traditional, small-scaled, well controlled technically. He has no great flair, and the readings could not be called imaginative, but his approach is sensitive and musical. The recording is dated in sound but generally clear in detail.

BARERE, SIMON

Chopin: Ballade No. 1 in G minor (Op. 23); Scherzo No. 3 in C sharp minor (Op. 39). Liszt: Faust Waltz; Gnomenreigen; Liebestraum No. 3. Rem 199-17.

With all of its monkeyshines, I like the *G minor Ballade* on this recording better than any other LP version except Hofmann's. It displays a certain daring quality, abetted by the great Barere fingers. It is given to few pianists in any generation to make their own rules. Hofmann was one; Novaes is another. Barere is in that company—in the romantic repertoire, at any rate. (His classics were unconvincing, and he seldom played music composed before 1830.) The *Scherzo* is romantic playing at its most personal, but playing of a sort that is its own reason for being. And for thoroughbred Liszt-playing the pieces above are untouchable. Barere was an extraordinary pianist who never achieved the recognition due him. It is a shame that this recording does not reveal his tone in a more favorable light. The disc has a sandpaper surface and thin piano sound.

"Barere Farewell." Rachmaninoff: Preludes in G minor (Op. 23, No. 5) and G sharp minor (Op. 32, No. 12); Polka de W. R. Blumenfeld: Étude for the Left Hand. Balakireff: Islamey. Schumann: Toccata; Traumeswirren. Liszt: Rhapsodie Espagnole. Rem 199-141.

All of these were taken from actual Carnegie Hall performances. The recorded sound is not very good, but it will serve. Some fantastic virtuoso playing is encountered here; playing that is, at times, more a tribute to Barere's fingers than to his taste and musicianship. Nevertheless, pieces like *Islamey* and the *Rhapsodie Espagnole* can take almost any amount of undiluted virtuosity, and that is what Barere gives them. In a way this disc is an oddity and may develop into a collector's item. I wouldn't give my copy away for anything.

BIGGS, E. POWER

"Bach's Royal Instrument." Vol. I: Toccata, Adagio, and Fugue in C; "Schübler" Chorale Preludes. C 4284. Vol. II: Trio Sonatas Nos. 1 and 2; Preludes and Fugues in G and B minor. C 4285. Vol. III: Fugue in C; "Little" Fugue in G minor; Passacaglia and Fugue in C

minor; Toccata and Fugue in D minor; Concerto in D minor (after Vivaldi). C 4500.

Bach: Prelude and Fugue in E flat ("St. Anne"); Fugue in D minor; Fantasy and Fugue in G minor ("The Great"); Toccata in F. C 4097.

The three "Royal Instrument" discs devoted to Bach's music were recorded in Symphony Hall, Boston. The other was recorded at St. Paul's Chapel of Columbia University. On all of the discs the sound is imposing: large volume without reverberation, clear bass, no muddiness of polyphony. Biggs's performances are all of a piece. He keeps steady rhythm, the notes are accurate, he never is very imaginative, and he is likely to plod metronomically along (as in the Vivaldi-Bach work on C 4500). That Bach's organ music can be played with more subtlety is attested to by the Walcha (Decca) and Viderø (Haydn Society) discs.

"French Organ Music." C 4195.

Music by Widor, Gigout, Boëllmann, Dupré, Alain, and Vierne makes up the selection here. They are standard organ pieces, most of them musically second-rate. Energetic performances are played by Biggs, and the recording has extremely rich, imposing sound.

BOLET, JORGE

"Recital Favorites." Bos 301.

Some old favorites that have almost dropped out of the repertoire are heard here—pieces like the Saint-Saëns *Étude en forme de valse* and Moszkowski's *En automne,* as well as Mendelssohn's "Hunting Song" and *Rondo Capriccioso.* Also played are Liszt's *Funérailles* and Beethoven's *Andante in F.* A big order of virtuosity is here. The playing itself is rather bleak and colorless, but anybody who can get over the keys with this kind of ease and security is a rare technician indeed. The recording is inclined to be clangorous in sound.

CHASINS, ABRAM

Bach: Chromatic Fantasy and Fugue; Mozart: Fantasy in C minor (K. 475); Brahms: 3 Rhapsodies. Mer 10062.

Chasins's piano version of the Bach work is discussed under the composer; it remains the preferred version. The Mozart is played with plenty of strength; there is nothing prissy about Chasins's ideas, and he conveys the drama and turbulence of the piece. In the Brahms he stresses the pianistic elements, making the music sound much more elegant than do many pianists who have been intent on bringing out the rugged aspects of the music. A fine disc, with good quality of piano sound. Heavy surfaces, unfortunately.

CORTOT, ALFRED

Chopin: Waltzes in A minor (Op. 34, No. 2), D flat (Op. 64, No. 1), C sharp minor (Op. 64, No. 2), A flat (Op. 69, No. 1), G flat (Op. 70, No. 1), and F minor (Op. 70, No. 2); Barcarolle (Op. 60); Étude in F minor (Op. 25, No. 2); Nocturnes in E flat (Op. 9, No. 2), F (Op. 15, No. 1), and C sharp minor (Op. 27, No. 1). V HMV 1032.

Style is present, if not much accuracy. Cortot must have been about seventy years old when he recorded these, and his fingers no longer obeyed his bidding. (Cortot always was a careless technician, though when aroused he was capable of some imposing feats.) This disc is a memento of a great artist, even if the holding-back and delayed-action pianism of pieces like the *E flat Nocturne* will bring a sneer to the face of the younger generation. The recorded sound is not very good. It is dull, with a thick bass and a noticeable hum in the background.

DEMESSIEUX, JEANNE

Bach: Toccata and Fugue in D minor; Prelude and Fugue in D. Franck: *Pastorale; Fantaisie in A (From Trois Pièces). L 319.*

Demessieux is a virtuoso organist. She plays with a good deal of throbbing intensity and likes flashy effects. Not all of these effects fit the Bach, where the line is broken up with all kinds of holds and effects. These are scarcely very subtle, though she builds up to some exciting moments. But why the negative, weak ending to the *Fugue in D?* The thick sound of the organ she plays is well reproduced.

DOLMETSCH, CARL, and SAXBY, JOSEPH

Recorder and Harpsichord Recital. Vol. I, 10" L 24. Vol. II, 10" L 278. Vol. III, L 1026.

In Vol. I are a Handel sonata, pieces by Elizabethan composers, and music by Couperin and Daniel Purcell (brother of Henry). Vol.

II contains music by Corelli, Loeillet, Telemann, and some traditional English tunes. The contents of Vol. III include a Telemann partita, a Handel sonata, music by Lawes, Pepusch, and a few early French composers, and a few anonymous pieces. The music often is interesting. Less can be said for the dogged, uninspired performances; and Dolmetsch is not invariably steady in matters of tone and pitch.

"EARLY ENGLISH KEYBOARD MUSIC"

Pieces by Byrd, Bull, Gibbons, Philips, Tomkins, and Farnaby, played by Thurston Dart (harpsichord and clavichord), Elizabeth Goble (harpsichord and virginals), Robert Donington (viola da gamba), and Geraint Jones (organ). L 712/13 [2].

An excellent, well-presented survey of keyboard music in the first Elizabeth's day. It is music that is intimate and even exotic-sounding, with a strong modal flavor and the characteristic harmonies of British folk song underlining all. The musicians engaged here know what the style and tradition are. Fine recorded sound. As a supplement to these two discs, one might mention Ly 37, which contains a group of Elizabethan keyboard pieces played by Chiasson. Most of the material has been taken from the *Fitzwilliam Virginal Book.* This disc is shared by Hugues Cuenod, who sings Elizabethan love songs. Charles Koenig, on EMS 236, also devotes a disc named "Elizabethan Keyboard Music" to pieces from the Fitzwilliam collection. His is a well-recorded disc of music by Morley, Farnaby (Giles and Richard), Bull, Johnson, and Pearson. Among the above discs a good deal of Elizabethan keyboard music is adequately covered. As with much early music, it is an acquired taste, and it is worth making the attempt to acquire it.

ELSASSER, RICHARD

"Organ Music by Modern Composers." MGM 3064.

These are the pieces: Britten's *Prelude and Fugue on a Theme by Vittoria;* Hindemith's *Sonata No. 2;* Cowell's *Processional;* Bartók's *En Bateau;* Copland's *Episode;* Milhaud's *Pastorale;* Messiaen's *Le Banquet céleste;* Thomson's *Pastorale on a Christmas Plainsong;* and Vaughan Williams's *Chorale-Prelude on the Welsh Hymn*

"Hyfridol." None of these is very stimulating, though the amusing Bartók trifle relieves the general monotony. Excellent recording, without blast or reverberation. Elsasser handles all of this varied material with a confidence that is not misplaced.

FRISKIN, JAMES

Bach: Chromatic Fantasy and Fugue; Two-Part Inventions (complete); Italian Concerto; Fantasia in C minor; Sonatina from the Cantata "Gottes Zeit" (arr. Friskin); Fantasia and Double Fugue in A minor; Chorale-Prelude "O Mensch, bewein' dein' Sünde gross" (arr. Friskin); Capriccio on the Departure of a Beloved Brother; French Suites Nos. 3, 4, 5, and 6; Fantasia and Fugue in A minor ("Moto Perpetuo"); Toccata in C minor. BG 543/4/5 [*3*].

Granted we don't know as much about Bach's way of playing his music as we would like to know, but of one thing we are sure: the music contains an emotional experience. And that is what is missing in these three discs. Friskin, generally clear and objective, seems to lack a concentrating focus. His rhythm is likely to be inflexible, there is little lift to his playing, and one misses the feeling of an imaginative musical mind. Conscientiousness can never be a substitute for re-creation. Bach Guild has supplied superb recorded sound to this enterprise, and the surfaces are noiseless.

GOLD, ARTHUR, and FIZDALE, ROBERT

"Modern Waltzes for Two Pianos." 10" C 2147.

Some seldom-heard music, all derived from the French school, is played here: *Second Avenue Waltzes* by Rieti; *Un Valse* by Auric; *Synthetic Waltzes* by Thomson; *Valse brève* by Sauguet; *Valses 1 et 2* by Tailleferre; and *Night Waltz* by Bowles. Pleasant music, most of this, and expertly played. The recording is thin in sound but fortunately without distortion.

"Music for Two Pianos—1900–1952." C SL 198 [3].

Not all of this is for two pianos; some four-hand music also is represented. All of this music has been discussed under the various composers. Here is the breakdown: Stravinsky: *Concerto for*

Two Solo Pianos; Hindemith: *Sonata for Piano Four Hands;* Rieti: *Suite champêtre* (all on C 4853); Poulenc: *Sonata for Piano Four Hands;* Debussy: *Six Épigraphes antiques;* Milhaud: *Concertino d'automne;* Satie: *En habit de cheval* (all on C 4854); Barber: *Souvenirs;* Haieff: *Sonata for Two Pianos* (both on C 4855). This is a fine, impartial, representative collection, in which many schools of composition are represented. It is one of the best sets of its kind, whether or not you may like all of the material.

"GREAT MASTERS OF THE KEYBOARD"

Vol. I. Debussy: Children's Corner, played by Debussy. Fauré: Barcarolle in A minor (Op. 26), played by Fauré. Ravel: Valses nobles et sentimentales, played by Ravel. C 4291.

Vol. II. Liszt: La Campanella; Chopin: D flat Prelude; Beethoven-Liszt: Fantasia on "Ruins of Athens," played by Busoni. Saint-Saëns: Valse mignonne; Finale from Act I of Samson et Dalila; Slow Movement from A minor Symphony; Le Rouet d'Omphale; Rhapsodie d'Auvergne, played by Saint-Saëns. C 4292.

Vol. III. Leschetizky: Two Larks; A minor Barcarolle; Arabesque in A flat; Heller: 2 Preludes, played by Leschetizky. D'Albert: Scherzo in F sharp; Excerpt from Tiefland, played by d'Albert. Grieg: Norwegian Bridal March; Little Bird; Butterfly, played by Grieg. Brahms: Hungarian Dances Nos. 1 and 4; Delibes: Waltz from Coppelia, played by Nikisch. Reger: Sostenuto; Humoresque in G minor, played by Reger. C 4293.

Vol. IV. Paderewski: Minuet in G, played by Paderewski. Chopin: Group of Preludes and Other Short Pieces; De Pachmann: Improvisation, played by De Pachmann. Scharwenka: Polish Dance in E flat minor, played by Scharwenka. Granados: excerpt from Goyescas, played by Granados. Falla: Aragonesa, played by Falla. Albéniz: Three Pieces, played by Marshall. C 4294.

Vol. V. Mahler: Excerpt from Symphony No. 4, played by Mahler. Reger: Two Piano Pieces, played by Reger. Strauss: Sections of Salome and Heldenleben, played by Strauss. Scriabin: Several Preludes, a Mazurka, and an Étude, played by Scriabin. C 4295.

Not all of these players are Great Masters of the Keyboard, and several have no business in this company—as executants, anyway. As musicians—that's another story. It is always interesting to hear a composer in his own music, no matter how poorly he plays it. Columbia recorded these five discs from Welte piano rolls made between 1904 and 1911. Frequently the repertoire is preposterous, and one cannot get too much of an idea of what goes on. Nevertheless, enough is heard to realize that Saint-Saëns did not get his reputation as a pianist for nothing; that De Pachmann played as erratically as he acted; that Ravel had trouble playing his *Valses nobles and sentimentales* ("trouble" is a mild word; but Ravel did not pretend to be a pianist). The Debussy is very interesting, especially for some accentuations that no pianist today bothers to follow. Busoni's ideas are strange by present-day criteria, but an entirely original and provocative musical mind is suggested. Leschetizky's playing is a surprise for its elegance and aristocracy, and both Scriabin and Reger also make a good impression. With all of its auditory faults, this series is unique and fascinating. Would that Columbia would dig into its warehouse and come up with some of the great vocal and instrumental items that flourished in its catalogue from 1903 until the advent of electrical recording (1925 or thereabouts)!

"GREAT PIANISTS OF THE PAST PLAY CHOPIN"

Nocturne in E minor (Op. 72, No. 1), played by Vladimir de Pachmann. Preludes Nos. 6, 3, and 7, played by Moritz Rosenthal. Mazurka in C sharp minor (Op. 63, No. 3), played by Ignace Jan Paderewski. Scherzo No. 3 in C sharp minor (Op. 39), played by Mischa Levitzki. Berceuse (Op. 57), played by Alfred Cortot. Waltz in C sharp minor (Op. 64, No. 2), played by Sergei Rachmaninoff. Polonaise in A flat (Op. 53), played by Josef Lhevinne. V LCT 1038.

All of these are early electrics, and several were recorded when the artists (De Pachmann, Paderewski) were past their prime. Prime or no, they play beautifully, and so does everybody else on this disc. Levitzki's ideas about the third *Scherzo* are more than interesting, and Lhevinne's performance of the *A flat Polonaise*, ever green in the memory, receives a stimulus through this recording. The other miniatures are stylishly handled by the pianists involved. You won't get hi-fi on this disc, but you will get a good idea of how an older generation of pianists played Chopin.

HARPSICHORD QUARTET

Couperin: Le Parnasse, ou l'Apothéose de Corelli. Rosenmüller: Sonata No. 2 in E minor. Frescobaldi: 5 Canzoni per Sonar. Es 517.

The Harpsichord Quartet is not a quartet of harpsichords, as the name might suggest, but a group consisting of Claude Monteux (flute), Harry Shulman (oboe), Bernard Greenhouse (cello), and Sylvia Marlowe (harpsichord). It has come up with some interesting pieces of music for the combination. Those on this disc are far superior to the humdrum run of many pre-Bach mediocrities. In the Couperin work Monteux recites, in French, the various sections of the composition before sitting down to join the ensemble in smooth performances. The recording is exceptionally clear and well balanced, especially in relation of harpsichord to the other instruments.

Bach: Trio Sonata No. 1 in C. Handel: Concertos a Quatre Nos. 1 in D minor and 2 in D; Sonata for Cello in C. Es 528.

Two of the three works are concerted. In the Handel sonata Greenhouse is the soloist. One wishes that the discs of the Harpsichord Quartet contained nothing but the ensemble work of the four musicians. They produce delicate sounds and precise balances. It is a pleasure to listen to such confident playing. Whereas, although Greenhouse plays well in his solo turn, it is the kind of playing that can be duplicated in many other sources. Bright recorded sound throughout the disc.

HEITMANN, FRITZ

"Christmas Organ Music." Tel 66009.

The contents of this disc of organ music are: Bach: *Fantasia in G;* three *Chorale Preludes* (from the *Orgelbüchlein*); *Pastorale in F; Canonic Variations on "Vom Himmel hoch";* Böhm: *Variations on "Gelobet seist du, Jesu Christ";* Walther: *Variations on "Lobt Gott, ihr Christen";* Buxtehude: *Variations on "Wie schön leuchtet der Morgenstern."* It is a fine selection, played in a masterly way. Heitmann was a sensitive and at the same time authoritative musician whose playing had a great deal of tradition behind it. He used an organ in a Berlin church—an instrument with clear sound that, when needed, could amass considerable volume without becoming muddy. This ranks with the Walcha (Decca) and Viderø (Haydn Society) discs as among the best organ records to be found anywhere.

HOFMANN, JOSEF

Chopin: Waltz in D flat ("Minute," Op. 64, No. 1); Ballade No. 1 in G minor (Op. 23); Berceuse (Op. 57); Waltz in A flat (Op. 42); Andante Spianato and Polonaise (Op. 22); Nocturne in F sharp (Op. 15, No. 2); Étude in G flat ("Butterfly," Op. 25, No. 9); Nocturne in E flat (Op. 9, No. 2). Rachmaninoff: Prelude in G minor (Op. 23, No. 5). Mendelssohn: Spinning Song (Op. 67, No. 4). Beethoven-Liszt: Turkish March. Moszkowski: Capriccio espagnole. C 4929.

A few words about Josef Hofmann, who is almost forgotten today. He was born in Poland in 1876, became the greatest piano *wunderkind* of all time (concerts at the age of six), made his American debut at the Metropolitan Opera at the age of eleven, retired for a while, studied with Anton Rubinstein, emerged as one of the supreme pianists of the day. He gave his last New York concert in 1946. At the point of writing (December 1954) he lives in Los Angeles. On November 28, 1937 he gave a golden jubilee at the Metropolitan Opera, playing two works with orchestra (conducted by Reiner, with players from the Curtis Institute, of which Hofmann was director) and a solo program. The entire concert was recorded on acetate discs, as part of a standard transcription service. Columbia, in 1954, persuaded Hofmann to release the solo piano portion of the acetates.

This LP disc is not hi-fi. It is noisy, has considerable distortion, and suffers from background noise (the entire audience seems to have had a cold). But the disc nevertheless is one of the great piano records of all time. I do not have the space to analyze every work on it. I do urge you to get the disc and discover for yourself how a supreme master plays Chopin. You won't get too good an idea of Hofmann's inimitably melting tone, but you will find in evidence a tremendous imagination, a perfect technique, an exquisite rubato, and a degree of dynamics that is breathtaking. Only Hofmann could get the sudden, tiger-like surges of tone you will hear in the *Andante Spianato and Polonaise*, or in the *G minor Ballade*. Only Hofmann could make so hackneyed a work as the *A flat Waltz* an altogether novel experience (notice the Viennese rhythm he slips into at one of the transitions). Only Hofmann would dare attempt the delirious type of virtuosity encountered in the closing measures of the *Capriccio espagnole.* It is a tragedy that he never made any electrical recordings (he made some acoustic shellacs, from 1915 to 1922 or thereabouts, that do not give much of an idea of his genius). This disc, at least, will give a faint idea of the impact that Hofmann made on the concert stage; and it will also illustrate a school of piano-playing that has virtually vanished from the earth.

HOROWITZ, VLADIMIR

Chopin: Andante Spianato and Grand Polonaise in E flat (Op. 22); Waltz in A minor (Op. 34, No. 2); Polonaise in A flat (Op. 53); Mazurka in F minor (Op. 7, No. 3); Waltz in C sharp minor (Op. 64, No. 2). V LM 1137.

The highlight here is an amazingly articulated performance of the *Andante Spianato and Polonaise*, though the rousing *A flat Polonaise* is not far behind. Horowitz is in top form; this is grand, large-scale Chopin-playing. The recorded sound manages to do justice to his bronze tone.

Chopin: Sonata in B flat minor (Op. 35); Ballade No. 1 in G minor (Op. 23); Nocturne in F sharp (Op. 15, No. 2). Liszt: Au bord d'une source; Hungarian Rhapsody No. 6. V LM 1235.

The Liszt-playing is as authoritative as the Chopin is weak. Both the *Sonata in B flat minor* and the *G minor Ballade* are among the most erratic things Horowitz has done. As always, tremendous control and bravura are present, but the chopped line, the artificial-sounding rubatos, and the fussy details are most uncomfortable. The Liszt is another story. *Au bord d'une source*, one of the composer's most charming works, ripples from the Horowitz fingers, and his performance of the *Sixth Rhapsody* is stupendous. Nobody else alive can turn on this kind of orchestral sonority.

Chopin: Ballades Nos. 3 in A flat (Op. 47) and 4 in F minor (Op. 52); Nocturnes in F minor (Op. 55, No. 1) and E minor (Op. 72, No. 1); Études in E (Op. 10, No. 3) and C sharp minor (Op. 10, No. 4); Impromptu No. 1 in A flat (Op. 29); Scherzo No. 1 in B minor (Op. 20). V LM 1707.

Some surprisingly erratic playing here, and to my way of thinking

Horowitz never has sounded less convincing. Most of the interpretations are overstressed, with arbitrary holds and pauses, strange accentuations, and long sections that sound overworked. It is as if Horowitz knows that the music demands certain things, but is not sure exactly which, and substitutes a febrile, even jittery, series of ideas instead of letting the music take its own course. He actually swoons over the *F minor Nocturne,* as glaring an instance of misinterpretation as you can find on any piano record. The only really successful performance is that of the *A flat Impromptu,* which Horowitz plays with a carefully shaped line. It is impossible to recommend this disc.

"Twenty-Fifth Anniversary Album." Schubert: Sonata in B flat (posthumous). Chopin: Nocturne in E minor (Op. 72, No. 1); Scherzo No. 1 in B minor (Op. 20). Scriabin: Sonata No. 9 (Op. 68); Études in B flat minor (Op. 8, No. 7) and C sharp minor (Op. 42, No. 5). Liszt-Horowitz: Hungarian Rhapsody No. 2. Debussy: Serenade for the Doll. Chopin: Waltz in A minor (Op. 34, No. 2). Prokofiev: Finale from Sonata No. 7 (Op. 83). V LM 6014 [2].

On February 25, 1953 Horowitz played his twenty-fifth-anniversary concert in Carnegie Hall. This recording was made at the event (at least, most of it was; there appears to have been some tape-editing and retouching). Horowitz is not the only pianist to be featured on records by an actual recital program. The Society of the Friends of Music in Bogotá, Colombia, sponsored a two-disc set of Rosita Renard's Carnegie Hall recital of January 19, 1949. It was handled by The Gramophone Shop in New York (the store is no longer in business, and the album will be hard to locate). Miklos Schwalb also has a two-disc Academy set of an actual recital, and some of Barere's Remington discs are repressings of acetates made during the late pianist's Carnegie Hall appearances. See also Collections: Backhaus (L 1108/9) for another "live" recital. Horowitz is one of the supreme virtuosos of all time, and in years to come this set may assume legendary aspects. He plays with his usual magnificence, though some of the ideas are debatable. His Schubert is an entirely different conception from that generally heard. Horowitz even manages to make the work sound pianistic, but it is an outsized conception, generally over-romanticized, with exaggerated pianissimos and fortissimos. To my taste, it is more planned and calculated than spontaneous. The Scriabin is formidable. Now that Barere has gone, Horowitz probably is the world's greatest Scriabin-player. In his own tinkering with Liszt's

Second Rhapsody he turns the cartwheels expected by his audience: and why not? Nobody does this sort of thing better. He also plays Chopin's *B minor Scherzo* more successfully than in V LM 1707, discussed above. The recorded sound is fine. Extraneous noises are at a minimum. Obviously the audience was co-operating with the Victor engineers.

JONAS, MARYLA

Chopin: Mazurkas Nos. 49 in F minor (Op. 68, No. 4), 19 in B minor (Op. 30, No. 2), 43 in G minor (Op. 67, No. 2), and B flat (posth.); Nocturnes Nos. 19 in E minor (Op. 72, No. 1) and 20 in C sharp minor (posth.); Waltzes Nos. 13 in D flat (Op. 70, No. 3) and 11 in G flat (Op. 70, No. 1); Polonaise No. 9 in B flat (Op. 71, No. 2). 10" C 2004.

Chopin: Polonaise No. 1 in C sharp minor (Op. 26, No. 1); Études in E flat minor (Op. 10, No. 6) and F minor (Op. 25, No. 2); Waltzes Nos. 7 in C sharp minor (Op. 64, No. 2) and B minor (Op. 69, No. 2); Berceuse (Op. 57); Impromptu No. 1 in A flat (Op. 29). C 4476.

All of the pieces on these two discs originally were released on shellac around 1947. The performances are extremely personal. Jonas, who is not a particularly strong technician, concentrates on works that do not give her fingers too much trouble. Within its slight framework, the music sounds sentimental, with a highly mannered rubato. And yet the pianist often achieves quite disarming playing. She walks a perilous tightrope, but here she does not fall off (as she does in her disc of *Nocturnes*), though her slow tempo in the *Berceuse* on C 4476 is hard to take. In view of many charming bits spread through this pair of discs, both are worth having. But bear in mind that this is a Victorian way of playing Chopin. He is a much stronger composer than Jonas's affected, small-scale performances would suggest. Good piano sound on these records, marred by a slight trace of "wow."

KAPELL, WILLIAM

"Memorial Album." Bach: Partita No. 4 in D (less gigue). Schubert: 8 Ländler; Impromptu in A flat (Op. 142, No. 2). Liszt: Mephisto Waltz; Hungarian Rhapsody No. 11. V LM 1791.

At the time of his death Kapell had not approved the gigue of the

D major Partita, and Victor respected his wishes by omitting it in this recording. The *Mephisto* originally was released by Victor in 1946; all of the other pieces are new. Kapell's Bach is indicative of a poise and maturity that he had not previously displayed. It has aspects of the Rachmaninoff style—incisive, masculine, rhythmic, sparse pedal, and a masterly shaping of phrase. Kapell would have developed into a supreme pianist, and one well understands the genuine grief that swept the music world when he met his untimely end in an airplane crash in 1953. His performance of the Liszt is a fleet-fingered *tour de force,* and the *Ländler* swing with grace. Admirable recorded sound.

KATCHEN, JULIUS

Chopin: Ballade No. 3 in A flat (Op. 47); Scherzo No. 3 in C sharp minor (Op. 39); Fantasy in F minor (Op. 49). 10" L 554.

Maturity is lacking from these conceptions. Katchen is too impulsive, and the lack of repose in his playing shows up in sections that can be described by no other term than spasmodic. This Chopin is a collection of pianistic effects rather than a unified conception. Good recorded sound.

KEENE, CONSTANCE

"Romantic Piano Favorites." Mer 10113.

Many short pieces are contained on this disc: three Rachmaninoff *Preludes,* three Chopin *Preludes,* works by Liszt, Debussy, and others. Keene goes about these in a remarkably exact manner. Every note is in place, every phrase mark observed, every difficulty, no matter how complicated, is instantly solved. The order of virtuosity that one hears in Liszt's *Gnomenreigen,* Chopin's *Prelude in G,* and Rachmaninoff's *Prelude in E flat minor* is something that one does not encounter every day. Fine recorded sound, poor surfaces.

Bach: French Suite No. 5 in G. Beethoven: 32 Variations in C minor. Brahms: Paganini Variations. Mer 10138.

At the time of writing, this disc contains the only good LP performance of the Beethoven *Variations.* Keene plays them in a note-perfect manner with plenty of snap and sparkle. She gets the

French Suite on a half-side by omitting the repeats. Some interesting ideas are present, including some really provocative accentuations. The only questionable thing is the tempo of the Gigue, in which the musical values are secondary to some amazingly fast and deft articulation. Five of the Brahms variations are omitted: Nos. 4, 8, and 14 from Book I; 7 and 9 from Book II. Somebody tried to get too much on this disc.

LANDOWSKA, WANDA

"Landowska Plays for Paderewski." V LM 1186.

A "gimmick" title if there ever was one. Landowska supplies the notes to the disc. Writes the great lady, casting her eyes to heaven: "The pieces included in this record are those Paderewski loved most. I played them often for him and—at his request—repeated them." And thus Landowska has selected music that stems from Poland: two polonaises by Oginski (a minor Polish composer who had some influence on Chopin); her own *Bourrée d'Auvergne* and *The Hop;* pieces by Rameau and others on Polish rhythms; three Polish traditional dances; and, of all things, Chopin's *Mazurka in C (Op. 56, No. 2).* Why not Paderewski's *Minuet in G* to round it out? Anyway, the thought of Chopin being played by Landowska on the harpsichord should be enough to send you rushing out to get the disc. A curiosity, but an utterly adorable one.

"Treasury of Harpsichord Music." V LM 1217.

It is indeed a treasury. The contents include: Bach: *Prelude, Fugue, and Allegro in E flat; Fantasy in C minor;* Scarlatti: *Sonatas in D and D minor;* Chambonnières: *Sarabande in D minor;* Rameau: *Le Dauphine;* Couperin: *L'Arlequine; Les Barricades mystérieuses;* Purcell: *Ground in C minor;* Anon: *The Nightingale;* Handel: *"Harmonious Blacksmith";* Mozart: *Rondo in D* (K. 485); *"Turkish March"; Minuet in D* (K. 355); Vivaldi-Bach: *Concerto in D.* All were released around February 1948, and the performances constitute a lexicon of what can be done on the harpsichord in matters of nuance and color. The cultivated art of Landowska shines through all this varied repertoire—through the grandeur of the Bach and the delicacies of Scarlatti, through the intense, moody Purcell and the lightweight French pieces. Low-level recording, but perfectly satisfactory. Most current harpsichord recordings are too loud, anyway.

LIPATTI, DINU

Chopin: Sonata in B minor (Op. 58); Barcarolle (Op. 60); Nocturne in D flat (Op. 27, No. 2); Mazurka in C sharp minor (Op. 50, No. 3). C 4721.

The *Sonata in B minor* has been discussed under Chopin. Lipatti gives the *Barcarolle* a beautifully paced, stylish performance, and he is equally the artist in the two shorter pieces. This disc must be highly recommended despite a tubby recording. It dates from the mid-1940's and lacks life. I had best results on the Columbia 78 equalization.

Ravel: Alborado del Gracioso. Liszt: Sonetto del Petrarca No. 104. Scarlatti: 2 Sonatas. 10" C 2216.

These were made between 1946 and 1948, and were not successful tonally. The heavy sound is difficult to equalize out, and the quality in general is poor. Through it all shines the playing of an artist who had already achieved greatness, and who was to die in 1950 at the age of thirty-three. Lipatti had everything: unlimited technique, taste, musicianship, ability to achieve a consecutive sequence, and interesting ideas. This disc will serve not as a souvenir of what was to be, but of what already was.

MILSTEIN, NATHAN

Pergolesi: Sonata No. 12. Schumann: Intermezzo. Brahms: Allegro in C minor. Suk: Burleska. Bloch: Nigun. Paganini-Milstein: Paganiniana. Accompanied by Carlo Bussotti, Cap 8259.

Some of the pieces in this little recital are rarely heard. The Pergolesi work, originally for two violins, was transcribed by Longo; and the last movement will be recognized as part of Stravinsky's *Suite Italienne.* The Brahms and Schumann pieces are part of the so-called *F.A.E. Sonata* that those two composers and Dietrich wrote for Joachim (Stern plays the entire work in his two-disc set of the Brahms *Sonatas,* C SL 202). Milstein often plays his *Paganiniana* in concert; it is one of those feats of violin topsy-turvydom which find a parallel in some of the arrangements that Horowitz has cooked up for himself on the piano. The kind of pluperfect virtuosity that Milstein exhibits leaves one gasping. Throughout the disc, indeed, Milstein plays with a poise and tonal splendor that very few other living violinists could match and none could surpass. A sensational disc of violinistics, beautifully recorded.

MOISEIWITSCH, BENNO

Chopin: Preludes Nos. 11–24; Scherzos Nos. 1, 3, and 4. V LBC 1038.

What got into Victor on this disc? Instead of presenting Moiseiwitsch in a complete recording of the *Preludes*, the American company cut the British set about in half—something like reproducing the *Mona Lisa* without the smile. Moiseiwitsch, even if he is no longer the pianist he was before the war, can still play nearly anybody else under the table. His work here is poetic, with immense finish and a secure tradition; and let's forget about a few smeared passages. Clear recorded sound.

"MUSICIANS OF THE PAST"

Vol. I. Liszt: Hungarian Rhapsody No. 13; Chopin: "Black Key" Étude; Nocturne in F sharp, played by Ferruccio Busoni (recorded c. 1915). Chopin: Waltz in A flat (Op. 42), played by Eugen d'Albert (recorded 1915–20). Grieg: Au Printemps, played by Edvard Grieg (recorded 1903). Saint-Saëns: Marche militaire française; Rêverie à Blidah, played by Camille Saint-Saëns (recorded 1919). Debussy: 3 Ariettes oubliées; Aria from the Tower Scene of Pelléas et Mélisande, sung by Mary Garden, with Claude Debussy at the piano. AM 1203. Vol. II. Sarasate: Introduction and Tarantella; Habanera; Caprice basque; Ziguenerweisen; Bach: Prelude in E, all played by Pablo de Sarasate (recorded 1905). Brahms: Hungarian Dance No. 2, played by Joseph Joachim (recorded 1905). Bruch: Excerpts from First Movement of G minor Violin Concerto, played by Franz Drdla (recorded 1903). 10" AM 0079.

Unlike Columbia's "Great Masters of the Keyboard" series, these are *not* piano rolls. It is amazing how much can be derived from these two discs. Busoni sounds much more convincing than he does on Welte rolls, and in the *Thirteenth Rhapsody* the listener can get an idea of the personality and pianistic power that his reputation suggests. The Debussy-Mary Garden series is eternally fascinating. Drdla (he of the *Souvenir*) apparently was not much of a violinist; or, at least, he wasn't when he recorded his excerpt from Bruch. Joachim was seventy-four years old when he stepped before the horn to record the Brahms *Hungarian Dance in D minor*. His bow arm was not too steady, but one is startled by the force and breadth of his conception. Grieg and Saint-Saëns play their pieces prettily, and D'Albert goes through the Chopin *Waltz* with a good deal of command (he could not have been in practice at the time). The revelation on these two discs is Sarasate, who displays elegance, purity, and facility that are spectacular. This is a species of transcendant virtuosity (a few slips in intonation notwithstanding; but Sarasate was over sixty at the time). The recording stands up surprisingly well, too. Why don't we get more instrumental records like these two discs? The vocal field has been pretty well covered, but the record companies have not investigated the work that Hofmann, Godowsky, Backhaus, Szigeti, Casals, and a good handful of Liszt pupils were doing on flat discs in the first two decades of this century.

NEF, ISABELLE

"French Masters of the Keyboard." OL 50028.

Harpsichord music of the seventeenth and eighteenth centuries. Composers represented on this disc are D'Anglebert, D'Andrieu, Rameau, Louis and François Couperin, Chambonnières, and Daquin. Nef plays this material in a learned, accurate manner that does not have much inner life, and this despite some varied registrations and the obvious care she takes to set each section off. Much superb and witty music is contained in this collection, and one wishes it emerged with more imagination. Fine recorded sound. Claude Chiasson has, on Ly 19, a disc with the same title: "French Masters of the Keyboard." Here the composers are Atteignant, Grevaise, Chambonnières, Daquin, D'Andrieu, De Grigny, Balbastre, and Rameau. I find the playing, like Nef's, accurate but routine, and Chiasson's choice of repertoire is not as interesting as that on the Oiseau-Lyre disc.

NEW ART WIND QUINTET

Berezowsky: Suite. Fine: Partita. Milhaud: 2 Sketches. CE 1003.
Modernism of a quiet sort here, distinguished by smooth writing and enhanced by the rich sounds of a wind group. The players are fully up to the technical demands of the music, and the disc is lifelike in tonal balance.

"The Mannheim School." Mozart: Cassazione in E flat. Stamitz: Bläserquartett in E flat (Op. 8, No. 2). Reicha: Bläserquintett in E flat (Op. 88, No. 2). Danzi: Bläserquintett in G (Op. 67, No. 1). CE 2010 [2].
Mannheim, in the last quarter of the eighteenth century, had the greatest orchestra in Europe and was a center of musical activity. The so-called Mannheim School, which evolved there, was an important influence in the emergence of a musical style that departed from the baroque. When Mozart heard the Mannheim orchestra he nearly died of excitement; he never had heard anything like it. Mannheim influence was in part responsible for the *Cassation* played in this set (though it is disputed Mozart; see entry under the composer). Of the other works, the Reicha is the most brilliant and the emptiest, the Danzi has a faint touch of romanticsm (with anticipations of Weber in particular), and the Stamitz is a fine, melodious work by a minor composer. The New Art Wind Quintet expertly threads its way through the music. This album has a bit more than mere historical interest. It is a welcome addition to the catalogues.

"American Woodwind Symposium." CE 2003 [2].
The Americans are contemporary. These are the scores: Carter: *Quintet for Woodwinds* (1948); Cowell: *Suite for Wind Quintet* (c. 1935); Dahl: *Allegro and Arioso* (1942); Goeb: *Quintet for Woodwinds* (1949); Persichetti: *Pastorale for Winds* (1943); Piston: *Three Pieces for Flute, Clarinet, and Bassoon* (1926); Riegger: *Quintet for Woodwinds* (1952). Listening to this symposium is, in one respect, stimulating; in another, depressing. Stimulating because the music is unfamiliar and (to be chauvinistic) American; depressing because of its basic uniformity and conformism. Exceptions are the unabashedly French treatment that starts the Persichetti work, and the relaxed, non-party-line (I'm talking here about the modern-music lobby; no politics intended) writing of Cowell. Otherwise the listener is going to be in for a session of objective, neurotic-sounding music. The material is intelligently

handled by the New Art Wind Quintet and also by the recording engineers.

NEW MUSIC STRING QUARTET

Gibbons: Two Fantasias. Locke: Consort for Viols No. 6. Purcell: Pavane and Chacony in G minor. Bar 913.

Music like this demands a specialized taste from the listener. It lacks the distinctive melodic contours of, say, a romantic score; it is delicate, murmurously flowing, and to some ears may lack variety. But it is worth making an attempt to know. These fine performances will help the cause. The New Music String Quartet, which seems equally as at home in pre-Bach music as in Bartók, is especially careful to keep the inner voices of the polyphony clear. Gratifying balance results. Excellent recorded sound.

Boccherini: Quartet in A (Op. 33, No. 6). A. Scarlatti: Quartet in D minor. Tartini: Quartet in D. Bar 911.

The disc could be subtitled "The Development of the String Quartet." Alessandro Scarlatti's *D minor Quartet*, a short, dignified work, is one of the very first specimens of its kind. The Tartini carries harmonic elements away from modality into something approaching classicism of a recognizable nature; and the Boccherini work, with certain romantic elements and a philosophy of opposing themes, is the string quartet as Mozart knew it. Intelligent performances by the New Music String Quartet are supported by the concrete virtues of well-integrated ensemble, pleasant tone, and admirable balance.

NOVAES, GUIOMAR

Chopin: Scherzo No. 3 in C sharp minor (Op. 39); Berceuse (Op. 57); Waltz in D flat ("Minute," Op. 64, No. 1); Impromptu No. 2 in F sharp (Op. 36); Nocturne in F sharp (Op. 15, No. 2); Fantasy in F minor (Op. 49); Etude in E (Op. 10, No. 3). Vox PL 7810.

By now, I should imagine, I have managed to make the point that I think Novaes is a very special pianist. In these Chopin pieces, especially in the miniatures, she is all spontaneity. And how she plays the piano! Her technique is natural and unforced, she never smites, and she can get all the effects she wants. Put this Chopin disc high up on your list. The recording is fine, too.

"Encores." Bach: Organ Prelude in G minor. Gluck-Saint-Saëns: Melody and Dance of the Blessed Spirits from Orpheus; Ballet Music from Alcestis. Purcell: Hornpipe. Brahms: Intermezzo in B flat minor (Op. 117, No. 2); Capriccio in B minor (Op. 76, No. 2); Waltz in A flat (Op. 39, No. 15). Philipp: Fireflies. Vuillement: Hornpipe. Vox 7500.

On most Novaes concerts you will find one or more of these turning up on the program or as an encore (she *always* plays the Philipp *Fireflies*). All of them she does with typical elegance. The Saint-Saëns transcriptions usually sound boring—but not when the Novaes fingers are at work, and the delicately colored articulation she achieves is altogether enchanting. As an illustration of how the piano should be played rather than hammered, this disc is Exhibit A. Bright-sounding recording, with nothing artificial or truer-than-life about it.

PEETERS, FLOR

"Old Netherlands Masters." Ren 39.
"Old English Masters." Per 578.
"Old Italian Masters." Per 586.

Three collections of early organ music. The composers on the Netherlands disc are Dufay, Ockeghem, Obrecht, Isaac, Des Près, Willaert, Demonte, Sweelinck, and Van der Kerckhoven. On the English disc are Byrd, Bull, Philips, Purcell, Craft, Greene, and Stanley. The Italian disc is devoted to the Gabrielis, Palestrina, Brignoli, Cavazzoni, Guammi, Frescobaldi, Zipoli, and Martini. Much of this music will be of interest only to specialists or students. Each disc contains an unexhilarating succession of pieces that have a tendency to sound alike and which are played very much the same way. Peeters does not bring much variety, either in registration or tempo, to his playing. And, except in the Italian disc, there is very little variation in dynamics.

PRESSLER, MENAHEM

"Piano Music for Children." Prokofiev: Music for Children (Op. 65). Shostakovich: Children's Pieces. Bloch: Enfantines. Milhaud: Touches blanches; Touches noires. Starer: Lullaby for Amittai. MGM 3010.

A fine collection. Prokofiev's little set is one of the few compositions that can be mentioned in the same breath as Schumann's pieces for children. The other composers here, while their music is not on a comparable level, write simply and attractively. Pressler plays similarly: simply and attractively. According to the notes, he himself was in the first delirious flush of fatherhood when he made the disc. Clear piano sound; but the recording has annoyingly noisy surfaces.

RACHMANINOFF, SERGEI

Rachmaninoff: Melodie in E (Op. 3, No. 3); Moment musical (Op. 16, No. 2); Preludes in C sharp minor (Op. 3, No. 2), E (Op. 32, No. 3), F minor (Op. 32, No. 6), G flat (Op. 23, No. 10), and F (Op. 32, No. 7); Études in E (Op. 32, No. 3) and E flat (Op. 33, No. 7); Daisies (Op. 38); Oriental Sketch; Étude-Tableau in A minor (Op. 39, No. 6); Humoresque (Op. 10, No. 5); Polka de W. R. Chopin: Nocturne in E flat (Op. 9, No. 2). Mendelssohn: Spinning Song (Op. 67, No. 4). Schubert-Liszt: Serenade. Kreisler-Rachmaninoff: Liebesfreud. V LCT 1136.

We are likely to forget that the piano could be played with this type of mastery. I unhesitatingly nominate this as one of the great piano records of all time. Rachmaninoff's technical armor was complete; anything that could be done on the piano, he could do. In addition, he could shape a phrase and organize a piece of music in an incomparable manner. He had great intellectual intensity, a prominent streak of poetry, and the most unerring fingers that ever were. As for the music on this disc, it may not rank high in the ultimate scale, but to hear Rachmaninoff play it is an experience that none should forgo. To single out two pieces: the *Moment musical* has the most exciting left-hand work that ever has been recorded; the *Polka de W. R.* is an example of how a fine musical mind can take second-rate material and make it enchanting. The recorded sound is not very good, but forget about it.

RECORDER CONSORT OF THE MUSICIANS' WORKSHOP

"Recorder Music of Six Centuries." CE 1018.
"Recorder Music of the Eighteenth Century." CE 1051.

The first of the two discs contains recorder music from the tenth to the seventeenth centuries. Composers include Reuenthal, Machault, Landini, Des Prês, Suzato, and Praetorius. None of this music, the notes point out, was specifically composed for recorders, but in its time the music *could* have been so played. Some unusual, exotic-sounding material is present. Exceptionally clear recording, perfect definition. Altogether a charming and successful job. On the accompanying disc is music by A. Scarlatti, Loeillet, Bach, and Telemann, played on recorders with a continuo of harpsichord and cello. A violin and an oboe help out, too. If CE 1051 lacks the interest of the disc devoted to early music, that is because we are on ground that has been trodden by many players and many record companies. The music has been prepared with care, however; the performances are expert; and the recording is as lifelike in sound as you can hear today.

RUBINSTEIN, ARTUR

"Encores." V LM 1153.

Old favorites here: pieces like Liszt's *Liebestraum*, Mendelssohn's *Spinning Song*, Chopin's *Nocturne in E flat* (Op. 9, No. 2) and *Fantasy-Impromptu*, a Schubert *Impromptu*, Rachmaninoff's *Prelude in C sharp minor*, and others. All are nonchalantly tossed off with the deceptive mastery that Rubinstein brings to his playing. A pleasant disc, admirably recorded.

SCHWALB, MIKLOS

Czerny: 6 Études from The School of Velocity. Clementi: 4 Études from Gradus ad Parnassum. Cramer: 13 Études. Ac 303.

At one time or another most piano students have had some of these études assigned to them. Who would ever consider them music? Yet Schwalb makes a good case, and his playing reminds us that Czerny, Cramer, and Clementi were highly respected composers in their day, and that their writing was far from devoid of ideas. Schwalb plays these attractive trifles with independent fingers, a strong wrist, and considerable rhythmic flexibility. An unusual and interesting disc, very well recorded.

SCHWEITZER, ALBERT

Bach: Toccata, Adagio, and Fugue in C; Fugue in A minor; Fantasy and Fugue in G minor; Preludes in C and D; Canzona in D minor. Mendelssohn: Sonata in D minor (Op. 65. No. 6). C SL 175 [3].

Nobility of conception is present—enough nobility to make one almost forget that the playing is that of an artist out of practice. Dr. Schweitzer, who spends most of his time as a missionary-doctor in Africa, was nearly an octogenarian when he made these recordings, and technically he is no longer equipped to compete with organists well over a generation his junior. But music is not all technique, and through these interpretations breathe the conceptions of a master. If, however, you find these performances too slow for your taste, there is Biggs for the *Toccata, Adagio, and Fugue* (C 4284) and several of the other Bach works in this set.

SEGOVIA, ANDRÉS

"Andrés Segovia Guitar Solos." D 8022.
"An Andrés Segovia Recital." D 9633.
"An Andrés Segovia Concert." D 9638.
"An Andrés Segovia Program." D 9647.
"An Evening with Andrés Segovia." D 9733.
"Andrés Segovia, Guitar." D 9751.

A good portion of the guitarist's recital repertoire is contained in these six discs, which cover musical ground from Milán to Villa-Lobos. Original music for the guitar alternates with many of Segovia's popular transcriptions of Bach and others. Segovia remains the old master; none of his competitors gets such a variety of color and effects. Good choices to start a Segovia collection are D 9647 and 9638, both of which contain many of his specialties. There is some pretty Spanish music on D 8022. Each of these recordings is good in sound, and the pressings I played had noiseless surfaces.

SKOLOVSKY, ZADEL

Scriabin: Sonata No. 4. Hindemith: Sonata No. 2. Berg: Sonata, Bartók: Sonata. C 4871.

Skolovsky, with fine impartiality, has selected four important twentieth-century piano works representing four acutely different styles of composition. An able, though not very colorful pianist, Skolovsky sweeps through the music with plenty of technical skill. If you are primarily interested in Bartók's barbaric-sounding

Sonata, a more forceful and idiomatic performance is contained on Vox 6620 *(*Concerto No. 2)* played by Foldes. This is preferable, though the recorded sound is nowhere near as good. I would avoid Scarpini's version of the Bartók on Col 1025; in this piece he is the typewriter sort of pianist whose percussive attack gets me down after a while.

STEFANSKA, HALINA

*Chopin: Fantasy-Impromptu (Op. 66); Mazurkas in C sharp minor (Op. 6, No. 2), B flat (Op. 7, No. 1), and C (Op. 68, No. 1); Nocturne in C sharp minor (Op. 27, No. 1); Polonaise No. 8 in D minor (Op. 71, No. 1). V LBC 1031 (*Beethoven: "Appassionata" Sonata, played by Nicolas Medtner).*

Stefanska, who has not yet appeared in America, sounds like a fine artist. Her performance of the *Fantasy-Impromptu* is as good as any on records, and she plays the other music in a romantic, flowing, and sensitive manner, with a good deal of technical freedom and a way of phrasing Chopin that sounds most authoritative. Her tone, too, is colorful. In short, this is a pianist with whom one would like to become better acquainted, and since she has made a number of recordings for HMV in England, it is possible that such a wish may be gratified (pending her eventual appearance in this country). Clear, well-articulated recording here. It is unfortunate that the reverse of this disc is occupied by a version of the *"Appassionata"* played by Medtner in little more than routine fashion.

SUPPER, WILLIAM

"Monuments of Baroque Organ Music." Ren 202 [2].

Many composers get a hearing on these two discs: Walther, Sweelinck, Buxtehude, Bach, Steigleder, Pachelbel, Simon, and Bruhns. Supper splits the playing among four European organs. This is an impressive set, both for the music and the performance, to say nothing of the resonant, full-scale reproduction. Supper has a direct way with the music, and keeps it from lagging. A set of Sweelinck *Variations* and Walther's *Partita on "Jesu meine*

Freude" are masterpieces which we can thank Supper for making available. All of the above repertoire is also available on two single discs—Ren 53 and 54, with the addition of a few short pieces by Lübeck (played by Eva Hoelderein).

VALENTI, FERNANDO

"*Spanish Keyboard Music.*" *W 5312.*

Composers like Matteo Albéniz, Anglés, Casanovas, Gallés, and Serrano are represented. All are eighteenth-century composers. None of their harpsichord music—on this disc, at any rate—is of much interest, though an aria by Padre Rafael Anglés does speak with a personal voice not heard elsewhere. Valenti's playing is typically vigorous and rhythmic. Close-up recording that is fine if played at low volume.

WATTERS, CLARENCE

"*French Baroque Organ Music.*" *CE 1008* [2].

Almost all the pieces included in this album are short, and a succession of short pieces by minor composers can be a long haul for the average listener. Watters plays music by Clérambault, Dandrieu, Marchand, Du Mage, Couperin, Siret, Daquin, Le Bègue, Jullien, Raison, Loeillet, and Balbastre. As in most baroque composition, strongly in evidence are workmanship and probity that refuse to let the music be canceled out entirely. And in several cases—Couperin's *Benedictus*, Daquin's *Noël 9*—the writing is of real beauty. The organist handles this varied repertoire with taste and, often, command. He is scholarly without being pedantic. He also has a good measure of technical security. This authoritative performance is backed by brilliant recorded sound.

ZABALETA, NICANOR

Harp Music, Vol. I. Caplet: Divertissement. Pittaluga: Danza de Hoguera. Tournier: Lolita la Danseuse. Halffter: 3 Short Pieces. Mudarra: Fantasy. Navraez: Popular Variations. Cabezon: Pavane with Variations. Polero: Romance. Anon.: Villancete. Es 509.

Harp Music, Vol. II. Prokofiev: Prelude. Tailleferre: Sonata. Tournier: La Source. Roussel: Impromptu. Hindemith: Sonata. Glanville-Hicks: Sonata. Es 523.

Harp Music, Vol. III. C. P. E. Bach: Sonata. Beethoven: Variations on a Swiss Theme. Mayer: Sonata. Rosetti: Sonata. Krumpholz: Andante con Variazione. Es 524.

An exploration of the harp literature. Vol. I is divided between sixteenth-century Spanish music and contemporary French and Spanish. Vol. II is all contemporary. Vol. III is eighteenth-century. None of this music has been arranged. Zabaleta is dedicated to the proposition that the harp has a literature of original music and that he is the man to play it. Not many harpists, it must be admitted, could do better. He achieves remarkable clarity of texture, sweeping up and down the strings with complete assurance. With musicianship, too. He avoids all of the salon tricks and the obvious effects beloved of salon harpists. That said, it remains to note that much of the music he plays is second-rate. Esoteric's recording puts the harp right into your lap, and virtually non-existent surfaces help the illusion.

INDEX OF PERFORMERS

The text of this book was set on the Vari-Typer, in the Bodoni Book Style (by Coxhead). Composition by *The Science Press*, Lancaster, Pennsylvania. Printed by *The Murray Printing Company*, Wakefield, Massachusetts. Paper manufactured by *S. D. Warren Company*, Boston, Massachusetts. Bound by *H. Wolff*, New York. Designed by Harry Ford.